Human Rights in Youth Sport

The human rights of children have been recognized in the 1989 UN Convention on the Rights of the Child, and ratified by 192 countries. Paulo David's work makes it clear, however, that too often competitive sport fails to recognize the value of respect for international child rights norms and standards.

Human Rights in Youth Sport offers critical analysis of some very real problems within youth sport and argues that the future development of sport depends on the creation of a child-centred sport system. Areas of particular concern include issues of:

- Over-training
- Physical, emotional and sexual abuse
- Doping and medical ethics
- Education
- Child labour
- Accountability of governments, sports federations, coaches and parents

The text should be essential reading for anybody with an interest in the ethics of sport, youth sport, coaching and sports development.

With a foreword by Mary Robinson, former President of Ireland and UN High Commissioner for Human Rights.

Paulo David works at the Office of the United Nations High Commissioner for Human Rights (OHCHR) as Secretary of the Committee on the Rights of the Child. He began his career as a sports journalist before moving into the human rights field.

Ethics and Sport
Series Editors
Mike McNamee
University of Wales, Swansea
Jim Parry
University of Leeds

The Ethics and Sport series aims to encourage critical reflection on the practice of sport, and to stimulate professional evaluation and development. Each volume explores new work relating philosophical ethics and the social and cultural study of ethical issues. Each is different in scope, appeal, focus and treatment but a balance is sought between local and international focus, perennial and contemporary issues, level of audience, teaching and research application, and variety of practical concerns.

Also available in this series:

Ethics and Sport
Edited by Mike McNamee and Jim Parry

Values in Sport
Elitism, nationalism, gender equality and the scientific manufacture of winners
Edited by Torbjörn Tännsjö and Claudio Tamburrini

Spoilsports
Understanding and preventing sexual exploitation in sport
Celia Brackenridge

Fair Play in Sport
A moral norm system
Sigmund Loland

Sport, Professionalism and Pain
Ethnographies of injury and risk
David Howe

Human Rights in Youth Sport

A critical review of children's rights in competitive sports

Paulo David

Routledge
Taylor & Francis Group

LONDON AND NEW YORK

First published 2005
by Routledge
2 Park Square, Milton Park,
Abingdon, Oxon OX14 4RN

Simultaneously published in the USA and Canada
by Routledge
270 Madison Ave, New York, NY 10016

© 2005 Paulo David

Typeset in Goudy by
GreenGate Publishing Services, Tonbridge, Kent
Printed and bound in Great Britain by Cromwell Press, Trowbridge,
Wiltshire

British Library Cataloguing in Publication Data
A catalogue record for this book is available from the British Library

Library of Congress Cataloging in Publication Data
A catalog record for this book has been requested

ISBN 0–415–30558–6 (hbk)
ISBN 0–415–30559–4 (pbk)

This book is dedicated to Emily, my daughter, and to all other
young athletes whose experience of competitive sport should be
summed up in three letters: joy.

Contents

Tables

Foreword

Since its adoption in 1989, the United Nations Convention on the Rights of the Child has made an enormous impact on how the world thinks about the well-being of children. The Convention is the most widely accepted international human rights instrument, ratified by 192 countries. It has helped shape the policies and views of almost every part of society, from schools to social agencies, from labour unions to non-governmental organizations (NGOs), from private corporations to professional groups and cultural associations.

But as Paulo David's work makes clear, one of the few areas that has yet to recognize the value of respect for international child rights norms and standards is competitive sports. This book represents a significant step in deepening our understanding of the links between competitive sport and its implications on the rights of young athletes.

It contains numerous examples of the abuse that some children and adolescents, in particular, experience in the name of sport. Abuse such as that suffered by footballer Luciano Djim, who was 'traded' like a commodity between his home in the Central African Republic and Belgium. Djim – and so many others like him – was brought to Europe illegally, lured by false promises of a career with a professional football club. He ended up abandoned on streets that were not paved with gold.

Human rights can play a crucial role in preventing and combating unacceptable sport-related abuses. Those who are committed to advancing this cause must do more to convince those in positions of authority that human rights are more than just good ideas or abstract objectives. States have freely accepted legal obligations under international human rights law and have agreed to be held accountable for their implementation.

The specific status of children requires us to be even more vigilant. Competitive sports can fail children and be the cause of child abuse, exploitation, violence or other violations of rights. Paulo David's book reminds us that if we hope to see human rights norms realized in the lives of all people everywhere, we must begin by recognizing the potential for abuses close to home, even in an organized activity such as competitive sports.

Mary Robinson

Mary Robinson was President of Ireland (1990–7) and United Nations High Commissioner for Human Rights (1997–2002). She is currently Executive Director of the Ethical Globalization Initiative.

Series editors' preface

In this first full length book treatment of the ethical issues surrounding youth's engagement in sport from a Human Rights perspective, Paolo David breaks new and important ground. The exploitation of children in sport is critically charted from its roots in the elite sport systems of Ancient Greece through to the twenty first century where pressures of commercialisation have forced academics, coaches, educators, parents and policy makers to view the engagement of children in sports with greater gravity.

David's book is a sophisticated elaboration of the way in which a legally enforced and universalistic moral language can help us both to detect abuses and prevent them. The central tool in his armoury is the United Nations Convention on the Rights of the Child. David comprehensively gathers data on children's experiences in sport from a range of social scientific research fields. In this way, he articulates the economic, psychological and social dimensions of abuse, exploitation, harassment, neglect and even violence that have at times characterised children's engagement in sport, especially at the elite level.

Perhaps the most important contribution of this book to the ongoing debates about children's sporting experiences is the clear ethico-legal framework for the protection and promotion of children's well-being in sport that it sets out. In addition to charting the rights that children should enjoy in sports, he also articulates key obligations or responsibilities that are held, knowingly or otherwise, by parents, coaches and officials alike. David argues, with considerable force, that sports organisations and individuals involved in their coaching, teaching and governance must wake up to the fact that the rights he articulates and contextualises here are not the product of naïve idealism, but rather the a matter of urgent moral and legal moment.

Mike McNamee, University of Wales, Swansea
Jim Parry, University of Leeds

Acknowledgements

This book is the result of a decade of reflection and work on an unexplored issue: the human rights of young athletes. Its objective is to explore the human rights dimensions of youth sports and the way these rights are, or are not, respected.

A decade ago I often felt lonely and isolated when debating this issue. It was simply taboo, in both the human rights and the sport worlds. In this context, I am indebted to Judge Jean Zermatten who, from the beginning, encouraged me to persevere in my work on this subject, which he felt was important. My recent, but crucial, meeting with Professor Celia Brackenridge was decisive in persuading me to publish this book and I thank her for her support.

Over the past ten years, I have also received the support and advice of many friends, relatives and colleagues, too numerous to list here. My thanks go to all of them, but especially to Nigel Cantwell for having introduced me to children's rights and for always faithfully supporting my projects. I am also grateful to all those who convinced me of the importance of human rights, whether through their knowledge or their behaviour, and who constantly inspired me. They include Eric de Decker, Massimo Lorenzi, Ricardo Leonardi, Soussan Raadi-Azarhkhchi, Thomas Hammarberg, Jaap Doek, Theo van Boven and the late Pierre Dufresne. In particular, I greatly appreciate and acknowledge the support of Professor Jaap Doek, whose dedicated efforts led to the presentation of this study as a PhD thesis in law at the Vrije Universiteit Amsterdam (Free University of Amsterdam).

During her five years as United Nations High Commissioner for Human Rights (1998–2003), Mrs Mary Robinson demonstrated her immense courage, competence and commitment to defend the cause of the victims of human rights violations. I greatly appreciate having had the privilege to work closely with her on child rights issues and having been inspired by her powerful personality.

I also wish to thank Sue Pfiffner, who had the challenging task of being the first reader of my manuscript. Her substantive contribution, editorial advice and cheerful support have been critical.

I will be forever grateful for the love and inexhaustible support of my late mother Kati David and my wife Jean Milligan. My mother, who was also an author, taught me the meaning of perseverance, without huge doses of which this book would certainly never have seen the light of day. She always insisted that many of our perceived limits are simply imposed by our mental barriers, barriers that each and every one of us can break down if we but dare to try. Finally, without Jean's patience and support, I would not have been able to complete this book, the fruit of a long process of reflection and research. Working on this project in my spare time, mostly early in the morning or late at night, I was fortunate enough to be able to count on Jean, who was always ready to go that bit further to give me the time and space I needed. Her ability to provide sound advice, expert guidance and constructive criticism on the most diverse issues is impressive and often saved me from total intellectual loneliness. I am grateful to her and to our three children, Simon, Emily and Owen, for having been so generous during this adventure.

Finally, I would like to emphasize that the opinions expressed in this book, as well as any mistakes or misinterpretations, are mine and mine alone.

Geneva, September 2004

Abbreviations

ADR	alternative dispute resolution programme for amateur sport (Canada)
AFC	Asian Football Confederation
AFM	African Football Management
AIS	Australian Institute of Sport
ASA	Amateur Swimming Association
ASI	Anti-Slavery International
ATP	Association de Tennis Professionnel (Professional Tennis Association)
BBC	British Broadcasting Corporation
BFC	Brazilian Football Confederation
BMA	British Medical Association
CAF	Confederation of African Football
CAN	Canadian Association of National Team Athletes
CAS	Court of Arbitration for Sport
CASA	National Commission on Sports and Substance Abuse
CAT	Convention against Torture
CDDS	Committee for the Development of Sport (Council of Europe)
CPSU	Child Protection in Sport Unit
DCI	Defence for Children International
EFTA	European Free Trade Association
ENGSO	European Non-Governmental Sports Organisation
EPO	erythropoietin
EU	European Union
FFT	Fédération Française de Tennis (French Tennis Federation)
FGM	female genital mutilation
FIFA	Fédération Internationale de Football Assocation (International Football Federation)
FIG	International Federation of Gymnastics
FINA	Fédération Internationale de Natation (International Swimming Federation)
FIS	International Ski Federation
FIVB	International Volleyball Federation

FMH	Fédération des Médecins Suisses (Swiss Doctors' Federation)
GDP	gross domestic product
GDR	German Democratic Republic
GMC	General Medical Council (UK)
HCG	human chorionic gonadotrophin
HGH	human growth hormone
HIV	human immunodeficiency virus
IAAF	International Athletic Federation
IABA	International Amateur Boxing Association
ICCPR	International Covenant on Civil and Political Rights
IFJ	International Federation of Journalists
IIHF	International Ice Hockey Federation
ILO	International Labour Organization
IMG	International Management Group
INSEP	Institut national du sport et de l'éducation physique (French national sports institute)
IOC	International Olympic Committee
ISF	International Snowboard Federation
ISO	International Organization for Standardization
IT	information technology
ITF	International Tennis Federation
LPGA	Ladies' Professional Golf Association
MLB	Major League Baseball
MLS	Major League Soccer
NASO	National Association of Sports Officials
NATA	National Athletic Trainers Association
NBA	National Basketball Association
NCAA	National Collegiate Athletic Association
NFL	National Football League
NFHS	National Federation of State High School Associations
NGO	non-governmental organization
NHL	National Hockey League
NOC-NSF	Dutch Olympic Committee and Dutch Sport Federation
NSPCC	National Society for the Prevention of Cruelty to Children
NYSSF	National Youth Sport Safety Foundation
OHCHR	Office of the United Nations High Commissioner for Human Rights
PAYS	Parents Association for Youth Sports
PCA	Positive Coaching Alliance
STDs	sexually transmitted diseases
TAC	American Track and Field Federation
TOYA	Training of Young Athletes Study
TSSAA	Tennessee Secondary School Athletic Association
UAE	United Arab Emirates
UEFA	Union of European Football Associations

UN	United Nations
UNDCCP	UN Office for Drug Control and Crime Prevention
UNDP	UN Development Programme
UNESCO	UN Educational, Scientific and Cultural Organization
UNICEF	UN Children's Fund
UN INCB	UN International Narcotic Control Board
USOC	United States Olympic Committee
USSR	Union of Soviet Socialist Republics
WADA	World Anti-Doping Agency
WHO	World Health Organization
WMA	World Medical Association
WTA	Women's Tennis Association

Part I
The conceptual frame

1 Introduction

> The right policy in regard to physical training is to avoid an excessive early training, which stunts the proper development of the body ... In the lists of Olympic victors there are only two or three cases of the same person having won in the men's events who had previously won in the boys'; and the reason is that early training and the compulsory exercises which it involved, had resulted in loss of strength.
>
> (Aristotle 1995: 303)

At a time when the sports world is plagued by excessive commercialization, doping, corruption, illicit behaviour and blind ambition, can human rights improve the quality of youth sports and the status of young athletes? This book is a first attempt to understand the human rights implications of involving children in competitive sports. It clearly demonstrates that human rights and competitive sport are closely interwoven, despite the fact that they have ignored each other for decades. It also reveals that, of all domains, sport is one of the few that has not yet been penetrated by children's rights. If we are to understand better how human rights can improve the protection of all young athletes' rights, the link between human rights and sports must be explored attentively.

For the past 30 years, the sports community has to a large extent avoided asking itself the fundamental questions that emerge from young athletes' involvement in elite sports and to which human rights can provide unique guidance and responses. Questions such as: does participating in competitive sport put children at risk? Does intensive training qualify as child labour? Is four hours of training a day truly beneficial for a four-year-old? Is it normal for a 16-year-old gymnast, who has dropped out of school and trains seven hours a day, to be only 1.30 metres tall and weigh less than 30 kilograms? Do physical and sexual abuse and anorexia occur more frequently in sports than in other environments? Should promising young football or basketball players be harassed by companies who want to put them under contract or traded between clubs for thousands of dollars without being properly informed and consulted? Should they be punished for absorbing illegal performance-enhancing drugs? Do young athletes have a right to privacy and, if so, what does this amount to?

Looking at the human rights of young athletes leads us to an unexpected paradox: although the issue is becoming increasingly controversial, it has not yet reached the point where it is openly debated and researched. Many questions are still taboo, carefully swept under the carpet; others are timidly beginning to attract polite attention. As yet, we cannot evaluate the beneficial and harmful aspects of competitive sports for young people, nor do we have the scientific tools necessary to understand the exact situation across the entire spectrum of human rights. In some fields, we can evaluate the level of respect for rights; in others, we rely on speculations or are simply unable to go beyond raising questions.

In addition, both public and sports authorities have so far turned their backs on the debate concerning the rights-based dimensions of sports. The result is that they often find themselves paralysed and feel threatened when faced with difficult issues, and therefore lack the power to react constructively to prevent situations in which children are put at risk. But human rights law can make a major contribution to competitive sports by virtue of its legal nature, from which obligations, responsibility and accountability ensue and which provides objective procedural, analytical and management tools (Kidd and Donnelly 2000).

Human rights can greatly contribute to improving the quality of support given to young athletes; competitive sports can in turn reinforce the human rights system.

CHILD RIGHTS IN SPORTS: ENSURING FUTURE SUCCESS

In 1990, the United Nations Convention on the Rights of the Child[1] entered into force and generated immense hopes for those working for and with children and adolescents. Obviously, to think that an international human rights treaty alone would solve all child-related problems was naïve; but it was right to expect an unprecedented innovative and dynamic approach to young people through the explicit recognition of their human rights for the first time ever.

The Convention has, for example, helped raise awareness about violations of children's rights. Until the late 1980s, authorities still considered reports of such violations – including sexual abuse and exploitation, child labour, trafficking and sale, forced military recruitment, early and forced marriages, children living in poverty, etc. – as false or largely exaggerated. The Convention has generated the emergence of a loose, but not negligible, child rights community bringing together individuals – practitioners, activists, lawyers, government officials, academics and many others – who refer in their daily work to the international norms and standards it recognizes, which are legally binding in all states of the world (with the exception of Somalia and the United States). This is partly the result of the systematic and expert involvement of non-governmental groups, first in welfare – and later in child rights – programmes and policies (David 1993a).

Since its adoption in 1989 by the United Nations (UN) General Assembly, the Convention has made an impact on a wide spectrum of groups in society, from families to schools, courts to labour unions, associations to public authorities. But amazingly, one of the few areas – if not the only one – that has yet to integrate international child rights norms and standards is competitive sports. To understand why sports authorities have failed to consider the rights of young athletes, we need to look at some long-standing, widespread practices and beliefs in the sports world.

Part I of this book sets the conceptual framework to explore the signification of considering competitive sport for young people from a human rights perspective. Part II questions whether the key principle of the 'best interests of the child' is compatible with their early involvement in competitive sports, while Part III examines the abuse and violence to which children are sometimes victim and which threaten their integrity and dignity. Part IV explores economic exploitation: whether competitive sport can be considered child labour for some young athletes, to what extent they are instruments of sport's commercial interests, and the occurrence of trafficking and sale of child and adolescent athletes. Empowering each human being to ensure that they are treated with dignity is a fundamental human rights principle and Part V analyses whether young athletes benefit from this basic right. Part VI addresses the responsibilities of adults in respecting the rights of young athletes and the book concludes in Part VII by suggesting some key measures to improve guaranteeing the human rights of youth in competitive sport.

POSITIVE IMAGE VERSUS NEGATIVE TRENDS?

With a few exceptions, this book is not based on new research, facts and information; rather it suggests a new analysis of competitive sports from an angle that has so far been neglected: child rights. For, whilst an impressive wealth of research on the impact of competitive sports and intensive training on young athletes now exists, we are still incapable of gauging whether and how these athletes benefit from their rights.

Today, the status of children and their living conditions are given more political and academic consideration than before and much information on the subject has become available and is easily accessible. The media is full of stories of child abuse, sexual molestation, violence, child soldiers, and so on. One consequence of this mass of information is that it is all too easy to believe that never before have children been treated so badly. But, in fact, the reverse is true: the further back one goes in history, the lower the level of child care (de Mause 1974; Fletcher and Hussey 1999). Similarly, in reading this book, the reader might feel overwhelmed by the magnitude and variety of abusive situations described. This merits clarification: the book's focus is limited to the respect of rights and it therefore emphasizes violation of those rights; consequently, it reflects only one specific aspect of a wider, more positive context. Also, the sporting world is not immune (although it often tries to pretend otherwise) to similar phenomena that affect children outside sports, such as sexual abuse, economic exploitation, etc.

The mistreatment of children in sports is not new, either. In Ancient Greece, children took part in sports competitions from an early age, and little attention was paid to possible negative effects. In the sixth century BC, child athletes, aged about 12 years old, were selected and sent to sport schools to become professional athletes. Boys – and also girls in some sports – had to endure intensive training, follow strict discipline and diets, take drugs and obey the sexual demands of their trainers. In the fifth century BC, both child and adult athletes changed clubs for a better salary, even if it meant changing their nationality (Vanoyeke 1992).

Another significant problem is the failure of the human rights and sporting communities to interact; both are poorly informed of the other's activities. Discussion of the rights of athletes often overlooks the human rights of these individuals, although as abuses come to light, problems such as doping and labour rights are forcing people to take a hard look at the treatment of athletes. Finally, as the image of children's sports is overwhelmingly positive (Coakley 1998: 96–102; Papp and Pristoka 1995), sports institutions, which are traditionally self-regulating and independently financed, have tended to brush aside any problems and been able to escape formal scrutiny or questions of accountability.

Individual empowerment has never been part of the sporting culture as it has in, for example, the arts or politics. This is perhaps one of the reasons why the sports world resists outside examination and reacts negatively to those evoking the human rights of all athletes, whether children or adults. One example was the sports community's reaction to the Bosman case in 1995, in which the European Court of Justice overturned the European football authorities' rules in order to protect footballers' right to freedom of movement. The European Union's image in the eyes of many was irrevocably tarnished.

Rather than viewing critics as disgruntled detractors out to harm the phenomenal success of sports in general, sports authorities would do well to accept that criticism can be constructive and that problems are not taboo. If they do not, they run the risk of seeing the ideal that sport represents – and its lucrative business deals – destroyed. Enhancing the promotion and protection of athletes' human rights should not be perceived as a threat, but as a way to increase the confidence of athletes and the general public in the integrity of sporting institutions.

A GROWING AWARENESS

As I repeat elsewhere in this book, researching and understanding this topic was often a lonely endeavour, especially a decade ago when I began to look at the implications of children's rights in sports. It was, however, a subject I felt drawn to, having experienced – at a modest level – elite competitive sports as an adolescent, before becoming a sports journalist and then specializing in children's rights. I began to view sports from a broader social perspective, using human rights as the basis.

My passion for sports began at a young age, but even as an adolescent, certain activities troubled me. I was a member of the Swiss under-21 field-hockey team and was surprised to be given two pills, 'vitamins' according to my coach, before an important match. I discreetly discarded the pills, as did a team-mate, although the other 14 players swallowed them with no qualms. I still have no idea of the specific ingredients of those tablets or the effect that taking them would have had. I could not understand how an adult could expect me to swallow pills without proper explanation or discussion. In Switzerland, field hockey was, and is, very much an amateur sport. If this could happen in field hockey, what about in more popular or even professional sports?

During my career as a sports journalist, my articles frequently upset the sports world, which was more accustomed to being honoured than criticized for its often unethical, sometimes illegal, practices. Suspicion about the illegal use of performance-enhancing drugs was already widespread but discussion on how to put a stop to it was non-existent. What shocked me most was the complicity of much of the media in promoting a distorted picture of professional sports to the general public and, as sports became big business, many reporters sought to develop privileged relationships with stars or large corporate sponsors rather than protect their professional integrity. Later, when I specialized in children's human rights, I came to realize how little those rights were given attention and protected in competitive sports.

AVOIDING THE GREY ZONES

This book does not debate the value of sports competitions nor advocate an end to them. Competition is a long-standing reality, neither good nor bad. It is a social process (Martens 1978: 104) involving children and adolescents in which adults need to enforce proper safeguards to prevent systematic patterns of abuse and exploitation. Building an ethical and sustainable form of competitive sports system is not exclusively a human rights matter, but human rights do provide a theoretical and operative framework, including the critical role of participation, to address the complex issues raised.

Although insufficient in-depth knowledge and data exist in the field, I would estimate – very roughly – that some 70 per cent of children involved in competitive sports greatly benefit and are empowered by their activity; 20 per cent are potentially at risk of different types of abuse, violence and/or exploitation; and 10 per cent are victims of some form of violation of their human rights. This is, of course, not a scientific estimation; it is an approximate attempt to understand the global benefits and shortcomings of the sports system for children. In view of the unprecedented number of children participating in competitive sports, even if only 1 per cent of them are victims of some kind of abuse, that still represents, worldwide, tens of thousands of young athletes every year. Numbers such as these justify mobilization and action. By its very nature, this book focuses essentially on the 30 per cent of young athletes whose human rights are challenged by competitive sports. My own sports experience was extremely beneficial throughout my youth and, in my social and professional life today, I still profit from the knowledge and experience I acquired.

It is obviously impossible to reach the zero-risk target and avoid all grey zones; nevertheless, due to the fact that little has been done as yet, a huge potential exists to improve the struggle against and prevention of child rights violations in competitive sports. One of the Convention's main strengths is to provide high visibility to children and to place them at the centre of decision-making processes; this is urgently needed in the sports world, where too often adults see first and foremost the athlete and only afterwards the child.

Competitive sports frequently reveal major tensions between the interests of the child and those of adults. In sports, the principle of the *best interests of the child* should always be a primary consideration, as enshrined in the Convention on the Rights of the Child (see Chapters 17 and 18). Experience shows that the measures necessary to guarantee child rights are often wrongly perceived as being a threat to political and sports authorities and interests. But if they are not properly addressed today, how will these groups face the possible emergence of the genetically engineered athlete tomorrow (see Chapter 10)?

NOTES

1 The full text of the Convention on the Rights of the Child can be found in the Appendix on page 265.

2   A black hole

Absence of debate, data and research

Perhaps never in the history of sport and leisure studies has so much interest [in sexual abuse in sport] been generated by so few data.

(Brackenridge 2001: 8)

Statistical indicators are a powerful tool in the struggle for human rights ... developing and using indicators for human rights has become a cutting-edge area of advocacy. Working together, governments, activists, lawyers, statisticians and development specialists are breaking ground in using statistics to push for change – in perceptions, policies and practices.

(United Nations Development Programme 2000: 89)

Since the early 1990s, academic and popular literature on the involvement of children and adolescents in competitive sports has flourished, reflecting the increased importance given to the practice of sports by young people. Scientific research from a wide variety of fields, ranging from the medical to the sociological, has without doubt contributed to our understanding of the implications for young athletes of their participation in sports. Popular literature provides parents and coaches with practical advice on how to improve the quality of services given to young athletes and avoid abuses. Despite the amount of knowledge available, however, studying the human rights of athletes is still problematic, in part because no tradition of applying human rights to sport has ever existed.

A particularity of human rights is that – in addition to identifying emerging issues – it looks at well-known situations from its own specific perspective, often revealing new dimensions. For example, the human rights community may not be the only one examining the health status of a population, but it will do so from a rights-based perspective. The medical community might be satisfied with a statistic indicating that 93 per cent of children are immunized in a specific country. The human rights community will want to study the 7 per cent remaining in order to understand whether patterns of discrimination prevail. If, among this 7 per cent, it finds that 93 per cent are girls belonging to indigenous families, the community will signal its concern and try to propose solutions.

The same rationale applies to competitive sports. We can find out how many children join football clubs in a given country, and perhaps the percentage of young athletes who reach the top and make an adequate living from the sport. We cannot determine, however, how good the training and supervision are in sports clubs, nor what happens to those – the majority in this case – who drop out of the system. In addition, scientific data on prohibited or illegal behaviour or activities – in the case of sports, these include doping, trafficking and sale of athletes, and physical, psychological or sexual abuse – are poorly documented in part because they are difficult to gather. But these are precisely the subjects that the human rights community must examine.

This book covers a multitude of human rights issues; almost all of them could justify a separate publication. Racial discrimination among young athletes is a perfect example; it is an issue already addressed in the literature (see Chapter 16) though rarely from a rights standpoint. Similarly, from a rights perspective, it is not enough to study in isolation the health status of very young athletes who train four or five hours a day; rather, their situation with regard to education, discrimination, family and social relations, sponsors, civil rights, etc., also needs to be taken into consideration. One of the reasons for examining young athletes' human rights as a whole is to emphasize the principles of interdependence and indivisibility of all human rights.

Limited awareness about the human rights of young athletes in the context of competitive sports results logically in limited research and data on the issue (see Table 2.1 opposite). In turn, awareness is hindered by the weakness of data collection and research. Some important issues remain entirely undocumented and, consequently, a number of topics developed in this book are supported with scarce, fragmentary or, at worst, anecdotal information. In this last case, no hasty conclusions are provided, rather issues are identified and questions raised.

Part III of the book, dealing with the physical and psychological integrity of the athlete, benefits from a substantial body of academic research on health and sport issues. At national and international levels, a wealth of academic journals covers almost all health aspects of sports, ranging from psychology to legal and ethical issues. Whilst these tools are important in assessing to what extent young athletes *enjoy their rights*, they are not sufficient. Monitoring children's rights and monitoring childhood might require different tools and serve different purposes (Casas 1996: 49–56). Traditional health indicators and statistics support analysis about *health status*, but not necessarily about correctly assessing the exercise of the *right to health*. Tools to understand issues such as access, accountability and the general levels of enjoyment of the right to health – especially by vulnerable and discriminated groups in the population[1] – are still scarce, sometimes non-existent. A UN expert body considers that four elements need to be addressed when assessing the right to health: availability, accessibility, acceptability and quality (UN Committee on Economic, Social and Cultural Rights 2000: para. 12).

Similarly, scientific knowledge and evidence are lacking in other aspects of human rights in sport. While the academic world has upgraded its work since the

Table 2.1 Child rights violations in competitive sports: scope, knowledge and awareness

Situation	Convention on the Rights of the Child	Geographical scope	Estimated number of children yearly affected[a]	Identified in high level and/or mass sport	Empirical research studies	Level of awareness and knowledge in society[b]
Health-related risks of intensive training	Article 24	Mainly in the Western world as well as Eastern European and some Asian countries	Several thousands	High level	Since the 1970s	Medium
Physical abuse	Article 19	Worldwide	Several thousands	High level and mass sport	Very scarce still, only since the 1990s	Very low
Psychological abuse	Article 19	Worldwide	Several thousands	High level and mass sport	Very scarce still, only since the 1990s	Very low
Sexual abuse	Article 19	Worldwide	Several thousands	High level and mass sport	Increasing body of research since the 1990s	Low to medium
Violence	Article 19	Worldwide	Unknown	High level and mass sport	Very scarce, mainly since the 1990s	Low to medium
Doping	Article 24	Worldwide	Several tens of thousands	High level and mass sport	Increasing body of research, only since the 1990s	Low to medium
Economic exploitation	Article 32	Worldwide	Unknown	High level	Non-existent	Non-existent
Trafficking and sale	Article 35	Mainly the Americas, Africa, Western and Eastern Europe	At least 1,000	High level	A few isolated studies	Almost non-existent
Transfers and freedom of association	Article 15	Mainly the Americas, Africa, Western and Eastern Europe	Unknown	High level and mass sport	Non-existent	Non-existent
Right to education	Articles 28 and 29	Worldwide	Unknown	High level and mass sport	Non-existent	Non-existent
Civil rights and freedoms of athletes	Articles 12 to 17	Worldwide	Unknown	High level and mass sport	Non-existent	Non-existent
Discrimination	Article 2	Worldwide	Tens of thousands	High level and mass sport	Important body of research, especially since the 1970s	Medium

a Conservative estimates.
b The level of knowledge and awareness in the academic world is obviously higher than in society as a whole, especially with regard to health-related issues.

1980s in fields such as sport sociology, sport ethics and sport law, human rights is not directly covered by these new sciences. This suggests that the academic community needs to involve itself to a far greater extent if we are to understand holistically the human rights implications of youth competitive sports.

The paucity of existing tools to monitor the rights of young athletes is not unique to the sports world. Despite the fact that most countries have a central agency to collect population statistics and data, few are as yet capable of collecting data required to monitor either adequately or, most importantly, independently all the areas covered by the Convention on the Rights of the Child (UN Committee on the Rights of the Child 2002). This may be due to a number of factors: political, technical, budgetary, scientific and cultural.

Most of the information sources used in this book are of North American and Western European origin simply because a significant number of studies, investigations and media coverage on the general topic of children and sport exist in these countries, which is not the case in other parts of the world. Therefore, the fact that a country is or is not mentioned in this book is not intended to reflect in any way its relative overall achievements in regard to the implementation and protection of the human rights of young athletes.

MONITORING: THE WINNING WAY

As monitoring and accountability are crucial aspects of the human rights system, the quality of assessment methods plays a key role in properly determining the levels of respect for human rights standards and norms. Sound human rights work is built on reliable information, qualitative and quantitative data, statistical indicators and independent fact-finding, inquiries and research; without them, improved policies and programmes cannot be designed and progress cannot be monitored. Set up by the Convention in 1991, the Committee on the Rights of the Child is an international and independent UN expert body that monitors progress made by states in implementing the treaty. The Committee (2002: para. 27) stresses the importance of data collection, which is 'a fundamental prerequisite for ensuring sound monitoring of child rights. It is a means of obtaining a picture of the child population, as well as providing a basis for designing policies and programmes and evaluating their effectiveness.' A national review of sport policy in Australia made the same point:

> Without data, it is impossible to make progress (or at least to know if progress is being made and, if so, whether it bears any resemblance to the intended outcomes). Without that data, a junior policy will not be accepted as serious and will, if only unconsciously, be significantly marked down in the minds of those whose behaviour and attitudes it must ultimately change to be successful.
>
> (Australian Sports Commission 1999: 9)

Identifying human rights indicators still remains a major challenge despite important efforts undertaken since the adoption of the Universal Declaration of Human Rights in 1948 (Lindholt and Sano 2000: 58). While it is relatively straightforward to identify, collect and analyse indicators in fields such as birth registration, immunization, detention or provision of social security, it remains a challenge to do so on issues such as the feeling of insecurity within a given population, the quality of education, respect for cultural values, mental abuse or violence, the right to food or housing, freedom of expression or religion, or interference with the right to privacy.

Economic, social and cultural rights are still poorly equipped to be scientifically monitored (Lindholt and Sano 2000: 57). Nor are civil and political rights better off – especially when it comes to children: they are often considered a 'non-measurable' field (Santos Pais 1996: 142–3). As competitive sports cover the five main groups of rights (civil, political, economic, social and cultural), they also suffer when indicators or statistics either do not exist or are insufficient or inadequate to provide instructive analysis. By their nature, human rights are not systematically quantifiable:

> Rights can never be fully measured merely in statistics: the issue goes far beyond what can be captured in numbers. But this is true of all uses of statistics. Nevertheless, as a tool for analysis, statistics can open the questions behind generalities and help reveal the broader social challenges.
> (United Nations Development Programme 2000: 90)

Ennew and Miljeteig (1996: 214), among others, argued that:

> the Convention [on the Rights of the Child] established rights and conditions that are very difficult to measure, whether in terms of achievement or violation. In general statistics directly related to childhood are either non-existent or of limited utility in this context.

The specific rights of children also rely on monitoring tools. Indications that domestic law, policies and institutions have been reformed in light of the Convention's provisions do not suffice to prove that the rights enshrined in the Convention are enjoyed by everyone under 18 in a specific country. Data, indicators and research are indispensable in understanding the achievements and limitations encountered by countries in implementing their obligations under the Convention. In 1992, only a year after its establishment, the Committee on the Rights of the Child (para. 32) declared that:

> the use of appropriate indicators could contribute to a better assessment of how the rights covered by the Convention on the Rights of the Child were guaranteed and implemented and to an evaluation of progress achieved over time towards the full realization of those rights.

Today, child rights researchers, experts and advocates still struggle to identify satisfactory information tools. After ten years of evaluating countries' commitments to child rights, the Committee observed:

> Many States have yet to establish mechanisms to collect data of persons under-18, and covering all the areas of the Convention. Moreover, data disaggregated by various criteria (e.g. sex, age, nationality, etc.) are often unavailable, as are statistics relating to vulnerable groups of children.
> (Committee on the Rights of the Child 2002, para. 27)

Ennew and Miljeteig (1996: 221) noted that:

> A vast amount of statistical data that could be collected about children's lives – time budgets, economic activities, domestic duties, *leisure activities* – simply do not exist. Children are studied with respect to institutions of childhood, such as schools and families ... Statistics are of little use to the human rights community if not properly disaggregated. Issues such as access, discrimination and equity are difficult to assess in the absence of a breakdown by groups of population. It is crucial in this context to be capable to understand to which age, gender, ethnic, social and other groups children belong. [emphasis added]

No culture of monitoring exists in the sports domain, where authorities traditionally consider sport to be a private activity that is not open to public scrutiny and interference. They often perpetuate the same arguments to justify this as those used in situations where children need to be protected within their family or community, but in many Western countries, public authorities may interfere with parents' right to privacy to protect the best interests of the child.

Very little research has been undertaken to study the effects of intensive training on child and adolescent athletes, though some progress has been achieved. McPherson and Brown (1988: 274) considered that: 'To date, there is little empirical support for the many beliefs and hypotheses concerning the positive or negative outcomes for character and personality development that are alleged to be derived from involvement in competitive sport.' Coakley (1993: 85) agreed with this opinion:

> Children construct definitions of success and failure primarily through social interaction during or after practices or games ... Unfortunately, these relationships and what happens in them has been overlooked in nearly all the research on children in sport. This leaves a large void in our knowledge about risks and the benefits of intensive training and participation in youth sports.

The absence of independent monitoring in sports handicaps the capacity of both private and public authorities to improve service and programme quality and to assess their effectiveness. The Convention sets legally binding obligations upon all countries, which constitutes the fundamental added value of human rights over other approaches or measures. Alston (1996: 30) noted that: 'There is a presumption that States Parties, in establishing a monitoring mechanism, intended to establish an effective means for achieving accountability in relation to the obligations contained in the Convention.'

Neither the sports world nor the human rights community have addressed the issue of young athletes' human rights adequately. Debate is practically non-existent and research by and large unsatisfactory. Those wishing to pursue the accountability of private and public authorities with regard to young athletes will only be able to do so when proper data collection, analysis and monitoring are achieved.

NOTES

1 Such as girls, indigenous and minority groups, children living in poverty or remote areas, children living in institutional settings, children with disabilities, street children, etc.

3 The rule of law enters the sports arena

It is clear that [European] Community law, and in particular the principle of non-discrimination, the principle of free movement and the competition rules apply to sport.

(Viviane Reding, European Commissioner for Sports, Culture and Education, in European Commission 2000)

Rules do not get in the way of the game, they make it possible.

(Rt Revd George Carey, Archbishop of Canterbury, in Grayson 2000: 7)

Sport has developed phenomenally since the 1970s and this has had a direct impact on children. The evolution from amateurism to professionalism, despite the long and hypocritical resistance of the International Olympic Committee (IOC), changed the face of sports, as did increased financial, political and media interests. Improved access to television worldwide brought sports into a new arena and changed the meaning of winning, not only for athletes but also for financial, social and political interest groups.

In 1970, Avery Brundage, then IOC president, called for a ban on Alpine skiing, ice hockey, football and basketball in the Olympics because of commercialization (Arlott 1975: 735). This radical threat did not prevent some sports from rapidly moving to all-out professionalism, although, until the fall of Communist regimes in Eastern Europe in 1989, the IOC pretended that no Olympic athlete gained personal profit by competing. Significantly, it was only in 2001 that the International Amateur Athletic Federation, the track and field world governing body, agreed to drop the word 'amateur' from its name, while leaving the abbreviation, IAAF, unchanged. In 1999, the Council of Europe estimated that 3 per cent of world trade concerned sports, while the European Commission (1999: 5) evaluated at 2 million the number of jobs created in member states by sports activities from 1990 to 1999. Television rights for the 2006 World Cup in Germany are estimated to be worth over US$ 6 billion; in the 1960 Rome Olympic Games, they were sold for US$ 700,000.

Professionalism has undoubtedly permitted athletes to improve the quality of their preparation and training. But it has also reduced the age of athletes who train for and compete in high-level sports. During the 1970s, intensive training programmes started to be systematically applied to child and adolescent athletes in sports such as gymnastics, figure skating, diving, football, basketball, ice hockey, swimming, athletics and tennis.

In gymnastics, for example, the average age of the three best gymnasts in Europe dropped from 25 years in 1965, to 20 in 1969 and 18 in 1973 (Baumann 1976: 26). At the 1976 Montreal Olympic Games, Nadia Comaneci, 1.50 metres tall and weighing 39 kilos, was only 14 when she won her gold medals and symbolized the birth of 'baby-trained' champions. Nowadays, the average age of female gymnasts participating in senior world championships varies between 16.5 and 17.5 years, although some athletes are much younger when they compete in the adult category[1] (Leglise 1997: 8).

Research on the involvement of children in sports has traditionally focused on their role in and access to sporting activities and the medical implications of such practice. Only during the 1970s, as youngsters were increasingly perceived as potential champions and therefore involved in intensive training schemes, did a few practitioners and researchers go beyond the traditional medical or psychological approaches and begin to raise the alarm about abusive situations. Marty Ralbovsky's provocative *Lords of the locker room* (1974), for example, criticized children's sports programmes and described coaches as dictators, fanatical about winning, who encourage cheating and promote blind obedience and warped values. He asked why 'no group or individual has come forward to speak out on behalf of the civil rights of one of America's largest and most vulnerable minorities: young athletes'. Ralbovsky was probably the first person to articulate the concept of young athletes' human rights and to denounce their violation publicly.

Another major breakthrough was American sports psychologist Rainer Martens's *Joy and Sadness in Children's Sports*, a key compilation of 36 articles published in 1978. Although none of the articles explicitly discussed athletes' human rights, the publication was the first to present a wide range of emerging issues, such as fanatical behaviour by parents, coaches and sports officials; racism and violence; excessive pressure; young athletes' opinions about competitive sports; and the influence of the media. The book ends with a remarkable and visionary 'Bill of Rights of Young Athletes': ten rights to protect the physical, social and psychological health of young athletes. Drafted more than ten years before the adoption of the Convention on the Rights of the Child, the document recognized fundamental human rights principles such as non-discrimination, human dignity, protection from physical abuse, freedom of choice and of opinion, and the specific status of children.

During the 1970s, researchers also discovered precocious intensive training schemes and new methods to detect potential champions at an early age, mainly – but not solely – developed under state responsibility in the USSR and its satellite countries in Eastern Europe (Riordan 1980). Although the first sport 'factories' were established as early as 1949 in the German Democratic Republic and in 1962 in the USSR, it was the 1970s that saw an explosion of special sport schools in most Communist countries. While this system may have allowed unprecedented access to sport, it remains an abhorrent example of a manifest state policy which encouraged the manipulation of children and blatant violation of their fundamental human rights. Forced doping of young athletes, compulsory and abusive training programmes, and removal from the family environment were among the worst abuses recorded in the race for medals and state prestige (Ungerleider 2001).

It is estimated that between 1970 and 1989, East German officials forced between 8,000 and 10,000 athletes, many of whom were under 18 years of age, to take performance-enhancing drugs. Since the fall of the Berlin Wall, a number of high-level officials have been prosecuted and condemned. On 10 February 2000, for example, the German Supreme Court rejected the appeal against a 1998 court decision by Dr Bernd Pansold, who was for a long time one of the East German swimming team's doctors, and convicted him of causing actual bodily harm in nine doping cases, including to eight minors aged between 13 and 18 years (Haas-Wiss and Holla 2003). As at 30 March 2003 – the deadline for submitting claims – some 300 East German sportsmen and women had claimed reparation under a special law which set up a compensation fund for athletes who experienced health problems caused by the country's systematic doping system. Among them, 185 former elite athletes had been granted financial compensation as of 1 February 2004. Many athletes did not submit a claim, fearing that it would reopen painful wounds, force them to disclose information about their private lives and risk damaging their careers (Associated Press 2004).

In the West, critical analysis of children's involvement in competitive sports was delayed for at least 20 years largely by cold war rhetoric, even though Western governments were also engaged, although more subtly, in the blind race for medals and established their own detection and training systems that are still questionable today. In 2000, in a court case that is still pending, a judge, Pierguido Soprani, accused the Italian authorities of financing from 1981 to 1996, through the Italian Olympic Committee, a national medical centre in Ferrare that researched and administered drugs to elite athletes (Rodeaud 2000). The end of the cold war (1989) offered new opportunities to question established sporting methods and policies and their impact on the development of children and adolescents.

THE CONVENTION ON THE RIGHTS OF THE CHILD: ADDED VALUE AND AN INNOVATIVE APPROACH

The origins of human rights can be traced back at least as far as England's Magna Carta (1215), although this document dealt only with the rights of barons. The English Habeas Corpus Act (1679), the American Bill of Rights (1791) and the French Declaration of the Rights of Man and Citizen (1789) have, among others, contributed to a consolidation of the concept of human rights. But the first *international* instrument adopted by the international community was the 1948 Universal Declaration of Human Rights, although a number of other international treaties that were accepted earlier, such as the 1926 Convention against Slavery, clearly included some human rights elements (Weissbrodt 1988).

International law developed sharply during the twentieth century; this normative work resulted in the form of treaties, including in the field of human rights. Seven international legally binding human rights treaties constitute today the core of the human rights body.[2] They impose legal obligations on those states that have ratified them, and states commit to implement the provisions of the treaty to which it is party (Steiner and Alston 1996: 31–8, 709). Each of these seven treaties also establishes an independent and international expert body, serviced by the United Nations, which is mandated to monitor periodically the implementation of each treaty by states parties.

Human rights can be defined as legal guarantees intending to protect individuals from any form of state interference or negligence resulting in abuse or neglect. They imply individual entitlements between the duty-bearers (state) and the rights-holders (individuals). As human rights law is evolving, it is increasingly accepted that non-state actors can also carry some level of *indirect* responsibility to respect human rights (see below). Many consider that there are three generations of rights (Harris 1991). The 'first generation' consists of the civil and political rights that emphasize individuals' freedoms, which have traditionally been given priority by Western states. The 'second generation' covers economic, social and cultural rights, which initially were recognized mainly by socialist states. The 'third generation' emerged during the 1970s and has been claimed predominantly by developing countries. These rights affirm that, in addition to the first two generations, collective rights exist that need to be recognized and enforced. Examples include the right to development and the right to self-determination. Some believe that human rights are the first universal ideology of human civilization (Weissbrodt 1988).

Human rights aim at offering the possibility to any human being to claim his or her rights, and when violation occurs, to have access to a fair and impartial redress procedure. Human rights ideology is composed of several fundamental pillars. The Office of the UN High Commissioner for Human Rights (OHCHR) considers that five overarching principles are essential to guarantee a rights-based approach: accountability, empowerment, linkage to human rights treaties, participation and non-discrimination (OHCHR 2004). These principles imply other values. For example, accountability also refers to the principle of transparency and to combating impunity.

Child protection and welfare policies are nothing new. But children and adolescents had to wait until 1989 for a full set of their human rights to be recognized by public authorities. On 20 November 1989, the United Nations General Assembly adopted the Convention on the Rights of the Child. Within a decade, the Convention had been ratified by 192 states, making it the most ratified international treaty in the world. Its norms and standards are therefore almost universal. The Convention, a legally binding instrument and one of the seven main international human rights treaties, defines the child as any human being under 18 years of age, unless domestic law sets a lower age (article 1).

Despite the existence of a legal definition referred to in the Convention, no unique and absolute definition of childhood exists (Davin 1999). Although other classifications have been elaborated, Jean Piaget, the pioneer of cognitive psychology, identified four specific developmental stages from birth to approximately 16 years (Piaget 2001) that are of interest in the context of sports. The first stage, which runs from birth to 18 months, is called the motor-sensorial phase, during which children adapt to life requirements using their practical intelligence and immediate perception. The second stage, from 18 months to six years, is the acquisition phase. Children build on what they have learned in the first stage to construct and increase their knowledge with the support of language and mental representation. The third phase, called 'operational', from seven to 11 years, is the stage when children are able to project themselves in space and time, although they still need a concrete representation of the object to use their intelligence to the full. Adolescents aged 12 to 16 years are in the last stage, called the formal phase, during which they are able to function and think on the basis of abstract parameters.

The Convention's adoption was an important benchmark as it moved children and adolescents away from old-fashioned welfare and charity policies by turning needs into legal rights (see Table 3.1), to which all children are entitled by law irrespective of their social or other status (Freeman 1992a; Verhellen 1992; Cantwell 1998).

Fundamentally, the Convention suggests a new status and role for society's youngest members. The child is acknowledged as a *fully fledged subject of rights* to whom public authorities are accountable (Verhellen 1992; Newell 1998; David 2002), rather than as a vulnerable individual in need of protection. By ratifying this legal instrument, states not only recognize that, due to their vulnerability, children are entitled to special protection measures, they also commit to guaranteeing indiscriminate access for all children to a number of provisions (health, education and other social services) and recognizing their right to participate, in accordance with their age and maturity, in all decision-making processes. The right of children to express their opinions freely and have them taken into account (article 12) is obviously one of the most innovative and challenging rights recognized by the treaty (Freeman 1992).

The Convention's ultimate objective is to guarantee sound development and progressive empowerment of children and adolescents, and it provides a wide range of safeguards to ensure their protection from all forms of abuse, neglect, violence and exploitation. By recognizing a young person's *evolving capacity* and *legal capacity*, the Convention also provides that they can – in accordance with their age and maturity – *exercise* their own rights (Hodgkin and Holmberg 2000). The treaty guarantees young people a *progressive* autonomy that should develop in the context of the rights, responsibilities and obligations of parents, or any other persons in charge of their care (article 5).

The Convention is an international public law treaty. By ratifying it, states have agreed to reform their legal system accordingly and have committed to adopt the policies and programmes and establish the institutions and mechanisms

Table 3.1 From the needs-based to the rights-based approach

	Needs-based approach	*Rights-based approach*
Objective	Meeting needs	Realizing rights
Nature and process	Reactive: based on charity and paternalistic motivated goodwill, and political decisions	Preventive: legal obligations under domestic law
	Potential space for arbitrary decisions	Non-discriminatory and equality guarantees
Status of the child	Passive object	Subject of rights
		Exercise rights, according to age and maturity. Recognition of the child evolving capacities
Universal definitions	No guarantee. Definition of needs can vary arbitrarily due to socio-cultural factors and considerations	Universally recognized rights under international law (Convention on the Rights of the Child and other international human rights treaties)
Scope of action	Focuses narrowly on specific needs when problems are identified	Wide range of human rights Holistic and multi-sectoral interdependence and indivisibility of social, economic, cultural, civil and political rights
	Addresses restrictively child protection issues by addressing situations identified as problematic	Addresses rights linked to child protection, child participation and empowerment and all other child-related situations in society
Focus	Superficial – emphasizes the social and emergency context	Structural – emphasizes the legal, institutional and policy context
Accountability	Political and moral (at best)	Political and legal
	No clear identification between duty-holders (obligations) and claim-holders (entitlements)	Clear identification under law between duty-holders (obligations) and claim-holders (entitlements)
Empowerment	Needs can be meet without empowering	Realizing rights empowers
	Unchallenged power relations	Strives towards equal power-sharing
Redress and remedy	Arbitrary (no legal basis guaranteed)	Access to judicial or non-judicial redress guaranteed under law

necessary to ensure that all children and adolescents are able to profit from their human rights. The Convention reflects the legal principles of *indivisibility* and *interdependence* of all human rights as recognized in the 1993 Vienna Declaration and Programme of Action. It is the only international human rights treaty covering in such a comprehensive manner all groups of rights – civil and political as well as economic, social and cultural (World Conference on Human Rights 1993). Consequently, the Convention needs to be understood as a homogenous entity; a single provision cannot be implemented or interpreted in complete isolation from all the others, nor can its provisions and principles be properly implemented if all the others are not respected. This particularity is often referred to as the *holistic approach* to human rights (Santos Pais 1996).

The Convention was adopted a little more than a decade ago and it will take at least a generation before its impact can be fully assessed. The few existing studies, although instructive, do not provide clear indications of how successful the Convention has been in protecting children from human rights violations and guaranteeing freedoms (Lurie 1998; Woll 2000a; Heyns and Viljoen 2002). We can safely say, however, that it has placed crucial issues that were still negated, ignored or neglected during the 1980s on the agenda of many politicians, legislators and administrators. These issues include domestic abuse and violence, economic exploitation, sexual abuse and exploitation, trafficking and sale, children in detention, child soldiers, refugee and migrant children, children with disabilities, etc.

The Convention has certainly given force in many countries to the concept of children capable of progressively exercising their rights. It has also proven to be an indispensable working tool for anyone working with and for children, providing meaningful guidance in the proper design and implementation of legislation, policies and programmes.

The traditional welfare and charity approaches to children's rights (see Table 3.1, page 21) have given way, under the impetus of the Convention, to a much wider recognition of the scope of their rights, including:

Accountability

The Convention sets *legally binding obligations* on public authorities (and their agents). The child's care, needs and interests do not, therefore, merely rely on generosity and political will, but are a right and an obligation established by law. It provides clear identification between *duty-bearers* (the state and its agents, and indirectly those caring for the child) and *rights-holders* (children).

Normative clarity and detail

The Convention provides a full set of *universally recognized norms and standards* that can be applied in any situation and in all social–cultural environments and are agreed upon by the international community.

It is, nevertheless, recognized that full measurement of the implementation of rights can fail to give a scientific indication of the level of respect of rights in some specific areas (see Chapter 2). At worst, human rights norms and standards can still serve as useful benchmarks.

Empowerment, ownership and participation

According to their *evolving capacities*, children are *progressively empowered* and recognized as actors with their own rights instead of being simply perceived as powerless and passive objects in the hands of adults.

Comprehensive and holistic analytical tool

Traditional research on children is usually fragmented, being rarely undertaken from a *multi-sectoral* angle. By covering the most essential developmental rights of children, the Convention frames analysis within a holistic dimension of the child. In general, the child is examined from a medical, psychological, sociological, legal or pedagogical angle, rather than from a holistic approach covering the child from a multi-disciplinary angle.

Remedy

When guaranteed rights are not enforced, children, or their legal representative, have a legal basis to complain and claim for redress in or outside the formal judicial setting. However, at a time when almost any disagreement, even of 'low intensity', can end up in a court case, redress and remedies for children and respect for their rights should first be considered outside of traditional judicial proceedings and only reach the courts as a last resort.

International scrutiny

In 1991, the Convention established the UN Committee on the Rights of the Child, an international and independent expert body, which *monitors the progress* achieved by all states parties in their efforts to implement the treaty's provisions and principles. By ratifying the Convention, states accept the obligation to report to the Committee periodically and thereby to be under *international scrutiny* (Lansdown 2000; Woll 2000b).

The Committee, which began its work in 1993, examines the child rights' situation in state parties and adopts recommendations, issues general comments to help interpret the Convention's provisions and principles, and identifies patterns of human rights violations and emerging trends. However, not having been endowed with an international tribunal's legal authority, it has to rely on 'constructive dialogue', expert advice and its moral authority to enforce respect for the Convention.

The Committee has identified four major principles in the Convention that should always be taken into account whenever a provision is implemented or simply referred to: non-discrimination; the best interests of the child; the right to life, survival and development; and the right of children to express their views freely in all matters affecting them.

RESPECTING THE RULE OF LAW IN SPORT

Like almost any other activity undertaken in modern society, sport functions within a recognized legal framework. Whether it is paying a membership fee or a salary, building a stadium or imposing a sanction, all sport-related actions need to respect the established rule of law. Nevertheless, during the twentieth century, sport more or less developed in a legal loophole, with sports federations establishing their own rules, administrative bodies and tribunals. For a long time, most sports organizations and authorities believed that they were free from legal obligations – or even above the law (Grayson 2000: 3).

The sporting movement grew up and matured under the principles of self-organization and self-regulation, which is perfectly acceptable as long as an association's internal rules and practice are defined and applied in conformity with national and international law. The European Commission (1999b) recognizes the need for sport 'to keep its operational autonomy safe from any political or economic manipulation'.

Since the beginning of the twentieth century, legal conflicts have occasionally flared up in the sporting world, especially in the field of labour rights (Dabscheck 2000). But it was mainly during the 1990s that a pattern of legal conflicts emerged, largely because of the increasing ineffectiveness of sport bodies to regulate their own affairs in a satisfactory manner (Mangan 2000). These conflicts essentially opposed domestic and international law with rules and decisions enforced by sports federations.

The Reynolds case illustrates the strong resistance of sport organizations to recognizing and applying legal decisions taken outside of their own internal jurisdiction. In June 1992, American athlete Butch Reynolds was suspended for two years by the IAAF and the IOC for having absorbed illegal performance-enhancing drugs. But at the same time, Iowa's Supreme Court and the American Track and Field Federation (TAC) pronounced Reynolds innocent. These decisions resulted in a paradox: Reynolds was allowed to compete at national level but, at international level, the IAAF and IOC sanction had force of law. Reynolds then sued the IAAF for loss of gain for the two years he was prohibited from running outside the United States and for applying unfair sanctions (the IAAF had declared that any athlete competing with Reynolds in the US would be sanctioned and banned from international races). Although the IAAF retracted the latter sanction, Reynolds won his case at the US Supreme Court and the IAAF was condemned to pay almost US$ 7 million for loss of gain and more than US$ 20 million in compensation. The IAAF refused to pay, but the US Supreme Court confiscated the fine from IAAF's US-based sponsors (Mack 1995).

Another example is the 'Bosman ruling'. In 1995, the European Court of Justice ruled that the transfer regulations imposed upon football players by the

Union of European Football Associations (UEFA) and the International Football Federation (FIFA) violated articles 48, 85 and 86 of the Rome Treaty (1957) by severely restricting the fundamental right of freedom of movement of citizens. UEFA was obliged to adapt its regulations to comply with European law and to allow European football players to play in any European club. This judgement was a key decision in that, in situations of conflict, it clearly reiterated the superiority of international law over internal sports regulations and reaffirmed the undeniable dimension of human rights in the sports domain.

Although the first sports case was put before the European Court of Justice in 1974, it is only since the Bosman ruling that the European Union (EU) has been seriously involved in the sporting world. The European Commission stated in 1999 that:

> Provisions in the EC Treaty [Amsterdam Treaty], secondary legislation, Community policies and decisions have increasing impact on sporting practices and activities. These developments have caused a number of problems for sport in Europe ... The increase in the number of [legal] actions also reveals that there is a gap between the real world of sports and its regulatory framework.
>
> (European Commission 1999a: 1)

It further affirmed (1999: 7) that:

> While the [Amsterdam] Treaty contains no specific provisions on sport,[3] the Community must nevertheless ensure that the initiatives taken by the national State authorities or sporting organisations comply with Community law, including competition law, and respect in particular the principles of the internal market (freedom of movement of workers, freedom of establishment and freedom to provide services, etc.).

In a system strongly based on self-regulation, the rule of law in sports protects athletes from any form of abuse generated by unfair rules or decisions by sport organizations. In the past ten years, athletes have sought to uphold their rights in three main areas: transfers from one club to another, including labour rights; disciplinary sanctions and the right to due and fair process[4] (in particular, athletes often have difficulties in ensuring that their right to appeal is upheld); and access to justice. Other issues have also reached the courts recently, including matters related to sexual abuse, freedom of association and doping.

Sports organizations, afraid of losing both control and power, have in general been reluctant to allow any litigation to reach the courts. Sports federations have long operated in an authoritarian manner and have been qualified by the EU's sports commissioner as functioning in a 'defensive shell' (European Commission 2000a: 3). In an attempt to prevent the intrusion of civil and penal law into sports and to deal with ever-increasing lawsuits, the IOC established the Court of Arbitration for Sport (CAS) in 1983. But from the start the court was seriously criticized for its lack of independence. Indeed, until overwhelming criticism led to a full review of its status in 1994, the CAS was not only financed by the IOC, but its members (judges) were nominated by the IOC itself.

Until the mid-1990s, some sports organizations included in their by-laws a provision prohibiting a club or an athlete from bringing any matter before the jurisdiction of a civil or penal court, threatening them with exclusion if they did not respect this interdiction. Some federations, such as the IAAF, even considered life suspension for any athlete seeking judicial remedies (Blanpain 1993: 162).

During the 1990s, the CAS did become more independent and certainly proved its worth. But, contrary to the wishes of several international sports bodies, it did not become the sole mechanism for athletes to appeal against sanctions imposed by sports federations. This was confirmed in 2002 when the *Tribunal cantonal vaudois* (Vaud cantonal court), a civil court in Switzerland under whose jurisdiction UEFA falls, ruled in a case between the Dutch football star Frank de Boer and UEFA regarding a sanction imposed by the latter for doping (*Le Temps* 2002).

THE CONVENTION AND SPORTS

The Convention on the Rights of the Child does not include any direct reference to sports. Even during the treaty's long and laborious drafting process, no one ever suggested debating the issue of competitive sports and its impact on children's human rights (Detrick 1992). This was due to the positive image of sports, a lack of awareness within governmental circles and the absence of advocacy groups in this field. Sport is one of the few situations frequently encountered by children that is not directly reflected in the Convention, even though it is the international human rights treaty that covers by far the widest range of issues.

The Convention's strength, however, is that it clearly suggests links with practically any situation. Of its 42 substantive provisions, 37 are of *direct* relevance to child athletes. They include:

- the right to non-discrimination (article 2);
- the principle of the best interests of the child (article 3);
- the right to be provided appropriate direction and guidance (article 5);
- the right to development (article 6);
- the right to an identity and nationality (article 7);
- the right not to be separated from their parents (article 9);
- the right to have their views taken into account (article 12);
- freedom of expression and association (articles 13 and 15);
- protection of privacy (article 16);
- the right to access appropriate information (article 17);
- protection from abuse and neglect and other forms of violence (article 19);
- the right to health (article 24);
- the right to education (articles 28 and 29);

- the right to rest, leisure, recreation and cultural activities (article 31);
- the right to be protected from economic exploitation (article 32), illegal drugs (article 33), sexual exploitation (article 34), abduction, trafficking and sale (article 35), and other forms of exploitation (article 36);
- the right to benefit from rehabilitative care (article 39); and
- the right to due and fair process (article 40).

Increasingly the human rights community is realizing that private for- and non-profit associations – including private sports entities – can have some obligations under legally binding international human rights treaties (Clapham 1993, 1995; Addo 1999; International Council on Human Rights Policy 2002). This level of responsibility is sometimes referred to as the 'horizontal effect', i.e., the effect that human rights have on relations between private parties, as opposed to the effect they have on the vertical level between the individual and the state (Detrick 1999: 31). The UN Committee on the Rights of the Child (2002b, para. 653) considers that states

> … have a legal obligation to respect and ensure the rights of children as stipulated in the Convention, which includes the obligation to ensure that non-State service providers operate in accordance with its provisions, thus creating *indirect obligations* on such actors. [emphasis added]

Another UN expert body distinguishes three fundamental types of obligations under international human rights law: the obligation to *respect* rights requires states to *refrain* from interfering directly or indirectly with people's enjoyment of their human rights; the obligation to *protect* requires states to take *measures that prevent* third parties from interfering with human rights; and the obligation to *fulfil* requires states to adopt appropriate legislative, administrative, budgetary, judicial, promotional and other *measures towards the full realization* of human rights (UN Committee on Economic, Social and Cultural Rights 2000: para. 33; UN Development Programme 2000: 93). These three fundamental type of obligations also apply to all sports authorities and organizations (see Figure 3.1).

State authorities are responsible for guaranteeing children's human rights and are directly accountable under domestic and international law. Responsibility cascades down from the top, so other stakeholders have some liability under the Convention. Therefore, sports bodies, whether publicly subsidized or privately managed, and all adults in charge of the care of children, are also accountable.

The Convention clearly engages non-state actors as it recognizes in article 18 that parents (or legal guardians) have the primary responsibility for the upbringing and development of the child, with the necessary support of the state, and that the best interest of the child will be their basic concern. Parents' rights, duties and responsibilities are recognized in article 5, but article 19 requires that states take all measures to protect the child, should parents fail to protect their child's rights.

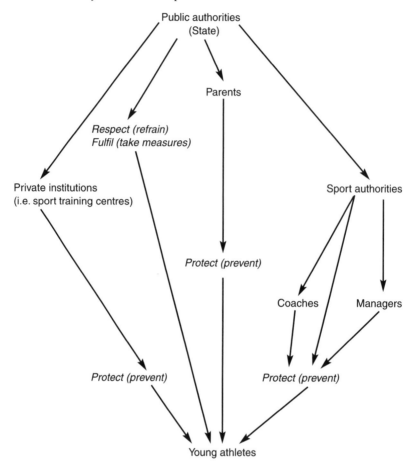

Figure 3.1 Convention on the Rights of the Child: human rights obligations

POLITICAL INERTIA

If the European Court of Justice, the Council of Europe and the EU have taken the protection of some of the human rights of athletes seriously, other regional and international political bodies have remained remarkably discreet. Neither the Organization of American States' Inter-American Court of Justice nor the Commission on Human and People's Rights of the Organization for African Unity (now called the African Union) have seriously addressed such issues. The UN Commission on Human Rights has not done much better, adopting a resolution in 1996 on the 'Olympic Ideal' which reaffirmed the 'mutually beneficial cooperation between the IOC and the UN', and paying lip-service to non-discrimination in sports (UN Commission on Human Rights 1996).

The seven UN human rights treaty bodies (established by the related human rights treaties), including the Committee on the Rights of the Child, have never addressed athletes' human rights violations systematically, even though this would fit perfectly into their monitoring mandate. This is probably due to the overwhelmingly positive image of sport in these international forums, as well as to the fact that, with a single exception, no major human rights treaty refers directly to sports[5] and that there are no independent advocacy groups active at the international level in this field. The only sport-related treaty adopted by the UN General Assembly (resolution 40/64) was the 1985 International Convention Against Apartheid in Sports, which banned all South African teams and athletes in order to combat racial discrimination in sports and prohibited contact between non-South African athletes, teams and officials and those competing under the apartheid regime.

To promote and protect the rights of young athletes adequately, the Convention's standards and norms need to be fully integrated into all sporting rules, by-laws, regulations, administrative and court decisions, policies and programmes and at local, national, regional and international levels.

In 1979 already, the Council of Europe proposed a European Charter on the Rights of the Child whose contents were both forward-looking and innovative. Although the Charter did not cover as wide a spectrum of rights as the Convention, the text it proposed included a visionary provision on sports. At a time when the concept of children's human rights was ignored if not rejected by most states and contrary to other treaties, which refer mainly to access to mass sports, the proposed Charter focused on abuse and exploitation issues in competitive sports and stressed related civil rights issues. It declared that:

> a. It should be ensured that high performance sports remain a voluntary undertaking, that no coercion of any sort be indulged in and that human dignity be respected at all time; b. To reduce health hazards and educational disadvantages, regulations should be introduced in training methods and training periods; c. Supervision should be exercised on the use of certain drugs which can prematurely stop growth or affect sexual development; drug detection tests during competition ought to be increased; d. The possibility for handicapped children to participate in sporting activities should be improved.
>
> (Council of Europe 1979: para. 17)

Although the Charter was never adopted, it had a significant impact on the growing recognition of children's human rights during the 1980s. It also influenced the drafting of the Convention, although the Charter's specific provisions regarding the rights of children in sports were, regrettably, lost in this process. No significant international child rights treaty has since been as explicit in its text in relation to the rights of child and adolescent athletes.

NOTES

1 However, when Russian gymnast Svetlana Khorkina won the 2001 world championship, she was 22 years old and 1.64 metres tall. Dutch gymnast, Verona van de Leur, aged 15 years 10 months, was the youngest participant at this competition.

2 In addition to the Convention on the Rights of the Child (1989), the other six major human rights treaties are the International Convention on the Elimination of All Forms of Racial Discrimination (1965); the International Covenant on Economic, Social and Cultural Rights (1966); the International Covenant on Civil and Political Rights (1966); the Convention on the Elimination of All Forms of Discrimination Against Women (1979); the Convention against Torture (1984); and the International Convention on the Protection of the Rights of All Migrant Workers and Members of Their Families (1990).

3 In 1997, however, the Intergovernmental Conference set up to revise the Maastricht Treaty did adopt a brief declaration on sport which recognized its specificities and was annexed to the Amsterdam Treaty.

4 See the definition of the 'right to due and fair process' in article 14 of the International Covenant on Civil and Political Rights (available at http://www.unhchr.ch/html/menu3/b/a_ccpr.htm).

5 Only the Convention on the Elimination of All Forms of Discrimination Against Women (1979) refers in its article 10 to sports: 'States Parties shall take all appropriate measures to eliminate discrimination against women in order to ensure to them equal rights with men in the field of education and in particular to ensure, on a basis of equality of men and women: … (g) the same opportunities to participate actively in sports and physical education.'

Part II

In the best interests of the child?

4 Winning at any cost

Winning isn't everything – it's the only thing.
(Vince Lombardi, former American football coach, in CASA 2000: ii)

Competitive sport begins where healthy sports end.
(Bertolt Brecht, German author, 1928: 145)

It is widely accepted that the practice of sports is beneficial to children and adolescents and has a positive impact on their physical, mental, psychomotor and social development (Bouchard *et al.* 1994; Metzl 2002: 3–16). Sport can help young people to become more confident and progressively more autonomous, evaluate their own progress and set objectives. It reinforces their self-esteem and concentration, and teaches them to discipline themselves, work in a team and handle defeat and victory, as well as encouraging fair play and socialization.

The medical world largely sees sport as a favourable activity for children's physical and mental well-being (Pellegrini and Smith 1998) and as essential for the prevention of health problems (Alpert and Wilmore 1994). In addition, sport is almost unique in that it encourages the integration of children, including those with disabilities, of all social, cultural and ethnic origins and is an instrument to promote gender equality.

If sport in general is widely considered a beneficial leisure activity, many specialists agree that *competitive sports* are not necessarily healthy for young people. 'Health is not the objective of competition; it's winning,' said Lucio Bizzini, a former Swiss football star and today a sports psychologist (Télévision Suisse Romande 2000). In July 2000, the American Academy of Pediatrics published a policy statement on the seriousness of the health-related risks of intensive training and competitive sports for young people, and qualified children engaged in these activities as 'at-risk populations'.

Even public authorities are beginning to consider that sports may potentially present harmful side effects. 'For the first time our region has ceased to regard sport as a health-related factor, and instead considered it as an activity linked to risk behaviour,' said an Italian academic involved in state-sponsored research on doping in sports (Solerti 2000: 69).

Once the fact that risk factors do exist in competitive sports has been accepted, they should be carefully identified and evaluated. The human rights framework can be of use in analysing these factors and can help to avoid unfounded and excessive judgements. The definition of risk, too, is often based on subjective criteria, as Frank Furedi, a British sociologist, pointed out (2000: 8–9):

> Virtually every aspect of life today is seen as inherently dangerous, whether it relates to health, food, technology, the environment, the Internet or personal relationships … The new concept of being 'at risk' lays emphasis on vulnerability and denies human beings their capacity for resilience … Immunising children to risk makes them more vulnerable to danger: they never learn to handle and to manage those factors.

Scientific evaluations of the economic impact of sport on society are still very scarce. In Switzerland, government institutions and a national health insurance plan published an official study in 2001, which estimated the direct and indirect economic benefits of sporting activities on health in the country at approximately 2.4 billion euros. It also revealed that the 'cost' of sports, mainly due to expenses related to accidents, amounted to 2 billion euros (Government of Switzerland 2001).

For the purpose of this book, competitive sport is broadly defined as any physical activity whose main objective, for participants, is victory. Such activity is practised by amateur or professional athletes and organized by a defined, structured and recognized authority. It takes place in an environment strictly codified by established rules. Although there is no standard definition of elite sports, it can be considered to include young athletes who train a minimum of one to two hours a day, at least five days a week. Amateur and professional levels are closely interwoven, with the vast majority of the sporting world's elite having been amateur athletes at some point in their career.

Competitive sports are not systematically harmful to health and they can be practised safely by talented young athletes, as long as appropriate safeguards are in place. Many children are gifted in a particular field – whether sports, arts, music or another subject – that they can develop in a conducive environment and if they are properly encouraged by adults. Children with a talent for sports have the right to expect support and guidance from their community. The Convention on the Rights of the Child affirms in article 29(a) that: 'States Parties agree that the education of the child shall be directed to: (a) the development of the child's personality, *talents and mental and physical abilities to their fullest potential*' (emphasis added).

To avoid becoming frustrated in 'regular' schools and to nurture their exceptional talent, gifted children are often placed in special schools and/or training centres. Sports stars such as Steffi Graf, Boris Becker, Dominique Monceanu, Ian Thorpe, Marion Jones, Michael Owen, Marco van Basten, Michael Jordan, Martina Hingis, and Serena and Venus Williams all left the standard education system at an early age to join special training and educational programmes. But, although these intensive sports programmes are intended to help young athletes progress, in reality they often put the children at risk as they are expected to accept great sacrifices to attain outstanding results rapidly (see Chapter 12). The Dutch football club Ajax Amsterdam, for example, is famous for 'producing' talented players and, for decades, its trainers have hammered home their motto: 'At Ajax, we are never satisfied' (Van Wijnen 2000: 9).

NEVER ENOUGH MEDALS

Elite youth sport often claims to respond to the needs and wishes of children. Far too often, however, it exists largely to satisfy adults. Even more than their peers, children involved in competitive sports grow up in a world dominated by adults with little space for freedom, self-initiative and creativity. Adults – parents, coaches and trainers, officials, managers and agents, journalists and sponsors – control competitive sports at all levels. They each have their own set of interests. Parents often live their own, sometimes frustrated, ambitions through their children or hope their success will alleviate financial burdens (Donnelly 1993: 102; Tofler *et al.* 1996: 281). Coaches and trainers need to justify their involvement and often prepare their professional future by obtaining successful results. Officials have to achieve satisfactory results to ensure the sustainability of their organization and, ultimately, of their sport. Career managers and agents need to get a return on their investment. The media wants positive results to ensure successful television ratings and print sales, while the sports goods industry speculates on attractive events and successful athletes to gain high visibility to market their products.

Competitive sports also have great political significance despite the end of the cold war (1989) and the dissolution of the East–West race for results and prestige. With victories being a source of great pride in most countries, sport has long been politicized. A few months before the Sydney Olympic Games (2000), Alexander Lukashenko, the president of Belarus, promised victorious Belorussian athletes:

> Just produce the results and you'll have an apartment and thousands of dollars and you'll be able to provide for yourself for the rest of your life. I'll buy you anything you need, be it guns, boats, swimming trunks, undershorts. But God forbid if I hear any complaints or questions on the eve of your departure for Sydney. If you get good results, I'll have the grounds to reward you …
>
> (Associated Press 1999f)

In elite sports, many trainers or officials, whose expectations are often very high, do not tolerate lack of achievement by child or adult athletes. When French figure skaters did not win any medals during the 2001 European championships, Didier Gailhaguet, president of the French Skating Federation, complained: 'I am fed up. We have created an environment that leads to performance. Athletes have rights, but also obligations. Pleasure is a trendy word. Athletes are not here to enjoy themselves, but to win' (*L'Equipe Magazine* 2001b).

Despite the overwhelming emphasis on victory in competitive sports, some champions still see winning in a much wider sense: competing against themselves and trying to improve constantly until they attain excellence. Andre Agassi, one of the most outstanding tennis players in history, commented: 'I think I don't really like competing, except against myself. I love the beauty of the game, the perfect move that generates euphoria when each stroke is efficient and just right' (*L'Equipe Magazine* 2001a: 39). And four-time Olympic champion, Russian swimmer Alexander Popov asked: 'Why should losing be different to winning? An athlete should be strong enough to accept it, as long as he or she did everything to avoid it' (Donzé 2000a: 21).

Since the 1970s, sport has become a global, multibillion-dollar affair, which benefits not only companies that produce clothes, toys and dietetic food and vitamins, construct stadiums and manage training centres, but also the media and the entertainment business. It is estimated that, in 2000, the sports industry generated over US$ 120 billion in the United States, making it one of the country's top ten industries (Murphy 1999: 32).

This overwhelming and apparently ever-increasing economic success has to be carefully studied from the perspective of the *best interests* of young athletes. The fundamental consideration must remain the developmental rights of the *child* – not the athlete nor his or her sports entourage. 'My coach's desire to win seemed stronger than mine at times,' said 16-year-old Danielle Herbst, a top American gymnast during the 1990s (Ryan 1995: 216). Adults' obsession with victory can overwhelm all other considerations and feelings. During the 1992 Barcelona Olympic Games, 15-year-old Shannon Miller, an American gymnast who became world champion in 1994, admitted that 'we don't enjoy training. The only pleasure is the results, the medals' (Monnard 1992: 36).

The identification and selection processes for gifted young athletes are frequently governed by result-oriented criteria alone. Some children and adolescents are traumatized by the cruel selection system applied in competitive sports, in which only the toughest will make it. For every champion, a large number of young hopefuls are unable to survive the harsh requirements and are rejected by the system. Dr Lyle Micheli, a paediatric orthopaedist at the Harvard Medical School and former president of the American College of Sports Medicine, considers that: 'Some of the biggest offenders are the elite coaches. If they have to sacrifice seven kids to get a champion, some will do it' (Ryan 1995: 234). His opinion is confirmed by Bela Karolyi, the world-renowned American-Romanian trainer, who said of 'his' little gymnasts: 'These girls are like little scorpions. You put them all in a bottle, and one scorpion will come out alive. That scorpion will be the champion' (Ryan 1995: 22).

Nowadays, the financial, social, media and political pressure on athletes, including the youngest ones, is immense. 'You don't win the silver; you lose the gold' was the slogan of the multibillionaire manufacturer Nike just before the 1996 Atlanta Olympics. Even golfer Tiger Woods, an elegant and fair sportsman, once said to the press: 'Second place sucks'; three decades earlier, golfing legend Jack Nicklaus also denigrated second place: 'I didn't win. Nobody ever remembers who finished second at anything' (Owen 2001). In the eyes of many, an athlete who finishes second is a loser; there is only room for winners in a world tailored by competition.

Is this the message the sports community wants to get across to help adolescents to fulfil themselves and to build a prosperous and peaceful society? What about the Olympic ideal 'to contribute to building a peaceful and better world by educating youth through sport practised without discrimination of any kind and in the Olympic spirit, which requires mutual understanding with a spirit of friendship, solidarity and fair play' (IOC 2002)? What safeguards exist to protect these values? Where and by whom are the ambitions and limits set?

Political prestige – not necessarily public health considerations – often pushes states to invest heavily in elite sports, even in developing countries. The Kenyan authorities, for example, admitted in 2001 that their government:

> has continued to invest in the development of sports infrastructures. This investment is aimed at the development of youth character, health and values that strengthen teamwork and national pride. As a result of past government support for sports, Kenya has become a regional and international power in various sports.
>
> (Government of Kenya 2001: para. 23)

During the Olympic Games in Sydney (2000), the Dutch team won worldwide acclaim and admiration by finishing eighth overall in the country medal tables, its best-ever result. The Netherlands were classed ahead of Great Britain and Cuba, two traditional sporting nations, and obtained only one Olympic title less than Italy or France and two less than reunified Germany. But in the minds of Dutch sport officials, the perfect score can never be attained. 'Too good does not exist; too many gold medals can't happen,' said the Dutch volleyball coach after his country's historic success in Sydney, having previously led his team to victory at the 1996 Atlanta Olympics (Vandeweghe 2000: 6).

Corporate business has taken over much elite sport. When a professional athlete wins or loses, the implications are not just human but also commercial – especially now that sport stars not only serve as a vehicle for commercial advertising, but also increasingly carry ideological life-style messages imposed by multinational corporations (Klein 2000: 50–61). 'Adidas makes you better' was the slogan used by the sponsor of top player Martina Hingis, during Roland Garros, the French Open tennis tournament, in 2001. But would it still have been a good slogan had Hingis lost in the first round? Marie Gérard, director of communications at Adidas France, admitted that: 'Our slogan is ambitious. If Martina had lost during the first round, our brand would have lost credibility' (Buss 2001: 24).

In the contemporary sport system, champions with no media profile may find themselves pushed aside. Winner of the 2002 and 2003 World Cup for skiing,

Austrian Stephan Eberharter, has been ostracized by sponsors and the media because they perceive him as boring. Marc Biver, former director of International Management Group (IMG) for Switzerland, stated:

> I respect Eberharter's personality, but apparently he doesn't want to be involved. Sponsors expect strong personalities, attractive to the media so that they can show them with their brands, as is the case in tennis, athletics, Formula One, football and so many other sports.
>
> (Payot 2002: 30)

Businesses are battling to dominate the huge sports market – and young athletes are increasingly caught up in the turmoil. American Sonny Vaccaro, who was one of the masterminds of Nike's development and is now a top Adidas executive, said in 1998:

> Sponsoring high school teams [15–18 years old] is a big part of keeping Adidas visible to the people who buy our product. And the people who we're trying to stay visible to are kids. I admit it is unfortunate that we have to put high school athletes in the middle of this. They're just the pawns in a big corporate fight. But Nike is not going to stop. So we can't stop either.
>
> (Wetzel and Yaleger 2000: 242)

Sport clearly mirrors society. In previous years, especially during the cold war, many children were directed into competitive sports to gratify the need for political prestige. Today, political competition has partly been overshadowed by the logic of the new economy and corporate business. But, whether for political prestige or commercial gain, very young athletes still risk being pushed by adults to win, whatever the cost to the children.

5 The age of innocence

Minimum ages for competing

> Our kids have gotten younger, and many leave home to train with an elite coach.
> So we are taking them out of their fundamental support system. Our window of
> competition is very small, and I think the kids, the coaches and the parents get
> caught up, knowing a career might be over at 16.
>
> (Board member of the US Gymnastics Federation, in Drape 1997: E16).

At what age can a child begin to take part in competitive sports? Since the
1970s, several authors have tried to find an answer to this question. They agree
that before the age of six or seven, a child cannot understand the concept of
competition (Sherif 1976: 18–36; Martens 1978: 190–1; Roberts 1980: 37–50;
Maffuli 1998: 298). Children under the age of nine are incapable of differentiat-
ing between the concept of effort and that of ability. This means that they
believe that winning can only be achieved through effort and that losing is the
result of not trying hard enough (Murphy 1999: 146).

Babies of just a few months may develop and express a competitive personality and, from a very early age, children may enjoy playing games (Hughes 1999;
Frost *et al.* 2001). These – normal – responses should not be confused with a
child's capacity to understand the meaning of competitive sports and the stakes
involved, both of which require a more sophisticated cognitive development. As
Martens (1978: 279) pointed out: 'Joy and sadness are not synonymous with winning and losing in the minds of young athletes – at least not until adults teach
them so.'

Article 1 of the Convention on the Rights of the Child defines the child as
'every human being below the age of 18 years unless, under the law applicable to
the child, majority is attained earlier'. Crucially, this means that every individual
under 18 is entitled to specific human rights, including that of special protection
measures due to their vulnerability. Whilst article 1 includes an escape clause
which allows states to set a lower age of majority, the Committee on the Rights
of the Child systematically recommends that all countries abide by the internationally defined age of majority, set at 18 years (Office of the UN High
Commissioner for Human Rights 1997: 414). States and other authorities aim to
set minimum ages for specific activities in order to find a proper balance between

children's right to protection and their right to progressive emancipation and autonomy. The Convention recognizes the *evolving capacity* of the child as a fundamental concept. The maturity and capacity of discernment of children need to be taken into account when enforcing their rights (articles 5 and 12).

The Convention (article 31.1) also refers to 'the right of the child to rest and leisure, to engage in play and recreational activities *appropriate to the age of the child*' (emphasis added). Applied to the world of organized sport, the Convention implicitly calls for a *child-sensitive* and *child-centred* approach to competitive sports and intensive training, in which the child's developmental stages are recognized and respected.

The intensity of training and the form it takes should be adapted to the child's physical and mental capacities and motivations, and not the other way around. Many specialists believe that until the age of 11 or 12 (Weiss 1993; English Sports Council 1998: 9; Rowe and Champion 2000: 170–1), the child athlete puts as much, if not more, importance on factors other than winning: on pleasure, action, informal games, social interaction, improvement of skills and personal involvement (see also Chapter 18) and that ranking, medals and titles could be abolished for competitors under the age of 14 (Bizzini 1989). The child is potentially in danger when adults impose – rather than adapt – their own values, perceptions and physical and mental demands (Maffuli 1998: 298).

Since the 1970s, the age at which children start to participate in competitive sports has dropped drastically. When the US Soccer Federation announced an agreement with the sporting goods manufacturer Nike to identify and recruit talented young players, its president, Alan Rothenberg, stated: 'The average age of a World Cup player is 28, which means that we have to be dealing with 9 to 16-year-olds right now' (*USA Today* 1998: 13C). Despite the fact that children cannot assimilate the concept of competition before the age of six, some are involved in intensive training from a very early age, often between four and six years old – which is lower than the minimum age for starting compulsory education in most countries.

SETTING MINIMUM AGE LIMITS TO PROTECT CHILDREN IN SPORT

The Convention on the Rights of the Child explicitly requires states parties to set legal minimum ages in certain areas: admission to employment (article 32); voluntary enlistment and conscription in armed forces (article 38 and its related Optional Protocol); and criminal responsibility (article 40). The Committee on the Rights of the Child also monitors different legal minimum ages set by states in various fields, such as legal and medical counselling and medical treatment without parental consent; minimum age to create or join associations; age for sexual consent; age for lodging complaints and seeking redress or participating in administrative and judicial proceedings; etc. (UN Committee on the Rights of the Child 1996: 8–9).

With the exception of voluntary enlistment and conscription in armed forces, the Committee – rather than the Convention – sets specific minimum age limits according to the principle of the best interest of the child (article 3) and his or her evolving capacities. Neither the Convention nor the Committee (for the time being) has addressed the issue of setting a minimum age for engaging in early intensive training, competing with adults, or in competitive or professional sports (although the minimum age for employment could deal with this situation, see Chapter 11). The Convention does, however, contain provisions that could tackle these fundamental issues, such as article 31 ('the right of the child to rest and leisure, to engage in play and recreational activities appropriate to the age of the child').

American child development experts agreed already in 1938 that competition could negatively affect young athletes' health. During a convention that year, they adopted the following resolution:

> Inasmuch as pupils below tenth grade (14 to 15 years old) are in the midst of the period of rapid growth ... be it therefore resolved that the leaders in the field of physical and health education should do all in their power to discourage interscholastic competition at this age level, because of its strenuous nature.
>
> (Murphy 1999: 30)

Some sports present more risks than others, so minimum ages for participation will also depend on the type of sport practised. In this respect, sports can be divided into four main types: non-contact sports (for example, volleyball, track and field, tennis, table tennis, swimming); contact sports (basketball, football, handball, field hockey, water polo); collision sports (ice hockey, American football, rugby, judo); and combat sports (boxing, karate and other martial sports).

The International Olympic Committee (IOC), despite being the supreme international sports authority, does not provide for a minimum age for participation in the Olympic Games, nor does it limit participation to adults only (over 18 years). The IOC leaves it to the different international sports federations to set such minimum ages, if they deem it necessary. During the 2000 Sydney Olympics, for example, Fatema Gerashi, a 12-year-old from Bahrain, took part in the swimming competitions, while 16-year-old American Cheryl Haworth won the bronze medal for weightlifting in her category.

In 1996, the Council of Europe's parliamentary assembly, alarmed by the abuse of young athletes in competitive sports, adopted a recommendation (resolution 1292) which states that:

> The Assembly ... calls on sports federations and the International Olympic Committee to review national and international competition systems involving young people with a view of raising minimum age limits or, where already appropriate, enforcing them. The Assembly sees several advantages in drawing a clearer distinction between juvenile and adult competition

classes. This could be achieved by raising the age limits for participation in certain competitions to 16 or 18 years, depending on the sport, particularly in international competitions and championships.

(Council of Europe 1996)

Similarly, in 1998, the European Non-Governmental Sports Organisation (ENGSO), a regional umbrella organization whose membership includes national Olympic committees and national sports federations and unions, adopted 'guidelines for children and youth sport' which recommended that:

> competitions for children below 13 years of age should normally be held domestically ... the member organisations of ENGSO and ENGSO as such should work towards an agreed joint minimum age limit for participation in international championships (Olympic Games, World Cup, European and World Championships). European sports federations and the Olympic movement should be involved in this work.

(ENGSO 1998, recommendation 3)

But both inter-governmental and non-governmental standpoints on minimum age limits have, for the time being, had little impact on sports organizations. In this regard, the IOC's passive attitude has permitted, since the 1980s, the participation of athletes as young as 12 in adult competitions, especially in sports such as gymnastics, diving, tennis and figure skating. In female gymnastics in particular, athletes are often programmed to reach their peak between the ages of 16 and 18. To reach athletic maturity at such an early age, children obviously need to start intensive training at the earliest possible age, between four and six years old at the very latest.

In the 1990s, some of the international sport authorities most concerned with the issue of minimum ages of participation did try to address it, but only as a reaction to widespread media criticism and serious pressure. After 13-year-old Chinese diver Fu Mingxia won a medal at the 1992 Barcelona Olympics, the International Swimming Federation (FINA) raised the minimum age of participation to 15 for the 'Olympic Games, World Championships or World Cups' (FINA 2001). This does not stop younger divers from competing in other senior competitions, such as the European, American or Asian championships.

Gymnast Nadia Comaneci was only 14 when she won her Olympic medals in 1976; but it was not until 1996 that the International Federation of Gymnastics raised to 16 the minimum age for participation in the Olympics. However, to qualify for the Olympics, a gymnast must take part in the world championships, which are organized the year before the Olympics and in which athletes of 15 can participate. To get to the world championships, the gymnasts will have had to qualify for the major junior contests between the ages of 11 and 13 in order to be eligible to compete in the senior ('adult') national championships when they are 13 or 14. The International Figure Skating Federation raised its minimum age for the Olympics from 14 to 15 in 1997. In both female gymnastics and figure skating, only girls who are not fully grown and whose bodies are small and very light can perform the technical skills required to reach the top. Consequently, high-level careers in these sports generally last no longer than three to five years, with top competitors reaching their peak between the ages of 15 and 20.

Another sport that attracted negative publicity concerning the age of players was tennis. The International Tennis Federation (ITF) was slow to react, despite the apparition during the early 1980s of 'baby champions', such as Tracy Austin and Andrea Jaeger, who suffered from burn-out and chronic injuries and had to give up competitive sports at a very young age. In 1995, at the same time as a new generation of very young champions was appearing on the scene (Martina Hingis, Anna Kournikova, Venus and Serena Williams, etc.), the ITF's Age Eligibility Commission, set up in 1994, fixed the minimum age at 15. But it permitted players aged between 14 and 15 to play, each year, in a maximum of four professional tournaments with prize money of more than US$ 10,000. Players were not allowed to participate in Women's Tennis Association (WTA) tournaments, which are the most important in terms of both prestige and prize money.

This rule has been criticized by the parents of some young, talented players. In 1999, Croat Mirjana Lucic won a court case in which she challenged the rule, and the father of a talented American player, Monique Viele, aged 14 at that time, threatened to take legal action against the WTA if it did not agree to let his daughter play the full schedule of professional tournaments (Doherty 1999: 144). The case did not reach court as the ITF gave in to pressure in 1999. It changed its eligibility rules to allow 14-year-olds to participate in seven ITF tournaments and the possibility to obtain a wild-card for one WTA championship a year. Rules for 16-year-old players were also changed: the maximum number of ITF and WTA championships was raised to 17 in 1999, from the 11 set in 1995.

In order to guarantee a child protection policy, the IOC should address this issue, undertaking independent, comprehensive research on the compatibility of existing minimum age limits, where they exist, set by different sport federations with international child rights standards. The study should look at the issue from a wider perspective, examining closely the age at which children are involved in intensive training schemes in relation to the age at which they should reach their peak in competitions. According to the results of its study, the IOC could set a minimum age for participation in the Olympic Games and encourage sports federations to set age limits for participation in competitions.

Some sport officials or researchers challenge the use of the concept of age to determine different categories for competition (Leglise 1997: 3). They give preference to the physiological age of the child, as they rightly assume that two young athletes of the same age do not necessarily have equal physical and psychological levels of development, especially during puberty (Maffuli 1998: 298). Even where age limits for participation have been set, there will still be an age difference of almost 12 months between a child born at the beginning of one year and another born at the end – a significant difference in the context of a child's development, which may have a considerable impact on the child's right to equal opportunities. This 'relative age effect' has been shown to occur in the sports and school systems (Grondin and Musch 2000).

Though far from perfect, the criteria of age generally seems the most fair – and the easiest to enforce – as it enables sport organizers to define categories on the basis of clear, objective and non-discriminative criteria. The Convention considers seriously, however, the concept of the child's *evolving capacity* (rather than the concept of age), which appears to be most relevant in situations where the child's opinion is sought by parents, teachers or a court judge (Limber and Melton 1992: 167–87; Morss 1996; Davie 1996).

Training and participation in adult competitions can put children at risk both physically and psychologically. Some countries have passed laws to protect young athletes, by fixing a minimum age of participation for some sports. In France, for example, weightlifting and bodybuilding are forbidden for children under 14 (André-Simonet 2000: 33). In Latvia, a minimum age for intensive training is set for each sport: for example, the age is six years for gymnastics and ten for volleyball (Council of Europe 1999a).

In Belgium, two minimum ages have been set for cycling, a leading sport in the country: 12 years of age for competing in races of short distances and 16 for very long races, although some political groups challenged the latter limit before the Belgian (Flemish) parliament, suggesting it should be lowered to 14 to help bolster Belgium's national sport. The parliament asked the independent Flemish Commissioner for Children to provide expert advice. Basing her position on the Convention, she emphasized that children should not be treated as adults and competition should be adapted to their physical and psychological capacities. She concluded that in order to protect children, existing ages should not be lowered (Government of Belgium 2000).

In the United States, the eligibility rules of some sport federations have been challenged in recent years. In many sports, the possibility for gifted young players to play in professional teams was limited to athletes having at least finished high school (i.e., aged about 17 or 18 years old). In baseball, basketball and ice hockey, these rules have recently been modified. The National Football League (NFL) rule only allowed players to join the professional Amercian football league three years after graduating from high school (aged about 20 or 21), in order for them to finish their education and to protect them from physical injury. This rule was challenged for the first time on 5 February 2004, when a federal judge at the US District Court in Manhattan ruled that the NFL rule violated anti-trust laws by restricting young football players' access to work. The court stated that the claimant, 20-year-old Maurice Clarett, was eligible to join a team in 2004, even though, under the NFL rule, he would have had to wait another year before qualifying for selection. The judgement received mixed reactions. Harris Barton, a former San Francisco 49ers player, said:

> I think the NFL was trying to protect these kids, making them stay in school, get an education. I think that was the right thing to do. It's a shame that the courts ruled like that, but the precedent was set in the NBA [National Basketball Association] and baseball. That's the way it works.

Bob Griese, a broadcaster and former Miami Dolphins player, said:

> I have two feelings on it: No. 1, this is America, and you have a right to work, and if you need to work, you should be able to go out and get a job. Having said that, I think that rule has been very good in terms of the NFL. I think playing in the NFL is a whole lot different for a high school kid going pro, skipping college, than it is for any other sport. If you see these kids trying it, they're either going to get hurt, or they're not going to be successful.
>
> (Hack 2004)

SPORTS OF COMBAT: A MINIMUM AGE?

The whole debate about the age at which children can participate in competitions and intensive training is particularly sensitive when it comes to high-risk sports, especially combat and martial sports. Mountaineering, rock climbing, parachuting, horse riding, car and motorcycle racing, bullfighting, scuba diving and combat sports can all be considered at-risk activities for young people and authorities have slowly begun to put in place safeguards, including minimum age limits.

Bullfighting, for example, is a traditional sport, very popular in Spain, Argentina and France, that raises serious ethical and protection issues. The minimum age for competing in bullfights in France is 16; until 2001, when it was raised to 16, the minimum age in Spain was 14. At the end of the 1990s, a promising young French matador, Jean-Baptiste Jalabert, under 16 at that time, changed his name to Juan Batista Jalalabert, went to Spain and was thus able to compete in bullfights. The raising of the minimum age in Spain, however, did not please everyone: bullfighter Miguel Cubillo declared that: 'If someone is ready, the least important issue is age. One could be more ready at 15 than at 20' (Wilkinson 2001).

No minimum age limits existed until recently in car and motorcycle racing. Since 2002, drivers under 18 are banned from participating in the prestigious American NASCAR car competitions for safety reasons. In 2001, however, a 16-year-old driver, Kyle Busch, competed in six races and Mike Helton, NASCAR's president, told CNN: 'Younger competitors need as much experience as they can accumulate before competing in NASCAR's professional levels. They need to hone driving skill knowledge, a judgment that is best learned at the local level' (CNN/SI.com 2001). Motorcycling authorities seem not to have followed NASCAR's moves: in 2002, a 15-year-old British competitor, Chaz Davis, took part in several races of the world's most renowned motorcycling event, the World Championship. In 2003, two other under-age motorcyclists also took part: Swiss Thomas Lüthi (16) and Mike de Meglio (15) from France.

The most controversial sports, however, are combat and martial sports. Since the early twentieth century, the practice of boxing and the injuries it can cause have been debated endlessly. Some countries, such as Sweden (since 1970) and

Norway (since 1981), have outlawed this Olympic sport on medical grounds. As Dr Bill O'Neill, an expert from the British Medical Association (BMA), pointed out: 'In boxing you aim to punch your opponent's head. If you do that in football, you get sent off' (BBC 1999a).

In medical terms, a knockout, boxing's ultimate winning move, is the equivalent of a brief coma (Jordan *et al.* 1997). 'The ultimate objective of every boxer is to knock his opponent out, conduct that almost inevitably involves the infliction of grievous bodily harm on the opponent,' stated the British Law Commission in 1994. 'Under the present law it is murder to cause death by an attack intended to cause grievous bodily harm.' The Commission pointed out that, according to the BMA, between 1945 and 1994, 561 deaths occurred during boxing matches worldwide. In Indonesia alone, eight boxers are reported to have died of injuries sustained during boxing matches since 1990 (Agence France Presse 2001).

Boxing authorities usually justify their sport by claiming that athletes are free to choose their sport; accidents are isolated cases and not more frequent than in other at-risk sports; and boxing is now medically controlled. They also affirm that banning boxing would be dangerous, as it would be forced into clandestinity, which would increase health risks.

Whilst the debate about the dangers of boxing continues and rages anew after each serious accident, it is evident that – at best – children should only be involved in fights progressively. From a child rights perspective, it is hard to justify combats involving boxers under 18, with the possible exception of fights where strikes to the head are totally prohibited. It could be argued that most mature and informed adolescents (aged over 16, for example) should have the right to decide on their involvement in boxing, but this needs to be balanced with the obligation of public authorities to protect everyone under 18 from harmful and risky activities.

The BMA's Dr Vivienne Nathanson told the BBC in 2000 that:

> Boxing should be banned ... There are those occasional tragedies where someone is killed or critically injured, plus there is the chronic problem that when someone is hit on the head they have a minor degree of injury to the brain. This becomes cumulative ... In extreme cases, severe Parkinson's disease can set in. There is no safe level of boxing ... The thing that separates boxing from all other sports is the chronic and continuing damage of the brain that is inflicted on almost every participant in the sport.

Many consider that the image of a shaking Mohammed Ali, destroyed by Parkinson's disease and calling for stronger safeguards in the sport that made him famous, should be sufficient to limit and strictly regulate the participation of young people in combat sports. While the sport's training schemes are usually safe and healthy, fights are controversial. But the major boxing federations have not set a minimum age for participating in combats, although many national associations have established safeguards, such as a ban on hitting the opponent's head for boxers under a certain age (usually nine) and close medical monitoring. For combats opposing boxers aged between 9 and 15, many national federations strictly regulate hits to the head and oblige any fighter, child or adult, who has been knocked out to take a period of rest. International championships, such as the European Cadet Championships, involve young fighters aged 14 to 16, but the International Amateur Boxing Association (IABA) does not permit boxers under 17 years of age 'to take part in the Olympic Games, World or Continental Championships or international matches' (IABA Rules, XXV). In female boxing, adolescents of 17 can participate in the Women's European Championships.

In many countries, although medical supervision of fights is compulsory, professional medical groups advocate to prohibit boxing. In the United States, boxing was banned as a school sport in the 1950s, and medical associations have opposed boxing for children since the 1970s (Martens 1978: 223–4). In the United Kingdom, after boxer Paul Ingle suffered catastrophic brain injuries in December 2000, the BMA sought to make boxing illegal by withdrawing the medical support it gives the sport (BBC 1999a). In Australia, controversy about young athletes involved in boxing raged in 1998 following a boxing competition in Queensland involving girls as young as 11, and the Australian Medical Association strongly supported an initiative to ban all forms of boxing for children aged under 14 years (Research Centre for Injury Studies 1999).

During 1999, a passionate debate arose in Thailand about establishing a minimum age for participation in Thai boxing or *muay Thai*, the country's national sport. An ancient, traditional martial art and part of Thai culture for centuries, it is considered more violent and dangerous than European boxing as combatants are allowed to use both hands and feet to knock their opponent out. Children aged between five and nine take part in the sport, with the best joining training schools and starting professional fights at around 12 to 14 years old. The sport has also recently been opened to young women; the first nationwide televised combat was held in 1998 and, since then, many girls under 18 have joined intensive training programmes.

In 1999, some Thai politicians, supported by human rights activists, such as Vitit Muntarbhorn (UN Special Rapporteur on the sale of children, child prostitution and child pornography from 1991 to 1994), challenged the fact that such young children were involved in professional fights and proposed a bill to set the minimum age for combat at 18 (the age of majority in Thailand). A compromise was reached: a law was passed setting the minimum age at 15, although younger children could fight if their parents consented. To the frustration of child rights activists, public authorities enforce the new law very poorly, although the debate it generated permitted all concerned to reflect for the first time on the impact of the sport on children's physical and psychological development.

Had the proposed bill (setting the minimum age at 18) been passed, however, it would have had major economic implications. The sport attracts enormous gambling activities, but also brings in badly needed money to poor families. Raising the minimum age from 15 to 18 would have meant that 'hundreds of thousands of rural families would be in trouble', said Sonchart Charoenvacharavit, chairman of the

Professional Boxers Association (Assavanonda and Susanpoolthong 1999). Fahkamron Watdirang, a 12-year-old who has fought 40 professional combats since he was eight, said: 'I make about 3,000 baht for each combat and if the law stops me from boxing I don't know where I would get the money for my school and family' (Sapsomboon 1999).

DO CHEATS PROSPER? FALSE IDENTITY AND CHEATING BY ADULTS

Children experience several distinct phases of development and competitive sport has been organized accordingly, with several age categories so that the same individuals and groups learn progressively and compete together. In principle, nobody is given an artificial and unfair advantage just because he or she is older, or physically and mentally superior. Usually, entry into adult competition is set at the age of majority (18 years in most sports and most countries), but the most talented sportsmen and women often jump age categories to compete with older opponents.

Some competitors try to cheat this system, based on age groups and on the minimum age requirements set by different sports federations. Adults are generally to blame for dishonest and illegal behaviour, and often the child athlete is not even aware of it (see also Chapter 17). The most common form of cheating is when parents or sport officials try by all possible means to arrange for young athletes to compete in a lower age category than they are eligible for, in order to increase their chances of winning.

Such practices occur all over the world and in international, national and local competitions. For example, as early as 1976, an American woman altered her 17-year-old son's birth certificate so that he could play in an American football team composed of players aged 14 and under. She explained that her son 'needed a chance to be a winner' (Martens 1978: 70). In 1993, the Moroccan national under-15 football team was excluded from a friendly tournament in France when its officials deliberately tried to include older players in the team (*L'Equipe Magazine* 1993). In fact, in some sports and countries, there have been so many instances of cheating that players must now present their birth certificate to obtain a licence, such as in the US Little League baseball championships (for children aged between 5 and 12) (Martens 1978: 176–8).

More serious abuse takes place when sport officials deliberately alter or acquire fake birth certificates or other official papers, such as sport licences or passports, so that over- or under-aged athletes can compete in competitions for which they are not authorized.

The Convention guarantees every child the right to a name, a nationality and an identity. Countries are therefore required to register the child 'immediately after birth' (article 7). A birth certificate is not just another piece of paper: it attests to the official registration of children and as such allows them to benefit from the human rights to which they are entitled throughout their entire life.

Children who are not registered usually become invisible citizens, who live on the edge of society and who, legally, do not exist. UNICEF estimates that, annually, one-third of all births are not registered and that more than 70 per cent of births in sub-Saharan Africa and 63 per cent in South Asia go unregistered; some countries, such as Afghanistan, Cambodia, Eritrea, Ethiopia, Namibia and Oman have no birth registration system at all (UNICEF 1998; UNICEF 2002).

In most countries, children need a birth certificate to enrol in school and, in some, to have access to health-care services. It is evident, therefore, that the weaker a country's birth registration system, the greater the chances of abuse and exploitation. Assessing the ages of, for example, Ethiopian long-distance runners is often difficult, as their country does not have an established birth registration system (Government of Ethiopia 1999: para. 40). The level of corruption and the presence of organized crime in some countries or sports associations may also create an environment in which some officials are tempted to cheat on the identity and age of athletes to increase chances of victory.

In the 1970s, Wanderley Luxemburgo was a member of Brazil's junior football team. But in fact he was three years older than the age shown in his passport. At the end of the 1990s, Luxemburgo became the Brazilian team's trainer and it was only then that he admitted his football licence was falsified (Damato 1999: 24). In 1979, Eduardo Bordon, head of the Chilean Football Federation, altered the licences of 16 juniors – out of a team of 18 – so that older players could participate in the junior World Cup qualification games in Uruguay. His brother, Humberto Bordon, chief of the secret police under Pinochet, helped him (Damato 1999: 24).

During the 1980s and 1990s, such forms of cheating multiplied worldwide and the International Football Federation (FIFA) had to take draconian measures to combat them. In 1988, Mexico was suspended from all international competitions, including the World Cup qualifying games, after having falsified the dates of birth of young players. In 1989, it was the turn of Nigeria to be suspended from all international competitions after over-aged players played in the under-20 World Championships in Saudi Arabia. In 1995, Togo was banned from the 1996 Atlanta Olympics for contravening the age-limit rules in the preliminary competition (FIFA 1995) and was again prohibited from participating in the preliminary competition for the 2000 Sydney Olympics. After the Brazilian under-17 team won the junior football World Cup in 1999, it was discovered that four of the players had presented falsified birth certificates and were, in fact, aged between 18 and 20. This practice is so frequent in Brazil that players who have cheated by changing their age are called 'cats', an allusion to the fact that they have a well-developed moustache for their 'age'. More recently, Luciano Siqueira de Oliveira, a Brazilian professional playing for Chievo Verona (Italy), admitted having falsified his identity and age when he was 19, under pressure from an agent who told him he would only be given a chance if he were three years younger (FIFA 2002).

In Asia, too, sports officials falsified the identities of players during the Asian under-16 football championships organized in 2001 in Viet Nam. No fewer than

16 players (six from Oman, five from Iran, three from Bangladesh and two from Thailand) were caught by the Asian Football Confederation (AFC), which resorted to bone X-rays of suspected players to determine their true ages. Some proved to be 19 and 20 instead of under 16. The AFC suspended the players, team managers and national football associations concerned. AFC secretary general, Dano Peter Velappan, said: 'For 15 years we have been asking national associations not to cheat, to teach the players to be honest but unfortunately this advice was ignored' (Reuters 2001a).

Age falsification has also affected gymnastics. In 2002, four Romanian gymnasts denounced these practices, including Gina Gogean, 1992 Olympic champion, who was given a false date of birth so she could compete in senior competitions for which the minimum age was 15 when she was not even 14. According to the president of the Romanian Gymnastics Federation: 'Falsifying the age of gymnasts is a worldwide practice. We copied what the others were doing' (Associated Press 2002).

Though it was never proved, North Korea's gymnasts were suspected of cheating about their ages during the 1998 Asian Games (Associated Press 1998) and 1999 World Championships. They appeared to be much younger than the minimum age (15 years) required to compete in these events.

Some professional football clubs seek the help of medical doctors to assess the age of talented players they would like to recruit. Players might be tempted to lie about their age so as to increase their chances of fitting the required profile. Bone-density control (usually using X-rays) – for medical and political reasons a highly controversial technique used on young asylum seekers by administrative authorities determining refugee status in many Western countries (Bochud 2000: 12–14; Rongé 2002) – is also practised by football clubs to double-check the age of talented young players, especially from Africa. For example, the Dutch club Ajax Amsterdam used this technique in 2000 when selecting young African players in Ghana (Van Wijnen 2000: 5).

The setting of minimum age limits is a critical tool in the protection of the rights of young athletes. Age limits should be established clearly and should carefully balance the right of the child to participate in sports and competition with the right to be protected from all harmful side effects. Minimum ages should not be fixed only to satisfy the priorities of adults or the interests of sport organizations. The principles of non-discrimination (article 2), the best interests of the child (article 3), the right to life, survival and development (article 6), and children's right to have their opinion duly taken into account (article 12) need to be taken into account when discussing and establishing minimum age limits for children's participation in competitive and/or dangerous sports.

Part III

Abuse and violence

The integrity of the young athlete

6 Sharp practice

Intensive training and child abuse

Most of the injuries I see are over-use injuries. Young players come with elbow, shoulder and back problems ... Kids never used to get these kinds of injuries in the past. These are new diseases we have created for children.
(Dr Lyle Micheli, director of the Boston Children's Hospital, in Kleinhenz 2000: 24)

Today young girls of nine train four hours a day. It's scandalous!
(Martina Navratilova, in Elian 1994)

Part III of this publication examines abuse and violence towards children in the context of competitive sport. While the forms of abuse covered in Chapters 8–10 are self-explicit, the subjects of Chapters 6 and 7 require some clarification. Chapter 6 examines child abuse in general and looks at whether some extreme forms of early intensive training can be qualified as child abuse. It also looks at how the right to rest relates to competitive sports and how its negligence can lead to child abuse. Chapter 7 covers more specifically different forms of physical abuse and violence that can negatively affect young athletes.

By nature, competitive sport is a physical activity based on training, sacrifice and effort, with no exception for the youngest practitioners. Success in sports is the result of a complex mixture of qualities, including gift, motivation, family and sport environment, physical and mental capacities. When very young children are involved in *intensive training*, adults are faced with a number of difficulties. A very thin line divides intensive training that allows children to fulfil themselves from that in which they are abused and exploited. It is not easy for adults to assess constantly whether the child's full development is benefiting or not from intensive training.

In extremely demanding competitive sports such as tennis, gymnastics, figure skating, diving, ice hockey, basketball or football, children as young as four years old may have already been pushed by adults to train frequently and some, at around the age of six, may be starting systematic intensive training programmes and competition (Maffuli 1998: 298). At this age, is training two to three hours a day healthy? Too often coaches and parents perceive child athletes as miniature adults and treat them accordingly, forgetting that children are vulnerable and in a state of perpetual physical and psychological evolution.

Both the World Health Organization (WHO) (1998) and the European Commission (2000b) have warned that the potential for abuse exists in intensive training regimes and of the importance of guaranteeing the health and protection of young athletes. In 1997, WHO warned that: 'Organization of children's sports activity by adults does have a potential for abuses to occur if those who set the amount of sports participation and the training regimen are inexperienced and use adult models' (WHO 1998).

Unfortunately, many coaches are not sufficiently aware of children's complex physical and psychological developmental needs and the stages they go through (David 1993: 13–16). A survey among 150 British elite coaches showed that an important gap exists between the age at which children actually start intensive training and the coaches' estimates of when they *should* start. In football, gymnastics, swimming and tennis, coaches suggested 14, 10, 12 and 11 years respectively as the age to start intensive training, but the average actual age was, respectively, 11.3, 8.6, 9.2 and 9.5 years (Training of Young Athletes Study (TOYA) 1993: 13).

Although it is obviously necessary for athletes to train a minimum number of hours a week, many top trainers still emphasize the quantity of training rather than focusing on the quality and often base training intensity on that of adults (Bizzini 1993). Scottish cyclist Graeme Obree, world hour record-holder in 1993, admitted focusing mainly on the quality of his training:

> I cannot see the point of training five hours a day; the quality of training is the priority. For me, three or four rides a week of maximum 90 minutes are sufficient. My body doesn't ask for more. When I see the training programmes that are given to kids when they join teams, I am alarmed.
>
> (*L'Equipe Magazine* 1993a)

Some top athletes now believe that it is not humanly possible to train more. Frenchman Jean Galfione, for example, Olympic pole-vault champion in Atlanta (1996), thinks that 'people won't be able to train more; we have reached the maximum' (*L'Equipe Magazine* 2000). In a position statement on intensive training, the American Academy of Pediatrics (2000) stated that:

> To be competitive at a high level requires training regimens that could be considered extreme for adults. The ever-increasing requirements for success create a constant pressure for athletes to train longer, harder, more intelligently, and in some cases, at an earlier age. The unending efforts to outdo predecessors and outperform contemporaries are the nature of competitive sports.

Top sports stars are idolized, not only by their fans but by sports institutions and entire nations. Such emulation is natural, but can easily lead to a dangerous escalation of ever-more training in an attempt to beat opponents, with excessive and abusive demands being put on young athletes. For example, Li

Hongping, a Chinese trainer who coaches in the United States, was asked about the domination of young Chinese divers in a competition. 'The Chinese and Russians are not more gifted or talented,' he said, 'but they train eight hours a day and we [the Americans] train four' (Litsky 1998).

According to a 1992 Canadian study of 45 retired high-level athletes, one skater had trained 56 hours a week between the ages of 15 and 17 and a swimmer calculated that he had spent 15,800 hours in the water training, which amounts to 22 months of his life at 24 hours a day (Donnelly 1993: 99). When children train this much, it is in the vast majority of cases because they are at best stimulated or at worst forced by adults (especially parents and coaches). 'No child ever thinks of doing 25 hours of practice per week,' said Peter Donnelly, a Canadian sports sociologist at Toronto University (Kleinhenz 2000: 23).

Today, unless a child starts training at a very early age, it is almost impossible to reach the top in many sports, such as gymnastics and figure skating, and increasingly in athletics, diving, tennis, basketball, ice hockey and football. As explained in Chapter 5, children do not fully understand the concept of competition before the age of six or seven. But this does not stop some parents from involving their children in a sport as early as three or four years of age, or even planning what sport their child will take up before they are born.

American Dominique Monceanu, gymnastics champion at the 1996 Atlanta Olympics, told *L'Equipe Magazine* (1996), 'When I was a year old, my father suspended me by my feet to a bar fixed to our door to exercise.' And, according to an authorized biography, her parents decided to 'test' her at six months by placing her tiny hands around a clothesline strung across the kitchen to see if she could hang on: 'Remarkably, tiny Dominique firmly gripped the makeshift bar and did not waver. "See," he [the father] said to his wife, "I told you she's going to be a great gymnast"' (Quiner 1997: 5).

The Slovak father of Swiss former number-one tennis player, Martina Hingis, said his daughter started playing tennis at the age of two (Agence France Presse 2001a) and, according to her mother, Jennifer Capriati's father decided before her birth that she would be a tennis player (Baupère 2001). Earl Woods, the father of golf legend Tiger Woods, believes that his son reacted positively to the game when still in his mother's womb, because when 'a golf ball hit the green, it reverberated against the volcanic surface [of the golf course] and produced a thumping sound, similar to a drum' and Tiger 'would suddenly be very still and quiet' (Owen 2001: 60–1).

Sports authorities have rarely questioned the practice of intensive training among very young child athletes, although they are fully aware that it exists and know that it may lead to abuse. After the 1992 Barcelona Olympics, during which 13-year-old Chinese Fu Mingxia became Olympic diving champion, Juan Antonio Samaranch, then president of the International Olympic Committee (IOC), made an ambivalent statement:

[He] was not in favour of intensive training at such a young age … we [the IOC] believe in the value of models set by champions to develop sports within a country. After the victories of Boris Becker and Steffi Graf [both became champions while they were still adolescents] thousands of tennis courts were built in Germany and millions of Germans began playing the sport. We need to avoid the artificial moulding of champions by all means, but sports is part of education and can become a lifelong discipline.

(Albuy 1993)

CHILD ABUSE AND SPORTS

In any situation, children are by definition more at risk of abuse than adults, due to their vulnerability and dependence upon others. Competitive sports can create factors that increase the child's vulnerability to abuse (see Table 6.1).

Many definitions of child abuse exist, but they vary little. In 1999, WHO defined child abuse or maltreatment as constituting:

all forms of physical and/or emotional ill-treatment, sexual abuse, neglect or negligent treatment or commercial or other exploitation, resulting in actual or potential harm to the child's health, survival, development or dignity in the context of a relationship of responsibility, trust or power.

According to the US National Center for Child Abuse and Neglect, maltreatment exists when:

through purposive acts or marked inattention to the child's basic needs, behaviour of a parent or substitute or other adult caretaker causes foreseeable and avoidable injury or impairment to a child or materially contributes to unreasonable prolongation or worsening of an existing injury or impairment.

(Loe 1998: 472–3)

Table 6.1 Typology of main forms of abuse, neglect and violence in competitive sports

Physical	Sexual	Psychological	Neglect
Excessive intensive training	Verbal comments	Excessive pressure	Failure to provide proper care and attention
Systematic insufficient rest	Physical advances	Verbal violence	Deliberate negligence
Corporal punishment	Abusive touching	Emotional abuse	Imposed isolation
Severe food diets	Forced intercourse and rape		
Peer violence, including 'hazing' or 'ragging'			
Encouragement of 'play hard' or 'play hurt' attitudes			
Imposed usage of doping products			

Abuse and violence against children were long a subject of taboo and only since the 1960s and 1970s have historians started to look closely at the way civilizations treated their children:

> The history of childhood is a nightmare from which we have only recently begun to awaken. The further back in history one goes, the lower the level of child care, and the more likely children are to be killed, abandoned, beaten, terrorized, and sexually abused.
>
> (De Mause 1974: 1)

In the United States, academics began to speak openly about the high occurrence of child abuse in 1962, after the publication of *The battered child syndrome* (Kempe *et al.* 1962). In many other countries, it was only in the last two decades of the twentieth century that child abuse became public knowledge (Gelles and Cornell 1983). For example, in the United Kingdom, a large government-sponsored survey revealed that almost one in six children had experienced 'severe' physical punishment; the vast majority – 91 per cent – had been hit (Nobes and Smit 1997; Nobes *et al.* 1999). A study of Australian primary schoolchildren found that 81 per cent of boys and 74 per cent of girls had been hit by their mother, 76 per cent of boys and 63 of girls by their father (EPOCH Worldwide and Save the Children-Sweden 1999), while, in Switzerland, 11 per cent of children are beaten, of whom 2.5 per cent are beaten with an object (Government of Switzerland 1992). In 1983, research in Canada, the United Kingdom and the United States estimated that domestic violence occurred in between 25 and 28 per cent of marriages and that the children of those families were as much as 15 times more likely also to become victims of the abuse of one or both of their parents (Shupe and Stacy 1983).

For a long time, protection of the privacy of the family sphere did not allow this issue to be adequately addressed by public authorities. Protection from interference has been a traditional justification for not intervening in cases of domestic violence (Kelly and Mullender 2000). Today, it is increasingly accepted that child abuse in its many forms – physical, psychological, sexual, etc. – affects a large number of children in every society and social group (Gelles and Cornell 1983). The UN Committee on the Rights of the Child's monitoring work also clearly confirms this global trend (Hodgkin and Newell 2002: 257–75).

The harmful consequences of child abuse are widely acknowledged – and they are devastating. They include physical injury, gynaecological problems (for girls), headaches, asthma, depression, fear, low self-esteem, poor school performance, inability to trust, guilt, anger, sexual dysfunction, eating and sleeping disorders, fear of intimacy, post-traumatic stress disorder and ultimately suicide (UNICEF 2000: 9; UN Commission on Human Rights 2000; WHO 2002: 69).

In sports, some very specific consequences of abuse and violence against young athletes can be identified, such as obsessive and compulsive behaviours with regard to excessive training; eating disorders relating to diets imposed in certain sports; and self-injurious behaviours regarding the risks of accidents and injury.

As the child athlete's training becomes more intensive, he or she will gradually spend more and more time with adults in sports facilities. Indeed, some children board during the week in training centres where, at the age of ten, they train at least six hours a day. As in a family, the sports environment is a closed world where children usually create strong emotional and dependency bonds with the adults in charge of them; discipline and obedience are also key elements of the relationship (David 1999: 62–4; De Martelaer *et al.* 2000: 6). Nothing suggests that abuse and neglect is more or less frequent in sport halls and training centres than in families, but it is increasingly recognized that young athletes are potentially vulnerable to serious abuses of trust and power, which may lead to severe forms of violence. Especially vulnerable are children who begin intensive training at a very early age and thus spend more time in the care of coaches than with their own parents.

Some experts consider that, in extreme cases, intensive training in itself constitutes a form of child abuse, especially in demanding sports such as gymnastics. For example, in an article published in the *New England Journal of Medicine* in 1996, four leading child health specialists stated that:

> The development of gymnastics champions involves hard training, stringent coaching, and often parental pressure, ostensibly in the best interest of the child. Over-training, injuries, and psychological damage are common consequences. Parents and coaches, in collusion with the young athlete, may seek to experience vicariously the success of the child, a behaviour that could be called 'achievement by proxy' ... Its hallmark is strong parental encouragement of a potentially dangerous endeavour for the purpose of gaining fame and financial reward. We suggest that in its extreme form 'achievement by proxy' may be a sort of child abuse.
>
> (Tofler *et al.* 1996: 281)

The increased awareness of the past 20 years and the multiplication of preventive and protective measures in Western societies regarding domestic and child abuse have not yet sufficiently reached the sports world. Parents and coaches often assume that abuse cannot occur in such a leisure-oriented activity; others believe it is part of an ultra-competitive culture in which sacrifices are essential and inevitable if the athlete is to reach the top. This belief prevails in societies, such as in Eastern Europe, where abuse awareness is low and insufficiently protected by laws that are sometimes weakly enforced. In many countries, too, it is still considered normal that children should be educated and disciplined through physical or psychological intimidation and force. The father of a nine-year-old Romanian elite gymnast explained in a television programme:

> The French, the Americans, they've tried everything. Nothing worked. It doesn't work there. Why? Because this sport [gymnastics] is very hard and children need to be taken care of. Here [in Romania] we push them; this sport is very hard. But with existing laws there [in the West], it would not be possible

to do this with the kids. Otherwise we would be working illegally, and this must be an explanation [of the fact that Western gymnasts are not the best]. Look the hands of my daughter, they are covered with calluses; she has got more than me and I've been working for years with scrap metal … I am convinced that she will succeed, as long as nothing happens to her health.

(Arte 2001)

Article 24.1 of the Convention on the Rights of the Child requires states to ensure 'the right of the child to the enjoyment of the highest attainable standard of health', but article 19 also obliges them to:

> take all appropriate legislative, administrative, social and educational measures to protect the child from all forms of physical or mental violence, injury or abuse, neglect or negligent treatment, maltreatment or exploitation, including sexual abuse, while in the care of parent(s), legal guardian(s) or any other person who has the care of the child.

The Convention is articulated around the concept of the *inherent dignity of the person* which needs to be respected in all situations.[1] It also recognizes that parents have the main responsibility to bring up, care for and protect their children (articles 5 and 18), but if they fail to do so, responsibility falls to the state.

In situations where children are constantly in the company of their coaches or trainers and where they spend more time with them than with their own parents (or may even live with them), the coach/trainer becomes the main caregiver under article 19 of the Convention and as such is responsible for the protection of the children. Even in less intensive situations, where children train several hours a day, they are considered to be in the care of their coach, who therefore has *de jure* the responsibility to protect the child from all forms of abuse, violence and exploitation. Parents quite often abdicate a substantial part of their responsibilities to a coach when their children train intensively. For young female athletes, a male coach can become a surrogate father, a role model, a source of strength and inspiration. A teenager or college-age athlete may be infatuated with or attracted by their coach (Doherty 1999: 132).

Both public and private sports authorities have a shared responsibility in ensuring that the young athlete's environment is favourable to the enjoyment of their human rights. When discussing the right to health, the UN Committee on Economic, Social and Cultural Rights (2000: para. 42) considered that not only public authorities have responsibilities and obligations in this regard:

> While only States are parties to the Covenant and thus ultimately accountable for compliance with it, members of society – individuals, including health professionals, families, local communities, intergovernmental and non-governmental organizations, civil society organizations, as well as the private business sector – have responsibilities regarding the realization of the right to health.

On the basis of article 19 of the Convention, the Committee on the Rights of the Child systematically advocates for 'zero tolerance against violence' (Hammarberg and Newell 2000: 127). Most countries have legislation to protect children from abuse, neglect and violence. Nevertheless, its enforcement greatly depends on the specific grounds that these national laws cover, particularly with regard to mental and emotional violence, and the political will and capacity of governments to enforce them, especially in the private sphere.

LOST CHILDHOOD

One common characteristic of seriously abused children is that they feel that they had to grow up too soon and that they 'lost' their childhood. Many young athletes involved in precocious intensive training, whose days are spent training, learning and sleeping, do not have the time to enjoy their childhood. This feeling may fuel anger, bitterness and frustration. Although it is far from an objective, quantifiable and scientific criterion, the feeling of 'lost childhood' among young athletes is nevertheless a powerful potential indicator of sport-related abusive trends.

Many former young athletes who underwent intensive training from an early age empathize with this concept. For instance, Olympic figure-skating silver medallist Rosalyn Summers had a nervous depression the year after winning her title. She explained:

> I'd been on ice six hours a day since I was six years old. I turned pro after the Olympics, when I was 20, and I began to wonder: When's my time? When am I going to relax? When am I going to have a boyfriend and go to the movies? I was touring with a professional show, moving from one hotel to another, in bed at eight o'clock and getting up at four to train. I was burnt out, totally burnt out. I wanted to kill myself. I was making a lot of money but I had no life.
>
> (Doherty 1999: 121)

American Dominique Monceanu, who was, at 16, Olympic gymnastics champion in 1996, also felt frustrated: 'I would think: don't you guys know anything besides gymnastics? Can't we go out for ice cream?' (Doherty 1999: 121). During the 1980s, American Chris Evert was one of the world's top tennis players. Now the mother of three boys, she is happy that:

> none of them are tennis players ... Once in a while we'll have a junior tournament here [in her tennis club] and I'll see two ten-year-olds play. I'll see the strained look on their faces, and their parents hovering over them. Would I want to do it all over again myself? No way.
>
> (Kleinhenz 2000: 23)

In a study of 46 elite US athletes preparing for the 1988 Olympic Games, more than half said that, if they had a five-year-old child, they would not raise him or her as they had been and would involve the child in activities other than sports (Murphy 1999:115).

Russian Alexei Nemov emerged as the world's best male gymnast during the 2000 Sydney Olympics, winning two gold, one silver and two bronze medals. When he was 14, he joined a full-time training centre in Krugloye, 50 kilometres from Moscow. Just before the 1996 Atlanta Olympics, he admitted:

> You become crazy here. We train three times a day, 30 hours a week. We train up to eight hours a day during intensive preparation phases. I train, I sleep, I train, I sleep. That's my programme. I don't remember the last time I went home. I have never been healthy. My back always hurts. One of my vertebra has moved; I need injections in my hand. I think it is due to working far too much. We do a lot of power-lifting. All gymnasts are like me: destroyed. This must be the price to pay to be at the top.
>
> (Donzé 2000b: 21)

Tennis player Mary Pierce was asked whether she felt she had had a happy childhood. 'No, certainly not,' replied Pierce, who has also reported having been abused by her father during her childhood. 'I left school at 13 ... Childhood is a time to live a carefree life. This is a stage I have never really known. Or maybe only before I started tennis' (Sainte-Rose 2000: 82).

Despite great advances in addressing child abuse and violence in many countries, these issues are still considered taboo in the sports world. Adults involved in sports tend to be defensive when questioned about the issue, just as parents often are when confronted with domestic violence. Nonetheless, in many countries, especially in the West, attitudes towards child abuse in general have evolved slowly and new laws, policies and programmes have been put in place to protect children.

THE RIGHT TO REST

The Convention also guarantees 'the right of the child to rest' (article 31.1), although this provision is one that countries and adults in charge of children neglect the most. The right to rest is as important as other fundamental rights, such as to nutrition, clothing and housing; not respecting this right can be considered a form of abuse. Children who habitually suffer from insufficient or poor-quality sleep can be made more vulnerable to physical and psychological health problems and to social and learning deficiencies. Two International Labour Organization (ILO) conventions specifically protect children from working at night and stipulate the number of hours of consecutive rest children should have: children under 14 or in full-time education should have 14 hours' rest; those aged 14 to 16, 12 hours; and adolescents aged 16 to 18, at least seven hours

(ILO Conventions Nos. 79 and 90). The Committee on the Rights of the Child (1998) expressed its concern in some instances when monitoring children's right to rest, as in Japan, for example, where 'children are exposed to developmental disorders due to the stress of a highly competitive educational system and the consequent lack of time for leisure, physical activities and rest'.

Intensive training and competitive sports are by nature activities that require important physical and psychological efforts. The right to rest is crucial for young athletes who train on a daily basis, sometimes spending more time in sports halls than on school benches. Young competitors often have to get up early to train before school and then train again in the evening; between sports and school they have no time for themselves and not enough time to rest. In 1997, Dr Michel Leglise (1997: 10), at that time chairman of the International Federation of Gymnastics' medical committee, reiterated:

> Another vital point is the need for rest periods and plenty of sleep ... Children need far more sleep than adults; this must be taken into account not only in daily life, by avoiding late training sessions, but also by avoiding early morning qualifying sessions and evening competitions.

Recent research tends to show that, contrary to popular belief, adolescents (aged ten to 17) need as much sleep, if not more, than children under ten (National Research Council and Institute of Medicine 2000). This research recognizes the complex and demanding developmental needs of adolescents, from both an internal (biological) and an external (social, educational, environmental) point of view.

Irrespective of their own interests and perceived obligations, it is crucial for coaches, sports officials and parents to fully acknowledge, understand and respect the right to rest of young athletes in order to ensure their sound and holistic development. Even adult athletes regularly complain of competition schedules that are too demanding, thus increasing their vulnerability not only to serious injuries but also to taking illegal performance-enhancing products. It is essential, therefore, that sport authorities understand that, for a healthy development, children need sufficient rest periods and that they organize programmes, regulations and policies accordingly.

NOTES

1 The concept of the dignity of the child is referred to in the Preamble and articles 23, 28, 37, 39 and 40 of the Convention on the Rights of the Child.

7 Bearing the brunt
Physical abuse and violence

> The biggest sacrifice I made for gymnastics is my body.
>
> (Kim Zmeskal, gymnast at the 1992 Olympics, in Monnard 1992)

> Because training has become more sport-specific and nearly continuous, overuse injuries are now common among young athletes. Recent data indicate that 30 per cent to 50 per cent of all pediatric sports injuries are due to overuse.
>
> (DiFiori 1999)

Competitive sports can expose young athletes to at least four types of physical abuse and violence: excessive intensive training; peer violence; physical violence by adults, including corporal punishment; and violence due to participating in competitions. Some people also consider that sport legitimizes certain forms of violence.

Fundamental to all major international human rights treaties is the recognition of the right to have full and free control over one's own body. Article 19 of the Convention on the Rights of the Child clearly obliges ratifying states to:

> take all appropriate ... measures to protect the child from *all forms* of physical or mental violence, injury or abuse, neglect or negligent treatment, maltreatment or exploitation, including sexual abuse, in the care of parent(s), legal guardian(s), or *any other person* who has the care of the child. [emphases added]

The World Health Organization (WHO) defined violence as:

> The intentional use of physical force or power, threatened or actual, against another person or against oneself or a group of people, that results in or has a high likelihood of resulting in injury, death, psychological harm, maldevelopment or deprivation.
>
> (WHO 2001: 2; 2002: 5)

It is generally assumed that it now takes at least ten years of intensive training for a talented athlete to reach the top at national level and to take part in international competitions. It follows that today's top athletes began intensive training before adolescence. In sports such as gymnastics, figure skating, diving and swimming, in which champions regularly reach their peak between the ages of 16 and 20, children will usually start training between the ages of four and seven. This is also increasingly the case for tennis, basketball, football and ice hockey.

Children are fully dependent upon adults, some of whom might exploit this situation, pushing children beyond their limits, especially as they tend to be more obedient and easier to control than adult athletes. The line dividing difficult, but tolerable, training schemes and exercises and those that are intolerable and harmful is fine indeed. Parents and coaches sometimes justify the excessive amount of time a child spends training by telling others – and themselves – that it is the result of the child's enthusiasm and passion for the sport. But this may be little more than self-deception and an abrogation of their responsibilities, for adults do not hesitate to limit the amount of time children spend on other activities they enjoy, such as playing or television. Under the Convention, parents have the duty to provide 'appropriate' direction and guidance to the child (article 5).

Some children who train intensively work so hard to please adults that they do not develop the critical sense that will allow them to say 'no' to their parents or trainers when they feel they have reached their physical and mental limits (Coakley 1993: 74–94). Some trainers abuse their position of power, exploiting the young athlete's trust in their competence and authority, imposing adult norms upon them, which can lead to work rhythms that are too rapid with exercises that are too difficult (De Knop and De Martelaer 2001: 42). 'I was let down by my inability to say no,' said Elena Moukina, a top gymnast from the former USSR. In 1979, she was told to compete despite being injured (Ryan 1995: 24). She fell and broke her neck and is now paraplegic.

Talented children can be like putty in the hands of over-ambitious adults who see them not as children, but as potential champions ready to be moulded as required. Young children, especially, will often do almost anything to please their adult mentors: 'The young ones are the greatest little suckers in the world. They will follow you no matter what,' boasted Bela Karolyi, the American-Romanian coach who trained many of the great gymnasts, such as Nadia Comaneci and Dominique Monceanu (Brennan 1993: D5).

HARMFUL CONSEQUENCES OF INTENSIVE TRAINING

Since the early 1990s, researchers have acknowledged that early intensive training can have harmful consequences and seriously threaten the physical development of young athletes (Dalton 1992: 58–70; Rowland 1993: 168–87; Tofler *et al.* 1996). Over-use injuries in children and adolescents are a serious risk (Oneill and Micheli 1988; DiFiori 1999) that is not always understood and addressed by adults.

Once again, it is female gymnastics that represents a radical illustration of this trend. Over the past few decades, and with the complicity of its international authorities, gymnastics has gone from being a graceful sport practised by women to a highly technical one involving 'miniature' adolescents who are usually less than 1.5 metres tall and weigh less than 40 kilos. Artistic ability and femininity have given way to extremely difficult jumps and moves that can only be performed by girls whose bodies are kept artificially small (Daly *et al.* 2001: 9). With body fat kept to a strict minimum to enhance performance, most top gymnasts menstruate for the first time only when their career has ended. It has traditionally been assumed that young gymnasts' physical growth is retarded because training programmes are so intensive (Malina 1994: 389–434). In their recent research, however, Baxter-Jones and Maffuli (2002) have challenged this, asserting that, 'Data are insufficient to warrant that intensive training may delay the timing of the growth spurt in female gymnasts.'

In demanding sports such as gymnastics, diving, figure skating, swimming, tennis and football, children over ten are often encouraged by their parents and coaches to train four to six – sometimes even up to eight – hours a day, six days a week (Dixon and Fricker 1990; Kolt and Kirby 1995). And at the age of five, some gymnasts train up to four hours a day (Ryan 1995: 110). To compete internationally, training must be the main activity in the child's life. What little time is left is taken up by studies and socialization, so the lives of young athletes rarely extend beyond school benches and sports arenas. No time for ice creams, outings, social life, parties and boy- or girlfriends; if the athlete goes on holiday, it is usually sport-related. One group of athletes involved in intensive training described their daily life as a feeling of 'the rest of their lives being on hold' (Brackenridge and Kirby 1997: 411).

Child athletes may have to sweat and suffer for hours in intensive training sessions – the slogan 'no pain, no gain' is regularly applied to them – but that is still no guarantee for success. For the more an athlete trains, the greater are the chances of injury, especially for adolescents, whose growth may render them fragile (Mandelbaum 1993: 217–33; Daly *et al.* 2001: 8). Given the complexity of jumps, and with their bone density weakened by the absence of the menstrual cycle, gymnasts are extremely vulnerable to a whole host of injuries, especially stress fractures. Many athletes just do not make it, not because they lack talent, but simply because their bodies cannot take the intensity of training. Some researchers argue that this is a process of natural selection and have found evidence that:

> young athletes who were able to compete and train at a high level are a naturally gifted group ... [with] a low rate of injury. Young athletes at the sub-elite level, however, who train intensively to reach the elite standard, may not be so fortunate. These children may suffer serious injuries that cause them to abandon their sport and experience significant problems in everyday life.
>
> (Maffuli 1998: 298)

A study of 48 elite football players, all belonging to the Swiss under-15, under-17 and under-20 teams, showed significant levels of serious injury (Tschopp *et al.* 2001). Over a period of two years, 18 players (including 16 under 17 years of age) had to stop their sporting activity due to injury for a period ranging between 12 and 104 weeks. Of these 18 players, six went on to become professional footballers, ten continued playing as amateurs and two retired due to the gravity of their injuries.

Some retired champions, looking back on the way they trained, suffered and the violence they inflicted upon themselves, would not wish the same on younger athletes. Czech athlete Jarmila Kratochvilova, 1984 world record-holder for the 800 metres, said of her compatriot, Ludmila Formandova, 1998 world champion: 'I don't want Ludmila to experience what I went through. Our training was too hard and I don't want her to sacrifice everything for athletics' (*L'Equipe Magazine* 2000a). Similarly, former Swiss tennis champion Jakob Hlasek affirmed:

> I have a young son and I will never make him take part in high-level sports … Competitive sport is not a healthy activity … I know that I personally risk having many health problems as I get older … We ask far too much of the body, both during training and during competition.
>
> (Oberli 2000: 2)

Olympic judo champion in Los Angeles in 1984, Japanese Shinji Hosokawa admitted 15 years later that he would not allow his two sons to go to Koudou Gakusha, the judo school in Tokyo that he attended, because 'they want to shape a character too different from the conception I have of judo … The president is very strict. Judokas have to fight even when they are injured, despite the pain' (Ben-Ismaïl 2000: 64).

Children can be extremely resilient, and some can withstand a considerable amount of physical and mental suffering without harm. Some researchers and trainers also believe in the 'immunization' phenomenon: that the more children train, the more they can take (Gould 1993: 28). Every individual has a limit to the suffering he or she can bear, however, and in sports, exceeding that limit generally leads to physical injury and/or mental burn-out. Young athletes cannot withstand pain and suffering to the same degree as adults. In its jurisprudence regarding torture and ill-treatment, the European Court of Human Rights recognizes that age must be taken into account when assessing pain and suffering (European Court of Human Rights 1980; European Court of Human Rights 1997).

Adult pressure on young athletes can be so strong that even when they are suffering from pain or injury they are tempted to continue training or competing. Four American child health specialists declared: 'The pressure to practise and compete injured compounds the risk of impaired skeletal development and permanent deformity' (Tofler *et al.* 1996). A study in New Zealand showed that 39 per cent of rugby players of all ages said that, one time at least, they had played injured and against medical advice (Gerrard *et al.* 1994).

Among the elite, pressure to compete is often present, even when injured. As coach Bela Karolyi once said: 'With or without injury they have to compete; they must compete without any kind of doubt' (Ryan 1995: 209). One of his gymnasts, Betty Okino, claimed that, at 15, even when doctors told her to stop and to take some rest following an injury, she remembered that 'that wasn't really an option. It was just like, either you are paralysed and you can't move or you train' (Ryan 1995: 35). A 1993 survey undertaken by the Minnesota Amateur Sports Commission in the United States revealed that 21 per cent of the athletes interviewed admitted they had been pressured to compete with an injury.

Athletes undergoing intensive training learn more and more about their own bodies and their physical aptitudes and limits. But this knowledge is acquired slowly after years of training and requires a great deal of experience and maturity; indeed most athletes admit they understand their body and capacities best only towards the end of their sporting career, at about the age of 30. Young athletes, however, remain largely dependent on proper guidance from their trainers, although even that is not always sufficient to make a young athlete, under pressure to get good results, listen to reason. In 1996, Olympic gymnast Dominique Monceanu, aged 14 at the time, explained why she was competing despite a 10 cm stress fracture in her right leg: 'What else can I do? I have to bite my teeth and somehow make it through. This is the Olympics you're talking about here. This is the big meet, the biggest in anyone's life' (Coakley 1998: 153). Under pressure to confirm her supremacy, she also decided to compete in the 1998 US championships despite a serious injury (hyperextension of the knee) and against the repeated advice of the team's medical staff (Associated Press 1998a).

Many athletes admit to taking huge amounts of painkillers, up to eight Aspirins or Advil a day, to practise and compete despite injuries. Erica Stokes, a top US gymnast in the early 1990s admitted, 'We'd all have these huge bottles of painkillers in our bags' (Ryan 1995: 40). And, when a famous American football player was asked about how he dealt with pain, he replied: 'You take bottles of Advil and then you go out and smash some more heads' (Coakley 1998: 153).

Competitive sport is characterized by a permanent and obsessive search for perfection which leads to perpetual improvement of results. Today a huge number of teenagers perform as well as the Olympic champions of the first half of the twentieth century. The junior (under-18) world champion in 2000 of the 100-metre sprint would have won all the Olympic gold medals until 1972 (inclusive) and in 1980 with his winning time![1] Success in any elite sport has become a catch-22 situation: each season, it becomes more and more difficult to win, so young athletes have to train more intensively, which makes them more vulnerable to injury and may, in the long run, seriously threaten their health.

Randy Pendergast, a head coach in New Jersey, USA, said that 'his' 'nine- to 14-year-olds are doing more than 1972 Olympic champion Olga Korbut did in floor exercises', while Elena Chankelia, a coach at the Romanian national gymnastics centre at Onesti, admitted, 'Exercises get harder and harder. For these little girls it's becoming difficult to reach perfection. We try to help them get there' (Arte 2001). But gymnast Ivan Ivankov who won the silver medal in the

1988 Goodwill Games warned, 'Gymnastics is dangerous. It's getting more difficult and too hard on the body' (Guzman 1998: C5).

In the most at-risk sports, athletes are repeatedly told from the moment they start training that injury is part of the game. Romanian Olympic champion gymnast, Andrea Raducan, stated: 'From the moment I went to the gymnastics hall for the first time, I knew that without the will, without getting injured and without being courageous, you cannot reach the top' (Citroen 2001).

Gymnastics is often considered one of the most risky sports, due to the combination of several factors: extremely precocious involvement; violent body movements; high technical difficulties requiring very intensive training; and low weight and weak bones due to the absence of menstruation (amenorrhoea) (Yeager *et al.* 1993). Prevalence of amenorrhoea is much higher among young athletes (between 3 and 66 per cent) than amoung the general population (between 2 and 5 per cent) (Writing Group for the PEPI Trial 1995). A 1992 study by the National Collegiate Athletic Association (USA) found that female gymnasts suffered from the most injuries in college sports, except for American football. Male gymnasts, who generally reach their peak when they are adults, ranked only eighth (Ryan 1995: 45). Gymnastics has received much media coverage and sustained academic attention for over two decades. Other high-risk sports for children, such as American football, football, ice hockey, boxing, rugby, horse racing and horse riding, have not yet received the same level of attention, though a respectable body of knowledge about their negative health implications exists (Kujala *et al.* 1995; Roberts *et al.* 1999; Roberts 1999; Waller *et al.* 2000).

Many leading medical researchers and practitioners have noted since the 1990s an increase of over-use injuries among young athletes (DiFiori 1999). Dr Lyle Micheli, co-founder (in 1974) and director of the world's first sports-medicine clinic for children at Boston Children's Hospital and former president of the American College of Sports Medicine noted that: 'The fact that most of these injuries are preventable raises troubling questions about children and organized sports' (Micheli *et al.* 2000). He considers that 80 per cent of children visiting his clinic for sport treatment suffer from injuries due to over-use (Bigelow *et al.* 2001: 118) and points out that, 'Until recently, "runner's knee" (pain caused by the kneecap not tracking or sliding along its groove properly) was unheard of in kids. Now it is the number-one diagnosis in my practice' (*USA Today* 2000).

The US National Athletic Trainers Association (NATA) identified youth sports injuries as a public health issue:

> As more and more children participate in organized sports every year, it is important that a study of this type be undertaken to determine who is at risk and enable more effective injury prevention and management ... [research should be undertaken to] help identify the consequences of intense physical activity on developing young adults.
>
> (NATA Research and Education Foundation 1998)

CORPORAL PUNISHMENT

Children and adolescents involved in intensive training may also be vulnerable to another form of violence: corporal punishment. Although many studies have been undertaken to document it and, since the adoption of the Convention on the Rights of the Child, an increasing number of countries have legally banned it,[2] corporal punishment remains a common phenomenon all over the world. Research in the last ten years in countries as diverse as Chile, Egypt, Kuwait, Romania, South Korea and the United Kingdom has shown that a majority of parents reported physically punishing their children. 'Physical punishment' included whipping, hitting, beating and kicking children, who may suffer from physical injuries ranging from fractures and loss of consciousness to permanent disability (Vargas *et al.* 1995; Nobes and Smit 1997; Qasem *et al.* 1998; Salah-el-din-Attia *et al.* 1998; Nobes *et al.* 1999; Halm and Guterman 2001; Browne *et al.* 2002).

The Committee on the Rights of the Child advocates in favour of legally prohibiting all forms of corporal punishment within the family, at school and in any other environment (David 1999a; Hodgkin and Newell 2002: 265–9). Such prohibition covers the so-called more acceptable forms of physical punishment, such as smacking, lawful correction or light chastisement. The Committee bases its position on the legal provisions of the Convention, such as the best interests of the child (article 3), the right to be protected from all forms of violence (article 19), that school discipline is administered in a manner consistent with the child's human dignity (article 28) and the right to be free from cruel, inhuman and/or degrading punishment or treatment (article 37). In 2001, the Committee reiterated that it had 'repeatedly made clear in its concluding observations that the use of corporal punishment does not respect the inherent dignity of the child nor the strict limits on school discipline'.

In 1998, the European Court of Human Rights judged that corporal punishment of a young English boy by his stepfather constituted degrading punishment in breach of the European Convention of Human Rights. In 1982, the same court delivered a judgement outlawing the use of corporal punishment in state schools.

Though specific research is still scant, corporal punishment is sometimes inflicted in the sports world on young athletes who do not perform as well as expected and on those who do not conform to the strict discipline. Aware of the potential risk of abuse by trainers, the Australian Sports Commission, the government agency for sports, declared in 2000 in one of its major policy documents that: 'Training techniques that give extra physical loads to children as "punishment" can be dangerous to the health of children who are already physically tired.'

Physical punishment can also be used as a threat to force young children to train harder. Chonnatee Padungkit, a 15-year-old professional Thai boxer, said:

I am afraid of being punished if I skip training. Once I didn't train hard enough and I was exhausted before the end of the fight. I got slapped on the head for that ... I wish I could go out play with my friends, but I can't do that or I'll be punished.

(Sae-Lim 1999)

Nothing leads to the conclusion that adults resort to corporal punishment less frequently in the sports world than at home or at school. Competitive sport is result-oriented and success increases the standing of coaches and trainers, who may abuse the confidence athletes put in them. A 1993 survey undertaken by the Minnesota Amateur Sport Commission (USA) concluded that 17.5 per cent of athletes surveyed said they had been hit, kicked or slapped while participating in sports. Two studies undertaken in Switzerland and Germany in the late 1990s revealed that the use of violence in sports by coaches is far from being an isolated phenomenon (Klein and Palzkill 1998; Kohler 2000).

Although the case of 11-year-old Romanian gymnast Adriana Giurca, who was beaten to death by her trainer in 1995 because, for once, she could not perform an exercise, is an extreme and isolated one, it nonetheless shows that over-ambitious coaches might lose their perspective and self-control.[3] The case also revealed more systematic physical abuse. A team-mate of Adriana Giurca's said:

We were regularly beaten when we did not perform perfectly during training, as it was expected. Our trainer told us it was the best way to reach the height of performance. It was normal, but we didn't tell our parents or anyone else. We wanted to be gymnasts and we accepted it.

(Willsher 1995: 37)

After Romania won the 1994 world championships, its head coach, Octavian Bellu, said: 'Bulgaria and Russia lost their place in world gymnastics when they lost their iron discipline' (Willsher 1995: 39).

Examples of physical abuse of young athletes are sometimes revealed despite the wall of silence around the issue and almost inexistent data and research. A 1996 French television report on gymnastics in China showed adult trainers sitting on the back of gymnasts aged six to seven, while at the same time lifting their legs in opposite directions to increase their flexibility. During an interview, in answer to the question, 'Is he [the trainer] strict?', one of the girls replied, 'Sometimes he beats us.' These types of imposed exercises to increase the body's flexibility – by force if necessary – have been reported in many countries, including by young Swiss amateur gymnasts (Kohler 2000). Former French gymnast and 1993 European junior champion, Elodie Lussac, who left gymnastics at 16 after a serious back injury, declared that some of her friends had been hit by their (Romanian) coaches employed by the French state. She added that they remained silent because they were afraid of being thrown out of the French national team (Hirzel 1996: 51).

In 1995, Ma, a Chinese athletics coach with a string of successes in women's track and field events, publicly revealed using physical punishment. Suspicions of abuse and doping were voiced after every international victory by a member of the 'Ma Family Army', as his team of young athletes was referred to. It was not until the 'army' was dismantled for unexplained reasons that Ma finally admitted:

> my management style was too simple sometimes. I would scold them [the athletes] or beat them when they were lazy or disobedient. But I only did it for their own good. If we are not prepared to suffer bitterness ... how can China catch up with the world levels in track and field? How can we win the world championships?
>
> (Reuters/*International Herald Tribune* 1995)

PEER VIOLENCE

Quite frequently when talented young athletes start to do well, their coaches upgrade them to a higher category, usually composed of older children. While this might help them to develop their capacities, it can also increase their vulnerability to peer violence, such as physical violence, jealousy and ridicule, and separate them from their friends and their environment. These experiences can have a positive effect, but they can equally be negative, leading to a loss of motivation and enthusiasm and, in some cases, to giving up the sport entirely. The decision to incorporate a young talent in a group of older athletes should not be motivated by the ambitions of adults alone, but in the light of two key principles of the Convention: the child's best interests and his or her involvement in the decision-making. Adults are responsible for taking all possible measures to prevent and protect children from peer violence.

Little research exists on peer violence among young athletes and it is hard to evaluate whether it is more prevalent in sports than in other contexts, such as in school. In a 1992 study of 45 retired Canadian elite athletes, one-third of them reported physical and mental abuse and peer pressure. Two athletes who took part in martial sports said they had been physically abused after winning contests against older competitors. A swimmer who, at the age of seven, trained with athletes aged between 14 and 17, admitted, 'I used to cry ... they put me in a locker for fun' (Donnelly 1993: 103).

In sports, peer violence can also take the form of 'hazing' or 'ragging'. Although little research has been carried out, available data tend to show that sport-related initiation rites exist in many countries and in most regions of the world (Kirby and Wintrup 2002). People have always initiated new members into groups through ceremonies and rituals to foster a sense of belonging. Rites of passage are not necessarily harmful, but some forms of hazing can definitely threaten the physical and mental health and integrity of young athletes, in addition to being illegal in many countries.

Many definitions of hazing exist, but differ little. One definition states that it is 'any humiliating or dangerous activity expected to join a group, regardless of your willingness to participate' (Hoover and Pollard 2000: 5). Another defines it as:

> any activity expected of someone joining a group that humiliates, degrades, abuses or endangers, regardless of the person's willingness to participate. This does not include activities such as rookies carrying the balls, team parties with community games, or going out with your team-mates, unless an atmosphere of humiliation, degradation, abuse or danger arises.
>
> (Hoover 1999: 8)

Hazing, to some extent, shares a few common points with harmful traditional practices. The Convention does not refer to hazing explicitly, although article 19 on all forms of violence is certainly relevant. Article 24.3 refers to 'harmful traditional practices', but this provision was adopted in order to address issues such as female genital mutilations (FGM), early and forced marriages and forced scarring, tattoos, diets or feeding, but not hazing. Both health practitioners and human rights activists campaign to prohibit the harmful aspects of initiation rites and traditions such as FGM and scarring, and to find alternative ways to keep these rites positive and safe. The same applies to hazing: it can play an important role in building social identity and sense of belonging, but its dangerous and harmful aspects need to be prevented and prohibited. Anti-hazing groups usually adopt this approach by promoting positive, constructive and safe initiation rites.

Cases of hazing in the sports context have been reported in Australia, Canada, the United States and Western European countries and perpetrators have in some cases been sanctioned by sport authorities or judicial courts. Hazing in sports probably occurs in many other countries, but information is lacking. According to Joel Fish, director of the Center for Sport Psychology in the United States, 'Hazing behaviors are deeply rooted in American athletic culture' (National Collegiate Athletic Association 2001).

In 2001 in New Jersey, USA, for example, 14 girls, aged between 16 and 17, were suspended by their field-hockey team for having hazed a dozen younger players (Gaudiano 2001). They ordered their younger team-mates to practise with syrup in their pants and simulate oral sex with bananas. In 1998, 14 athletes pleaded guilty in a US juvenile court to criminal charges of harassment against a peer player and each was ordered to perform 50 hours of community service (Gaudiano 2001). In 1990, Nicholas Haben, an American teenager, died in a lacrosse team initiation (Farrey 2001). The issue, however, is still very much taboo and frequently neither coaches nor officials are very talkative when questioned about these practices. Responding to a national questionnaire on hazing in sports in the United States, a coach declared, 'It's not an issue, it doesn't happen here ... If it happened, it would be an isolated case' (Hoover 1999: 23).

A study undertaken by the Alfred University (New York) in 2000 on hazing in high schools revealed that 48 per cent of the 20,000 students surveyed (aged

15 to 17) reported being subjected to activities that they considered hazing, half of them in the sporting context; 22 per cent qualified their hazing experience as 'dangerous'. Hazing often starts at a young age: 10 per cent of students declared that they first experienced hazing before they were 9 years old, 15 per cent between 10 and 12, 61 per cent between 13 and 15, and 14 per cent between 16 and 18. Interestingly, the study also revealed the feelings of those being hazed: 27 per cent had negative feelings (anger, embarrassment, confusion, guilt, sadness); 32 per cent shared both negative and positive feelings, 27 per cent had positive feelings only (part of the group, pride, strength, trust) and 14 per cent had a feeling of revenge.

Another study undertaken by the Alfred University covered college sports which are under the authority of the National Collegiate Athletic Association (NCAA). It concluded that approximately 250,000 college athletes every year are subjected to hazing, among whom 50,000 experience 'unacceptable and potentially illegal hazing' (Hoover 1999: 6).

Anti-hazing laws are in force in 42 American states and in a number of other countries, such as France and the Philippines. In 1998, the French parliament revised its penal code in order to forbid hazing:

> the fact that a person forces another, with or without their consent, to be subjected to or to commit humiliating or degrading acts during school or other social meetings or events is punished by six months' detention and a fine of 50,000 French francs [approx. 10,000 euros].

LEGALIZED VIOLENCE?

Performance in competitive sports is based on a legitimized level of aggressiveness, which is regulated by rules and enforced by referees. However, in many collision sports (for example, boxing, American or Australian football, ice hockey and rugby) or contact sports (such as football, basketball, baseball, wrestling, field hockey, handball, etc.), it is easy to slip from the side of accepted and encouraged levels of violence to that of violent and intolerable aggressiveness.

If children are involved in competitive sports at an early age, they will, as they grow, learn about both the written and the unwritten rules. What they acquire depends mainly on the ability, culture and mentality of their adult coach. Sport represents an important educational tool for young athletes and offers an interesting opportunity to learn to control physical strength and channel aggressiveness. A British study showed that between 50 and 79 per cent of young elite athletes described themselves as 'fairly' or 'definitively' aggressive in their sport, but that two-thirds of them perceived competitive aggression as 'honest' (TOYA 1993a: 6–8). Sport-related violence usually reflects, and sometimes magnifies, wider societal violence. Therefore, when training young athletes, adults are responsible for sending a clear message about the limits of aggressiveness and teaching them the rules of sportsmanship and fair play.

Competitive sport is one of the few social situations where aggression, and in some instances violence, deliberately directed at another, may not only be condoned but even rewarded (TOYA 1993a: 2). It is not rare that in collision sports, coaches advocate a 'play hurt' or 'play hard' attitude among their young players in the hope of instilling a so-called 'winning mentality' among their teams (Roderick *et al.* 2000). As one scholar noted, 'Young players are taught that violence is an acceptable and successful method of achieving victory' (Clarke 2000).

Adult coaches and officials often encourage young athletes to play to the limit. Sometimes their violence is rewarded, even if it exceeds the accepted limit. In non-contact sports, too, adults urge athletes to develop their aggressiveness in the hope of improving results. A young swimmer noted, 'Dad says some people want to win more than I do, [he says] I should be more upset when I lose – I could be more aggressive' (TOYA 1993a: 10).

Young athletes are influenced by older role models who, in contact sports, are often encouraged to 'play hurt' simply to reaffirm their masculinity and increase supporters' and television's interest. Dr Robert Huizinga, a former player in the US National Football League (NFL) and former president of the NFL Physicians Society, affirmed that many sports fans 'want people to play hurt, and when someone doesn't play hurt, he's no longer our hero' (Coakley 1998: 155).

American sports are certainly not alone in struggling with the desire to control and even decrease violence without prejudicing their success. Since the 1980s, the four sports that attract most spectators and are the most financially successful – American football, basketball, baseball and ice hockey – have all seen violence become one of the most difficult issues to control, despite referees and sport organizations having increased power to sanction violent behaviour. An American sports expert explained:

> Each of the four major American sports has its own brand of senseless violence. As far as criminal law is concerned ... given the major role that professional sports plays in American culture, the sports violence problem must be controlled; without some type of restraint, the future of sport may hold grave possibilities for our society.
>
> (Nielsen 1989: 681)

Although the media, among others, regularly asserts that aggressive behaviour and violence are on the rise in youth competitive sports, most experts note – although relevant data and statistics are not available – that violations of fair-play rules and other forms of violence are not necessarily more frequent today than they were in the past (Coakley 1998: 160; TOYA 1993: 2). The debate about the alleged increase of violence among young participants in sport resembles that regarding claims of an important rise in youth crime. In fact, available data regularly point to a decrease in violence among young people (Roberts and Stalans 2000). Dan Macallair, vice-president of the Center on Juvenile and Criminal Justice, a Canadian organization whose objective is to find alternatives to youth incarceration, confirmed the absence of data on violence in sports:

We really don't know because we don't have the evidence ... My guess is that it's probably less than we think ... My gut feeling is that it's being reported more frequently and more widely just because of modern-day media practices and media technology.

(James and Ziemer 2000)

Sport is regularly perceived as an allegory to war and therefore shares similar terminology and symbols (Brohm 1981: 146–56). Tara Van Derveer, the coach of the US national women's basketball team during the 1996 Atlanta Olympics, declared, 'I think we have some warriors. I think they are ready for the battle.' During the 1990s, *Sports Illustrated*, the most respected American sports magazine, gave every new subscriber a video tape, *The Hidden NFL*, that proudly announced: 'We have revealed a side of pro [American] football that is savage.' The video began with the statement:

There is more violence per square foot in the pit than any other sport ... It is only through [special video technology] that the savagery of these raging struggles can actually be seen. [The video shows an interview of a player saying:] 'There's things going on in there that would be illegal off the football field. I mean you can literally kill someone with the things we're doing in there.'

(Coakley 1998: 194)

Also in the 1990s, Reebok, one of the world's top sport shoe manufacturers, launched an ambiguous slogan: 'Life is short. Play hard.' In France, the French Football Federation was criticized in 2001 for promoting the games of its national team through poster campaigns showing historical battle symbols: for the France–Japan game, a Samurai with French players screaming in the background, and a Teutonic knight symbolizing the France–Germany match (*Le Courrier* 2001). Almost two years later, the federation declared that it had not intended to incite violence.

In the past few years, there has been considerable controversy concerning the levels of violence in collision and contact sports. In the United States, dozens of National Hockey League (NHL) and NFL players have had to retire early because of repeated concussion which can result in permanent brain damage. Tim Green, who played in the NFL for eight years and suffered almost a dozen concussions, said:

My parents told me when I was a boy that if I was going to play the game of [American] football I had to expect to get hurt ... Blood is a beloved thing in the NFL. If a player can draw blood from another, it's like winning the big stuffed bear for your girl friend at the fair. It means you've hit someone so hard that they burst. If a coach sees blood all over his players at the end of a game or a practice, he knows that some serious hitting has been going on and it warms his soul.

(Green 1996: 68–188)

Alarmed by the reported increase of head injuries in elite sports, the International Ice Hockey Federation (IIHF), the International Football Federation (FIFA) and the International Olympic Committee (IOC) organized in 2001 the first international conference on concussion in sport in order to improve knowledge and prevention.

According to some experts, collision and contact sports are getting physically tougher every year and athletes are required to become ever stronger and bigger in order to perform better. The number of NFL players weighing over 136 kilos (300 US pounds) increased from 50 in 1990 to more than 3,000 in 2002. During the summer of 2001, a 27-year-old NFL player, Korey Stringer, who weighed over 160 kilos, died of a heat stroke. Tim Green strongly criticized this trend, 'The pressure to be as big as you can possibly be in the NFL is enormous. The bigger you get the bigger advantage you have on everyone else' (O'Connor 2001: C1).

Research has often shown that aggressive play is not necessary to win games. But belief that it is a prerequisite for success is still strong, a myth that is kept alive by some trainers who believe in the 'winning at all cost' mentality (Engelhardt 1995). Many outstanding champions, such as Joe Montana, Michael Jordan, Diego Maradona, Johan Cruyff, Michel Platini and Wayne Gretzky, did not base their game on aggressiveness and violence. But a famous American basketball trainer, Pat Riley, admitted that he fined his players US\$ 1,500 in the 1990s if they failed to give a hard foul to an opponent driving to the basket (Coakley 1998: 192).

In some martial sports, such as boxing, full contact and Thai boxing, aggressiveness is encouraged even more strongly, albeit within established rules and limits. Several professional medical organizations have requested without success a total ban on these sports for children (see also Chapter 4). Although there are regularly fatal accidents in boxing – 561 deaths reported worldwide in the past 100 years (British Law Commission 1994: para.10.20) – many doctors believe that the sport 'does not pose an acute risk of death' for young boxers (Pearn 1998: 312; Leclerc and Herrera 1999).

The danger for children resides more in the fact that boxing institutionalizes a violence that can lead to chronic brain injury, a serious risk that few children are aware of. Even doctors in favour of banning boxing as a sport for children do not deny the important positive social and psychological role that the sport can play for young underprivileged and deprived males, nor the fact that it can be the only way for young males to channel their aggression. But the violence on which martial sports are based carries, they say, too high a health risk. Australian paediatrician John Pearn, who strongly advocated for a boxing ban, reported the case of a 23-year-old boxer who had been fighting since the age of 11 and whose autopsy revealed 'dramatic neuropathological changes' despite the fact that he did not appear to be clinically impaired. Every violent hit on a boxer's head leads to 'microvascular and contusional injury of small but multifocal extent. Not surprisingly this results in neuronal degeneration and neurofibrillary tangles and is cumulative' (Pearn 1998: 312). The increased involvement of girls aged under 18 – based on the principle of gender equality – is also of great concern to the medical field, especially as girls are reportedly more vulnerable to certain injuries: risk of traumatic hits to breast tissues and higher risks of brain injury due to the fact that adolescent girls' skulls 'are thinner than those of males and the protective effect is, of necessity, less' (Pearn 1998: 312).

CONSENT TO VIOLENCE

To what extent do athletes consent to participate in the violence of the sports they practise? According to Gardiner (2000: 102), 'Legal issues surrounding consent to physical force in both the civil law and the criminal law are not unproblematic. When this is within the context of sporting endeavour the issues become increasingly complex.'

For a long time, courts have applied the risk doctrine in sport injury, considering that violence was part of the game and that, by practising a sport, athletes consented implicitly (Nestel 1994: 3). Nevertheless, in many countries, and especially since the 1990s, cases of violence among athletes have reached the courts. In most cases, courts have recognized that athletes consented only to force to an extent that could reasonably be expected to occur in competition, but not to 'over the limit' violence. Participants in most sports, but especially contact sports, know that a reasonable risk of injury exists and consent to it. But sports regulations, together with coaches and officials, should indicate clearly to young athletes the limits they should not infringe. Injuries may be part of sports, but intentional or reckless infliction of injury cannot be tolerated by sports organizations and judicial courts (Gardiner 2000: 105). For example, in Australia, a court ruled that recklessness is not a requirement for civil liability between competitors, and that a competitor could be held liable for an injury 'caused by an error of judgement that a reasonable competitor, being a reasonable man of the sporting world, could not have made' (Wenn 1989: 3).

To what extent, we might ask, have athletes under 18 years of age fully given their consent to practise a sport? Certainly not in the same way as adults do, as children who are not capable of discernment cannot provide sound, informed consent; more mature adolescents, however, can give at least partial consent. Adults are responsible for the involvement of children in high-risk sports, such as boxing, American football, ice hockey or even rugby or football. How can 13-year-old children objectively assess the risk incurred through boxing and exposing their head to blows? Coaches and officials should systematically and objectively inform parents and young athletes about the dangers involved and ask them if they understand what they may risk when playing.

Child athletes and especially their parents also need to be informed that some sports are considered dangerous and/or violent and are therefore not covered by health insurance plans. For example, in Switzerland, SUVA, the national accident insurance, does not provide full coverage for athletes practising sports considered as 'high risk', such as boxing (fights), full contact (fights), car and motorcycle racing (including training), mountain biking, bungee-jumping, downhill skiing (training and competing), speed skiing, canyoning and roller-skating races (SUVA 2001). If an athlete is injured in one of these sports, the insurance will cover costs related to search and rescue and treatment, but not for pension allowances or other indemnities.

Intentional and violent incidents usually concern post-puberty athletes rather than very young children. Some experts mainly blame adults and the media. Frank Smoll, professor of psychology at the University of Washington (Seattle), declared:

> I am surprised there isn't more violence in youth sports given the current underlying phenomena that feeds this violent system, particularly in hockey. During the hockey season, the sportscasts ... show the fight of the night. That's sick, flat out. Is it any wonder kids are going to see that and say, 'Hey, I'm going to be a better fighter, I've got instruction'?
>
> (James and Ziemer 2000)

In case of serious incidents resulting in injury of another player, young athletes are generally considered by courts to have at least a partial criminal responsibility with regard to the victim. The minimum age for criminal responsibility is a subject of controversy among politicians and legislators and ranges from 6 to 18 years of age, depending on the country. In a few states there is not even a clear minimum age set by law, so court decisions can be totally arbitrary (UN Committee on the Rights of the Child 2000; 2001a). In many Commonwealth countries, the minimum age for criminal responsibility has for a long time been set at seven. At the other extreme, Belgium and Bolivia, for example, have set this age at 18. A majority of countries have now established an age limit between these two extremes. The Convention itself fixes no minimum age limit for criminal responsibility, but obliges states to establish one. The Committee on the Rights of the Child has systematically condemned countries having established very low ages (under ten) and advocates for a minimum age of at least 12 years, if not older (Hodgkin and Newell 2002: 601–3). It believes that under a certain age, children in any given situation should not be sentenced under the penal or criminal code but should have their case diverted away from judicial proceedings, as foreseen in article 40.3(b) of the Convention.

Cases of excessive violence among young athletes have reached criminal courts in some instances and the trend could increase in the future. In 1984 a Swiss court fined a junior ice-hockey player US$ 3,000 for hitting another player with his hockey stick; the victim had five teeth knocked out (Gardaz 2001). In 1999, a 15-year-old American ice-hockey player was charged with two counts of aggravated battery and condemned for having cross-checked from behind an opponent resulting in spinal injury and paralysis of his opponent (Swift 1999: 35–6). But on the whole, judicial remedies are only used as a last resort to remedy violence in sports. In many countries, most people consider that it is up to sports associations themselves to solve such problems.

NOTES

1 British athlete Mark Lewis-Francis won the 100-metre race in the 2000 junior world championships in 10:12 seconds and Darrel Brown from Trinidad and Tobago won the 2002 race in 10:09 seconds. Valery Borzov from the Soviet Union won the 1972 Olympic Games in 10:14 seconds; Hasely Crawford (Trinidad and Tobago), the 1976 Games in 10:06 seconds; and Allan Wells (Great Britain), the 1980 Games in 10:25 seconds.

2 Countries such as Austria, Croatia, Cyprus, Denmark, Ethiopia, Finland, Israel, Italy, Latvia, Namibia, New Zealand, Norway, Seychelles, South Africa, South Korea, Sweden, Uganda and Ukraine have taken legal steps to ban corporal punishment. See http://www.endcorporalpunishment.org

3 The trainer, Florin Georghe, was convicted of manslaughter, sentenced to eight years' imprisonment and ordered to pay the equivalent of US$ 5,600 to Adriana Giurca's parents. He was released on parole for 'good behaviour' after three-and-a-half years.

8 Below the belt

Psychological and emotional abuse

> In time of pressure, which not a day passed without … I was yelled at, screamed at, and had things thrown at me … Somehow my coach had convinced himself, and constantly reminded me, that I was a fat imbecile, a bloody idiot, no good and worthless.
>
> (Danielle Herbst, former top US gymnast in Ryan 1995: 216)

> There is little doubt that those involved in children's sport are concerned with the competitive stress placed on the young athlete. Problems arise when we attempt to discuss this issue.
>
> (Daniel Gould, in Cahill and Pearl 1993: 20)

The general public generally views sport only as a physical activity. Those involved in competitive sports, however, know that performance is also closely linked to mental and psychological capacities (Maffuli 1998: 298). To take part in intensive training and competition, athletes need to have the ability to concentrate and persevere, to accept self-sacrifice and self-denial, to withstand suffering, and to abstain from specific activities and food. In modern sports, athletes can only succeed at the highest level if they combine the necessary physical and mental qualities. Athletes' performance tends to improve significantly after mental training (Weinberg and Comar 1994; Solberg et al. 2000). Experienced trainers and educators have often seen naturally talented young athletes fail in their performances due to a lack of mental abilities while less gifted youths succeed because of their exceptional mental will and strength.

Young athletes can be victims of mental violence and psychological abuse when they participate in sports, just as they can at home or in school (Gerbis and Dunn 2004; UN Committee on the Rights of the Child 2001b: paras. 674–745). But, according to the World Health Organization (WHO 2002: 64–5): 'Psychological abuse against children has been allotted even less attention globally than physical and sexual abuse … evidence suggests that shouting at children is a common response … cursing children and calling them names appear to vary more greatly.'

Regrettably, many areas relating to the psychological consequences of involving children in intensive training and competitive sports are still insufficiently studied. Young elite athletes evolve in an adult environment and may be driven to perform not for their own satisfaction and to reach their personal targets, but to respond to the high expectations of adults, who might be motivated by their ego, earnings, glory or even by political motives. Young athletes may not only be subjected to stress related to sport, but to pressure at school – if they have not already dropped out. The need to perform in any field naturally generates an environment in which the level of pressure is proportionate to that of the expectations. The high popularity and visibility of competitive sports, often resulting in tremendous financial, media and political interests, creates a high-pressure world in which young athletes are sometimes caught up.

The National Youth Sport Safety Foundation (NYSSF) is an American non-profit, educational organization dedicated to reducing the number and severity of injuries that young people sustain in sports and fitness activities. NYSSF, in dedicating its 2001 national campaign to emotional abuse in sports, pointed out that: 'Certain behaviors and philosophies [in youth sports] have been found to create a destructive environment, causing some children to be scarred for life' (NYSSF 2001). For the NYSSF, 'emotional abuse' includes rejecting, ignoring, isolating or terrorizing a person; calling them names, making fun of them or putting them down; saying things that hurt feelings; yelling; forcing children to participate in sports; and punishing or not speaking to them if they have played poorly (NYSSF 2001).

Sport psychology has developed rapidly since the 1970s, with 1,100 sport psychologists now practising in the United States. In many countries young athletes are seeking support not necessarily because they are suffering, but often to learn how to deal with the pressure to win, how to become tougher or how to increase their capacity to concentrate. American sport psychologist Alan Goldberg affirmed, 'When kids have problems in sports, it's often not mechanical. The problem is between their ears' (Wen 2001). But although psychology is increasingly part of elite athletes' preparation, another psychologist has warned that 'when kids are brought to a sport psychologist, they can view it as just more pressure to perform' (Wen 2001).

The international community has only recently acknowledged mental violence and psychological abuse, which are still poorly recognized by public and judicial authorities in many countries. As opposed to most forms of physical violence, psychological abuse cannot systematically be demonstrated with concrete evidence. Therefore, courts and society often challenge its definition and, in most countries, very little – if any – legislation covers mental violence. Article 19 of the Convention on the Rights of the Child recognizes mental violence. This provision represents a real breakthrough in international law: it is the first time that a major human rights treaty refers explicitly to this type of violence. Nonetheless, it fails to provide a detailed definition: 'States Parties shall take all appropriate legislative, administrative, social and educational measures to protect the child from all forms of physical or mental violence … '

Article 39 also refers to the child's right to 'psychological recovery'. In its jurisprudence, the Committee on the Rights of the Child has given a clearer meaning to 'mental violence' referring, among others, to acts such as deliberate humiliation, harassment, verbal abuse and the effects of isolation (Hodgkin and Newell 2002: 260–4).

Sports authorities and organizations are, therefore, bound to prevent and protect young athletes from all forms of psychological violence.

EXCESSIVE PRESSURE AND STRESS

Many researchers have noted how resilient children are, even in the most extreme situations (Loesel and Bliessener 1990; Rutter 1992; Cyrulnik 2002). In growing up, they learn to deal with certain stressful situations. One of the goals of early intensive training is precisely to teach young children coping mechanisms, including self-control techniques, to enable them to function efficiently under pressure (Gould 1993: 33–4).

But the level of stress that an individual can take varies from one person to another: some are positively stimulated and perform even better under stress, others can't take it at all. For athletes, the ability to deal with stress is a critical selection criterion. All champions have developed a variety of means to perform in situations of high pressure. Increasingly they are turning to specialists in, for example, relaxation therapy to help them handle stress. The American gymnastics federation recognized that, 'How such [young] athletes view and respond to stress in some ways will determine their success in gymnastics as well as the quality of their gymnastics experience' (Duda and Gano-Overway 1996).

Competitive stress has been defined as 'negative emotions, feelings, and thoughts that one might have with respect to their athletic experience, such as feelings of apprehension, anxiety, muscle tension, nervousness, physical reaction, thoughts centred on worry and self-doubt, and negative statements' (Scanlan *et al.* 1991: 105). While stress is not necessarily always negative, competition can create very high levels of anxiety and some leading researchers consider that approximately 10 per cent of young athletes suffer from excessive stress (Weinberg and Gould 1995).

Parents are often at the origin of stress-related problems. A study of 46 top American athletes preparing for the 1988 Olympic Games showed that, although most parents (95 per cent) were supportive of their children's involvement in sports, 35 per cent of the athletes admitted suffering from excessive pressure from their mother and 25 per cent from their father, which was considered a source of discouragement. One Olympic athlete said:

> I didn't understand my dad's harsh attitudes. I just wanted to go out and have fun, basically, and of course my dad wanted me to go out there and kick ass and take names. That took all the fun out of it. That meant that you had to be mad all the time and I didn't want to play like that.

(Murphy 1999: 93)

Some sports, such as tennis, gymnastics, basketball, ice hockey, football or figure skating, subject young athletes to high levels of stress as they combine early intensive training, commercial and financial interests and strong visibility through sustained media interest. A 1995 British study of 453 young elite athletes showed that 4 per cent of gymnasts and swimmers and 3 per cent of footballers admitted suffering from severe and constant anxiety due to sport-related pressure; 12 per cent of gymnasts and 10 per cent of footballers, moderate and inappropriate anxious behaviour; and 33 per cent of gymnasts, 27 per cent of swimmers and 22 per cent of football players said they regularly had sleeping problems due to anxiety before competition (TOYA 1995: 6–8).

Stress can be overwhelming for these athletes and as a result victory does not necessarily bring what it should: happiness and self-esteem. After she won the US figure-skating championship in 1995, Tiffany Chin was asked how she would have felt had she not won. 'Devastated. I don't know. I'd probably die … I didn't feel happiness winning. I felt relief. Which was disappointing,' she replied (Ryan 1995: 8).

Chin is not the only athlete to react this way. Others, including some who never achieved top results, have expressed similar feelings. A study on the origins of competitive stress covering 75 young (9 to 12 years) elite American gymnasts showed that stress was caused by:

- fear of unsatisfactory performance and of new and dangerous skills (38 per cent, 'I feel stress falling off the beam and doing new, scary skills');
- apprehension of being evaluated (25.7 per cent, 'I feel stress being in front of judges, people video taping me, and I'm afraid I'll mess up and embarrass myself');
- the environment during competition events (14 per cent, 'I feel stress when I try my hardest and my coach says I'm doing bad');
- making mistakes (4.1 per cent, 'I get stressed when I work over and over on something and just don't do it right');
- expectations from self and others (4.1 per cent, 'I feel stress when my coach puts pressure on me. Like if you don't do it, you can't go to the meet'; 'I feel stress when your coach is depending on you to win'; 'I feel stress when you have to do something you don't want to do');
- time pressure (3.5 per cent, 'I feel stress rushing in timed warm-ups'); and
- fear of injury (2.9 per cent, 'I feel stress when doing a new trick and thinking you're going to kill yourself').

(Duda and Gano-Overway 1996a)

VERBAL VIOLENCE AND EMOTIONAL ABUSE

Bringing up children requires a great deal of patience, self-control and dedication from parents and other caregivers. Coaches involved in intensive programmes need, in addition to their knowledge of sports, these same qualities to train children properly. The key to success is the trainer's capacity to recognize a child's potential and to allow that child to develop his or her full potential in a healthy manner. Just as there are many methodologies in education, ranging from the conservative to the progressive, so a wide range of approaches exists in competitive sports training. Some national sport federations and their trainers believe that training for elite sports requires harsh – almost spartan – and authoritarian discipline, often inspired by military methods. Others promote at an early age a sense of responsibility and autonomy among athletes.

Competitive sport is usually based on an unbalanced relationship of power between trainers and athletes, which is even more apparent when it comes to youngsters, and empowerment is rarely valued. Coakley (1998: 503) explained:

> In coach–athlete relationships, it is generally accepted that coaches can humiliate, shame and derogate athletes to push them to be the best they can be. Athletes are expected to respond to humiliation by being tougher competitors willing to give even more of themselves in their quest for excellence.

Irina Viner, a successful Russian gymnastics trainer, once said, 'My relation to the young girls is like master–slave until 14, then it looks like general–soldiers until 16, after that we enter in a partnership' (Losson 1994).

Young children involved in intensive training often spend more time with their trainers than with their parents. This situation reinforces their emotional bonds with their coaches, so that young athletes often refer to their 'second mother or father'. Some coaches, anonymous or famous, do not hesitate to abuse young athletes verbally and emotionally, using insults and humiliation to provoke their charges' anger, which they consider a powerful stimulant and a prerequisite to character building, and pushing them to the limit and beyond. While this phenomenon has as yet been the subject of little research (Klein and Palzkill 1998; Kohler 2000), Joan Ryan published in 1995 a shocking account of such abuse during young girls' intensive training in gymnastics and figure skating.

Excellence in sports requires high levels of self-control, not only physical but also emotional. Therefore, coaches prepare their athletes mentally to cope with stress, emotions and pain. When properly taught, this instruction can contribute to the sound development of children and adolescents. But the strictness and toughness of intensive training can lead to very abusive trends. Elite athletes are sometimes taught to stifle their emotions and be stoical about pain.

When children are too young to have developed their own values, their obedience might be abused by authority figures. Chris Reid, the father of Karen Reid, a top US gymnast during the 1990s, said:

> he [the trainer] could be so cruel to the children, calling them 'fat', 'you idiot'. I used to think, 'What is this going to do to my daughter when she starts dating? Will she choose an abusive partner?' She was always trying to please this abusive man … It's disgusting, all these men with their huge egos dealing with little girls.
>
> (Ryan 1995: 217)

A 1993 survey undertaken by the Minnesota Amateur Sport Commission (USA) revealed that almost half (45.3 per cent) of the male and female athletes surveyed said they had been called names, yelled at or insulted while participating in sports. Some trainers also use threats to ensure that accounts of their abusive methods remain confidential. 'If you tell others what happened I will go to jail ... if you leave, I'll commit suicide,' said one coach in a 1999 Swiss study (Kohler 2000: 27).

Sport authorities are ultimately responsible for preventing all forms of mental abuse. In 1998, the Australian Sports Commission, in collaboration with Active Australia, prepared guidelines for athletes on a harassment-free sport system, which stated that: 'The coach should refrain from using profane, insulting, harassing and otherwise offensive language, refrain from making sexual innuendoes about athletes.'

IMPOSED DIETS

All top athletes have to keep a close eye on their diet in order to stay physically fit and to prepare their sporting careers properly. This is particularly the case in sports that include an artistic and aesthetic evaluation (such as gymnastics, ski jumping, equestrian sports, diving and figure skating). Not only do young champions have to master the skills of a demanding sport, but they must also focus on their body image, appearance, charm and sense of beauty. This is especially challenging as these entail two very contrasting apprenticeships and are not necessarily acquired at the same pace by young athletes who are still in a most sensitive phase of their development.

Athletes today follow scientifically researched training methods and are required to adhere to strict lifestyle rules. Nothing is left to the whim of fate. Close attention is paid to what they eat, for both research and practice have shown the benefits of proper nutrition (Steen 1998). Child and adult athletes are sometimes obliged to follow rigid diets to prepare themselves for competition. This is often hard on children, whose nutritional needs are very specific due to their physical development, but who have to overcome the temptation to eat foods that are forbidden for them – chocolate, biscuits, ice creams and other sweets – but that might be considered 'normal' for their non-sporting peers.

Little scientific research has been undertaken on the diets imposed on children in competitive sports, although anecdotal information seems to confirm their existence. For example, in the United States in 1994 the mothers of two high-school gymnasts reported being asked by the girls' coach to give them only one meal a day, advice which they ignored (*Columbus Dispatch* 1994). In Belgium, symptoms of dehydration were detected in a 14-year-old gymnast, who trained three-and-a-half hours a day, five days a week, and who was forbidden to drink during training sessions (Symposium on talent detection in sport 1997). Rainer Martens, an American sport psychologist, pointed out in

2001 that, 'For 25 years we've known that depriving athletes of water during intensive competition or practice is foolish, yet coaches continue to do it today' (Martens 2001: 49).

Accounts of young athletes secretly eating forbidden food are legion. More serious, nevertheless, is the risk that imposed diets and almost obsessive references to food limitations create an environment favouring the development of eating disorders in child athletes. Silent Edge, an American advocacy group protecting the rights of figure skaters, reported that one mother had said:

> I wish someone would have told me how unfair this [figure skating] sport is, how prone to eating disorders the girls are ... I know of many girls who have sought treatment. Basically, I wish my daughter would have never started skating. I think it is a very unhealthy environment.
>
> (Silent-Edge 1999)

Preparation periods for major competitions are especially difficult as young athletes are forced to diet very strictly. American gymnast Betty Okino explained that just before the 1992 Olympics, for which she, aged 16, had qualified, 'we were eating very little ... we were eating much less than we normally eat. I don't think it was even 1,000 calories a day' (Ryan 1995: 72).

The Committee on the Rights of the Child and the UN Commission on Human Rights' Special Rapporteur on harmful traditional practices against women and children have identified excessive food taboos and imposed diets as harmful traditional practices (Hodgkin and Newell 2002: 367). UNICEF also considers that denial of food is a form of violence (UNICEF 2000: 2). The phenomena referred to are traditional, cultural and religious beliefs and take place in a completely different environment to that of competitive sports, but the most radical diets and food constraints sometimes imposed by adults on young athletes can also be considered abusive.

EATING DISORDERS

Individuals can be considered disordered eaters if they engage in bingeing, purging, food restriction or prolonged fasting, use diet pills and/or diuretics, have a strong preoccupation with food and develop a distorted body image (DePalma *et al.* 2002). Eating dysfunctions, especially anorexia and bulimia, are present in competitive sports, probably due to a complex combination of factors, including the following:

- Increased competitiveness depends, among other things, on a proper diet.
- Intensive training attracts people coping with eating disorders and willing to lose weight.
- Athletes are, by definition, constantly using and concerned with their own body and therefore often self-centred.

- Many sports are based on both aesthetic criteria and endurance and can only be performed by light athletes whose weight is controlled.
- Some sports are divided into weight categories (weightlifting, boxing, wrestling, judo, etc.).

In addition, adolescents, as a group, are recognized as being especially vulnerable to eating disorders. They are in a turbulent development phase involving enormous physical, emotional and psychological changes. Identity building and, for some, the search for absolute perfection are also crucial aspects of this phase. It is generally acknowledged that athletes are a population group with higher levels of eating disorders (Sundgot-Borgen 1999), but whether this is a direct result of the sporting environment or whether some athletes presented the pathology before taking up elite sport, is open to debate (Nativ *et al.* 1997; Khan *et al.* 2002).

The impact of society's trends on the sports world is an additional factor in dysfunctional behaviours. The view that 'thinner is better' has undeniably had an impact during the past two decades on both athletes and sport and its rules. By giving more importance to technical rather than artistic aspects, gymnastics, for example, has evolved into a sport made for exceptionally light, short and young athletes. In 1976 the average American Olympic gymnast weighed approximately 52 kilograms, whereas in 1992 the average was 42 kg. The 1994 world champion, Shannon Miller, weighed 40 kg (Propson 1995: 25). Alarmed by this trend, the European Parliament 'urged the International Federation of Gymnastics not to encourage extreme thinness, by penalising gymnasts and other sportspersons' (Council of Europe 2000). During the late 1990s, the International Federation of Gymnastics had considered imposing a minimum weight limit on gymnasts, but this measure proved not to be realistic and was dropped (Terrani 2001).

Some sports federations have tried discreetly to look into the problem of anorexia, but solutions are not easy to find for a problem that goes well beyond the borders and controls of sports. In gymnastics, improved information has been circulated to athletes and trainers explaining that thinness can be counter-productive for sports results.

Little research has been undertaken in developing countries (Chandra *et al.* 1995); in all Western countries, however, it is generally agreed that the incidence of eating disorders is on the increase and that they present a serious problem (Eagles *et al.* 1995). The Academy for Eating Disorders, the world's largest professional organization for those who work with people suffering from eating disorders, considers that between 0.5 per cent and 3 per cent of young women suffer from either anorexia or bulimia (Academy for Eating Disorders 2002). Evidence tends to show that eating disorders are higher among young elite athletes involved in intensive training than in the global population. In some sports requiring spartan diets and training, such as gymnastics, swimming, running, wrestling, rowing or figure skating, the levels of anorexia are much higher than in the general population. Studies reveal that between 15 per cent and 62 per cent of female athletes suffer from eating disorders (Skolnick 1993;

Smith 1996; Sundgot-Borgen *et al.* 1999; DePalma *et al.* 2002). Tennis champions such as Zina Garrison and Carling Bassett Segusso publicly revealed having experienced serious eating disorders.

In extreme situations, competitive sports can create a damaging environment for the child due to excessive pressure and expectations. Christy Henrich, a top US gymnast, died of anorexia in 1993. She missed the 1988 Olympic Games selection by only 0.118 of a point, a margin so small that only a computer could identify it. Fellow gymnast Kristie Phillips, who also suffered from anorexia, said:

> everyone goes through it [anorexia], but nobody talks about it, because they're [the gymnasts] embarrassed. But I don't put the fault on us. It's pressures that are put on us to be so skinny. It's mental cruelty. It's not fair that all these pressures are put on us at such a young age and we don't realize it until we get older and we suffer from it ... I weighed 45 kilograms and I was being called [by her coach] an overstuffed Christmas turkey.
>
> (Ryan 1995: 10)

In sports such as gymnastics, swimming and figure skating, some coaches systematically weigh athletes. The day starts and ends on the scales. Pressure can be so excessive that some young gymnasts frequently absorb diuretics or laxatives in order to maintain low body weight. Tiffany Cohen, a former Olympic swimming champion, developed an eating disorder while she was training at the University of Texas. A self-proclaimed perfectionist, she claimed that her coach 'knew that, and he knew who weight really affected. He played on that. He played on people's neuroses' (Doherty 1999: 137). She explained that, to avoid being a member of the dreaded 'fat club', many of her team-mates 'routinely fasted, induced vomiting, used laxatives and did extra workouts' (Doherty 1999: 137).

Athletes can suffer many forms of abuse by coaches putting too much pressure on them to lose weight. Now a coach herself, American Tonya Chaplin said that by the time she left gymnastics she was vomiting up to a dozen times a day. Her coach punished girls whose weight minimally exceeded requirements with verbal abuse, denying the 'fatties' meals and confining them to a 'fat room' (Propson 1995: 13). Jane Doe, a former international competitor in pairs figure skating, recalled:

> I used to dread having to wake up every day for the rest of my life worrying if I was going to gain weight ... Actually walking into the rink every Wednesday for weigh-in became a nightmare. When I first moved to the rink, everyone whispered behind my back that I was too fat (five feet, 100 pounds), and as I gradually starved my way down to 89 pounds, I lost my muscle strength and was perpetually injured, but at least nobody could tell me I was fat. In fact, the thinner I got, the more approval I felt in my coach's eyes.
>
> (Propson 1995: 3)

Bela Karolyi trained Nadia Comaneci, who also admitted having suffered from eating disorders. In the 1990s Karolyi came under fire for his quasi-militaristic training methods. According to him, it is normal in every sport for coaches to comment on their athletes' weight, but parents are responsible for athletes' eating problems. 'They are the ones feeding them,' he said (Ryan 1995: 8).

Even the parents of less-renowned athletes may also put pressure on their children to lose weight. In a British study on the health of elite athletes, the mother of a gymnast said: 'I'm very concerned about her weight. I told her to lose half a stone. I don't want her anorexic but she must lose weight' (TOYA 1995: 17).

Eating disorders more commonly affect women, but men are also affected and about 10 per cent of individuals with eating disorders seen by health professionals are male (Andersen 1999; Fairburn and Beglin 1990). In competitive sports, gymnastics, running, bodybuilding, rowing, wrestling, horse racing and swimming may render male athletes more vulnerable to eating disorders (Andersen *et al.* 1995).

One study revealed that 11 per cent of male rowers and wrestlers displayed eating disorders (Thiel 1993), another showed that 9.9 per cent of footballers were at risk of eating disorders and 42 per cent practised dysfunctional eating behaviour to meet the weight restrictions of their sport (DePalma *et al.* 1993). Rapid weight loss in wrestling, for example, has long been a tradition. In 1996, the American College of Sports Medicine updated its 1976 position statement on weight loss in wrestlers:

> Weight cutting is a half-century-old practice that can result in serious health problems ... Despite a growing body of evidence admonishing the behaviour, weight cutting (rapid weight reduction) remains prevalent among wrestlers ... Use of pharmacological agents, including diuretics, stimulants, and laxatives to reduce weight has been reported among a few of these athletes. The weight loss techniques have been passed down from wrestler to wrestler, or coach to wrestler, and have changed little over the past 25 years.

According to specialists, since the jumping style changed to the 'V style' during the 1990s, ski jumping has become one of the sports in which male athletes are most vulnerable to eating disorders. Athletes are required to be tall and light to remain longer in the air. The best jumpers are usually between 1.80 and 1.85 metres tall and weigh between 60 and 65 kilograms, if not less (Terrani 2001). German ski-jumping superstar, Sven Hannawald, is considered to have the perfect body size with a height of 1.84 m for a little over 60 kg. Suspicion of anorexia has often surrounded Hannawald, but no evidence has ever been found (Terrani 2001).

In 2003, Frank Löffler, world junior ski-jumping champion in 2002, was banned from the German team for his inability to keep to a strict diet and maintain a weight of 68 kg (for a height of 1.87 m). In an interview with *Der Spiegel*, Löffler referred to 'an absurd hunger diktat' imposed by his trainers that felt like 'permanent terror'. 'For two years I weighed only 64 kg. The only thing that remained was my skeleton,' he said (Grossekathöfer and Pfeil 2003).

BURN-OUT SYNDROME

By definition, children and adolescents are constantly and rapidly evolving. The Convention on the Rights of the Child strongly emphasizes the child's 'evolving capacity' (in article 5, for example), meaning that a child of seven and an adolescent of 14 cannot be regarded and treated the same way and that even children of the same age should be considered individually, as they might be at different developmental stages (Hodgkin and Holmberg 2000: 93–105). Competent trainers systematically adapt their methods and programmes to the changing capacities of a young athlete and would not train a seven-year-old as they would an adolescent.

The sports world has difficulties accepting that children might not always share adults' motivations. If the concept of victory is the primary stimulator in adult sports, the same does not necessarily apply to children. Children between six and 11 years old overwhelmingly prefer to play and lose than to sit on the bench of a winning team (Weiss 1993: 39–69).

Play, not winning, is a unique and key concept in the psychological and physical development of children (Huizinga 1950; Hart and Petren 2000: 107–21). Playing is associated with fun and when pleasure and fun are absent, children may no longer wish to participate in sports. An American study conducted in 1997 by the National Youth Sports Coaches Association clearly showed that the main reason given by children who drop out of sports is that 'the sport is no longer fun' (Doherty 1999: 130). A British study revealed that, of the elite athletes studied, 64 per cent who trained at least 15 hours a week and who retired from sports during adolescence did so because of their lack of enjoyment (TOYA 1995a: 6).

Key factors of motivation for the child are progress, self-improvement and personal empowerment. Though research and practice have shown that success is not only based on the amount of hours spent training, many coaches still privilege quantity over quality. They run the risk of pushing young athletes so far that they drop out of sports. This phenomenon is the burn-out syndrome and is relatively frequent in competitive sports. Motivation is a key aspect in modern sports that is surprisingly often overlooked, for the greater the gap between the motivations of adults and those of young athletes, the higher the risk of burn-out.

Another key parameter of the burn-out syndrome is the age of involvement in intensive training. Over-training has been identified as a leading cause of stress and burn-out, to which children are far more vulnerable than adults (Holander *et al.* 1995). By the time adolescent athletes are 16, they may already have ten years of intensive training behind them, especially in sports such as tennis, football, baseball, basketball or gymnastics. In 1985, an outraged John McEnroe, a former tennis champion, exclaimed:

> you talk about Bjorn Borg, burned out by glory at 26 years old. But who cares about 13-year-old kids, already burnt out by tournaments, travel, pressure

and who have nobody next to them if they lose … Not to mention parents who care only about the money!

(*L'Equipe* 1985)

Erik Johnson, a former professional baseball player for the San Francisco Giants, also warned: 'I see a lot of burn-out … It used to be high-school (15–16 years), but now it is 10-, 11- and 12-year-old kids. The kids get fried' (Bigelow *et al.* 2001: 97).

For every athlete reaching the top, there are thousands of anonymous young people who did not make it – some are burnt out at too young an age, others have bitter memories of abusive experiences, and still others will long struggle with psychological traumas and scars.

9 Foul play

Sexual abuse and violence

I wondered, if I'd killed myself, would they add that to his sentence?
(Anonymous teenage boy who became suicidal after being sexually
abused by his wrestling coach, in *Cleveland Plain Dealer* 1995)

If sexual exploitation is a symptom of failed leadership in sport, then leadership is
also the key to ridding sport of this problem ... empowerment strategies are
required to ensure that, regardless of the coach's motivation to harass or abuse,
the athlete has the confidence skills and opportunities to resist.
(Brackenridge 2001: 231)

Sexual abuse of children in and outside their family remains an area of taboo in
the field of child rights, although since the mid-1980s many studies have
revealed its widespread prevalence. Over the past two decades, epidemiological
studies have yielded prevalence estimates of child sexual abuse ranging between
6 and 62 per cent for girls, and 3 and 37 per cent for boys (Finkelhor 1989;
Dhaliwal *et al.* 1996). These statistics vary greatly depending on the definition
given to sexual abuse (i.e. verbal, with/without physical contact, with/without
penetration) and the way data is gathered. The World Health Organization
(WHO 2002: 149) defined sexual violence as:

> any sexual act, attempt to obtain a sexual act, unwanted sexual comments or
> advances, or acts to traffic, or otherwise directed, against a person's sexuality
> using coercion, by any person regardless of their relationship to the victim,
> in any setting, including but not limited to at home and work.

In its definition of sexual abuse, UNICEF (2000: 3) includes coerced sex through
threats, intimidation or physical force, forcing unwanted sexual acts or forcing
sex with others. Men who are, or who have been, in a position of trust, intimacy
and power are usually the perpetrators of sexual violence.

The Committee on the Rights of the Child considers that the legal age of sexual consent, when lower than the age of majority, should not be an obstacle in
the obligation of states to protect people under 18 years old from sexual abuse

(UN Committee on the Rights of the Child 2002a: 49b). The United Kingdom took measures in 1999 to adapt its policy to this requirement, specifying that those in need of protection include 'young people over the age of consent [16 years] but under 18 years of age and vulnerable adults where a relationship of trust with an adult looking after them exists' (Government of the UK 1999: 3).

The nature of the sexual abuse itself hinders research and the formulation of reliable estimations: it is difficult to obtain information when the abused are loath to speak out, due to taboo, confidentiality or fear of reprisal and revelation. In its second periodic report to the Committee, the Norwegian government put forward the figure of 5 per cent of girls having been victims of sexual abuse, although it indicated that this is a conservative figure and that higher figures have been revealed by researchers in Norway (Government of Norway 1998).

In 1986, a study conducted by the American Medical Association in the United States found that 25 per cent of girls and 13 per cent of boys had been molested before the age of 18 (Howard and Munson 1998). A comprehensive study undertaken in Canada revealed in 1997 that 12.8 per cent of females reported childhood sexual abuse (MacMillan *et al.* 1997), while in Finland, research indicated that 7.6 per cent of girls and 3.3 per cent of boys had experienced forced sexual contact by an adult (Halperin *et al.* 1996).

The Convention on the Rights of the Child explicitly recognizes, in articles 19 and 34, the right of the child to be protected from sexual abuse. Article 19 affirms that:

1   States Parties shall take all appropriate legislative, administrative, social and educational measures to protect the child from all forms of physical or mental violence, injury or abuse, neglect or negligent treatment, maltreatment or exploitation, including sexual abuse, while in the care of parent(s), legal guardian(s) or any other person who has the care of the child.

2   Such protective measures should, as appropriate, include effective procedures for the establishment of social programmes to provide necessary support for the child and for those who have the care of the child, as well as for other forms of prevention and for identification, reporting, referral, investigation, treatment and follow-up of instances of child maltreatment described heretofore, and, as appropriate, for judicial involvement.

Article 34 states that:

States Parties undertake to protect the child from all forms of sexual exploitation and sexual abuse. For these purposes, States Parties shall in particular take all appropriate national, bilateral and multilateral measures to prevent: (a) The inducement or coercion of a child to engage in any unlawful sexual activity; (b) The exploitative use of children in prostitution or other unlawful sexual practices; (c) The exploitative use of children in pornographic performances and materials. The latter provision concerns mainly children outside of the family environment; whereas the first one protects the child within the care of parent(s), legal guardian(s) or any other person who has the care of the child.

Article 19 applies to young athletes if, for example, they are in the care of a coach (who may become a surrogate parent) or are involved in an intensive training programme and spend many hours a day away from their family. In such situations, the coach takes over, in part, the role and responsibilities of parents. The building of a collective sense of identity and the existing hierarchical structure and patriarchal authority characterized by the sports system reinforce the similarity between teams and the family. Some authors have noticed that the concept of family is constantly rebuilt in the sporting environment. According to a Canadian expert, 'Time and again, players and coaches refer to the team as "family"' (Robinson 1998: 97).

Are children more at risk of sexual abuse and violence in a sports context than in other settings, such as at home or at school? Celia Brackenridge (2001: 4), the author of the most comprehensive study undertaken on sexual abuse in sport, believes that we know too little to draw any conclusions. So far, only one study (in Norway) has compared the prevalence of sexual harassment in and outside the context of sport. The result is of great concern: twice as many athletes as non-athletes have experienced sexual harassment from authority figures (Council of Europe 2000a: 6; Brackenridge 2000).

Most experts believe that sexual harassment, abuse and violence in sports are still widely under-reported due to the fact that many victims – mainly female, but also male – hesitate to reveal these abuses; they do not trust the system to respect their right to confidentiality, fear reprisal and appear to grow resigned to the frequent acts of verbal and physical harassment in the strongly male-dominated sport context (Seymour 1998; Donnelly 1999). In 1998, studies in Canada and Norway revealed that athletes (40 to 50 per cent, and 33 per cent respectively) experience a negative and uncomfortable environment, ranging from mild sexual harassment to abuse (MacGregor 1998; Fasting *et al.* 1998). A Danish pilot study (1998) also revealed that about 25 per cent of athletes under 18 knew about or had themselves experienced situations of harassment by a coach or trainer (Milling 1998). Research in Canada in 1996 found that over 20 per cent of the 226 elite athletes who participated in the study had experienced sexual intercourse with an authority figure in their sport, and that 8.6 per cent had experienced forced sexual intercourse; 3.2 per cent of the respondents stated that they had had upsetting experiences in a sporting context with a 'flasher' when they were under 16; and 2.6 per cent had experienced unwanted sexual touching when they were under 16 (Kirby and Greaves 1996; Brackenridge and Kirby 1997). Results from a comprehensive study in Australia in 2002 revealed that no less than 31 per cent of female athletes and 21 per cent of male athletes reported experiencing sexual abuse at some time in their lives. Of these, 41 per cent of females and 29 per cent of males had been sexually abused within the sports environment (Leahy *et al.* 2002).

There are as yet no specific studies on the prevalence of sexual abuse by females in sport, although research on the subject outside of sport reveals very low rates of incidence. In the absence of research, it is believed that in almost all cases of sexual abuse in the sporting context, males are the perpetrators, which reflects the unchallenged domination of men in coaching and other positions of power in sports (Elliott *et al.* 1995). A meta-analysis of eight studies published during the 1990s found that an average of 97.5 per cent of female victims and 78.7 per cent of male victims were abused by males (Fergusson and Mullen 1999).

In the sporting world, boys are almost as vulnerable to sexual abuse as girls, and sometimes they are even more isolated and powerless in these situations. Girls remain the largest group of victims of sexual abuse in general, but expert groups have noted that sexual abuse of boys carries even stronger societal taboos and, therefore, in most countries, legal and other protection measures are almost non-existent (UN Committee on the Rights of the Child 2001b: paras 678 and 689). After the revelations of abuse by ice-hockey star Sheldon Kennedy in 1997, the Canadian Hockey League commissioned a study of the scope of abuse in the sport. The resulting report recognized that 'harassment and abuse of males is largely overlooked and ignored' (Kirke 1997).

Boys are apparently less likely than girls to report abuse and consequently most official statistics in this regard are unreliable (Peake 1989: 3–18). Boys find it hard to reveal harassment and abuse experiences, mainly for fear of being labelled homosexual and perhaps because men rarely sympathize with other males who have been sexually abused (Messner 1992; Robinson 1998). As one abuse victim, who was raped by his baseball coach as a boy, observed: 'Women turn to other women in times like this. Men don't turn to other men. You're not going to go to another guy with something like this' (*Boston Globe* 1995).

Research on sexual abuse of disabled athletes is still scarce, but it is generally believed that young athletes with disabilities are more vulnerable to sexual abuse than others, and intellectually impaired children carry the highest risks of being sexually abused (Kerr 1999; Sobsey 1991). Some researchers consider that over 90 per cent of people with developmental disabilities will experience sexual abuse at some point in their lives, and that 49 per cent of them will experience ten or more abusive incidents (Valenti-Hein and Schwartz 1995).

A FAVOURABLE ENVIRONMENT FOR ABUSERS

The world of sports offers a conducive environment for the sexual abuser. As can be seen in Table 9.1, young athletes can find themselves in a number of situations in which they are potentially more at risk of sexual abuse. Sport can attract abusers, just as school, arts or religion do. It provides easy access to children in an environment that is usually based on a relationship of trust between parents, children and the coach. As the therapist of a male sexual abusers in sport explained:

Table 9.1 Characteristics of sports systems that potentially increase the vulnerability of young athletes to sexual abuse

Young athletes:	• are frequently in close physical contact, with coaches, masseurs, physiotherapists, etc.
	• undress and shower with others
	• are isolated from their families, their natural support and protection system
Sport:	• is a male-driven activity, run on strictly paternalistic and hierarchical systems
	• offers easy access to volunteers and professionals with the wrong intentions
	• is not open to independent monitoring and investigation
	• has a very positive image that might generate excessive confidence in the system
Coaches:	• feel a great ownership for their athletes
	• are authority figures, upon whom athletes are dependent
Intensive training:	• requires such an investment of time and energy that it limits and slows social development and the learning of coping strategies and life-skills
	• offers ample opportunity for abuse to take place, for example, during closed practices, travel, unsupervised team trips and overnight

The first thing to remember is that, regretfully, there are some men who go into sport to get access to children sexually ... if men are going to abuse children, they have to form a relationship first. Sport is a way of forming that relationship, and is a way of turning that relationship into an abusive one. A coach has power and authority over the children they're training, they have respect from the parents, respect from the community and because often their lives are dedicated to children, it's hard to believe that a person in that position can be an abuser. All of that can be used as a cover by a man who has sexual arousal and is oriented towards children.

(Brackenridge 2001: 68)

Young athletes know that they are completely dependent on the coach's knowledge and goodwill to improve their own performance and capacity, and that all decisions will be taken by the coach, so they need to establish a bond of strong mutual confidence in order to train properly. It is, therefore, almost impossible for young athletes to challenge the trainer's power. 'By then I was absolutely dependent upon him – he was God,' said a female athlete who was sexually abused by her coach. 'From 15 to 19 he owned me, basically' (Brackenridge 2001: 111).

Even athletes who have reached the legal age for sexual consent are not invulnerable to abuse and exploitation, again because they are entirely dependent on their coach. The UK government (1999: 3) considers that 'although young people can legally consent to some types of sexual activity, they may still be relatively immature emotionally ... It is essential that those looking after young people recognize this vulnerability and make sure it is not exploited.'

The relationship between young athletes and their trainer, often a combination of discipline and affection, can become so close and intimate that the trainer is regarded as a substitute parent and the sports club a surrogate family; some specialists have described sexual abuse in these types of environment as 'virtual incest' (Council of Europe 2000a). All these elements put the child in an extremely dependent situation in which the trainer is in a position of power and controls almost entirely the child's everyday acts and behaviour.

In a case reported in 1998 in the Netherlands, three young female judokas were sexually abused by their coach. One admitted that 'without judo and especially without him [the coach] I was nothing any more'. One of her peers said: 'There was only one way and it was the way of [the coach] ... You are so busy with that coach, you are a prisoner.' During a tournament abroad, they had to share the hotel room with their coach; one of the judokas explained: 'You did everything so he would not be angry' (Buisman *et al.* 1998: 29–61).

In fact, coaches and trainers sometimes behave as if athletes were their possessions. When abused athletes denounce their coaches, the latter usually feel betrayed because they feel they have a form of 'conjugal right' over the player whom they perceive as their property (Burke 1999). Sheldon Kennedy revealed to the police that he had been abused for almost 20 years by his junior coach, Graham James, who commented: 'Did I expect Sheldon Kennedy to do this? Absolutely not. Sheldon and I were close ... He legitimately cared' (Burke 1999).

This concept of the child owned by an adult strongly conflicts with the Convention's main message, which is precisely that children are rights-holders and are empowered gradually, and they should not be perceived as powerless objects in the hands of their parents and other adults (Flekkoy and Kaufman 1997; Van Bueren 1995).

The context of sports can attract sexual offenders, though it is still debated whether abusers come mainly from within or outside the sport system (Brackenridge 2001: 24). Too often, popular assumption, relayed by the media, has focused on the abuser as a monster from outside sport, rather than looking at sexual perpetrators inside the system who have had time to build relationships of confidence with young athletes.

Brackenridge and Kirby (1997: 409) suggest that young athletes are most vulnerable to sexual abuse when they reach the 'stage of imminent achievement', i.e. when they are close to joining the elite. This stage usually coincides with puberty and its related initiation to sexual activity. During this period most children experience their new identity at school and through social networks, but 'the elite athlete may well spend time separated from such contacts whilst he or she trains and competes'. Therefore, they may not be able to develop and strengthen coping strategies and life-skills that other more socially experienced and sexually active young people of their age possess (Australian Sports Commission 1995).

It is common that victims of sexual abuse feel pressure to remain silent because of the intimacy of the issue and the potentially negative impact of any revelation. In the sporting context, this feeling is usually mixed with the fear of damaging the relationship with the coach, the 'father figure' upon whom athletes are dependent if they want to achieve good results and have an opportunity for a decent career. In a survey undertaken in 1999 by Silent Edge, a group advocating for the rights of figure skaters, of a total of 182 athletes (84 under 18 years old) who responded to the online questionnaire, 45 declared having experienced sexual harassment by someone involved in skating. Approximately one-third believed that speaking out would definitely damage their career (16 athletes); one-third did not (15 athletes); and the others didn't know (14 athletes) (Silent Edge 1999a).

The impact of sexual abuse is devastating for victims. It may diminish ambition and self-confidence, destroy self-image, reduce the ability to concentrate and socialize, and generate sleeplessness, depression and physical aches and ailments (Brackenridge 2001: 66). Sexual abuse can lead to pregnancy and gynaecological complications, sexually transmitted diseases, mental health problems, suicidal behaviour and social ostracization (WHO 2002: 162–4). A female volleyball player who was abused by her coach when she was 16 explained:

> Even now, it's rare that a day goes by when I'm not haunted by that abuse. I often have drenching nightmares, sometimes five nights in a row. I dream he or a big, powerful man is chasing after me, trying to kill me slowly ... I felt ashamed and dirty and didn't want anybody to know ... The hard thing about coming forward wasn't that my parents wouldn't believe me, but that they would believe me but do nothing about it because [my] volleyball was too important ... I hated myself. I always had a lot of faith in God. I couldn't even face God.
>
> (*Los Angeles Times* 1995)

Her friends noticed the change in her; one said 'she became like this machine. She wasn't fun any more. [He] controlled every thought and emotion she had' (*Los Angeles Times* 1995).

Despite recent advances in addressing the issue, sexual abuse within the family still carries a very strong taboo, mainly because of the nature of the crime and a number of other factors: victims are often not willing or helped to speak out, families usually hide behind their right to privacy and state authorities are hesitant to intervene. Sports authorities are similarly reluctant to address the issue properly and in most sports and countries sexual abuse has not gone beyond the denial phase (there are nonetheless a few significant exceptions to this inaction, see Chapter 19). The Swiss Association for the Protection of the Child, an independent non-governmental body, organized in 1999 a seminar on sexual abuse in sports and invited 54 national sports federations whose members include young athletes. Only 12 federations replied to the invitation, and only half of these favourably (Imhof 1999). Similarly, a meeting on child protection organized by the Council of Europe in 2001 brought together governmental and non-governmental sport representatives from 23 member countries. Over half of them vigorously denied any occurrence of sexual abuse in their own country's sporting environment; about six acknowledged that sexual abuse might occur in sport in their country but admitted not having addressed the issue, and only a handful of national sports organizations had taken concrete measures to tackle this type of abuse.

Sexual abuse exists in most types of sports. In 1997, it was estimated that among the 37 American Olympic sports federations, nine had pending or had settled cases of sexual abuse (Burke 1999). In the United Kingdom, where a 'moral panic' about sexual abuse in sport developed in the mid-1990s, sport organizations reacted by taking proactive measures. According to one study covering 396 junior sports clubs in a large British county, knowledge about the issue and measures taken varied greatly from one sports organization to another: 43 per cent of sports clubs studied had a code of ethics and 39 per cent, a specific child-protection policy (Brackenridge 2000).

According to two specialists mandated by the Council of Europe:

> the greatest impediment to future research into sexual harassment and abuse of athletes is access to the community of sport. Very few sport organisations are yet persuaded of the importance of these issues and of the need to gather more data. Even those who are working towards policies for improving athlete safety in this regard are reluctant to open themselves to the gaze of the researcher and to risk the possibility of uncovered 'bad news'.
>
> (Council of Europe 2000a: 12)

On the positive side, some world champions have recently spoken about their own experiences of abuse in order to combat the existing taboo. In addition to Sheldon Kennedy, whose revelations shocked North America in the 1990s, Australian athlete Cathy Freeman, gold medallist at the 2000 Sydney Olympics, revealed that she was abused by her trainer at the age of 11. She explained that she wanted to help children speak out, so they would not be paralysed by their secrets. 'I spoke out to assist other victims, not for myself,' she told *L'Equipe Magazine* (2000b).

The UN Commission on Human Rights (2000: 15–16) recognizes sexual servitude as a contemporary form of slavery. Former Soviet gymnast Olga Korbut, Olympic champion in 1972 and 1976, told of how she was forced to become her trainer's 'sexual slave'. He threatened to exclude her from the team if she refused to have a sexual relationship with him and regularly beat her (*L'Equipe* 1999: 11).

MEASURES TO PREVENT AND COMBAT SEXUAL ABUSE

Under international human rights treaties, sexual harassment, abuse and violence are qualified as grave human rights violations (articles 19 and 34 of the
Convention on the Rights of the Child). These acts are serious threats to the
fundamental dignity and integrity of individuals. By ratifying the Convention,
states agree to address sexual abuse adequately in whatever situation it occurs and
are responsible for creating a conducive environment in which all forms of sexual
violence are clearly outlawed and where offenders are brought to justice.

Public authorities need to enact and enforce appropriate laws, policies and
programmes. They should also establish child-sensitive and efficient complaint
and reporting procedures to ensure that the measures are reliable and afford the
victims full confidentiality. When appropriate, access to courts for redress and
reparation should be facilitated.

The starting point of any measures to combat all forms of sexual abuse and
violence – in sports or elsewhere – should consist of a legal framework defining in
detail the crime of sexual abuse. It is equally important that potential abusers
realize that they cannot act in total impunity and that they will be prosecuted.
Sports authorities and organizations should adopt a comprehensive code of conduct (see also Chapter 19) that:

- includes a clear policy statement explaining the right of athletes to be
  protected from sexual abuse;
- indicates responsibilities of those engaged in relationships based on trust
  and/or power;
- defines prohibited behaviour;
- indicates the duty of all to report improper behaviour by staff, managers,
  volunteers, parents and others;
- lists the procedures that exist to protect victims; and
- includes a list of sanctions to apply to those violating the code of conduct
  (within the respect of the rights of the defence).

(Council of Europe 2000: 20)

Coaches, whether voluntary or professional, should undergo a mandatory screening procedure, and sports clubs and organizations should be able, if necessary, to
have the police records of potential coaches checked.

Although preventive measures are often expensive, they are an investment to
protect children – and their cost pales in comparison to fines that could be
imposed by courts' decisions to compensate victims. Since 1984, when the US
Volleyball Federation took one of the trainers it employed to court for having
abused many girls under 18, many victims in North America and Western
Europe have been seeking judicial redress. It is estimated that millions of dollars
are spent every year by sports federations to pay rehabilitation and medical support to victims (Deak 1999: 181).

Sexual harassment, abuse and violence in sports is a phenomenon that not only affects girls and boys, but also women. It can, therefore, only be efficiently addressed in the larger framework of gender equality and respect for the human rights of women in society. Not surprisingly, the countries in which the issue has been dealt with most seriously, such as Australia, Canada, Denmark, Finland, the Netherlands, New Zealand, Norway, Sweden, the United Kingdom and the United States, are usually those leading the social movement towards the advancement of the rights of women. But despite some positive developments, an enormous amount of work still needs to be done by all those involved in competitive sports.

Since 1997, the Council of Europe has taken steps to prevent and combat sexual harassment in sports, which resulted in 2000 in the adoption of a resolution 'on the sexual harassment and abuse of women, young people and children in sport' by the Council of Europe Conference of Ministers responsible for sport calling for, *inter alia*, 'the implementation of a national policy [by member states] within a context of an overall framework of support and protection for children, young people and women in sport' (Council of Europe 2000b).

A number of countries have also taken decisive policy measures, including Australia, Canada, the Netherlands, the United Kingdom and the United States (Council of Europe 2000: 11). The Swiss Olympic Association also adopted a code of conduct in 2002.

Significantly, for many of the experts who have studied the problem, one of the main prevention tools remains the empowerment of children. As sexual abuse of athletes strongly reflects an imbalance in the power relationship between the coach or another adult and the under-aged athlete, the latter needs to be empowered in order to be able to reduce the power gap with the adult and to resist any form of abuse. Empowerment is a key principle of human rights and is reflected in the Convention in articles 12 to 17 which recognize the civil rights and freedoms of children. Empowering young athletes requires a radical shift and an evolution of the sport system (see also Chapter 19). One expert asks: 'But how can power and self-interest, both of which appear to be unavoidable features of competitive sport, become successfully integrated with intimacy and care?' (Brackenridge 2001: 231).

10 Dicing with death
Doping and medical ethics

In the United States of America, a young boy of 14 who wishes to get seriously involved in sports knows that he will have recourse to illicit drugs.
(Frank Shorter, director of the American Anti-Doping Agency and former Olympic marathon champion, in Mercier and Miquel 2001)

If we are not successful in lowering the current levels of doping – an unacceptable level – we run the risk of losing credibility forever. What parent will still want to send their children to sports clubs if they realize that even at that age they are confronted with lethal drugs?
(Jacques Rogge, President, International Olympic Committee, in Fournier 2001)

Most people think that the use of illicit performance-enhancing drugs is a recent phenomenon triggered by money, television and the alleged deterioration of values. In fact, athletes have been using drugs for centuries, but what is new is the arrival of young athletes, 18 years and under, in professional sports.

In Ancient Greece, athletes ate special mushrooms to improve their performance while Roman gladiators took stimulants to overcome fatigue (Hainly 1983; Puffen 1986). In the 1850s, there were reports of Dutch competitive swimmers taking an opium-based drug and cyclists using a mixture of heroin and cocaine to increase their endurance (Voy 1991). Cyclist Arthur Lindon's death in 1869 is probably the first recorded fatality of an athlete from an overdose of drugs (Houlihan 1999: 34). Years of negligence and even cover-ups ensued; doping has only been taken seriously by sports and public authorities since the mid-1980s.

French cyclist and five-time Tour de France winner, Jacques Anquetil, was one of the few champions who confessed during their career to using illicit substances. In 1967, Anquetil, who died of cancer at the age of 53, admitted – 'in order to warn young people' – that he had taken amphetamines (Yonnet 1998: 159). Harold Connelly, 1956 Olympic hammer-throwing champion, testified in 1973, long after he had retired from sports, that the majority of athletes he had known 'would do anything, and take anything, short of killing themselves to improve athletic performance' (Coakley 1998: 167–8).

Doping is cheating, but cheats can only prosper when they operate behind closed doors or in front of blind eyes. The issue finally became part of the public debate after Ben Johnson failed a drug test a few hours after winning the 100-metre sprint in the 1988 Seoul Olympics and was stripped of his title. But it still took another decade before authorities acknowledged that athletes under the age of 18 were also affected by substance abuse, even though clear evidence had existed since the 1970s.

The first recorded case in which adolescent athletes were caught using illicit drugs was probably in 1959 when a Texan doctor allegedly administered an illegal substance (Dianobal) to a high-school football team (Yesalis *et al.* 1993). The German Democratic Republic's (GDR) scientific, state-sponsored doping programmes were only the tip of the iceberg (Franke and Berendonk 1997; Ungerleider 2001). Of the 10,000 athletes, some as young as 12, who attended the GDR's special sports schools at any given time, most were forced to use illicit substances. In 1993, the USSR's Olga Kareseva, 1968 Olympic gymnastics champion, reported that she had been forced to conceive a child and abort three months later. The objective was to exploit to the full the drastic changes in her body metabolism, especially to increase her red blood cells which improves the transport of oxygen, and consequently she was capable of much greater effort (Montaingnac 1993). In many other countries, too, doping was widespread, although not necessarily state-supported. From 1980 to 1996, for example, Italian sports federations, especially in cycling and cross-country skiing, were reported to organize systematic, scientific doping programmes for their athletes with the financial support of the state (Rodeaud 2000: 100).

This phenomenon affects both amateur and professional sports. It developed parallel to the dramatic growth of the pharmaceutical industry from the mid-twentieth century. In 1994, the International Narcotic Control Board (UN INCB), a United Nations specialized agency, expressed concern about the increased use of pharmaceutical products for non-medical use and public authorities' relative passivity towards this trend. It later highlighted the widespread use of 'life-style' drugs, including those to boost athletic performances (UN INCB 2000: 5). The increase in drug use seems difficult to control: according to preliminary work by the recently established World Anti-Doping Agency (WADA), the use of illicit substances by athletes doubled between the Atlanta Olympic Games in 1996 and the 2000 Sydney Olympics (Costa 2000). Long-distance runner and multiple Olympic champion Haile Gabreselassie, from Ethiopia, has admitted, 'Doping is everywhere; everybody knows it' (*L'Equipe Magazine* 2000a).

Since 1967, the International Olympic Committee (IOC) has been compiling a list of the performance-enhancing substances it has banned to serve as the main anti-doping tool. But anti-doping bodies face a number of problems, including their inability to keep up with the pace of pharmaceutical advance and the lack or insufficiency of political will, at the level of both public and private (sports) authorities. Cheats, therefore, have a head start on those trying to combat doping: they can use new substances that are difficult or impossible to detect, or are not yet included on the IOC's prohibited substances' list. During the prestigious Tour de France in 1988, the winner, Spanish cyclist Pedro Delgado, failed a drug test and subsequently admitted taking a new product, but he was cleared as it was not yet banned on the IOC list.

Article 33 of the Convention on the Rights of the Child states that: 'States Parties shall take all appropriate measures ... to protect children from the illicit use of narcotic drugs and psychotropic substances as defined in the relevant international treaties.' Most performance-enhancing products used in sports qualify under this provision. Article 19 of the Convention also requires countries to 'protect the child from all forms of ... abuse, neglect or negligent treatment, maltreatment or exploitation ... while in the care of parent(s), legal guardian(s) or any other person who has the care of the child'. In this context, the adults who provide children with illicit drugs in order to boost their performance not only abuse and exploit them, but also commit an illegal activity. Doping, especially when state-sponsored, is also a discriminatory practice under article 2 as it offers an added advantage over athletes who do not use illicit drugs.

Article 17 confirms that children have a right to be properly informed of the consequences of taking illicit drugs: 'States Parties shall ensure the child has access to information and material ... *especially those aimed at the promotion of his or her social, spiritual, and moral well-being and physical and mental health ...*' (emphasis added). Article 24 also requires states to 'recognize the right of the child to the enjoyment of the highest attainable standard of health ...' and 'to ensure that all segments of society, in particular parents and children, are informed, have access to [health] education ...'. Finally, article 36 specifies that states should 'protect the child against all other forms of exploitation prejudicial to any aspects of the child's welfare'.

Although other international treaties also broach the subject, the most sophisticated international treaty in the field of doping is the Council of Europe's 1989 Anti-doping Convention, which, as at 1 September 2004, had been ratified by 45 countries, including three from outside Europe. While the Convention does not distinguish between children and adults, article 6.1, which relates to education, targets children. Finally, the two most relevant United Nations international treaties to combat the abuse of drugs in society are the Convention on Psychotropic Substances (1971) and the United Nations Convention against Illicit Traffic in Narcotic Drugs and Psychotropic Substances (1988). The latter's article 5 is important as it recognizes the principle of aggravating circumstances when an adult induces a minor into doping. It requests states parties to:

> ensure that their courts and other competent authorities having jurisdiction can take into account factual circumstances which make the commission of the offences established in accordance with paragraph 1 of this article *particularly serious* such as: ... f) the *victimization or use of minors*. [emphases added]

THE OCCURRENCE OF DOPING AMONG YOUNG ATHLETES

For a long time, allegations and suspicion of doping were rife; but the subject was taboo and little precise, reliable information was available until the late 1990s. In addition, political and sports authorities were either too weak or deliberately closed their eyes to the reality of drug trafficking and abuse. It took the Tour de France scandal in 1998, with the prosecution and detention of almost an entire team of professional world-famous cyclists, to force attitudes to change and the political will to enforce laws to evolve. But resistance is still strong among athletes and sporting authorities. During the 2001 Tour of Italy (Giro), a court ordered the search of the hotel rooms of 86 people, including 64 professional cyclists, who were suspected of possessing illicit drugs. Indeed, massive amounts of performance-enhancing products were found and 52 of the 86 people were put under court investigation. But cycling teams claimed they were being treated like criminals. Judge Luigi Bocciolini, in charge of the case, said: 'I don't understand why the cyclists have expressed their outrage publicly. It means that justice has let cyclists off for too long and, more generally, that until now investigators have ignored the scourge of doping' (Prébois 2001).

Due to its clandestine and illegal nature, it remains difficult to evaluate the prevalence of the use of illicit drugs in competitive sports. According to the most comprehensive study published by the United States government – and depending on who was questioned – between 3 and 90 per cent of all athletes use doping products (CASA 2000: 3). The lowest figures usually reflect the opinion of sport authorities who refer to results of their own tests; the highest percentages are usually based on interviews with coaches and active and retired athletes. One month after the 2000 Tour de France, official doping tests revealed that 45 per cent of cyclists had taken prohibited products. Most teams participating in the race justified the use of illicit drugs for medical reasons (BBC 2000b).

Research carried out in North America, Australia and Western Europe concerning the number of young people using illicit drugs tends to show that between 1 and 10 per cent (3 to 5 per cent as an average) of young people under 18 – and not just athletes – take illegal drugs, with some studies quoting figures as high as 18 per cent in specific situations (Tanner *et al.* 1995: 109). Girls are also affected by the phenomenon, although to a lesser extent than boys. This may be due to the fact that there are still fewer girls engaged in competitive sports; it may also be because girls tend to be more inclined to respect established rules and may feel that cheating is socially less acceptable for them. Most research on drug use is based on anonymous answers to questionnaires, so the resulting data, especially in the case of forbidden activities, may be distorted or underestimate the problem.

Studies in the United States found that at least 500,000 adolescents were taking illegal steroids regularly, mainly in weightlifting and bodybuilding but also in American football (*US News and World Report* 1992) and that, of 12,000 high-school students (aged between 15 and 18), 4.1 per cent of the boys studied used steroids (Durant *et al.* 1995: 23). Elsewhere, studies in Canada (*La Presse* 1993), the United Kingdom (Williamson 1993; Clarke 1999), France (Flamand 1994: 2),

Australia (Brunel *et al.* 1998: 59) and Sweden (Kindlundh *et al.* 1998) all confirmed the widespread use of steroids and other illicit performance-enhancing drugs by adolescents. The Swedish study revealed that, of the 2,742 students (aged 16 to 19) interviewed, 2.7 per cent of boys reported having used doping agents, but this percentage rose to 8.1 per cent in the capital, Stockholm. In 2000, the Dutch Ministry of Justice voiced its alarm that an estimated 35,000 young amateur athletes apparently had regular recourse to doping (Van den Heuvel 2000).

Some sports, such as American football, weightlifting, athletics, swimming and cycling, seem to experience higher illicit drug use than others. Former American football star, Tim Green, explained that the only way to make it to the top in the National Football League (NFL) was to take massive amounts of drugs and that no professional player was ever impressed by possible health-related consequences (Green 1996). Research among American football players (aged 17 and 18) in Arkansas high schools showed that a total of 11 per cent were taking anabolic steroids (Hermann 1998). In 1999, the Italian cyclists federation carried out a study which showed that the level of red blood cells was much higher than tolerated in 58 per cent of a sample of 18-year-old juniors. A higher red blood cell count increases the oxygen flow in the blood, which enhances an athlete's performance. It is also most probably a symptom of doping with EPO (erythropoietin). In 1997, the same test revealed only 2 per cent of juniors had a higher level of red blood cells than permitted (Rodeaud 1999: 122).

The average age of using illicit drugs for the first time varies and depends on several factors, including family, medical and sporting environment, type of sport, and form of doping. In general, illicit drug use concerns adolescents aged between 14 and 18, although pre-pubescent doping does exist but has been the subject of very little research (Randall *et al.* 2002). A study of almost 1,000 high-school American football players revealed that, on average, they were 14 when they first used anabolic-androgenic steroids, but that 15 per cent of them had begun to take these strong illicit drugs before the age of 10 (Stilger and Yesalis 1999). In 1997, Dr Michel Leglise, at the time chairman of the International Federation of Gymnastics' medical committee, admitted: 'This is a criminal offence and a matter for the courts, even if we ourselves [gymnastic sport authorities] have an important part to play in the area of prevention and in improving information' (Leglise 1997: 9).

CONTEXT AND MOTIVATIONS AMONG YOUNG ATHLETES TO ENGAGE IN DOPING

Many complex factors may induce children to consume illicit substances in order to improve their sporting performances. Among them, societal trends, including the pressure to win, a hyper-medicated environment and the influence of role models, certainly have an important impact. Dawson (2001: 56) stressed that 'the patients who should concern the physician most are not the high profile, elite athletes, but the youth and other members of society who are being increasingly drawn to use of performance-enhancing drugs'.

Today, children and adolescents, particularly those involved in intensive training and competitive sports, often develop in a socio-cultural context which is achievement-oriented. The sports world and that of the market economy share strong common values, especially success, glory and economic profit. Many children and adolescents who participate in high-level sports are quickly caught up in this competitive environment and are confronted with serious physical and psychological challenges. The doctor of one French team, who wanted to remain anonymous, explained, 'It is not rare to see young players of 15 in professional football teams start progressively to get used to licit and illicit substances in order to adjust to the increase of physical charges' (Bonamy 1999: 11).

Ivan Waddington (2001: 17), the author of a number of articles on doping, asked:

> To what extent … are team physicians themselves constrained by the greatly increased importance which has come to be attached to winning and by a sporting agenda in which 'second place doesn't count'? To what extent do they experience pressure, perhaps not just from the athletes but also from coaches, managers and others, to supply athletes with performance-enhancing drugs? How easy is it to resist such pressures where the prescription of such drugs may mean the difference between winning and losing an important competition which may involve considerable international prestige? To what extent are doctors' decisions influenced by their knowledge that other competitors will almost certainly be using such drugs?

Winning is so strongly valued by society that it symbolizes all aspects of success: glory, wealth, access to academic and professional careers, and social recognition. Young athletes, like adults, might be tempted to use illicit means, including doping, to increase their performance and ultimately their chance to win.

A study undertaken in the United States in 1995 found that one in four adolescent athletes admitted that they had been tempted to take illicit drugs to earn a scholarship or to qualify for professional leagues (Bichon 1995). A survey undertaken during the 1996 Olympic Games in Atlanta revealed that, of 198 American athletes, half admitted that they would be willing to take a drug – even if it killed them eventually – as long as it allowed them to win every event they entered five years in a row (CASA 2000: 9).

Illicit products are now used in sports such as archery, bowling and paralympic sports (for athletes with disabilities), which long seemed to be free of drugs. At the 1996 Atlanta Paralympic Games, one athlete was caught using steroids, while at the 2000 Sydney Paralympics over a dozen were suspended for cheating (BBC 2000a).

The post-Second World War boom of the pharmaceutical industry has undoubtedly had an impact on the use of drugs by athletes. It has also to some extent legitimized drugs in sports (Lueschen 1993). In the Western world in general, people have become increasingly dependent on pills. Access to medicine is universal and easy – drugs are advertised and sold over the Internet. In its 2000 annual report, UN INCB raised serious concerns about the developed countries' 'pill-popping' culture. Children and adolescents are also affected by these trends – swallowing medicine, even for a minor cold or injury, is part of their daily life.

Most physical and psychological troubles are treated with drugs in the industrialized world, a practice that is not without risk of abuse. According to the Maryland School of Public Affairs (USA) (1999), approximately five million American teenagers take Ritalin, an amphetamine-derivative drug that is used to treat the so-called 'attention deficit disorder'. In Switzerland, a federal government study showed that the number of children (aged 5 to 14) taking Ritalin in one Swiss canton (Neuchâtel) had multiplied almost seven times between 1996 and 2000 (Government of Switzerland 2002). The UN INCB (2001: 3) is concerned about:

> the frequent long-term use (beyond one year and sometimes indefinitely) of psychotropic substances for treating psychological reactions to social pressure without a diagnosis for a specific disorder. There are different forms of insomnia, anxiety, obesity and child hyperactivity, as well as various kinds of pain, for which controlled drugs, the opioids, amphetamines, barbiturates and benzodiazepines (in order of their dependence liability) are extensively used in medicine today …

Ivan Waddington (1996; 2000) and Barrie Houlihan (1999: 32) see the sporting world as strongly influenced by this intensively medicalized society. According to Houlihan:

> It is unrealistic to expect athletes to insulate themselves from the culture which expects pharmacists and doctors to be able to supply medicines for all their ills whether physical or psychological. It is also unrealistic to ignore the importance of legitimate drugs in the intensively scientific training regimes of most, if not all, elite athletes in the 1990s.

For John Hoberman, author in 1992 of a key – but controversial – book on doping, sport serves the ends of science rather than the other way round. Athletes are mere guinea pigs used by the pharmaceutical industry to test and promote new products.

The search for excellence in sports is now so sophisticated that it relies on all the medical support it can get. It is a paradox: supported by scientists and sports science systems, the athletes' bodies are pushed to such extremes that they are increasingly vulnerable to physical and psychological problems and injuries (DiFiori 1999) and, in health terms, have become one of society's most fragile groups. Most professional teams and athletes have their own medical staff, upon whom the performances of athletes depend more and more, to the extent that in the pursuit of victory they are almost more important than coaches. Erwann Menthéour, a former French cycling talent who admitted using illicit drugs and stopped racing when he was 25 to campaign against drug abuse in cycling, remarked, 'The one that has the best physician always wins' (Bernard 1999).

Children are strongly influenced by role models as they grow up, and in most societies parents are the main role models. A survey in the United Kingdom, however, revealed that 70 per cent of young people ranked an athlete as the person they admire or look up to (Sport England 2001a: 174). A study in the United States showed that for 73 per cent of young Americans, sports heroes are the second most esteemed group after parents, but 52 per cent think it is common to see famous athletes using steroids or other banned substances to get an edge on the competition (Henry J. Kaiser Family Foundation 2000: 15).

Children love to mimic adults, but what happens when their heroes are cheats? Or when some sport federations offer athletes insurance policies to cover legal fees if ever they are accused of using doping?[1] Or when they sidestep the rules by exploiting the weaknesses of the regulations – like American baseball superstar Marc McGwire, who was not sanctioned in 2000 after admitting to taking androstenedione, which is a form of steroid? This drug, banned by the IOC and many other federations, is not prohibited by the Major League Baseball (MLB). But American Randy Barnes, Olympic shot-putt silver medallist in 1996, was banned for life by the IOC for using exactly the same product (CASA 2000: 10).

In these conditions, can one really expect talented young athletes to continue upholding the message of integrity, sportsmanship and excellence? From a purely human rights perspective, young athletes should be protected from using illegal performance-enhancing substances for at least three main reasons: the threat to their health; obedience and respect for sports rules and ethics (Leaman 1988; Rosenberg 1995); and their lack of maturity to take and assume appropriate and informed decisions, which renders them vulnerable to the harmful and abusive influence of adults.

SERIOUS HEALTH RISKS

A large majority – but not all – of banned substances are considered by medical experts to be capable of generating serious to severe health-related side effects (American Academy of Pediatrics 1997: 2). Among the main drugs used illegally in sports are: amphetamines (extensive and moderately serious side effects); cocaine (extensive and extremely serious); caffeine (serious), morphine (extensive and extremely serious); anabolic-androgenic steroids (extensive and extremely serious); diuretics (varied and moderately severe); HCG (human chorionic gonadotrophin – moderate to severe); HGH (human growth hormone – severe); blood transfusion and EPO (moderate to severe); marijuana (only significant with heavy and/or long-term use); and beta-blockers (in general only severe if pre-existing cardiac problems) (Houlihan 1999: 82). Although research reveals that athletes under 18 have not been spared by all these different products, they mainly use anabolic-androgenic steroids (for example, in American football and weightlifting), ephedrine, diuretics (for example, in gymnastics), beta-blockers and marijuana.

In 1993, the World Health Organization (WHO) reviewed the potential health risks of doping. It concluded that many of the substances used have negative health consequences and create a mild to strong dependence effect upon consumers and that doping should be considered a public health threat (WHO 1993). Steroids, for example, can impede growth and prevent young adolescents from attaining their potential adult height (though this has been recently challenged by some researchers) (Houlihan 1999: 70). Sharing contaminated needles – a possibility when illicit drugs are administered by injection – presents a risk for the transmission of, for example, hepatitis, sexually transmitted diseases (STDs) and HIV/AIDS (Tanner *et al*. 1995: 108).

Some researchers have also found a significant association 'between use of doping agents and use of psychotropic substances (cannabis oil, LSD, amphetamines, opioids, etc.)' (Kindlundh *et al*. 1998: 9) and between doping substances and the use of legal (for adults), addictive products such as alcohol and tobacco (DuRaunt *et al*. 1993; Tanner *et al*. 1995: 108).

A Swiss study conducted among 400 drug addicts found that 50 per cent had practised sports every day, 32 per cent had been involved in high-level competition at least at regional level, and 25 per cent had trained several hours a day (Schmid 1999). A similar study undertaken in the Monte-Cristo rehabilitation centre for drug addicts in Paris (France) revealed that 20 per cent of patients were former elite athletes who trained at least two hours a day.[2]

Not all adolescents are aware of the risks doping may have on their health. A 1995 study showed that over 60 per cent of students interviewed about doping use were not aware that liver disease is a potential risk; approximately 30 per cent did not know that heart disease and arrested growth are potential side effects; and about 20 per cent were unaware of the possibility of addiction, aggressiveness, cancer and breast enlargement (Tanner *et al*. 1995: 111).

Even some older athletes pretend not to know about the potential side effects of drug use. In 2000, French cycling star Richard Virenque said during his trial for doping, 'If I had known, I would have chosen a healthier sport' (Roger 2000: 9). Other athletes are more sensitive to the issue. When she was asked about the use of creatine by other players, such as Mary Pierce, and the fact that most successful players except her have a game based on strength, tennis player Martina Hingis replied, 'I'll never swallow anything to get physically stronger, I don't want to die before I'm 30' (Van der Meyden 2000).

MEDICAL ETHICS AND DEONTOLOGY

The act of doping raises many ethical issues, especially when it relates to under-aged athletes. Does the use of force-enhancing substances lead to unfair competitive conditions (Gardner 1989)? Is doping justified by the individual's right to choose his or her lifestyle, even if the choice involves health risks and violates sport regulations? Although the American College of Sports Medicine (2000) warned that creatine should not be taken as a dietary supplement by children and adolescents, it is not classified as illegal and has been taken by children as young as 11 (Cumming 2001). A study in Wisconsin high schools revealed that 15 per cent of student athletes (15–17 years old) had used the supplement (Hunt 2000). But getting the message across is almost impossible when sport role models, such as football star Zinédine Zidane, publicly announce that they use creatine 'as it is not prohibited' (Davet 2002).

Many athletes have privileged access to new illicit drugs that are extremely difficult to detect, such as HGH or synthetic testosterone. Others take advantage of the latest technologies and medical advances to improve their performance and their physical characteristics. Top golfer Tiger Woods, for example, benefited from laser technology to bring his eyesight close to perfection. Some athletes are able to train in high-altitude regions for long periods, which increases their red blood cells and therefore their capacity for sustained effort. Today, these conditions can be recreated artificially in a closed room. The number of such rooms has increased so rapidly that the IOC has ordered a two-year study (2002–4) to evaluate whether they boost physiological results and are dangerous for the health of athletes (Le Coeur 2001). Such facilities are perfectly legal in most countries (although they were banned in France in 1998), but they clearly advantage some athletes over others from poorer communities who cannot access them, due to financial considerations.

In some sports, the lifestyles of athletes competing against each other differ enormously. Some are generously supported by the public or private sector which enables them to train full time and have sufficient rest; others have to work full time and can only train in their 'free' time. General training conditions are usually better in industrialized countries than in developing nations, although this is not systematically an advantage. Nevertheless, the fact that many athletes from developing countries regularly migrate to Western universities or other settings tends to prove that this gap does have an impact.

From a human rights perspective, article 1 of the Universal Declaration of Human Rights declares that 'all human beings are born free and equal in dignity and rights…'. However, perfect equity is impossible to attain as each human being is an individual and different from all others. No one questions the fact that some athletes are genetically better predisposed to performance than others. One day, perhaps, sport categories will no longer be divided by age or weight, but by information on the genetic code of each athlete.

When sports authorities prohibit the illicit use of performance-enhancing drugs, it is not only to protect the health of athletes, but also to attain a certain equality among competitors. However, even this attempt at creating a level playing field for all is not without problems, as banned drugs have very different characteristics. An athlete systematically using steroids or HGH cannot be compared with one abusing caffeine or another taking a medicine against colds or asthma that includes ephedrine (a banned substance).

While some illicit drugs have been scientifically identified as having a very negative impact on health, others could potentially be used to cure injured athletes. Nevertheless, all athletes who use banned substances, whether innocuous or dangerous, are usually perceived and sanctioned in the same way. Should harmless doping be authorized, even for young athletes? Some authors believe so (Tamburrini 2000).

Sport stars who are caught using illicit drugs are usually disavowed, because drug abuse doesn't fit with the healthy image and values athletes are supposed to convey. The general public is, however, usually tolerant of artists, whether William S. Burroughs or Jean-Paul Sartre, who use illicit drugs to push their creativity to the edge; the same is true of other professional groups (media, politicians) who use drugs – including illegal ones – to improve their performance. The major difference between sports and other activities is that sporting authorities have adopted rules which strive to achieve values such as equality, reciprocity, solidarity and fraternity, and respect for these rules forms the bedrock of sports.

Increasing tension exists between ensuring that sport's rules and ethics are respected and the ever-growing pressure to guarantee that all sports events are spectacular and generate the profit necessary to ensure their sustainability. The need to guarantee a high-quality show and excellent TV ratings is often seen as a more important criterion than ethical issues (Tamburrini 2000; Munthe 2000). Who really cares whether the Hermann Maiers or the Marion Jones of sports use drugs or not, as long as they entertain and keep the profits rolling in?

When questioned about doping in 2001, 84 per cent of people in France said they wanted everything to be done to eliminate it from sports, but 48 per cent declared that 'the most important is the show and the performances' (TMO/Sportlab poll on doping 2001). Strong anti-doping policies, whether the IOC's or other sports bodies', certainly hurt the image and success of sports events, as is the case with the Tour de France since 1998 or in the Tour of Italy (Giro) in 2001. As Houlihan (1999: 15) explained, 'The IOC rules on doping appear to have been perceived as an impediment to success rather than as a reflection of Olympic values.' How would the movie industry react if it had to ban all films starring drug-consuming actors?

RESPONSIBILITIES AND DUTIES OF THE MEDICAL COMMUNITY

The medical world's involvement in the sports community and its relation to doping is a complex issue which also raises some ethical questions, especially regarding illegal drug use (Dawson 2001). Today, most professional teams have their own, often large, staff of medical specialists. But, if these specialists are employed by teams whose aim is performance and success, will they be able to remain independent and respect medical deontology (McCrory 2001; *British Journal of Sports Medicine* 2001: 141–2)? Yves Demarais, a doctor for several top French sports teams, admitted that 'it is difficult to keep in line with medical ethics' (Coadic 1998a: 70).

Interestingly, in 1996, the British Medical Association (BMA) defined sports medicine as covering the 'prevention, diagnosis, and treatment of exercise related illness or injuries' and the 'maximization of performance'. Sport doctors work under permanent pressure for results: they may receive substantial bonuses when their teams or athletes do well, or be fired if they don't. Successful physicians are known to earn as much as the sports stars. Some doctors compare their work to 'war medicine' – where the ends justify the means: 'There's a certain unease when you're an elite athlete's physician,' said doping specialist Jean-Pierre de Mondernard. 'You inevitably find yourself under pressure' (Terrani 2000a: 24).

In 1988, in an editorial entitled 'Sports medicine – is there a lack of control?', the leading British medical journal, *The Lancet*, noted that some doctors were 'showing more interest in finding new ways of enhancing the performance of those in their charge than in their physical well being' and suggested that sports medicine be brought 'beneath the umbrella of a recognised body within an accredited programme of professional training' (*The Lancet* 1988).

The World Medical Association (WMA), an international organization representing medical doctors, adopted in 1981 a 'Declaration on Principles of Health Care for Sports Medicine'. This declaration was revised for the third time in 1999 and states that:

> 2.1. The physician must ensure that the child's state of growth and development, as well as his or her general condition of health can absorb the rigors of the training and competition without jeopardizing the normal physical or mental development of the child or adolescent. 2.2. The physician must oppose any sports or athletic activity that is not appropriate to the child's stage of growth and development or general condition of health. The physician *must act in the best interest of the health of the child or adolescent, without regard to any other interest or pressure from any other source.* [emphasis added]

Some national medical associations in countries such as Australia, Finland, Germany, Norway, Sweden and the United Kingdom have taken the ethical aspects of sport medicine seriously and adopted general guidelines for their practitioners. For example, the United Kingdom's General Medical Council (GMC) states that doctors 'who prescribe or collude in the provisions of drugs or treatment with the intention of improperly enhancing an individual performance in sport' would contravene the GMC's guidelines and their 'continued registration' would be questioned (Monnat 2001: 1654).

As yet, no national medical code of ethics has recognized and incorporated the specificities of sport medicine. In Switzerland, a working group of the national medical association proposed in 2001 to amend the existing code in this sense (Monnat 2001). Although there was no follow-up, the code's proposed amendment was supplemented by guidelines that were entirely child rights sensitive. They recognized the right of the child both to special protection and to be clearly informed of what the doctor is doing or intends to do, and that children aged between 12 and 16 (and even younger under exceptional circumstances) should be involved in medical decision-making processes related to sport (Fédération des Médecins Suisses 2001).

Recent events showed that sport doctors are regularly confronted with the issue of doping. In the 1998 Tour de France drug scandal, for example, Bruno Roussel, the then director of the Festina cycling team, and team doctor, Eric Ryckaert, deliberately chose to engage in an ultra-sophisticated doping strategy. Other doctors are confronted with the professional dilemma of having an athlete – sometimes a minor – as a patient, who seeks assistance in obtaining banned substances. Health practitioners are well aware that obtaining these drugs clandestinely is far more dangerous than being supplied with them in a controlled medical environment. Dr R.T. Dawson, of the UK's Drugs in Sport Clinic and User's Support, said in 2001:

> This policy of prohibition [of doping] has also increased pressure on physicians who are struggling with the ethics of becoming involved with athletes taking performance-enhancing drugs. If we are to advise our patients on the use of performance-enhancing drugs are we then complicit in their drug use, or are we simply upholding our oath to do our best to protect their health? … For some there is an ethical dilemma, for the health monitoring and giving advice to patients using performance-enhancing drugs may be perceived as collusion in the patient's 'cheating'. But we must not forget that we are obliged to protect our patients from harm.

The standpoint that medical doctors are strictly bound by the Hippocratic Oath and therefore should not combat doping but rather 'treat' doped patients, is strongly challenged by Richard Pound, WADA's chairman. In a keynote speech given during a 2002 workshop on 'Genetic enhancement of athletic performance', he said:

> I realized [then] that the medical profession had abandoned any pretence of ethical engagement in sport and that, instead of being of assistance in the ethical involvement on an important dimension of social behaviour, it was as likely to assist cheaters as it was to help keep competition pure … I do not want to suggest that the medical profession is devoid of ethics. I am sure that many professional associations have developed ethical rules … My question is whether these organizations enforce the rules that they themselves have adopted as best practices … If they do not regulate themselves in such matters, then it may become necessary to look elsewhere and to have third-party enforcement.

It is almost cynical to see that some sports doctors will endanger the health of perfectly healthy athletes by proposing illicit substances. In 1998, Benoit Lombard, a French amateur cyclist, explained how he started taking steroids at the age of only 17, at the suggestion of his doctor, who was employed by his cycling team (France 3 Television 1998). In Italy at the end of the 1990s, an estimated 700 doctors prescribed illicit substances to athletes (Longman 1998: D2). A study undertaken by the University of Nancy (France) revealed that 61 per cent of amateur athletes (adolescents and adults) using illicit drugs received them through their physician (Coadic 1998b: 45).

THE LIMITED RESPONSIBILITY OF THE CHILD?

Children as young as eight years old have in some cases taken steroids, but – fortunately – this is the exception. The average age at which adolescent athletes start to use illicit drugs is generally between 14 and 16 (Kennedy 1992: 375; Tanner *et al.* 1995: 112). If an adult can be considered capable of making informed choices, children and adolescents, depending on their age, maturity and capacity for discernment, are much more vulnerable to misinterpret a given situation and to be influenced and manipulated. The risk of their being coerced into drug use is therefore considerable.

Young athletes obtain illicit substances through three main channels: legally, through, for example, a physician; through peers, coaches or family members; or 'directly' through dealers. In each situation the original provider of illicit drugs is always an adult, even if the drugs may transit at some stage through peers. Studies tend to show that the main group of providers are peers (44 per cent); the remaining 56 per cent are divided between parents, coaches and physicians (Tanner *et al.* 1995: 112). In another survey, more than 20 per cent of steroid users under 18 years reported that teachers and coaches actually encouraged them to take the drugs (Goldberg *et al.* 1996: 715).

In his book on children and sports (1999), American psychologist Shane Murphy explains that many of his patients are adolescents who were forced into doping by their parents. But the problem is not new: in 1976, two American football coaches were disciplined for giving weight-reducing pills to children under 14 years so they could be eligible for a weight category in which they had a better chance of winning (Martens 1978: 70). The act of providing or pushing a child into drugs is a violation of article 19 of the Convention which provides that the state, parents and any other person who has the care of the child shall protect him or her from all forms of abuse, ill-treatment and exploitation.

From a human rights perspective, athletes under 18 years who are caught using illicit substances should be considered victims rather than criminals and not be judged in the same way as adults. That individuals under 18 who have infringed penal law should always be considered *specifically* and not the same way as adults due to their age, maturity and vulnerability (article 40.3 of the Convention) is a fundamental consideration under international law.

If the notion of 'victim' of doping might be controversial for adult athletes, it is, in light of the Convention, appropriate when dealing with young abusers. In 1998 the French Minister for Sports, Marie-Georges Buffet, said: 'Athletes are victims of the system. If the word "victim" is too shocking for some, we could use the term "instrument"' (Coadic 1998: 62). Bruno Roussel, who was arrested in

1998 for having imposed systematic substance use on his team of cyclists, did not agree: 'Doped athletes are not victims,' he said. 'Doping against their will does not exist; they are not kids' (Gatellier 2000: 22).

Houlihan (1999: 119–20) believes that:

> the weaknesses of the argument based on coercion are clear. Unless one is referring to sport within a repressive political regime, athletes are always able to refuse drugs and simply to settle for fourth place or worse ... A variation on this argument suggests that coercion arises from the inability of the athlete to provide informed consent to the use of drugs. It can be argued that modern elite athletes are surrounded by an array of experienced professional advisors, coaches, physiotherapists, doctors, dieticians, psychologists, etc. and are locked into an unequal relationship of professional and client. The disempowerment of athletes is best reflected by the way they are treated in many sports as mere commodities to be traded between team owners with only minimal consultation and little regard for their interests. Athletes are, therefore, expected to fulfil a passive role within sport and the development of dependent relationships with professional staff is often encouraged. The weakness of this view is the profound difficulty in identifying the point at which the individual athlete cannot be held responsible for his or her actions. Even if athletes are locked into heavily dependent relationships, there has been so much publicity surrounding the anti-doping policy that it is hardly plausible for an athlete to deny knowledge of the policy and claim that they were unable to exercise their right to walk away from drug-based sports.

Governments have not taken unified measures to prevent and combat doping at national level. Some, such as the United Kingdom and Norway, penalize the supply, or possession with intent to supply, of doping, but do not penalize the use of performance-enhancing drugs. France (1999) and Italy (2000) have enacted new laws to prevent and combat doping in sports. They are based on the assumption that the athlete is the victim of a broader system and is not the only person responsible and sanctioned in case of doping; others, such as trainers, coaches or any other person indirectly involved, are equally responsible. In addition, adults will be subject to more severe penal sanctions if they are guilty of coercing a minor into taking illicit substances. In 2000, the Swiss government amended its sport legislation so that trainers or medical staff can be punished, rather than the athletes themselves, if the latter take illegal performance-enhancing drugs. The athletes can only be sanctioned (generally suspended) by their sports federation.

The situation of the child or adolescent athlete coerced into doping by adults is in some regards comparable to child prostitution. The Committee on the Rights of the Child (1994a) has systematically upheld that these children be considered victims and that they be accorded special protection and support. It has been relatively successful in advocating that, given that in almost all cases children under 18 are coerced by adults into prostitution or pornography, they should not be incriminated for such acts, even if the age of sexual consent is under 18 in their country of residence. A number of countries have reviewed their legislation to this end.

To be in line with international law, sanctions imposed on athletes under 18 who have used illicit substances in the context of competitive sports should not be the same as those imposed on adults. The Court of Arbitration for Sport (CAS) does not include in its jurisdiction specific provisions concerning athletes under 18, despite the fact that its judges are free to take this element in consideration when deliberating a case. When 16-year-old Romanian gymnast Andrea Raducan tested positive for 'drugs' and was stripped of her gold medal during the 2000 Sydney Olympics, she was treated and sanctioned, by the IOC and the CAS, as if she were an adult, even though it was proven that the medicine prescribed by her team doctor was a flu remedy which contained banned substances. The judges recognized that she was not directly responsible and the team doctor was also heavily sanctioned, but her sports authorities did not appeal the sanction on account of her being a minor. After the case, the CAS stated officially that it was conscious of 'the impact of its decision on a fine young elite athlete. It finds, in balancing the interests of Miss Raducan with the commitment of the Olympic Movement to drug-free sport, the Anti-Doping Code must be enforced without compromise' (Associated Press 2000). A few months later, the Swiss Supreme Court, responding to an appeal filed by Raducan, confirmed the sanction (Associated Press 2000a).

In 1972, a similar case took place during the Munich Olympics. Rick DeMont, a 16-year-old American swimmer, was stripped of his 400-metre freestyle gold medal, after taking an asthma medication that contained a banned substance. He had informed the United States Olympic Committee (USOC) in time that he was taking the medicine, but the USOC did not report it to the IOC. In 1996, DeMont sued the USOC for breaching its fiduciary duty and committing libel and negligence. In February 2001, as part of a settlement, the USOC reconsidered the case and finally decided to recognize him for his accomplishments. But the IOC restored neither his title nor his gold medal.

COMBATING DOPING AMONG THE YOUNG

In order to prevent the use of illegal drugs by young athletes, prevention programmes would have to take into account a number of factors specific to competitive sports: the enormous pressure put upon athletes to win, the impact of role models and sport federations' efforts to combat doping through law enforcement. However, until adults involved in elite sport set a clear and strong example, no programme will be able to convince young people to refrain from taking illicit substances.

The sports world often ends up seeming to impose double standards and merely paying lip service to the fight against doping. Two months before the 2000 Sydney Olympics Dr Wade Exum, for nine years USOC drug control administration director, was fired and criticized for declaring that half of American athletes used illicit drugs and for accusing the USOC of being passive towards doping (Janofsky 2000: D1 and D5). This was not the first time the USOC had dismissed drug control directors whom it perceived as being too militant: Irving Daedick was fired in 1985 and Robert Voy in 1989.

Frenchman Jérôme Chiotti, former world cross-country cycling champion, admitted in 2000 that, in the month before he won the 1996 world championship race, he swallowed and injected (49 times) various illicit drugs, including 12 doses of EPO, 20 doses of HGH and 400 milligrams of testosterone and other products (Gatellier 2001: 19). Giving back his world title and gold medal, he said he had decided to go public as he was disgusted by the amount of illicit drugs used in cycling. Despite his repentance – probably unique in the history of sport among active athletes – the CAS sanctioned Chiotti like any other dope-taking athlete (Ballester 2001: 9). In sport, it appears that, contrary to other fields, repentance is not (yet) rewarded and taken into account as a factor to decrease a sanction.

It is evident that appropriate information, guidance, education and awareness-raising are fundamental tools in combating doping. In the United States, a prevention programme entitled ATLAS has obtained interesting results by focusing on educating youths about alternatives to doping such as improved nutrition and training to increase strength. An important factor was that the programme was delivered by coaches and peers in order to highlight the fact that role models had rejected the doping option (Goldberg *et al.* 1996; Goldberg *et al.* 2000). Random drug testing in schools is another prevention method, although highly controversial, which is mainly used in the United States (Meldrum and Feinberg 2002). Though radical, this type of measure has not necessarily been an effective deterrent nor led to impressive results. It has been criticized for violating students' right to privacy (see Chapter 15).

WHAT THE FUTURE HOLDS: THE GENETICALLY ENGINEERED ATHLETE

Some experts believe that within a decade the golden age of traditional medical doping will be replaced by the science of 'gene-doping'.[3] Recent developments in bio-genetic medicine, including cloning, gene manipulation and the successful mapping of the entire human gene (Human Genome Project), seriously challenge the human rights community (Burley 1999). How will rapid scientific advances in this field impact upon competitive sports and more specifically upon young athletes? Will genetically modified athletes soon be a reality or is this merely science fiction? 'There is growing evidence that this might be possible … it would seem naïve to ignore such possibilities,' said Andy Miah (2001: 37), a leading expert in the field of genetically engineered athletes.

Genetic science is not intrinsically in opposition to the rights of the child. Genetic therapy might revolutionize medicine positively by curing hitherto incurable diseases and improving the quality of life. But its potential misuse as a human enhancement tool and its eventual political and economic exploitation could lead to gross human rights violations. The Convention on the Rights of the Child does not address directly the issue of bio-genetic use, experimentation and treatment, though children are protected by article 36 from 'all forms of exploitation' and by article 7 of the International Covenant on Civil and Political Rights, which protects all human beings from being 'subjected without his free consent to medical or scientific experimentation'. The Universal Declaration on the Human Genome and Human Rights (1997), which does not have the force of a convention as it is not a legally binding treaty but a political commitment adopted by the international community, states clearly in articles 10 and 11 that human rights and dignity need to be respected in any such experimentation or research. Article 13 prevents scientists, including researchers, from misusing the results of their work, for example, by helping athletes to cheat.

Finally, the Council of Europe adopted in 1997 a legally binding treaty which can also be ratified by non-member states, the Convention on Human Rights and Biomedicine.[4] This treaty integrates principles safeguarding the rights of the child such as children's evolving capacity and the need to have their views duly taken into account according to age and maturity. In article 13, it states that: 'An intervention seeking to modify the human genome may only be undertaken for preventive, diagnostic or therapeutic purposes and only if its aim is not to introduce any modifications in the genome of the descendants.' It does not, however, cover sport achievement as a legitimate ground for the use of genetic science.

All these treaties put the protection of the *dignity of the human being* as the core value justifying prohibition of certain forms of bio-genetics, especially cloning. But, as Malby (2002) has pointed out, it is not often clear how the concept of human dignity is defined.

A distinction needs to be drawn between gene enhancements made before and those made after birth. If parents or others decide during pregnancy to alter an unborn child's genes on order to create a better athlete, the child has obviously not consented to the decision. Have parents the right to select and impose specific traits on their unborn child (Thomas 1999)? In the case of genetic enhancement after birth, if the young athlete is mature enough, he or she must be adequately informed about its implications. It remains questionable whether such practice would be legal and ethical, though nothing at this early stage of bio-genetic development appears to affirm that it would not be (Anderson 1992; Koshland 1999; Miah 2000).

In the future, sports authorities and sponsors might use genetic testing at a very early age to verify the potential of every promising young athlete, and therefore avoid 'wasting' time and money on those who have no chance of becoming champions (Munthe 2000). But unrestricted use of genetic information in sports is problematic as it infringes on the right to confidentiality of individuals, just as it does in other contexts such as employment or admission to insurance schemes.

Bio-genetics could impact sport in at least two ways. First, gene alteration or transfer could potentially enhance the bodies of athletes in terms of strength and resistance (Munthe 2000; Miah 2001). Second, gene engineering could provide advanced technology for ensuring that injuries heal rapidly (Lansam *et al.* 1997; Martinek *et al.* 2000). Seriously concerned by the prospect of genetic modification used to enhance sport performances, WADA organized in 2002 the first conference on 'Genetic Enhancement of Athletic Performance'. Participants adopted a set of recommendations, one of which stipulated that the 'definition of doping used by WADA, the IOC, international sport federations (Ifs), and national authorities should be expanded to include the unapproved use of genetic transfer technologies'.

At the Royal Free and University College Medical School (London), bio-genetic scientists have already succeeded, by injected genes, in increasing the muscle volume of mice by 20 per cent in two weeks, giving the animals bigger legs. Professor Geoffrey Goldspink, who led the research team, believes the effects on human beings might be less dramatic, possibly 'only' 10 per cent growth in a month:

> But as only 5 per cent improvement in performance can turn a mediocre club athlete into an elite national athlete and potential gold medal winner, the temptation for athletes to abuse these breakthroughs is obvious... Anyone in sport who needs muscle bulk – American footballers, sprinters, shot-putters, discus throwers – may want to try this.
>
> (Campbell 2000)

Could genetic medicine be used to help seriously injured athletes to recover rapidly? Harri Syvasalmi, WADA's secretary general, has declared:

> This gene manipulation is not at all bad ... especially for athletes who are injured. The sports world was not prepared for anabolic steroids. We can't get behind [on a doping trend] again. By looking at gene enhancement now, we hope to raise the ethical issues and appeal to the ethics of athletes.
>
> (Swift and Yager 2001)

In the not-too-distant future, will it be possible for a badly injured athlete to recover in a week instead of six months? Dick Pound, at the time IOC vice-president, asked:

> Are we going to create a generation of monsters, of made-to-order humans, a race of specialised people who only do sport? Are we going to breed bigger and meatier people, such as 180 kilogram linemen to play American football, in the same way that we already breed cattle? The scientists, legislators and medical ethics people have to say, wait a minute, and stop this happening.
>
> (Campbell 2000)

Johann Olav Koss, a Norwegian doctor who won three gold medals in speed-skating at the 1994 Lillehammer Winter Olympics and is today a member of the

IOC's medical commission, cautioned: 'There is no knowledge about the potentially damaging side effects of genetic changes. Saying that, we also know some athletes don't care about long-term risk.' Koss went on to say:

> This is an ethical question, not only for sports, but for the human race. You are tinkering with nature. How far are you going to go? What is acceptable? What will be the effect long term? Why shouldn't we create something genetically that is much smarter, stronger and better than a human? Why shouldn't we put wings on a human? Or give humans the eyes of a fly? Then we are no longer human, we are something else. You could eliminate the human race.
>
> (Swift and Yager 2001)

Ahead lies a new world in which sport is dominated by those who can afford the best scientists using their knowledge and skills to prepare armies of the strongest and most sophisticated genetically engineered athletes. Jacques Rogge, the IOC president warns:

> At this point we are at the crossroads with biotechnology and the developments in the field of genetic manipulation. If tomorrow a mother is scared because her child is involved in sports, then it's too late, we will have lost it.
>
> (*De Telegraaf* 2002)

NOTES

1 The Dutch Olympic Committee and Dutch Sport Federation (NOC–NSF) offer insurance policies to Dutch athletes to cover legal fees if they are suspected or accused of doping (*De Telegraaf*, 16 August 2001).
2 Cited by Mr Nordmann of the Monte-Cristo centre during *Droit de Cité*, a Swiss public television programme, 16 September 2000.
3 This is discussed in A. Miah's *Genetically Modified Athletes: The Ethical Implications of Genetic Technologies in Sport*, published in July 2004 by Routledge (London).
4 The Convention for the Protection of Human Rights and Dignity of the Human Being with regard to the Application of Biology and Medicine: Convention on Human Rights and Biomedicine entered into force on 1 December 1999 and has been ratified by 18 states as at 1 September 2004.

Part IV

The economics of sports and its impact on the rights of young athletes

11 Work to rule

Economic exploitation and child labour

> Unlike many jobs, the road to become a professional starts from an early age, sometimes as young as nine, through involvement with a club ... It has become unusual for players above school age to be signed as professional footballers.
>
> (The Football Association, England 2001)

> It is ridiculous that nowadays huge amounts of money are put on the table to contract talents of 11 or 12 years old. The problem lies in the hands of parents. A child should stay with his or her parents. We live in a capitalist world ruled by money. I saw on television parents who were proud of having sold their child. It is a scandal because an 11-year-old football player is only a child.
>
> (Diego Maradona, one of the world's best football players in the 1980s, in *Voetbal International* 2000)

The rapid growth of sports since the 1970s has turned the activity into an important sector of the world's economy. In the United States alone, sport generates business worth approximately US$ 250 billion a year, making it one of the top ten industries in the country (Longman 2001a: 1). Consumers of the European Union's 15 member states spent almost 34 billion euros on sports goods in 1999 (Sports Industries Federation 2001). In the United Kingdom, the sports market has grown by 15 per cent in value and 31 per cent in volume since 1994 and in Japan, the industry was worth 1.26 billion yen (approximately US$ 10 million) in 1999 (Sports Industries Federation 2001a; 2001b). Three factors have been largely responsible for turning sports into a highly commercialized activity in the past 30 years: the change of Olympic eligibility rules in 1972, which formally opened the door to professional athletes; the development of leisure-centred societies in Western countries; and globalization.

Professional sports have expanded considerably since the International Olympic Committee (IOC) changed its eligibility rules, although they did exist prior to the change in some countries. While becoming professional allowed athletes to improve their preparation and performances and to make a living, it also indirectly reduced the age at which they start training intensively. Some adults were quick to realize that success could be achieved by exploiting children's unique capacity to learn well and rapidly at a very young age. Since the 1970s, sports training centres and schools for young athletes – which previously existed mainly in a handful of Communist countries – have flourished all over the world.

Since the Second World War, leisure activities have developed and become accessible to most people in Western societies and they are now rapidly gaining ground elsewhere. For most young people, sport generally begins at the community level in an amateur, volunteer environment. Nonetheless, even at this level, sports are influenced by and related to commerce and economics: local sponsors and media respond to sport's community-based roots and even amateurs are consumers who need to be equipped.

Today, sport attracts much financial and commercial interest as it offers a worldwide market for economic expansion. Many multinational corporations use sports as a vehicle for global expansion, exploiting today's open markets and the universal attraction of some sports and their stars. A basketball superstar such as Michael Jordan or a football icon like Zinédine Zidane have the same impact in Beijing, Santiago de Chile or Harare. But modern sport is not immune from the dark side of most economic systems, such as organized crime. In Italy, for example, a multimillion-dollar European traffic by organized crime of anabolic substances was uncovered in 1998 (Council of Europe 2000).

Today, many transnational corporations have stronger economies than countries. In 1998, for example, sport clothes manufacturer Nike's gross sales reached US$ 9.89 billion, an amount bigger than the individual gross domestic product (GDP) of 82 developing countries (Wetzel and Yaleger 2000: 12; UN Development Programme 2000: 206–9). Sport as a whole is an industry that generates 3 per cent of world trade (Council of Europe 1999). Television rights for football's 2006 World Cup in Germany have been traded at US$ 6.21 billion, which is equivalent to the cumulative GDP of eight poor countries with a total population of over 30 million people: Burundi, Guinea-Bissau, Eritrea, Gambia, Sierra Leone, Laos, Togo and Mauritania (UNDP 2002: 180–1).

IMPACT OF THE COMMERCIALIZATION OF SPORT ON CHILDREN

The impact of the massive development and commercialization of sport since the 1970s on young athletes is at least fourfold (see Table 11.1). First, the involvement of children in amateur sports directly or indirectly generates income and jobs at an important scale. Local administrators, coaches and other workers are hired to organize the activity; sport programmes, centres and schools are established; public health systems are used for sport-related prevention programmes and to deal with sports injuries; sponsors and public authorities support sports initiatives for youth, etc. In the European Union (EU), it is estimated that there are 500,000 professional coaches, officials or managers, 300,000 physical education teachers and another 300,000 people employed in the construction and maintenance of sport infrastructure (European Commission 1999). Former Canadian Olympian Bruce Kidd once described athletes as 'sweat-suited philanthropists, ensuring the careers of hundreds of well-paid coaches, sports scientists and sport administrators' (Kidd 1988: 23).

Table 11.1 Impact of the commercialization of sports on the human rights of young athletes

	Athletes as generating job creation	Athletes as advertising medium	Athletes as commodities	Athletes as workers
	Youth sports is a major industry worldwide generating many jobs, essentially for adults. Sustaining this multibillion-dollar industry depends on young people's continuing involvement in sports	Athletes, especially young athletes, are an attractive medium through which corporations appeal to their customers	Athletes have a commercial value, and bring added value to team owners, investors and agents through transfers. Some young athletes are vulnerable to trafficking and sale practices	Many young athletes involved in intensive training need to be recognized as workers and protected by labour rights
Athletes' human rights in need of protection	Best interests of the child (article 3) Freedom of choice (articles 5, 12 and 14) Protection against economic exploitation (article 32)	Best interests of the child (article 3) Freedom of expression and thought (articles 13 and 14) Protection of privacy sphere (article 16) Protection against economic exploitation (article 32)	Best interests of the child (article 3) Freedom of choice and opinion (articles 12 and 13) Freedom of association (article 15) Protection against economic exploitation (article 32) Protection from trafficking and sale (article 35)	Best interests of the child (article 3) Rights to join labour unions and to bargain collectively (article 15) Rights to social security (article 26) Right to education (article 28) and rest (article 31) Right to be protected from economic exploitation and hazardous work. Need for a minimum age for admission to employment. Right to appropriate regulation of the hours and conditions of employment (article 32)

In the EU alone, it is estimated that, in ten years, 2 million jobs were created in direct relation to sports (Council of Europe 2000: 5). Between 30 and 40 per cent of the EU's population are involved in the sport and leisure industry, though less than 10 per cent are directly involved in competitive sport (European Commission 1999: 5).

Children are also consumers of sports products: in the United States in 2000, young people aged between 12 and 19 years old spent an estimated US$ 155 billion on all kinds of goods (*The Economist* 2000a: survey 9). In the United Kingdom, consumer expenditure on sport in 1998 amounted to GB£ 13 million, equivalent to 2.5 per cent of total consumer expenditure (Sports Industries Federation 2001a). Adolescents are, especially in Western countries, an important consumer group, and sporting goods, including clothes, represent a significant item in their spending (Klein 2000: 63–85). Today, the strong image of sports and the high impact of athletes as role models among young people are more than ever attractive factors for the promotion of corporate symbols.

The second implication is that child and adolescent athletes, especially the gifted and committed ones, are gradually building up a commercial value, and the best among them are a potential 'commodity' that will be traded as soon as there is an interest. This phenomenon usually starts long before the child is considered an adult (18 years) and does not only concern a handful of very gifted youngsters in the world, but is systematic in most countries where competitive sport is developed and affects all young athletes who have a particular competitive edge. An adolescent athlete's move from one local club to another, for example, is often conditioned by financial requests, incentives and negotiations.

Third, child and adolescent athletes, depending on their success, but also on their visibility and personality, may be incited to sign agreements with corporations who will use their image to deliver a wide range of messages. Some young athletes, such as in gymnastics, tennis, basketball, American football, ice hockey and football, are also key elements of the sport entertainment system that generates millions of dollars through television rights.

Finally, since competitive sport has become highly professionalized and commercialized, young athletes are frequently obliged to participate in intensive training schemes from a very young age (see also Chapter 6). But, even though some earn a substantial amount through contractual arrangements and spend more hours training than they do in school, they are not given the status of workers. Even professional adult athletes have a very weak status in most countries. American sociologist Jay Coakley (1998: 350) has noted:

> Many people have a difficult time thinking of athletes in commercial sports as workers, and they hesitate to consider owner–player relations in professional sports as employer–employee relations. This is the case because people usually associate sports with play in their own lives: they see sports as fun rather than work. However, when sports are organized for the purpose of generating revenues and making profits, players are workers, even though they may have fun on the job.

SPORT AS CHILD LABOUR

Today, the commercialization of sports is a reality. The rule of supply and demand means that corporations will pay US$ 2.6 million for one minute of commercial time during the broadcast of American football's final, the Super Bowl (Coakley 1998: 13). Protecting the human rights of young athletes in this context can only be achieved if adequate safeguards, including legal ones where appropriate, are put into place. In this regard, article 32 of the Convention on the Rights of the Child provides that:

1   States Parties recognize the right of the child to be protected from economic exploitation and from performing any work that is likely to be hazardous or to interfere with the child's education, or to be harmful to the child's health or physical, mental, spiritual, moral or social development.
2   States Parties shall take legislative, administrative, social and educational measures to ensure the implementation of the present article. To this end, and having regard to the relevant provisions of other international instruments, States Parties shall in particular: (a) provide for a minimum age or minimum ages for admission to employment; (b) provide for appropriate regulation of the hours and conditions of employment; (c) provide for appropriate penalties or other sanctions to ensure the effective enforcement of the present article.

The main 'relevant provisions of other international instruments' referred to in this article are two International Labour Organization (ILO) treaties: Convention No. 138 on minimum age for admission to employment (1973) and Convention No. 182 on the elimination of the worst forms of child labour (2000). The Convention on the Rights of the Child and the two ILO treaties do not prohibit work *per se* for children under 18, but intend to regulate the age of admission to work and outlaw all abusive forms of child labour.

Finally, the International Covenant on Economic, Social and Cultural Rights recognizes the right to work in just and favourable conditions, to join unions freely and to bargain collectively (articles 6 and 7) for everyone, as well as the right of children to be protected from social and economic exploitation (article 10).

Surprisingly, no definition of 'labour' or 'work' exists under international law. This is mainly because, as working trends evolve with time, the ILO wishes to keep some flexibility in its work as guardian of international labour norms and standards. A rigid definition of labour would not permit this pragmatic approach. Much domestic legislation defines work through two large criteria: the payment of a 'salary' and the relationship of subordination between the employer and the employee. As seen earlier, 'child labour' and 'economic exploitation' are to some extent defined by the Convention on the Rights of the Child and ILO Conventions 138 and 182.

A majority of young athletes practise competitive sports as a leisure and recreational activity and derive no material gain; others, however, should be given the status of worker. The concept of 'child athletic workers' is not completely new, as some researchers have articulated it since 1976 (Donnelly 1997: 390), but it is a concept that is totally rejected by both public and sport authorities. Once more, the pure and candid image of sports makes it difficult for political authorities to admit that sports can generate abusive forms of labour and economic exploitation.

Child labour is usually associated with horrendous images of slave-like, exploited children in coal mines or carpet factories, and many would question why a young Western athlete should be considered a worker. But, of the estimated 100 million children under the age of 14 working worldwide,[1] not all suffer the same levels of economic exploitation. It is difficult to compare a ten-year-old child exploited as a sex worker with those working on a farm outside school hours with and for their own family. The same applies to sports workers: they cannot be compared to the children exploited in brick factories or coal mines. In this context, it is important to note that child labour is not necessarily abusive or exploitative and that 'it is important to distinguish between beneficial and intolerable work and to recognize that much child labour falls into a grey area between these extremes' (UNICEF 1997: 24).

ILO Convention No. 138 sets different minimum age limits: article 2 prohibits work for children under 15 years (14 years for developing countries), but article 7 tolerates 'light work' for children aged 13 (12 in developing countries). It also prohibits hazardous work for all children under 18 (article 3). In addition, it defines a number of conditions that qualify child labour: any activity 'likely to jeopardise the health, safety or morals of young persons' (article 3) and any activity that does not 'prejudice [their] attendance at school' (article 7). The scope of ILO Convention No. 182 is the 'worst forms of child labour' and is discussed in the context of competitive sports in Chapter 13.

While the practice of sport generally has a positive impact on children's physical and psychological development, intensive training and competitive sports carried out to excess can jeopardize the health of young athletes (see Part III). Intensive training is rarely designed with the developmental stages and capacities of children in mind: the rhythm and techniques used in imposed training programmes are often similar to those of adults. An ILO expert identified this similarity as potentially threatening to the child and as one that should be addressed by international conventions:

> These [ILO] instruments are aimed at work carried out by children *that life treats as adults before their time*, those that have the same working day as adults in conditions that are harmful to their health and physical and moral development, that are deprived of any serious educational or training opportunities which would offer them a better future. This is the type of work that indeed must be abolished.
>
> (Piccard 1995: 2, emphasis added)

HAZARDOUS WORK

When young athletes train between two to eight hours a day, their sporting activity can hardly be considered 'light work'. Indeed, it becomes their main occupation and not only seriously jeopardizes school attendance, but increases health risks (ILO 1992: 14). In some situations, intensive training can be considered hazardous work – and therefore prohibited for athletes under 18 – especially when:

- average training exceeds 25 to 30 hours a week (in some countries, the legal working week for adults is 32 or 35 hours);
- physical efforts are comparable to those undertaken by adults and therefore excessive;[2]
- insufficient time is allowed for rest and recuperation;
- working conditions are dangerous and risk of injuries and accidents much higher than normally accepted (this is sometimes the case in sports such as gymnastics, boxing, football, American football, etc.); and
- competitive stress is excessive and therefore jeopardizes the mental health of athletes.

According to the ILO, a certain number of 'extremely important indicators' characterize child labour (ILO 1992: 14). It is interesting to put these indicators in the context of precocious intensive training of athletes:

- **The age at which children are put to work**. As seen earlier, children aged between five and ten are already training intensively in some sports, such as gymnastics, figure skating, swimming, tennis or football.
- **Hours of work**. At the age of five to six, young athletes may train at least two to three hours a day[2]; at seven to eight years of age, the average training time can increase to four or six hours a day, five or six days a week, not counting time spent competing. Holiday time is often used to train, study and be with their families.
- **Schooling**. The education of top athletes is clearly affected and many do not complete their schooling. This does not mean that every elite athlete will drop out of school; some achieve excellent studies. But educational opportunities are clearly put at risk by too great a focus on sport.
- **Fatigue of child workers and risk of injury**. Sport is physically and psychologically demanding. Many young athletes are often tired, which increases the risk of injuries and accidents.
- **Physical, psychological and emotional risks**. As seen in Chapter 6, young athletes can be made very vulnerable by the environment existing in early and intensive training programmes.
- **Child slavery**. Some forms of child slavery exist in sports, such as the sale and trafficking of young footballers (see Chapter 13).

- **Poor salaries**. Young elite athletes may generate an important income for adults. However, a disparity exists between the salaries they are paid: most receive no pay at all or earn disproportionately low salaries, others may earn huge amounts of money.
- **No satisfaction**. Sport is supposed to bring high levels of satisfaction, but some young athletes drop out precisely because they no longer enjoy practising their sport. Others, under pressure from parents and other adults and sometimes against their will, remain in competitive sports.
- **Too high a level of responsibilities**. Some professional adolescent athletes, for example Thai boxers or African footballers, are their families' main income-earners and therefore cannot leave their sport. Even in rich countries, young athletes are expected to generate income for their families, especially those who may have borrowed large amounts of money to pay the child's sport-related costs. Whatever their age and level of development, young athletes who reach world-class competitions in highly publicized sports endure extreme levels of pressure and responsibilities in relation to their sports federation (which might also be their employer), corporate sponsors, fans, their government, the media and others who expect successful results.
- **Being subject to intimidation**. As seen in Chapter 8, some adult trainers or coaches demand absolute obedience and strict discipline from their young athletes.

Many contact sports, such as football, ice hockey, rugby, American football, boxing and other martial sports, are characterized by a relatively high risk of injury and, practised at the professional level, could constitute potentially hazardous working conditions. Kevin Young (1991: 6), a British sociologist, considered that: 'By any measure professional sport is a violent and hazardous workplace replete with its own unique forms of "industrial diseases".'

Children's earnings from sport vary enormously and may be acquired from a large variety of sources. In some countries, child athletes might earn an annual 'compensation' wage from a governmental body that promotes and supports elite sports. In others, a private body, such as a sports federation or club, may pay such a stipend. Child athletes can earn money through commercial endorsements that pay them a monthly fee. Sports clubs sign labour contracts with young players and pay them a salary – this is the case, for example, of teenage football players from Africa, Latin America and Europe.

The image of wealthy sport superstars – who are powerful role models the world over –and the possibility of social promotion encourage many children to try their luck in the world of competitive sports. With German Formula One champion, Michael Schumacher, earning US$ 45 million a year, the average salary in the US National Basketball Association championship reaching US$ 2.2 million and French football player Zinédine Zidane transferred for 75 million euros, many parents see sports as a way for their children and themselves to gain recognition and wealth. Some children are pushed into intensive training and competitive sports solely to earn money and perhaps ultimately support their family, regardless of their freedom of choice and opinion (see Chapter 15).

LEGAL LOOPHOLE

No country in the world has enacted specific and comprehensive labour legislation covering young athletes. At best, they are protected in some countries by legislation regulating the work of children in the entertainment industry, but these laws do not specifically cover young athletes or, when they do, are rarely applied to them. Despite the Convention's clear requirements, no explicit limitation exists under domestic law on the number of hours a young athlete can train a day or a week, nor is there any supervision of contractual arrangements, general working conditions or the methods used by coaches. The Convention affirms in article 32 that: 'States Parties shall take legislative, administrative, social and educational measures to … (b) provide for *appropriate regulation of the hours and conditions of employment*' (emphasis added) and article 3.3 declares:

> States Parties shall ensure that institutions, services and facilities … shall conform with standards established by competent authorities, particularly in the areas of *safety, health*, in the number and suitability of their staff as well as *competent supervision*. [emphases added]

Giving adolescent athletes, who train and compete professionally, the status of a worker would provide them more specific rights, such as to be protected from exploitation, the right to association, to collective bargaining and, when relevant, to claim compensation. It would also oblige public authorities to inspect athletes' workplaces to ensure full compliance with labour policies and legislation. In most countries, employers and unions have not yet accepted the right of legally employed youngsters under 18 to join unions, though the Convention does protect the right of children to freedom of association (article 15). In the context of sports, unions have, in general, not defended athletes' rights very effectively and there is little social tradition of sportsmen and women being unionized. The same applies to collective bargaining (see also Chapter 15).

The question of the right of young athletes to claim compensation has arisen a few times. In the United States, for example, courts are sharply divided over the question of whether college athletes (aged from 17 to 24 years) on scholarships fall within the scope of workers' compensation statutes. In approximately half of the cases, courts have recognized student athletes as employees who are therefore entitled to access compensation when seriously injured (Davies 1994).

In France, Elodie Lussac, a junior European gymnastics champion in 1993, sued and claimed compensation rights from the French Gymnastics Federation for having obliged her to compete in the 1994 World Championships despite the fact that she had a serious back injury and had repeatedly asked not to compete. Her injury deteriorated so much that she had to retire from competitive sports at the age of 16. In July 1999 the *Tribunal de Grande Instance* of Paris decided that the Federation had a responsibility in the incident, but nevertheless ordered it to pay only a symbolic sum (US\$ 2,000) in compensation to Lussac, who had claimed US\$ 250,000 (*La Lettre du Sport* 1999).

Athletes' workers' rights have hardly ever been discussed or monitored by the ILO, which has in general implicitly considered athletes as part of the entertainment business. No projects exist to study the phenomenon and there are no experts on the subject among its 2,000 headquarters staff. Among the several thousands of studies published by the ILO, none has ever discussed the rights of athletes in the context of labour, though the organization, in one of its very rare references to athletes, did recognize them as 'special purpose workers' (ILO 2002: para. 142). Every year, the ILO spends over US\$ 60 million to prevent and combat child labour (ILO 2002a: 68–71), but it still needs to explore the exploitation of young athletes, including their trafficking and sale (see Chapter 13). General international labour norms obviously apply to athletes, but more specific standards to regulate athletes' working conditions, including those under 18 years, would seem necessary.

THE SHOW MUST GO ON

In many countries, competitive sport has entered the realm of entertainment. The most popular sport events attract the highest television ratings and generate enormous profits. This creates a major tension between the rules and ethics of sports and those of showbusiness. Modern sport is caught between these two trends, but the combined pressure of the media, profits and politics has already modified the rules of the game and will do so to a greater extent in the future as sport authorities constantly need to compromise to ensure their sustainability.

The IOC has to juggle with the dilemma of defending the Olympic ideal as enshrined in its charter and satisfying the expectations of corporate sponsors and the media, both of whom invest heavily in sports for their own commercial benefit. Juan Antonio Samaranch, former IOC president, was wont to repeat: 'Money generated by sport shall benefit sport' (IOC 2001: 5).

Many highly commercialized sports such as beach-volley and tennis have recently been accepted as Olympic sports, mainly due to commercial pressure. But in the 1990s, the IOC threatened other traditional – but less commercialized – Olympic sports, such as table tennis, fencing, field hockey, volleyball, water-polo and handball, with exclusion from the Olympics unless they adapted their rules in order to become 'more attractive' to sponsors and the media.

This trend seriously affects young athletes as many are potential – or actual – players in the global sports show and may be under contract to sponsors despite their young age. Young athletes may be crushed by the interests of the corporate business and consumer demands.

Although it is not the case for all athletes, some are treated as a 'commodity' at a young age, with their 'price' being estimated by sports teams and sponsors according to their entertainment value and TV viewers' demand. Television long ignored youth sports events (with the notable exception of Little League base-ball, played by children aged nine to 12, which has been broadcast in the United States since 1953), but the 1990s saw the number of broadcasts covering junior championships increase substantially. Television companies no longer hesitate to pay large sums to screen, for example, the under-16 European football champi-onships. The more a sport is commercialized, the higher the value of young athletes. But turning professional at a very young age is not without risk for both athletes and sponsors: the latter cannot predict exactly how athletes will evolve, especially if they were signed up before adolescence. And the athletes will be confronted with incompatibility of professional sports and education.

Athletes may be extremely gifted at 14 but, as they get older, may no longer progress or find it hard to deal with the stress and pressure when they have a bet-ter understanding of the immense interests involved. Before the 2002 Salt Lake City Olympics, 20-year-old American Michelle Kwan was favourite for the Olympic figure-skating title. But the four-time world champion admitted that she suffered more from the pressure than when she was younger: 'I should behave like I was still 14 years old, have nothing going through my mind, not thinking about the consequences of a missed jump,' she said (Inizan 2001: 70). As had already been the case in the 1998 Olympics, the pressure was perhaps too much: Kwan did not win the gold medal.

Young athletes can also simply lose their motivation. American Monique Viele was only 14 when her trainer Rick Macci, former coach of tennis stars such as Jennifer Capriati and the Williams sisters, said that she was 'much better' and claimed that she was a future world number one. Four years later, Viele hadn't won any titles and seemed more motivated by singing than by tennis (*L'Equipe* 2001b).

Young athletes leave the world of children to join that of adults when they become professionals. Javier Saviola, a young Argentinean football star, felt this way when he was recruited at 16 by Argentina's most prestigious professional football team, River Plate. 'Since that day my life accelerated. I was no longer one among the young people of my age. My new world became the one of adults, contracts and money,' he said a few years later (Lions 2001: 9). Georgian volley-ball player, Victoria Ravva, is today one of world's top players. Her professional career began in 1989 when she was only 14. Under contract with a team in Baku, Azerbaijan, she had to leave her home in Tbilissi and later recalled feeling that she 'wasn't a child any more, but not yet an adult' (Bernès 2002: 18).

The media periodically reports on very young football players who are offered contracts by professional clubs. In 1993, a five-year-old British boy, Kene Jackson, was approached by a local club and offered a GB£ 10,000 contract to join the team. His parents refused the offer (*L'Equipe Magazine* 1993b). A year earlier, AC Milan, the football club owned by Italian president and media mag-nate Silvio Berlusconi, put an 11-year-old boy, Luigi Quarticelli, under contract (*France Football* 1992). Vincenzo Samo, a ten-year-old from Naples, hit the head-lines when he was offered the equivalent of 70,000 euros to join a professional team in Turin, almost 1,000 kilometres from his home (Pénouel 1999). In Germany, 12-year-old Marco Quotschalla was transferred in 2001 from Bayer Leverkusen to Cologne football club allegedly for some 120,000 euros (*L'Equipe* 2001b). In the United Kingdom, Jermaine Pannant (15), 'the most talented schoolboy player in England', was under contract with Arsenal football club for the equivalent to 3 million euros (Reuters 1999) and, in 1998, Stephen Bywater (16) transferred to another British team, West Ham, for 4 million euros.

But teams contracting such young players have no real guarantee that they will get a 'good return' on their investment. The transition from junior to adult teams is often difficult even for very talented young players. Most football coaches agree that it is very hard to predict whether a talented adolescent will become a professional player as an adult.

It is, however, still in the teams' interest to contract talented athletes early, when clubs can still afford them and before they are approached by others, so identifying new talents is essential in many sports such as football, basketball or ice hockey. But the market is a jungle: the richest teams usually have the most efficient detection methods and the strongest financial arguments to convince young players and their parents. While some minor clubs, which invest heavily in training young players, risk being plundered and seeing talented athletes move to other clubs or even foreign countries, for others this is part of their planned income-generating activities: they intend to transfer the best players to richer clubs after a few years and, in the process, reap part of the transfer money.

Talent spotting exists in many different sports, even in Formula One motor racing. In 1998, McLaren, one of the richest teams, contracted 15-year-old Lewis Hamilton, a talented go-kart driver, for US$ 2 million, even though he didn't have a driving licence. Commenting on this move, Jackie Stewart, former world champion and now Jaguar team manager, said, 'It's a very good idea and we do it too … It is a small investment that can become very profitable' (Hart 2000: 104–11).

Basketball has attracted major interest from the sport merchandise industry, because professional athletes are the ideal promoters of goods such as training shoes that are used by almost everyone. For example, as soon as Michael Jordan was acclaimed as a spectacular player, Nike offered him a contract to promote their sports shoes. The release of the 'Air Jordan' shoe in the early 1980s definitely helped Nike to build its worldwide financial empire. Multinational companies, especially in the United States, compete against each other to find a new Jordan: two young players, Kobe Bryant and Tracy McGrady, signed contracts worth US$ 5 million (in 1996) and US$ 12 million (in 1997) respectively with sports shoe companies (Wetzel and Yaleger 2000: 139–40). Although these are the biggest deals signed by adolescent basketball players, hundreds of other prospective stars sign more modest deals in the US every year. High-school and college coaches also enter into arrangements with shoe manufacturers to ensure that their teams play with the proposed brands. These deals are so crucial for the survival of multinational shoe manufacturers that Phil Knight, the founder and executive director of Nike, reportedly said during an internal meeting, 'We never want another kid to go professional out of high school again without Nike being involved' (Wetzel and Yaleger 2000: 5).

Corporate power is now so strong in several professional sports that multinational companies are sometimes suspected of influencing a team's selection of players. In 1997, the American Basketball Association selected a national junior team to tour Europe. It did not go unnoticed that an overwhelming number of players had endorsement deals with the same sponsor as the American association, leading to suspicions that contracts rather than ability determined the selection (Wetzel and Yaleger 2000: 99–100). Similarly, many suspected that Nike obliged the Brazilian trainer to force Ronaldo, at the time football's number-one superstar, to play the 1998 World Cup football final, even though he was clearly unfit. A parliamentary inquiry into the affair was carried out in 2000 and 2001 in Brazil, but no proof was uncovered.

Harassment of young athletes by professional teams or corporate companies to sign contracts is relatively common. Fifteen-year-old French goalkeeper, Mickael Fabre, signed a contract in 2000 with the Italian team, Bologna, after hesitating for four months. His father acknowledged that 'the managers of Bologna called me every day. In the end, they harassed us. They were ready to double his salary and the bonus upon signature. But for us it was a matter of principle, not one of money' (Champel 2000: 113). A promising basketball player at 16, Wesley Wilson was constantly harassed by agents who wanted to sign him up:

> In between games there would be people approaching me, saying play with my team ... 'I'll give you this. I'll give you that'. Shoes and stuff. Clothes ... Then they got the college coaches over there, looking at you like they're owners. 'Look at his teeth. Are his teeth good?' You just feel like cattle. That messed my mind. I didn't like the feeling.
>
> (Wetzel and Yaleger 2000: 118, 133–4)

SPORT AGENTS FOR CHILDREN

A new profession has emerged in elite sports: the agent. In the increasingly commercialized, cut-throat world of sports, they gauge the potential commercial value of talented youngsters and fight to be the first to get them under contract.

American Tara Lipinski, who was, at 15, Olympic figure-skating champion at Nagano in 1998, had her first agent at 13 years old. She didn't, however, know why she needed an agent: 'It was my parents' decision,' she said. Nor did she know what she would do with the US$ 60,000 she'd earned in two days of competition (Brennan 1999: 142).

Corporations accept that of the 100 athletes they contract, only a few will make a decent career and be worth the investment. To maximize the career income of athletes, some sport management groups do not hesitate to scour the world to detect and contract potential talents, just as others scout for young fashion models. IMG (International Management Group) first signed Russian tennis player Anna Kournikova when she was ten. The contract stipulated that she and her mother would move from Moscow and set up home in Florida (Finn 1992: B13–B18). Today, Kournikova is not the top female tennis player, but she is the highest-paid, earning over US$ 10 million a year, mostly from commercial endorsements.

Since the 1980s, many tennis champions have made millions of dollars while they were still minors. Jennifer Capriati, for example, was 16 when she earned her first million in prize money (Litsky 1999: 7). In 2000, aged only 20, Venus Williams signed a five-year, US$ 40 million deal with sporting goods manufacturer, Reebok. Martina Hingis had earlier signed a six-year deal believed to be worth almost US$ 30 million (Sandomir 2000). In 1999, four young female tennis players who had just turned 18, Martina Hingis, Anna Kournikova, and Venus and Serena Williams, earned US$ 12 million, 11 million, 5 million and 6 million respectively (Forbes.com 2000). Young female figure skaters, such as Ukraine's Oksana Baiul and American champions Tara Lipinski and Michelle Kwan, also earned millions of dollars, principally through television rights, before they turned 18 (*L'Equipe Magazine* 2001a).

But for some, the glory and gain can be difficult to assume at such a young age. In 1994, 16-year-old Oksana Baiul was Olympic figure-skating champion and she rapidly became wealthy once she was established in the United States. But four years later, she entered an alcohol rehabilitation programme suffering from depression (Brennan 1999: 410).

PARENTS: TAKE THE MONEY AND RUN ...

In most countries and legal systems (including common law), money earned by children and adolescents (under 18 years) is retained by the parent with legal custody. This rule applies whether a child delivers newspapers or makes millions starring in a film. Parents can manage the money earned by their child in any way they see fit, even if it means spending instead of saving or investing it.

Only a few countries have legislation that adequately protects these earnings. In the United States, California's Coogan's law was enacted in 1939 to protect the earnings and contractual relationships of under-aged actors (Heller 1999; Siegel 2000). The law was named after the child actor Jackie Coogan, who starred in Charlie Chaplin's *The Kid* and realized, when he reached adulthood, that his parents had spent all his earnings. Amended in 1999, this law now covers 'personal services in the entertainment and sports industries'. It specifies that minors are the owners of their earnings and foresees that at least 15 per cent of the earnings be placed in a trust fund monitored by a court.

Though most parents or legal guardians do manage their children's earnings properly, others have spent it all. In 1998, the case of Dominique Monceanu, gymnastics champion at the 1996 Atlanta Olympics, received worldwide media attention. At 17, she ran away from home and sued her parents for misuse of her earnings (Associated Press 1998b). She petitioned for and was granted emancipation from her parents, and the court recognized her right to be treated as an adult and to have full control over her earnings. But her parents had spent nearly US$ 4 million of her trust fund to build the largest gym hall in the US, without her permission. Her father claimed that he had informed his daughter, who insisted that she did not know about the trust fund nor did she have any idea of her earnings during her short career (Siegel 2000).

Other child athletes have also been abused by their parents. For the same reasons as Monceanu, Olympic gymnasts Mary Lou Retton and Shannon Miller both won legal emancipation from their parents through court decisions. Other parents were more careful with their children's earnings, as was case for American gymnast Jaycie Phelps who won the Olympic gold medal in 1996 along with Monceanu and Miller. Her parents invested her money efficiently and when she reached her majority, she was able to pay her college fees from her savings (Siegel 2000).

In Western Europe, there have as yet been no reported cases of young star athletes suing their parents for lost earnings. The European Union explicitly recognized sport as part of entertainment industry and adopted a directive in 1994 advising member states that:

> The employment of children for the purposes of performance in cultural, artistic, sports, advertising activities shall be subject to prior authorisation to be given by the competent authority in individual cases ... By way of derogation ... In the case of children of at least 13 years, Member States may authorise, by legislative or regulatory provision in accordance with conditions they shall determine for the purposes of performance in cultural, artistic, sports, advertising activities.
>
> (European Union 1994: article 5, paras. 1 and 3)

In the United Kingdom, The Children (Performances) Regulations of 1968 require that all children under the age of compulsory education (16) must be licensed when performances (including rehearsals) last for more than four days in any six-month period, if absence from school is required and when payment is received for the activity. Licences are, however, seldom issued for child athletes, even when they receive payment for their activities, as they are rarely assimilated as workers in the entertainment industry. According to British case law, income earned by young athletes can only be spent by their parents for maintenance, protection and education; additional revenue should be saved and at the disposal of the athletes when they reach their majority.

In Canada and France, laws require permits or authorization for children to work in the entertainment industry and protect their income. However, young athletes are not covered by these laws.

MARKETING THE KIDS

Like any business, commercial sport can only function properly if it is adequately marketed. In highly publicized sports, marketing has become a natural tool not only of management, but even for parents. This troubles some sports professionals, such as John Evert, who works at the Evert Academy in Florida (USA) with his sister, Chris Evert, a former world number-one tennis player. John Evert has declared:

> what worries me is the way parents are marketing their kids. Parents are now doing brochures on their kids. And when they lose sight of it being a game, and start to think more about it being business, about money, then it becomes more about winning. I see kids come in exhausted in the morning, and I say to parents – what are you doing at night? Are you taking them away and training them? Are you talking tennis all night? A lot are.
>
> (Kleinhenz 2000: 25)

Frank Marcos of the Major League Baseball scouting bureau, a service identifying young prospects, explained that he gets:

> letters, phone calls, faxes from parents, girlfriends, coaches, agents about players and sometimes it is very valuable information. Some guys are creative. We get videotapes, color shots of their swings. I guess they see it as an investment in their future and are willing to go to that extent.
>
> (Major League Baseball 2001)

Age is no longer a limit when it comes to scouting for talented youngsters. On its website, shoe manufacturer Reebok is full of admiration for Mark Walker: 'a threat from anywhere on the [basketball] court, and he's only three and half years old. Short on everything but talent, Walker is destined to the big league. With his trademark two-handed over-the-head shot, he owns the playground.' A video film shows Mark throwing the ball 18 times in a row into a net. The shoe manufacturer indicates it wishes to spot other diaper-generation talents: 'Young sensations wanted. Does your son or daughter have super talent? Share his or her special skills with the rest of us,' says Reebok, encouraging parents to describe their child's 'superior abilities' and send in a tape (Reebok 2003).

The most sophisticated and aggressive marketing is often undertaken by sports organizations and federations as well as commercial sponsors. For example, the International Volleyball Federation (FIVB) came under pressure from the IOC, its major sponsors and television companies to turn volleyball into a 'more attractive' game to ensure its sustainability. In 1998, therefore, the FIVB changed the rules to oblige female players to wear tight-fitting shorts and shirts so that they look more sexy and clearly prohibited loose or baggy shirts and shorts (FIVB 1998). Since 1998, female beach-volley players are also obliged to wear bikinis and the bikini bottom should not exceed 'six centimetres of tissue on the side' (Donzé 2000: 1). Nevertheless, following widespread protest, the FIVB amended the rules again in 2001; they are now less explicit and state that, for world and official competitions, 'Jerseys and shorts should comply with FIVB standards' (article 4.3.2, FIVB Rules) but the text fails to define what 'FIVB standards' are. As international teams are only allowed to use equipment from corporations affiliated to the Federation, they are systematically equipped with tight-fitting shorts and shirts and, in the case of beach-volley, with bikinis.

The Polish national basketball league also decided in October 2001 to invite all female players to abandon their traditional shorts for more sexy, tight-fitting outfits (Agence France Presse 2001c). The objective was to make basketball more attractive for television viewers. Wieslaw Zych, the president of the Polish Basketball League justified the decision, saying: 'We are not just copying the volleyball revolution, but we think that the shorts worn by our basketball players are old-fashioned and we invite them to show a little more of their long legs' (Agence France Presse 2001b).

Women's football seems to be following suit. The 2003 women's football World Cup was not as popular and successful as expected. A few months later, in 2004, FIFA's president Joseph Blatter suggested that female football players should be more attractive: 'Why shouldn't female players be dressed in a more feminine way, wearing tight-fitting shorts for example?' (Tschoumy 2004).

Tennis is another sport that, during the 1990s, made specific efforts to attract the attention of the media, sponsors and spectators. Female tennis was almost completely neglected by the media until the late 1980s when the rivalry between two exceptional champions, Chris Evert and Martina Navratilova, started attracting the public's attention. But the big change in female tennis occurred when a new generation of gifted and physically attractive teenage players emerged, from Martina Hingis to the Williams sisters and Anna Kournikova. 'Entertainment marketing' emerged as a new dimension in female tennis, enthusiastically developed by managers, players, sponsors, television companies and the Women's Tennis Association (WTA) alike. The idea was to involve these teenage athletes in non-sporting activities, such as modelling or advertising, so that the visibility of tennis and its popular success would increase. With everyone pulling at the same string, profits are multiplying. Today, some players, such as Kournikova, earn more through advertising than in prize money. More than sports events, female tennis tournaments are now shows that attract the attention of the general public and the media, with their dramas, intrigues, success and conflicts. Hingis, world number one for several years, said:

> It's good that people talk about us, about our personalities; in the end it valorizes the game. I see myself as an integral part of a spectacle, a show. You need to understand that people come to see us to have fun.
>
> (Sainte-Rose 2000a: 38)

At 17, Kournikova became a sex symbol in one of the most extreme examples of the marketing of players, when she posed in 2000 for a bra company's advertisements: 'Only the ball should bounce,' said the slogan. Many female tennis players are more often on the front page of magazines such as *Elle*, *Cosmopolitan*, *Vogue* or *Vanity Fair* than in specialized publications. In 1999, Hingis, then 19, appeared on the cover of GQ, a well-known men's magazine in the United States, in a strapless dress under the title: 'I am for sale'. Asked why she did this, Hingis replied: 'It's the business that wants this from us, and we're playing the game, me and Anna and Venus. We're the Spice Girls of tennis' (Kleinhenz 2000: 24). 'The frontier between sport and entertainment has exploded,' said Phil de Piciotto, the president of Advantage International, a career management company that manages, among others, the careers of Kournikova and Hingis (Sainte-Rose 2000a: 40).

In her book denouncing the system ruling tennis, French player Nathalie Tauziat revealed that, parallel to its official ranking list, the WTA has a confidential commitment list, which classifies players according to their capacity to boost ticket sales for tennis tournaments. On the basis of this list, some players are invited to play in tournaments where their presence is not necessary in terms of their sporting career (Tauziat 2000: 150). American Lindsay Davenport, former world number one and still in the top five, is one of the very few players to reject this system. She successfully finished secondary education and systematically refuses to deliver any information about her private life or to participate in non-sporting activities.

For sport organizers these recent developments are mostly appreciated. Liz Garger, a WTA director, explained:

> While the sporting aspect is our priority, we cannot neglect the side events … we have the chance to have among the best, pleasant and cute young women. For tennis fans, there are the sport pages, the results, but to attract larger and larger crowds, you need to know their [the players] personalities, what they do off the courts.
>
> (Sainte-Rose 2000a: 41)

The WTA, for example, sells on its website 'the 2001 Sanex WTA Tour Calendar featuring beautiful photos, facts and tour information on all favourite players' as well as 'the 2001 Anna Kournikova Calendar'. These promotional products feature sexy pictures of many female tennis players. The success of female tennis is so overwhelming that, for the first time in the history of sport (with the possible exception of figure skating), female competition is more attractive than men's in the eyes of the media and the public.

Athletes are the best marketing tools sports goods manufacturers have and so they pay special attention to the way their players are dressed in order to boost their own sales. During the 2001 Australian Open, 20-year-old Venus Williams wore the most provocative dress ever seen on a tennis court, showing the upper part of her breast: 'I love this design, which is the creation of Gianni Versace,' she said. A WTA official commented: 'She is a hostage of the merciless war among companies. We might have to establish rules to avoid any excess' (Dupuis 2001: 17).

Female tennis might not be Hollywood, but dress codes already seem more important than athletic performance. When 16-year-old American Ashley Harkleroad made her professional debut during the 2001 US Open, she attracted enormous media attention, because, even though she lost in the first round, she wore revealing, very tight shorts and a midriff-baring top. In the after-game press conference, she explained candidly why she wore such an intriguing outfit: 'Well, Nike is my sponsor, and I went to the Nike room earlier this week and I tried on all the clothes and they liked me in that outfit best, so …' (US Open official website 2001). *Sports Illustrated*, the respected US sport magazine, commented:

> So there it was: the moment when the panting search for the next Anna Kournikova hit rock bottom. Harkleroad's parents, her handler from Mike Ovitz's Artists Management Group and the folks from Nike can all slap one another on the back over the excitement they stirred up. Cameras clicked through Harkleroad's match, and 43 reporters packed a room fit for 10 for her post-match press conference. Three showed up for Tu's [her opponent who won the game]. She was the story of the day, but no one mentioned Lolita.
>
> (Price 2001)

Harkleroad, who is one of the best-ranked juniors in the world, is compared to Kournikova, the Russian Lolita of the tennis circuit. 'They just want me to be like a Kournikova, but from the US I guess. I hope I can be that,' said Harkleroad (Rodriguez 2001).

A few months earlier, during the Wimbledon tournament, Austrian player Barbara Schett, aged 25, agreed to pose in a sexy manner for the London tabloid *Daily Mirror* for the equivalent of US$ 50,000. Later she regretted it:

> They say it was great for me presswise, but I told them [her managers] that I wouldn't do it again, because I don't want people to see me as a sexy tennis player. I want them to see me as a tennis player.
>
> (Price 2001)

NOTES

1 Statistics concerning child labour worldwide are difficult to evaluate. In its 2002 report, *A future without child labour*, the ILO considers that 180 million children aged 5 to 17 years are engaged in the worst forms of child labour. Over 100 million children under 15 are estimated to be engaged in hazardous work.
2 American gymnast, Kristie Phillips, trained four hours a day at the age of five, although this was an exception rather than the rule (Ryan 1995: 110).

12 Factories of champions

Moulding athletes in specialized sport centres

> Not all players who are successful in gaining entry to Football Academies and Centres of Excellence, will make it as established professionals. Some will be 'released' by their clubs. Boys and parents/guardians need to be realistic and appreciate the extremely small chance of successfully overcoming all the obstacles to becoming an established professional.
>
> (The Football Association 2001b)

The success of major national and international sport events is ultimately based on the quality of the show offered and on the uncertainty of results, though well-conceived promotion campaigns alone can ensure success in the short term. If the Olympic Games or the football World Cup brought together only second-class athletes, their sustainability would be rapidly threatened, just as the film industry would collapse if only mediocre actors performed. Modern sport needs a continual succession of attractive entertainers capable of exciting supporters and TV viewers alike with their skill and outstanding results. To keep up the succession of successful athletes, sports organizations and public authorities in many countries have established training centres or schools for young athletes, sometimes referred to as 'baby champion factories' by critics.

These specialized establishments are not new – they already existed prior to the 1970s, but mainly in Communist countries. Today, they can be found all over the world: from Portugal to Ukraine, from Senegal to Chile, from North Korea to New Zealand, most countries have some type of specialized elite training schools. Trinidad and Tobago, for example, established a cricket academy in 2000 to improve the skills of its young players and maintain its excellent international results (*The Economist* 2000: 45). In the former German Democratic Republic (GDR), 14 of its efficient, but later unanimously criticized *Kinder- und Jugendsportschule* (child and adolescent sport schools) survived the collapse of Communism in 1990. They are now completely overwhelmed by the demand and have to refuse many young athletes every year. Many former GDR coaches are again training children, who enter these schools at six years of age for figure skating, at age eight for gymnastics, ten for swimming and 12 for other sports (Inizan 1999: 80–98). In the United Kingdom, 36 'specialist sport colleges' existed in 1999 but the government aimed to have over 100 sport colleges in

2003 in order 'to give pupils the opportunity to achieve their potential in sport' (Government of the UK 1999a). These institutions exist for most sports, from skiing to field hockey, football to swimming, cricket to badminton – France even has a full-time school for sport fishermen – and, although they differ from country to country in form, setting and structures, they are usually quite similar.

In some countries, such as China, the Czech Republic, Denmark, France, Italy, Portugal, Romania or Russia, sport is placed under the direct jurisdiction of the state. Privately owned sport centres, sometimes benefiting from public grants or subsidies, also exist in these countries, especially in very wealthy sport clubs. Other countries, such as Australia, Austria, Germany, New Zealand, Spain, Switzerland, the United Kingdom and the United States, place sports under the jurisdiction of sport authorities; all sport centres are therefore private entities, although they may receive state subsidies. No definitions exist of sport centres and they can vary greatly from one country to another. France is probably the only country where sport centres are defined, with detailed requirements set out in a specific law regulating these institutions (Government of France 2001: article 1).

Sport centres can give talented athletes unique opportunities to develop their athletic gift fully, just as special boarding schools do for intellectual, musical or artistic prodigies. Article 29.1 of the Convention promotes the fulfilment of the child and specifies that: 'States Parties agree that the education of the child shall be directed to: (a) the development of the child's personality, talents and mental and physical *abilities to their fullest potential...*' (emphasis added). In its general comment on this article, the UN Committee on the Rights of the Child (2001) specified that:

> 'education' in this context goes far beyond formal schooling to embrace the broad range of life experiences and learning processes which enable children, whether individually or collectively, to develop their personalities, talents and abilities and to live a full and satisfying life within society.

One of the main challenges for sport centres or schools is to enable children to benefit from privileged training conditions to develop their skills fully without hampering any of their human rights, such as their rights to physical and mental integrity, education and rest. But when the institutions' whole focus is on sports results, they tend not to consider the child's holistic development as a priority. Education is often perceived in these schools as a secondary activity, one that they are obliged to offer on moral grounds and because education is compulsory. This is particularly serious as the vast majority of young athletes leave these centres the day their performance is not as good as expected.

Many sport centres, especially in football, count on a 'direct return on investment' system: they need to 'produce' a minimum of professional champions who can later be traded with other teams so that, in turn, the money resulting from the transaction can be re-invested in the system. Football experts estimate that the global cost of forming one professional player is between 5 and 7 million euros (this includes the 'lost' investment in players who drop out of the system)

(Bielderman 2000: 57). These schools are therefore strongly oriented towards sports performances and young athletes are under constant pressure to succeed as they are key to the system's sustainability. The reputation of Dutch football team, Ajax Amsterdam, is largely based on its training centre. Arie van Os, the centre's treasurer, admitted, 'After three years you need to sell the player. Then at least you still can make profit' (Van Wijnen 2000: 4).

Many major professional sport clubs have invested heavily in their training programmes. Liverpool FC, one of the wealthiest British football teams, invested between GB£ 10 and 15 million to open its football academy in January 1999, the 'biggest of its kind in Europe' (Liverpool FC 2000). The academy accepts children from the age of seven, but only players aged 16 and above stay full time in the centre. According to Steve Heighway, a former top Liverpool player and director of the academy, 'The objective is to prepare players of a very high level and, to reach this level, you need to start very young, between 7 and 8 years old. This will require a lot of understanding from parents and teachers' (*Le Courrier* 1999: 17).

Based on a pyramidal approach, sport centres 'produce' only a few athletes who will turn professional and make a living from sports. In most sport centres, most athletes drop out at some stage of the process, simply because their performances are not considered good enough.

Adolescents 'released' by a sport centre may well be devastated by their experience: not only has their dream evaporated, but their education has often been so neglected that they will face major obstacles in reintegrating into society and starting a new professional career. Peter Donnelly, a sociologist at Toronto University, declared, 'The capitalist exploitation of children is far worse than it used to be in the Communist countries; there at least the kids got an education' (Kleinhenz 2000: 24).

The Convention on the Rights of the Child recognizes the 'right of the child to education' and obliges states to 'make primary education compulsory and available free for all…' (article 28). In most countries compulsory education ends between the ages of 12 and 16 years; the Convention encourages, but does not oblige, secondary education. In Belgium, France, New Zealand, Switzerland and the United Kingdom, for example, school is compulsory until the age of 16; up to this age, all sport schools or centres in these countries must include education in their programmes. While this obligation is usually respected, the problem is often the poor quality of education and the insufficient time given to it compared to the sports training provided.

In many sport schools, the demands on the child are often overwhelming. Even when sufficient hours of education are provided, it remains difficult, if not impossible, for young athletes to focus on both their sporting career and their schooling, especially in an environment geared towards sports results and performances. Lucien Legrand, basketball trainer at the French national sports institute (*Institut national du sport et de l'éducation physique* – INSEP), a state-sponsored institution where over 1,000 elite athletes aged between 14 and 30 years reside, admitted that athletes 'live at a crazy pace, they don't have enough time to recover … they face demands from their parents, their trainers, school-teachers … and the competition among them can be fierce' (Thomas 1998: 19).

Most students attending sports institutions will not make an adequate living from their sport. It stands to reason, therefore, that the education they receive should, on both intellectual and practical levels, be sufficient to allow them to enter the non-sport professional world without too much trouble. This, unfortunately, is rarely the case and some sport schools have even been suspected of delivering diplomas to students who have not reached the required level. In February 2000, for example, the French Minister for Sports opened a ministerial inquiry after two football training centres in Cannes and Nice were suspected of delivering falsified education certificates (Fritscher 2000).

TRAINING INTENSIVELY OVER 40 HOURS A WEEK

In most sport centres, athletes train between four to eight hours a day, five or six days a week, but there is no guarantee that such dedication will bring results and success. Not all athletes can physically endure so much intensive training and many will eventually drop out of the system. Others might be handicapped by chronic or serious injuries and will have to abandon their ambitions (see Chapter 7). Only in France does a law oblige sports institutions to specify in a written contract, signed by the athlete's parents and the school, the maximum number of training and competing hours a week, the minimum rest time between competitions, and the length of holiday leave (Government of France 2001b).

After winning a gold medal at the 1992 Barcelona Olympics, 15-year-old Ukrainian gymnast, Tatiana Goutsou, said: 'I don't remember the last time I had an ice-cream, it was a very long time ago. Holidays? I never had any' (Monnard 1992: 35). In Romania, where gymnastics is a national passion, talented children join part-time gymnastic schools at the age of six. A commission composed of trainers, medical doctors and psychologists identifies talented youngsters at about the age of four, before they start primary school. Octavian Bellu, Romania's top gymnastics trainer, explained:

> We test coordination, courage, capacity to learn rapidly, and we look at the personality. We also make detailed calculations about potential body size and, of course, we look at the size of the parents. If I see that the mother's height is 170 centimetres and the father's is 180 cm, I will not take the girl.
>
> (Inizan 2000: 55)

At the age of eight, gymnasts train three and a half hours a day. When they reach their peak (at about 14–16 years of age), they join the national training centre in Deva and train six to seven hours every day, except for Thursday mornings (dedicated to schooling) and Sunday afternoons, for family visits (Bucharest is five hours away by train).

In Australia, unlike swimming, field hockey, rugby, tennis and beach-volley, gymnastics is not a national sport. Nevertheless, at the Australian Institute of Sport (AIS), established in Canberra in 1981, young gymnasts trained 'six days a week before and after school or work, for a total of between 32 and 40 hours' in 2001. The first training session of the day usually starts at 7am and the last ends at 7:30pm (AIS 2001). The AIS is largely sponsored by private corporations and each sponsor can fund a programme according to its own interests. For example, pharmaceutical companies, such as Roche, Bayer and others, support the AIS's 'sport science and sport medicine programme' financially; Compaq and Microsoft sponsor the information technology department; and Nestlé sponsors the career and education programme, and the food service and nutrition programme (AIS 2001a).

In the Netherlands, where, like in Australia, gymnastics is not a traditional sport, gymnasts usually integrate the Zoetermeer training centre at around nine years old and train a total of 34 hours in a six-day week, while following schooling at the same time (*De Telegraaf* 2001a). The approach seems to bring results: in 2001, for the first time ever, a Dutch gymnast, Renske Endel, won a silver medal in the bars competition at the world gymnastics championships. A year later, another Dutch gymnast, Veronna van de Leur (16), came second in the floor exercises of the world championships.

In Japan, many judo training centres are famous for the rigour and discipline they impose on young judokas. Living conditions at Tokyo's Koudou Gakusha centre, for example, are so harsh that every year three or four youngsters run away. In addition to four hours of daily training plus schooling, young judokas have to clean the whole training centre every day. Posted on the walls are slogans inciting the youngsters 'not [to] lose from inside' and to 'uphold the fighting spirit' (Ben-Ismaïl 2000: 64).

In Thailand, professional Thai boxing is seen as an opportunity for the poor to wrest themselves and their families from their bleak living conditions. All over the country, thousands of Thai boxing schools have sprung up since the 1980s and there are now no fewer than 60,000 professional combatants, many of whom are under 18 years old (Béguin 2000: 52). Thai boxing is a very tough sport and the training regimes imposed in these centres are extremely demanding and discipline is harsh.

SEPARATION FROM PARENTS

Some very young children join a sport centre located a long way from their home, a situation – sometimes imposed upon them by their parents or sports officials – that can be very difficult for them to bear. But how can these young children fully understand what it means to leave home and break family bonds? Even if they are involved in the decision-making process, they might be too immature to take such an important decision, which will have repercussions for the rest of their lives. Children also want to please their parents or other adults and tend to give in easily to their wishes and submit to their pressure.

A study undertaken in 1983 among athletes in the Neustift sport school in Austria, a centre for elite competitive skiers, revealed that 64 per cent of children had been pushed by their parents to follow this particularly difficult education system (Suisse *et al.* 1990). In this context, article 12 of the Convention is fundamental as it requires states parties to:

> assure to the child who is capable of forming his or her own views the right to express the views freely *in all matters affecting the child*, the views of the child being *given due weight* in accordance with the age and maturity of the child. [emphases added]

Public and sport authorities should always ensure that the placement of a child respects article 9 of the Convention, which engages states parties to 'ensure that a child shall *not* be separated from his or her parents against their *will*' (para. 1, emphases added) and that 'States Parties shall respect the right of the child who is separated from one or both parents to *maintain personal relations and direct contact* with both parents on a *regular* basis...' (para. 3, emphases added). This provision is especially relevant in countries with authoritarian political regimes where public authorities might unilaterally decide to move a child to a sport school, therefore separating him or her from its parents. In China, for example, when discussing placing a nine-year-old gymnast in a sports centre 1,500 kilometres away from her home, a recruiter said: 'At first they miss their parents. But they get used to it' (Emmerson and Wehrfritz 1996: 49).

Some adolescents also find it hard to move away from home and friends and they leave sports centres after a short time. Relationships among athletes in these schools can be cruel and biased by the fact that every one of them knows perfectly well that they are competing against each other for one of the few places in paradise. Little mercy and low solidarity often characterizes their relations; friendship usually exists among the best or the worst groups as they know they are not fighting against each other.

The capacity of children to deal emotionally with the separation from their affective environment, including parents, siblings and friends, at an early age varies from one child to another. Former French football star Didier Deschamps regularly claimed that having to leave his family at 14 to join a training centre over 700 kilometres from home made him stronger and tougher. Some of his world champion colleagues felt differently. Christophe Dugarry explained that 'without my parents close to me I would never have made it' (Marchand 2000: 6) and Zinédine Zidane, the world's best footballer in the late 1990s, admitted that the separation from his family at 14 when he joined the AS Cannes training centre was painful: 'I cannot count the number of nights I spent crying. I missed my family. Football took away my youth, but also taught me to be ambitious, to put the limits always higher' (Terrani 2000: 19).

Disappointing results and unsatisfactory experiences have led some sport federations or clubs to abandon the system of full-time boarding schools and to establish programmes that do not separate children from their families. The

French Tennis Federation decided at the end of the 1990s to allow the youngest players to go home every evening: 'It isn't worth cutting the links with parents too early,' said Jean-Claude Masias, the Federation's technical director (*L'Equipe Magazine* 1999).

LACK OF MONITORING MECHANISMS

Although public authorities have direct or indirect responsibilities, depending on the status of sport centres and the country's policy of intervention towards private sport bodies, very few countries have set up serious monitoring and evaluation mechanisms. In most countries, such a system does exist for 'normal' public and private schools and other types of specialized education institutions, such as for children with disabilities. Article 3.3 of the Convention calls for a competent supervision of institutions:

> States Parties shall ensure that the *institutions, services and facilities responsible for the care* or protection of children, shall conform with the standards established by competent authorities, particularly in the areas of *safety, health, in the number and suitability of their staff, as well as competent supervision.*
> [emphases added]

Placing young athletes in specialized sport centres could make them more vulnerable to abuse and exploitation than when they stay in their own family environment with its specific natural protection mechanisms. All sport institutions must, therefore, conform to applicable norms and standards, including those recognized by the Convention. Rare are the centres that have put in place mechanisms to prevent and combat physical, psychological and sexual abuse as well as different forms of exploitation, including imposed doping practices. England's Football Association visits its 54 football academies and centres of excellence at least three times a year, though these visits are not undertaken by a fully independent body but by its own technical department (The Football Association 2001a).

The 1984 French law regulating sport organizations was amended in May 2001 in order to allow public authorities to carry out spontaneous visits to monitor centres (Government of France 2001a). Under this law, sport centres are given a governmental label, which they can lose if they do not respect a certain number of minimum standards related to the protection of children. These standards include quality of education, number of hours spent in training, competition and rest, medical checks and support, quality of sport infrastructure, equipment and competence of coaches, social and medical staff.

There is hardly any independent research on the quality of sport schools or centres and insufficient debate on which criteria should be used to establish a quality control system. In France, however, the French Football Federation establishes every year a classification grading the quality of sport centres and their efficiency. Quality criteria are mainly based on the infrastructure, coaches, medical staff, schooling and nutrition. But to calculate a centre's efficiency, the criteria focus on how many athletes secure a professional contract when they leave the centre, how many matches are played in professional and/or national teams and – to some extent – school results. Important elements, such as medical support and social reintegration of those who drop out, are not evaluated. Since 1997, The Football Association in England has established a training policy; to obtain the 'academy' label, football centres must follow established guidelines strictly and comply with a 'charter for quality', which includes a child protection policy, screening of staff, grievance procedure and periodic inspections. In Belgium, a project entitled 'Instrument for quality evaluation of gymnastics clubs' was launched in 1998 and a catalogue published, which provides parents with guidance and information on the quality of existing programmes (Van Hoecke and De Knop 1998).

No country has legislation that sets, for all sports, a minimum age to join special schools or sport centres. The only notable exception is France, which in 2001 set at 14 years the minimum age for joining an official sport centre (Government of France 2001: article 1). But the question remains of how this law is enforced in the case of French gymnasts who do join these centres before they are 14.

Some experts consider that no child should join a full-time sport centre before finishing compulsory education (i.e., generally between 12 and 16 years old) and preferably not before the age of 14 (Meier 1997: 284), which is in line with the Convention's recommendations. But some children are extremely young when they enter these structures: Chinese diver Fu Mingxia joined the national sport institute in Beijing when she was six. In 1992, at a press conference after winning the Olympic gold medal at the age of 12, she explained that she had only seen her parents half a dozen times during the two years before the Olympic Games. When asked what sort of job her father had, she couldn't answer (*L'Equipe Magazine* 1992).

Talent spotting often starts as young as six years old. Gifted youngsters may not be sent this early to sport centres, but they are systematically monitored and evaluated and may later be encouraged to join them. In Austria, where skiing is the main national sport, gifted children are identified at the age of six and the best join sport schools at 11 or 12 years old (Terrani 1999: 19).

There are sport schools that focus on children's overall development rather than just on their athletic performance and results, but they are the exceptions. In the Swiss canton of Geneva, for example, a specialized education system for elite athletes was set up in 1981 and has since been duplicated in many other Swiss cantons (see also Chapter 19). This system, which is aimed as much at elite athletes as at ballet dancers, gives equal importance to sport and education and both parents and trainers are requested to sign a charter that engages them to respect the fact that 'extra-curricular activities justifying the inscription of the child in the programme in a specialized school cannot undermine the quality of education, nor the physical integrity and the health of students (article 6)' (Meier 1997: 282). Under this programme, established in co-operation with the regular public education system, the physical and psychological well-being of the young athletes is permanently monitored. Geneva's innovative model has received major attention from many European states, but it should be noted that hardly any top international athletes have emerged from this system. Successful athletes from Geneva such as tennis player Marc Rosset or footballers Johan Vogel (PSV Eindhoven) and Patrick Muller (FC Lyon and, since 2004, FC Mallorca) followed parallel systems.

In the Flemish-speaking part of Belgium, the authorities launched in 1998 the 'top sport covenant' which is an agreement between the Ministry of Education and sport federations. The two parties agreed that elite athletes could train for 12 of school's 32 hours a week. Sport federations are responsible for the training programmes, while the school curriculum remains the same as for regular schools; the difference is in the organization of time and the working methods (De Knop 1998: 79).

NEO-COLONIALISM AND THE IMPACT OF GLOBALIZATION

Since the early 1990s and as a result of globalization, many major European and North American sport clubs have bought into established clubs or moved some of their training centres to developing countries. Some critics have qualified this a neo-colonialist trend (Regalado 2000); those involved usually justify it as offering unique development tools and opportunities to children living in poverty. The truth is probably somewhere in the middle, but the abusive and exploitative trends that exist in some sport institutions in the Western world are now duplicated – and probably magnified – in Africa especially, but also in Latin America and Asia.

In Europe, Ajax Amsterdam, the Dutch football club, pioneered this new trend by buying teams in South Africa (Ajax Cape Town) and Ghana (Ashanti Goldfields SC). In these clubs, Ajax has established centres to train young players and then bring the best to Holland to play for Ajax. The club's official website (2000) explained that the idea to work with 'certain clubs and organizations on various continents in an effort to increase Ajax's talent scouting network' originated in 1997 and that, by the end of October 2000, '700 boys from Khayelitsha and 1,500 from Nyanga [South Africa] will have had trials with us – they are all 15 and younger. We know the formula: when it comes to trying out boys from townships, it works.'

Jan Pruijn, Ajax's manager for international programmes, explained how countries are chosen: 'The decisive factor when Ajax chooses to work together with a particular club or country is the talent displayed by the youngest category of players' (Ajax Amsterdam official website 2001). Critics of this policy have claimed that in reality it offers few prospects for footballers from developing countries: by 2001 only one South African player had been brought to Amsterdam in order to pursue his career (Driessen 2001).

Other European clubs have followed suit, not necessarily buying foreign teams, but establishing or financing training centres, or signing exclusive agreements with existing centres. Examples include Manchester United, which has a co-oper-ation agreement with FC Fortune in South Africa, and FC Copenhagen, which owns a 'development centre' in Port Elizabeth (South Africa). AS Monaco, a top French football club, has its own domestic training centre as well as links with Aldo-Gentina, a training centre for footballers aged 13 to 14 in Dakar (Senegal), the Abidjan (Ivory Coast) football academy and another centre in Bamako (Mali). 'Our policy is mainly based on the productivity of our own training centre and, as we need to qualify each year for the European Championships, we recruit players that can help them [the young ones] to progress,' explained Louis Campora, president of AS Monaco (Glo 2000: 50).

As Michel Platini, former French football star and now special adviser to the president of the International Football Federation (FIFA) has pointed out, some young talents may be forced to move to Europe:

> If we [FIFA] establish, for example, a training centre in Benin that trains 50 kids aged between 15 and 18, and if there are no structured clubs in the country that can integrate them once they finish their training, we have failed. We should avoid creating a modern slave system which would benefit European clubs exclusively.
>
> (Leroux 1999: 17)

Since the early 1990s, another by-product of globalization has emerged: major manufacturers of sports equipment have established training camps for distance runners in poor countries with low standards of living. For the past few years, wealthy sports shoe companies, such as Puma, Adidas and Fila, have focused much of their attention on Kenya, a country famous for its long-distance runners, and set up high-altitude training centres for gifted young Kenyan athletes. One multinational admits spending US$ 3 million to train a few dozen young runners. But Brother Colm, an Irish missionary training young Kenyan runners, has declared:

> As there is no middle class here, running is one of the few ways leading to success. But I do not want to see young runners of 14 or 15 contracted by Puma or Nike. They are not for sale. I want them to be mature enough to choose.
>
> (L'Hermitte 2000: 59)

In baseball, delocalizing training facilities pre-dates globalization. As early as 1954, the Los Angeles Dodgers began a 'farm system' by establishing a sister team in the Dominican Republic (Regalado 2000: 16). In the past 30 years, baseball teams from the United States and Canada have established training centres, mainly in the Dominican Republic, but also in Mexico, Puerto Rico and Venezuela (Vargas 2000: 28). These 'farms' have set up 'academies', which iden-tify and recruit local talents in order to train them to become professional players in the US. Despite promises and commitments made when joining the centres, a large majority of youngsters do not make it to the promised land and the contracts offered to those who do have frequently been qualified as 'exploitative' (Regalado 2000: 11). One of the first Americans to scout young talented players aged between 12 and 18, Branch Rickey, introduced into Latin America the non-binding agreement, which he called 'desk contracts'. Rickey taught his scouts the art of 'signing thousands of amateurs on a purely tentative basis', using the 'quality out of quantity' principle; players could be sent to the US and 'released a few weeks later without money for transportation home' (Kerrane 1989: 27) (see also Chapter 13).

American baseball academies established in Latin American countries have often been described as a system mainly motivated by access to cheap labour (Marcano and Fidler 2003: 45). According to Angel Vargas, president of the Venezuelan Baseball Players Association and secretary general of the Caribbean Baseball Players Confederation, 'The appetite of powerful [American] Major League Baseball teams for Latino talent combined with the vulnerability of children and their parents in these countries is a recipe for exploitation' (Vargas 2000: 24).

For some experts, these baseball training centres function in the same way as major American companies, such as the United Fruit Company, did during the 1880–1930 colonial era in the region (Regalado 2000: 10). Professional American baseball teams still 'maintain the "boatload mentality" and see Latino children and young men as commodities – a boatload of cheap Dominicans, as if these human beings were pieces of exported fruit' (Vargas 2000: 27). Former American player at the Colorado Rockies, Dick Balderson, explained that the 'boatload mentality means that instead of signing four American guys at US$ 25,000 each, you sign 20 Dominicans for US$ 5,000 each' (Breton and Villegas 1999: 244).

During the 1980s, some baseball academies established in Latin America 'proved to be holding centres in which clubs could protect their investments … there existed cases where scouts virtually kidnapped players to prevent interlopers from interfering with their catches' (Regalado 2000: 18). And Papi Bisono, a former Dominican baseball commissioner, claimed that the academies were like 'hideouts because the scouts didn't want their kids seen by other scouts. It almost seemed like they were concentration camps' (Klein 1991: 54).

But the lower cost of forming champions in Latin America is not the only reason that motivates the existence of these academies. Another reason is the restricted number of visas available to Major League Baseball (MLB) teams from the US government for foreign players – 26 visas a year for each team. According to Vargas (2000: 29):

> MLB teams do not have enough visas to send all Latino players to the United States of America, so academies hoard the promising players by keeping them from other teams that might like to sign them. The visa bottleneck created by the US Government has driven development of the baseball academies.

A more subtle reason motivating MLB teams to maintain academies outside of the US is the aim of making baseball a universal sport and increasing revenues abroad (Marcano and Fidler 2003: 12). MLB teams collectively own broadcasting rights and those on all official MLB products that are merchandized in and outside the US. By increasing the number of foreign players in American teams, the interest in baseball in the countries of origin of these players (such as the Dominican Republic, Mexico, Japan, South Korea and Venezuela) has grown rapidly. When South Korean Chan Ho Park pitched for the Los Angeles Dodgers in 1997, for example, all his games were shown live in South Korea. A year later over 100 games were broadcast in the country (Marcano and Fidler 1999: 524). This expansion strategy fuels the baseball academies with talented children who are often desperate to turn their back on poverty.

MLB is not the only organization working to globalize its sport and brand. The American National Basketball Association (NBA), National Hockey League (NHL – ice hockey) and National Football League (NFL – American football) use similar strategies. Although the NBA and NHL scout talents abroad, however, their 'farming' systems are not so developed as those of the MLB. Ensuring a global impact also motivated the historical marketing deal in 2001 between two of the most powerful sports teams in the world, the New York Yankees (baseball) and Manchester United (football).

In 1984 the MLB fixed 17 as the minimum age limit for signing professional contracts. But it has set no age limit for joining a Latin American baseball academy and MLB clubs can freely recruit children aged between 12 and 16 for their teams' academies. According to Vargas (2000: 29), 'in many Dominican and Venezuelan academies, the persons responsible do not treat the players according to their ages. This means that 13 and 14-year olds are expected to complete workouts designed for players 17 years and older' – proof once again that 'Latino boys are regarded as cheap commodities'.

American baseball teams invest much more in their development programmes at home than abroad, even if compared using the same costs of living. Although these figures are extremely difficult to obtain from professional teams, it was estimated in 1981 that the Philadelphia Phillies' funding for their development programme in the US amounted to US$ 335,000 compared to US$ 25,000 for Latin American recruits (Kerrane 1989: 311). In 1987, the Los Angeles Dodgers' training centre in the Dominican Republic cost hardly anything to set up. Rafael Avila, the Dodgers' leading scout, said:

> It was a hill! There were cows and horses all over the place. It looked like a jungle … If you realize that we spent approximately $400,000 for the land, the construction of the entire camp, baseball fields, levelling of the hill, equipment, the bus, you see how far money goes, and what a good deal it was for the Dodgers. Imagine what that would cost in the United States.
>
> (Klein 1991: 64)

At the same time, MLB teams generate immense revenues every year; in 1998 they were estimated to range from the Montreal Expos' US$ 35 million to the New York Yankees' US$ 170 million (Marcano and Fidler 1999: 515). The same teams that invest as little as possible in their academies abroad do not hesitate to contract superstars for huge amounts of money: the Texas Rangers paid US$ 252 million to sign Alex Rodriguez for ten years in 2000.

According to Vargas, not only is education systematically neglected in these baseball academies, but nutrition is poor and medical treatment is minimal: 'Often, injured players are immediately released, and MLB teams try to avoid paying for medical costs that the player incurs treating the injury.' This is despite the fact that young players training hard need proper food and medical attention and that MLB rule 56(g)5(f) requires Major League clubs to 'provide qualified medical trainers or personnel to their minor league teams' (Vargas 2000: 30).

State authorities are often negligent in monitoring these types of institutions for children. In the Dominican Republic, a law regulating baseball academies was enacted in 1985 but only after abuses had been repeatedly reported, and it has not been vigorously enforced (Government of the Dominican Republic 1985).

It should nevertheless be acknowledged that not all Latin American baseball academies are abusive and exploitative. Standards of living are very low, especially in the Dominican Republic, and some children can benefit enormously from life in academies even if their chances of succeeding in baseball are not great. They do give most young players basic necessities that they may not get outside: food, shelter, basic education and medical service. But the fact that the academies' owners come from a much richer country than the Latin American nations in which they have established their institutions should not prevent both parties from respecting the Convention's minimum standards, just as multinational companies cannot justify slavery, abuse or exploitation in the factories they establish in developing countries simply because of the latter's weak economic development.

MLB authorities in the US admitted: 'We are aware of the problems, and we are working on them' (Vargas 2000: 34) and, at the end of 2000, they opened an office from which a new administrator for Latin America would oversee MLB operations. Breton and Villegas (1999) ask the fundamental question about discrimination: 'Would it be tolerated if underprivileged Americans were treated by major league baseball the way Latinos are?'

THE AMERICAN MODEL

Specific sport centres for young athletes in the United States exist but remain the exception. These privately managed centres, where annual fees can be a huge burden for parents (see Chapter 17), specialize in sports, such as gymnastics, tennis and figure skating, in which children start intensive training very young. Sports training in the US, as well as in Canada and Japan, is usually mainstreamed in the regular educational system, and becomes serious when children enter high school, usually at the age of 14. Gifted youngsters are trained through interscholastic sports and not in community-based clubs as is the case in Europe and Latin America (though community-based clubs are becoming increasingly popular in the US). Students aged 17 to 18 leave high school to join colleges, where interscholastic sports are often extremely important: some colleges spend US\$ 100,000 a year on sports, others US\$ 30 million.

In theory, this model allows elite athletes to evolve in an environment that reconciles the demands of competitive sports with those of academic achievement. While athletes studying in high schools and colleges are not necessarily under-achievers, they often struggle to manage both activities (Coakley 1998: 452–5) (see Chapter 14). Nowadays, intercollegiate sport is so commercialized that the educational value of sport programmes has faded. Shareef Abdur-Rahim, who left the University of California in 1996 to play in the NBA, explained: 'The reality is, you're going to miss classes, you're going to be behind in your schoolwork. You get caught up in taking finals on the road, taking them late, getting to class late' (*USA Today* 1996).

High-school and college sport programmes have attracted powerful media and business interests, including the sports good industry. College sports are now organized along the lines of professional sports, with well-prepared athletes, wide television coverage, full stadiums and corporate support. The paradox is that athletes are not entitled to any reward and are still considered amateurs (Byers and Hammer 1995). However, athletes may still 'gain' from their performances as the best are often offered attractive college scholarships and may be contracted by corporate sponsors or drafted by major professional teams. Professional basketball teams have been drafting ever-younger players since the 1990s. Between 1948 and 1995, only three players were drafted directly out of high school. Between 1995 and 2000, 11 high-school players received a contract with an NBA team (Wetzel and Yaleger 2000: 36).

Over the years, sport programmes have developed into a major feature of the US educational system. Some high schools and colleges have invested heavily in developing their sports programmes with the hope of achieving results and gaining visibility which helps to attract students. For example, Virginia's tiny and isolated Oak Hill Academy gained a national reputation and major financial support thanks to its successful basketball programme (Wetzel and Yaleger 2000: 114).

In many high schools and colleges, sport programmes have an independent budget, with much of the money coming from gate receipts, corporate support, television rights and donations from clubs. 'Big-Time Intercollegiate Sports' is the name given to schools that have a national profile and make substantial profits. It is an industry full of contradictions. On the one hand, it promotes amateur sports within a regular education system; on the other, it involves major financial interests and gain in a non-profit sector (education). In these programmes, the quest for victory needs to be reconciled with academic development; major financial interests with equality of access to education; corporative and media priorities with educational ethics and rules. American sociologist Jay Coakley (1998: 455) noted that:

Some athletes on those teams may be in school only to get the coaching they need to stay in amateur Olympic sports (such as swimming, track and field, volleyball, wrestling and rowing), or only to become draft prospects in professional sports (such as baseball, basketball, American football, and ice hockey). Coaches for those teams may view sports as businesses, and they may be hired and fired on the basis of how much revenue they can attract to the athletic programme. Even academic administrators, including college presidents, may use the programmes for public relations or fund-raising tools instead of focusing on them as programmes that should be educational in themselves.

American law professor Timothy Davies considered that two models compete in intercollegiate sports: 'the amateur/education model' and 'the commercial/education model'. Under the first model, 'the student athlete is viewed as an amateur, and college athletics is considered an integral part of the educational purpose of universities' (Davies 1994). This model is fully in line with articles 2 and 2.7 of the oft-debated and severely criticized National Collegiate Athletic Association (NCAA) Constitution which states: 'Student-athletes shall be amateurs in an intercollegiate sport … Student participation in intercollegiate athletics is an avocation, and student-athletes should be protected from exploitation by professional and commercial enterprises.' But, as Davies noted, 'this ideal [is] all but unobtainable' and is 'illusory and out of step with the contemporary realities of college athletics' which can generate millions of dollars a year through corporate sponsorship, gate revenues, licensing merchandise and television rights. The 'commercial/education model' is one where 'economics displaces the principle of amateurism as the controlling force in college sports'. The 'commercialism and the concomitant pressure to win results' compromises 'the educational value … and represents the ever-present tension between commercial and academic interests in college sports' (Davies 1994).

Big-Time Intercollegiate Sports attracts major sponsors as it is an efficient channel for corporations to reach young people and market their products. In basketball, for example, shoe manufacturers fight to sign deals with successful high-school teams to ensure that they wear their brands. Some education experts seriously question these practices that create inequality between schools that profit and those that do not. Others also argue that powerful sponsorship within the education system might also influence and shape the minds of students. Alex Molnar, an expert in the subject of corporate sponsorship of public education, noted that:

A lot of attention has been paid to these schools that sell advertising space to soft drink companies or accept computers for grocery receipts. But no one seems to be asking these questions about schools renting space on the bodies of their students for advertising purposes. In many ways, these apparel/shoe deals are much worse than what is happening with soft drink companies because they don't get a spot on the jersey worn by football or basketball team.

(Wetzel and Yaleger 2000: 240–1)

In 1996, for example, a multinational shoe manufacturer entered into a contract with the University of Wisconsin-Madison for a reported US$ 9.1 million, which included marketing rights to clothing designed like the university's athletic wear. But it also included a written clause that declared it a violation of the contract for anyone at the university to 'disparage' the sponsor's brand name. This happened at a time when major sporting goods manufacturers were publicly accused by independent groups of exploiting cheap labour in their factories based in developing countries. When the university administrators realized the significance of this clause, they successfully pressured the sponsor to drop it (Wetzel and Yaleger 2000: 246–7).

13 Play the market

Trafficking and sale of young athletes

> I thought that these cases of false passports were isolated but I was wrong ... the neo-colonialist practices of some people when it comes to transferring young players are inadmissible ... a new type of slavery ... we must protect young players and protect the clubs in which these young players develop.
>
> (Joseph Blatter, FIFA's president, in *L'Equipe* 2001 and Reuters 2001)

> We must not let young athletes lose their freedom and become dependent on agents who determine where, and against whom, they should compete.
>
> (Juan Antonio Samaranch, former IOC president, in IOC 2001: 5)

The trafficking and sale of human beings is a modern form of slavery that is practised all over the world. Different types of trafficking exist. While most cases relate to activities such as debt bondage, forced prostitution and pornography, or exploitation of migrant workers, others – for example, forced marriages, sale of wives and illegal inter-country adoptions – are also considered contemporary slavery (UN Commission on Human Rights 2000a).

Due to its illegal nature, it is by definition difficult to assess the number of human beings trafficked and sold every year. But the UN Office for Drug Control and Crime Prevention (UNDCCP) considered in 2000 that 4 million people are smuggled every year, which led Pino Arlachi, UNDCCP director at the time, to declare that it 'is the fastest-growing form of organized crime. Trafficking in human beings is one of the most globalized markets in the world today. Almost no country is immune from it.' Interpol considers that the criminals behind human trafficking make US\$ 9 billion a year (Reuters 2000a).

The phenomenon of trafficking and sale has not spared the world of sports, where it mainly takes the form of adolescent athletes trafficked and sold in the context of transboundary, illegal transfers between clubs. Unscrupulous intermediaries acting clandestinely usually handle these transfers.

Since the early twentieth century, international law has banned trafficking in human beings. The first instrument to do so was the 1910 International Convention on the Suppression of the White Slave Traffic, followed in 1949 by the Convention for the Suppression of the Traffic in Persons and of the

Exploitation of the Prostitution of Others. More recent human rights treaties have also included provisions outlawing this practice: the Convention on the Elimination of All Forms of Discrimination against Women (1979); the Convention on the Rights of the Child (1989); and the International Convention on the Protection of the Rights of All Migrant Workers and Members of their Families (1990).

In recent years, the phenomenon has undoubtedly increased due to the effects of globalization and the weakening of the concept of national borders. The international community has, therefore, adopted additional treaties with a specific focus on the trafficking and sale of children: the Optional Protocol to the Convention on the Rights of the Child on Sale of Children, Child Prostitution and Child Pornography (2000), ILO Convention No. 182 on the worst forms of child labour (1999) and the Optional Protocol to the Convention against Transnational Organized Crime (2000).

Although no international treaty explicitly defines trafficking and sale of children in the framework of sports, existing definitions nevertheless do apply directly to these types of crimes. Article 35 of the Convention on the Rights of the Child requires that, 'States Parties shall take all appropriate national, bilateral and multilateral measures to prevent the abduction of, the sale or traffic in children *for any purpose or in any form*' (emphasis added). Its Optional Protocol on Sale of Children, Child Prostitution and Child Pornography states that: 'Sale of children means *any* act or transaction whereby a child is transferred by any person or group of persons to another for remuneration or any other consideration' (article 2.a, emphasis added). ILO Convention No. 182 considers the worst forms of child labour comprises 'all forms of slavery or practices similar to slavery, such as the sale of children and trafficking of children ...' (article 3.a).

Finally, the most complete definition of trafficking is to be found in the Optional Protocol to prevent, suppress and punish trafficking in persons, especially women and children, supplementing the UN Convention against Transnational Organized Crime. Articles 3.a and 3.c of this Convention, which is not strictly speaking a human rights treaty but which focuses on crime prevention, state that:

> 'Trafficking in persons' shall mean the recruitment, transportation, transfer, harbouring or receipt of persons, by means of the threat or use of force or other forms of coercion, of abduction, of fraud, of deception, of the abuse of power or of a position of vulnerability or of the giving and receiving of payments or benefits to achieve the consent of a person having control over another person, for the purpose of exploitation. Exploitation shall include, *at a minimum*, the exploitation of the prostitution of others or other forms of sexual exploitation, forced labour or services, slavery or practices similar to slavery, servitude or the removal of organs ... The recruitment, transportation, transfer, harbouring or receipt of a child for the purpose of exploitation shall be considered 'trafficking in persons' *even if this does not involve any means set forth in subparagraph (a) of this article.* [emphases added]

Probably due to lack of awareness, the Committee on the Rights of the Child has not yet addressed the issue of trafficking of young athletes (with one notable exception: child jockeys). The only country that has so far objected to consider that 'sale of children' can apply to athletes is the United States, as its government stated during a UN General Assembly meeting that they were afraid that criminalizing the 'sale of children for any purpose' could prevent bartering in the sports industry for athletes under 18 (*On the record for children* 2002).

As is the case for most types of slavery, the sale and trafficking of athletes mainly occurs in situations of economic exploitation where those with an advantage – often economic – over others use their power to impose unfair practices. In sports, as in other domains, financial power is concentrated in the hands of North Americans and Western Europeans. Talented athletes from all over the world dream of joining a European or an American team in order to improve their economic situation. Globalization has accelerated this trend and most professional sports leagues and federations now include athletes from other regions of the world. The 'global village' has given rich sport teams an almost inexhaustible source of talented and cheap labour, especially from Africa and Latin America.

One feature common to all forms of sale and trafficking is that the individuals caught in the tentacles of criminals are perceived and treated as disposable commodities, with no rights at all. Their value is regulated by the crude law of supply and demand, as well as – in most cases – by their capacity for work. In sports, trafficking and sale is to be found mainly in football and baseball, but is probably also present in other sports such as basketball and ice hockey. Africa and Latin America, and to a lesser extent Eastern Europe, are the areas most affected.

When children are trafficked for prostitution or adoption, there is no sentiment of passion or pleasure for the victim. But when children are sold to rich football or baseball teams, their passion for the sport is at the origin of the criminal activity. Unscrupulous traders often rely on the fact that young athletes and their families are desperate to join a major sports team and have a lucrative career in the industrialized world, which complicates the prevention of trafficking and sale in sports.

As in most types of criminal activity, rapid financial profit is the main, if not the only, motive for the traffic in athletes. An intermediary agent or a team can increase its 'investment' in a young footballer a hundred or even a thousand times. Some agents succeed in keeping their rights over young players until they are recruited by major football teams. A child bought in Africa for a few thousand dollars might one day be transferred to a wealthy club for several million dollars. And the law of silence prevails: no one will denounce the fact that a child athlete was trafficked illegally if he or she becomes a sports star.

The first serious allegations of systematic trafficking of children in sports date from the early 1990s. Evaluating the number of victims of this type of traffic is not easy, not only because statistics are always difficult to collect in illegal and clandestine activities, but also due to the insufficient interest and awareness of public authorities and even non-governmental organizations (NGOs). Nevertheless, a conservative estimate is that at least a few hundred children are trafficked each year; some would suggest a few thousand youngsters a year.

One of the first official institutions to denounce the sale and trafficking of football players was the Belgian government's *Centre pour l'égalité des chances et la lutte contre le racisme* (Centre for equality of chances and for combating racism). In its 1998 annual report on human trade, the centre revealed the difficult situation of young footballers who were brought to Belgium illegally from Latin America and Africa to be tested in football clubs. According to the report, only a minority succeeded in signing a contract with a professional club, albeit for a very low salary and a short period of time. The majority were unable to find an employer and remained in Belgium illegally, often not even having enough money to fly back home.

Ofelia Calcetas-Santos, the UN Special Rapporteur on the sale of children, child prostitution and child pornography, denounced the trade in footballers in 1999. Her report to the UN Commission on Human Rights was the first time that the issue was brought up in an international political forum. It attracted a little media attention, but was ignored by state delegations. A year later, she again denounced the practice in her mission report (2000b: paras 14–16) to Belgium and the Netherlands:

> There are allegations that unofficial talent scouts and recruiters bring talented boy players from countries in Africa, notably Nigeria, as it is considered to be cheaper to recruit amateur players from a developing country than to train local players ... Once in Belgium, the boys are taken from one football club to another. The recruiter presumably makes a considerable profit if the boys are taken on by a club. If the boys are unsuccessful, they are usually abandoned. Having come to the country illegally, few legal options for their future in Belgium are then available to them ...

NEW SLAVE TRADE

During the late 1990s, allegations of the trafficking of young football players multiplied in media reports and in information from NGOs. Publicly, sport authorities remained very discreet about the issue although they were aware of the seriousness of the problem and the risk of a backlash on the success of football. In France, the Minister for Sports and Youth, Marie-Georges Buffet, alarmed by several reports on the number of adolescent footballers with no residence permits in French football training centres, ordered an administrative inquiry into the problem in 1999. The confidential report of the inquiry, which was made public after having been leaked to the media, revealed appalling shortcomings: structural dysfunction, illegal recruitment and, in some cases, a dire education system. The report denounced the fact that many unofficial training centres have emerged and that they 'are not the object of any adapted regulations nor effective controls'. Clubs 'test (without contract or licence) up to ten foreign players to recruit only one', it said, but 'nobody can provide reliable data on the whereabouts of tested players who have not been retained ... they enter the typically inhuman and sordid field of clandestine migration' (Government of France 1999).

During the 1998–9 football season, 58 young African players came to France, many of whom were under 15 years old. One year later, 108 non-European players migrated to France, among them 96 Africans. During the same period, strong evidence emerged that in Italy too, African and Latin American children were being brought into the country illegally by professional football clubs (Tshimanga Bakadiababu 2001: 295–6). An inquiry carried out by the Senate's Commission for Children revealed that 5,282 licensed players under 16 in Italy came from countries other than the European Union (EU), mainly from Africa, and that only 23 had their contract properly registered. Most of them were brought to Italy illegally (Bianchi and Curro 1999).

In 2000, many key actors finally began to acknowledge the problem of the 'new slave trade' (Sopel 2000). The African Cup of Nations, held in January 2000, helped attract the attention of both the media and the general public to the issue. John Fashanu, who was a football star in England before becoming Nigeria's ambassador for sport, strongly condemned the practice of importing young African footballers to Europe:

> Many of them are not really good enough so they find themselves as nothings still hoping to become professional footballers but never getting there … Instead they can find themselves in Israel or Russia cleaning cars or restaurants, with barely enough money to get back to their country of origin.
>
> (Stocks 2000)

A Belgian parliamentary committee investigating the trafficking of Brazilian players to Belgium considered that in the space of a few years, over 5,000 underaged footballers had flocked to Europe (Associated Press 2001). Pelé, one of the greatest football players ever, strongly denounced the new slave trade:

> In Brazil, Argentina and in Africa it is most dangerous. It is like with slave ownership. They go to parents to get the consent to bring 16- and 17-year olds to Europe and if the kids don't have instant success, they don't want to know and drop them. It is really high time to think seriously about these things.
>
> (Reuters 2000)

Since the landmark Bosman case in 1995, in which the European Court of Justice condemned FIFA for not respecting the freedom of movement of professional football players within the European Community, tension has been increasing between the European Commission and FIFA. In 2000, FIFA came under strong pressure from the Commission to modify its rules regulating the transfer of players between clubs, as a number of them were not compatible with European Community law, in particular those concerning the fact that players who wish (or are obliged) to transfer from one club to another usually have to pay financial compensation to the club with whom they are contracted. Such payments are not stipulated in their contracts nor are they in accordance with most domestic legislation, yet they are enforced even when the players have ended their term of contract.

At one point in the negotiations, FIFA proposed to ban all international transfers for players under 18. But the European Commission refused; the Commissioner for Education, Culture and Sports, Viviane Reding, explained that, even though she adhered to the idea behind the proposition – to protect young people – they cannot be protected by being unable 'to enjoy a fundamental Community right, that of freedom of movement' (Potet 2000a).

In March 2001, after several unproductive meetings, the Commission and FIFA finally agreed that 11 principles would be included in the new FIFA Regulations on the international transfer of players. Principles 1 and 2 concern respectively the protection of minors and compensation for clubs that invest in training young players:

1   In order to provide a stable environment for the training and education of players, international transfers or first registration of players under the age of 18 shall be permitted subject to the following conditions: a) the family of the player moves for reasons not related to football into the country of the new training club, or within the territory of the EU/EFTA (European Free Trade Association) and b) in the case of players between the minimum working age in the country of the new training club and 18 suitable arrangements are guaranteed for their sporting training and academic education by the new training club. For this purpose a code of conduct will be established by the football authorities.

2   In order to promote talent and stimulate competition in football it is recognised that clubs should have the necessary financial and sporting incentives to invest in training and educating young players. It is further recognised that all clubs which are involved in the training and education process should be rewarded for their contribution ...

(FIFA 2001)

In July 2001, FIFA amended its regulations concerning the status and transfer of players to reflect the principles adopted in March of that year. These new regulations might prove difficult to enforce properly and time will show whether they help to prevent and combat trafficking and sale. Much effort, political will and financial investment will be required to monitor clandestine moves of young players from outside Europe to the EU countries.

Article 12.1a of FIFA's new regulations states that only players having reached the 'minimum working age in the country of the new training club' may be transferred to that country. This provision has two main implications: one is that the players' status as workers is implicitly recognized; and the other is that the EU and FIFA have agreed that a minimum age should be established for international transfers, and that this age should refer to existing domestic laws. The 15 EU countries have set the minimum age for access to employment at between 15 and 16 years. Nevertheless, all these countries permit younger persons (usually aged between 13 and 14) to engage in 'light work'; but the EU and FIFA fail to indicate whether the minimum age referred to is the one concerning light work or that of access to employment. Nor do the new regulations specify how it will be possible to prevent young talents (and their legal guardians) from signing pre-contracts at the age of 15 that legally commit them to signing an 'official' contract with a club once they are old enough.

FIFA's regulations also state that 'suitable arrangements are guaranteed for their [the minor football players'] sporting training and academic education by the new training club' (FIFA 2001: article 12.1b). Experience shows that academic education is too often neglected by training clubs due to lack of time, interest, competence and finance (see Chapter 14). Enforcing such a generous principle will require very serious consideration and financial investment by sporting authorities.

THE BASEBALL MARKET

For almost 30 years, young baseball players have been traded between Latin America and North America, mainly the United States (see also Chapter 12). The neo-colonialist attitude did not escape baseball experts: Klein (1991: 42) argued that scouts in the Dominican Republic 'were reminiscent of those of the West African slave trade of three centuries earlier'; Breton and Villegas (1999: 83) noted that 'Almost all the nations and territories producing Latin American players today have been invaded by US troops in the last century' and that 'if it wasn't American troops, it was American businesses that organized the sport. In Venezuela, US oil interests helped popularize the game, and even today the United States muddle infielders and petroleum.'

According to Breton and Villegas (1999: 83), between 500 and 700 young Latin American baseball players are brought to the United States every year, usually when they reach the age of 17 or 18 but sometimes earlier, despite the fact that the minimum age set by the MLB (Major League Baseball) for such transactions is 17. Most of them will not make it either in the MLB or in minor leagues and will remain in the US with few qualifications and no legal resident permit. Felipe Alou, a former baseball star in the 1950s, asked, 'Why does this happen? Because of our Latin American roots ... Baseball is a 100 percent capitalist business, and as with all business, when there is room for exploitation there will be exploitation' (Breton and Villegas 1999: 48). Former Oakland Athletics general manager, Sandy Alderson, once admitted that the Latin American baseball market 'is favourable to entrepreneurs' (Breton and Villegas 1999: 36).

There is extremely little awareness and interest among the public and the media about the trafficking and sale of Latino baseball players to US teams. In November 1999, however, an incident retained public attention when it was revealed that the Los Angeles Dodgers signed a 14-year-old Dominican player,

Adrian Beltre, in a clear violation of the MLB rule, which set the age of 17 for all transactions (Associated Press 1999e). In their defence, the club's officials explained that other US baseball teams routinely violated this rule and that at least 50 under-aged players had been contracted illegally, not counting those playing in minor leagues (Vargas 2000: 26). The MLB commissioner fined the team US$ 50,000 and ordered it to close temporarily Dodgerstown, their training centre in the Dominican Republic (Associated Press 1999d).

UNSCRUPULOUS INTERMEDIARIES AND ILLEGAL MEANS

In sports, the trafficking and sale of adolescents usually relies on unscrupulous intermediaries attracted to this sort of 'get-rich-quick' activity. Obviously, not all sport agents, intermediaries or scouts are involved in illegal transactions and most respect very strict ethical and legal rules. But poverty, ignorance and corruption can engender fraud and exploitation. Competition is ferocious among the 1,000 or more licensed and non-licensed football agents to find and contract the best prospects and has led to a decrease in the age of players signing with them. 'In Germany, you need to identify young prospects and contract them at 16 or 17 years old,' said German agent Norbert Pflippen in 1998, 'as the market is hyper-competitive with 44 [88 in 2003] official FIFA agents' (Jouhaud 1998: 6).

Recruiters need to identify potential talents before approaching them. Fred Ferreira, a former minor league baseball player, now scouting young players in the Dominican Republic, explained that he gets:

> recommendations from everywhere ... I never say no to prospects; you have to look at that kid. You can't always evaluate someone on what you see initially. Some of these kids are so poor they may not have the correct shoes on, or they may have two different sizes. You see a kid catching balls with the worst piece of leather you ever saw, but give him a nice glove – comfortable, soft – and you see a better player come along.
>
> (Daniels 2001)

Traffickers will use coercion, deceit and fraud in an attempt to convince talented athletes and their parents to try their chance in Europe or North America, which is the dream of many of them, especially in the poorest countries. A minor from Burkina Faso who ended up in France with no club interested in contracting him and no residence permit explained in a French television programme: 'We are obliged to accept whatever conditions we are offered. We come from Africa and we have nothing to offer...' (France 2 Television 2000). This dream of playing in Europe or North America, combined with inexperience, lack of education and naïvety, makes them easy targets. 'When you are a youngster in Africa you watch television and you see the beautiful football stadiums and you want to wear the football strip like the real professional players,' said Serge Nikji Bodo, who left his home in Cameroon aged 17 to go to Belgium on a tourist visa in 1996. 'All I ever wanted was to play football so when I was approached by an agent who promised me big clubs and professional status I signed a contract with him' (BBC 1999). What he did not realize was that he had signed away all his rights. He signed a contract, written in Dutch, with a third division (minor) team. He had no way of knowing that the agreement tied him to the club with no fixed wage (Henley 1998). In the end, he found himself stranded in Europe with no work and no papers.

Some recruiters do not hesitate to exploit the ignorance or illiteracy of parents and their children by making them sign contracts that are incomplete or in another language whereby they authorize their child to leave the country. Usually when American scouts recruit young Latin American baseball talents, neither the parents nor the adolescent receive a copy of the contract, which is always in English. Spanish translations are not proposed even though under the laws of many countries this is illegal (Vargas 2000: 27). As Michel Benguigui, one of France's top agents, has said: 'What child can resist a grown-up promising fame and riches?' (Sopel 2000).

In Brazil, a country that possesses an impressive reservoir of football talent, scouts scour remote areas for gifted youngsters aged between 11 and 14 to whom they offer the equivalent of US$ 10,000, an enormous amount for families living in poverty. The young footballers train in camps, often far away from their homes, set up by big professional clubs. Hardly any of them will ever qualify for professional teams or get a contract with a European team; most will drop out after two or three years with no prospects for the future.

Some very talented young Brazilians have been bought by teams for up to US$ 600,000, but they are the exceptions (Glo 2000a: 66). The price of footballers has increased constantly in the past two decades, boosted no doubt by the desire of managers and clubs to discover the new Romario, Ronaldo or Ronaldhino, Brazilian superstars who are worth tens of millions of dollars. According to the Brazilian Football Confederation (BFC), the number of young professional Brazilian players *officially* sold to European teams increased from 136 in 1990 to 733 in 2001 (Agence Télégraphique Suisse 2001; Huertas 2001). The BFC estimated that in 1999, 312 players went abroad clandestinely and without the required BFC registration (Osava 2001).

The business is so attractive in Brazil that some investors have established private training centres for footballers aged between 12 and 18 which are not affiliated to professional clubs. 'Project Soccer Brazil', for example, claims to be a 'farm system that creates elite players and conquers championships' (Soccer Brazil 2001). Pelé succeeded in 1999 in pushing a law through the Brazilian parliament that helps home clubs to keep young players, but enforcement is weak. 'That is the only way to control the market in new recruits,' he said. 'Agencies are even operating over the Internet today' (Reuters 2000).

In Africa, the business of identifying and trading young players has attracted numerous agents and investors. African Football Management (AFM) was set up in 1991 with offices in Europe and Africa to identify gifted youngsters and to facilitate their transfer to European clubs. In September 1999, Issa Hayatou, president of the Confederation of African Football (CAF), and Antonio Mataresse, at the time the Italian Football Federation's president, accused AFM of running a slave trade to exploit young players (Tshimanga Bakadiababu 2001: 123–5). AFM operates permanently in six African countries and affirms on its website (2001) that 'Young African players definitely want to leave Africa for Europe … It's not a matter of waiting, maturing, progressing. No. The password is let's go now, here we die … AFM is involved in a small part of this exodus.'

ILLEGAL WORKERS AND CLANDESTINE MIGRANTS

Of the thousands of athletes brought from poor countries to North America and Europe, a large majority will not find an acceptable arrangement with a sports club. In Europe, most African football players are 'imported' on a tourist or student visa and stay initially on a temporary basis to be 'tested' in professional football clubs. Luciano Djim, who left the Central African Republic for Belgium aged 17, explained that, 'Like many Africans, I wanted to try my chance in Europe, to make a good career, but mainly to support my family.' His manager had promised to find him a club and a school, 'but none of his promises were kept … he tried to place about 50 African players in clubs … today one is even playing in Malaysia!' Djim failed to find a team and, as he was an illegal immigrant in Belgium, he 'was afraid of being arrested at any time by the police' (*Le Soir* 2000).

In the Netherlands, an official inquiry by the National Labour Inspectorate concluded in November 1999 that eight professional football players aged under 18 years old and 18 just over that age had no legal working permit and were in violation of labour laws. Among the players under 18, two were already fairly famous, Feyenoord Rotterdam's Leonardo from Brazil and Nigerian Christopher Kanu from Ajax Amsterdam, the younger brother of top Arsenal player Nwankwo Kanu. The same inquiry revealed that 21 young foreign players had no residence permit. Half of these players did not receive the minimum wages foreseen by law (*De Telegraaf* 1999). In the United States, three young African basketball players were arrested in 1999 while playing for a New Jersey college team because they had no residence permit (ABC News 1999).

Young players living in Europe or North America have heavy responsibilities towards their families back home and are under pressure not to fail. 'Today, I am the father of my family, I have to go back with my arms full of goods,' said goalkeeper Carlos Kameni from Cameroon, who was only 16 when he and his team won the gold medal at the 2000 Sydney Olympics (Glo 2001: 46). Roger Milla, one of the most successful African football players, explained, 'A young player in Europe can send money back to his extended family. That's very important. It means far more than most Europeans can imagine' (Oliver 2000). The shame of not finding a job and being unable to support their families is also keenly felt by Latino baseball players, who usually prefer to stay clandestinely in the United States rather than go home.

The pattern repeats itself too often: young talents are illegally imported to Europe or North America and many of them end up in despair, having to live in clandestinity and sometimes forced to survive on the streets. Statistics are hard to come by, but very conservative estimates put the number of minors who stay illegally in Europe or the United States every year at a minimum of a few hundred. Marcos Breton (1997) has declared:

> Each year, hundreds of penniless, ill-educated boys from the Dominican Republic are brought to the United States by major league baseball. And each year, all but half a dozen or so end up embodying the underside of American's national pastime: living, breathing relics whose dreams of escaping poverty were turned to nightmares when baseball deemed them not talented enough, dissolved their contracts and their only means of living in the United States legally. No longer of use to win games or help train other prospects, the Dominican players are punched a one-way ticket home. But many – unwilling to face the certain shame and the certain poverty that awaits them there – sneak out of airport terminal to remain illegally in the United States.

AGENTS AND ORGANIZED CRIMINAL NETWORKS

The situation of trafficking and sale of children for competitive sports is similar in some respects to illegal adoptions. The key players in these criminal activities are usually intermediaries who are able to exploit existing poverty, ignorance, corruption and legal loopholes. Just as poor parents are approached to give up their child for adoption for a few hundred dollars, so parents of talented football players accept a handful of dollars to send their children to Europe 'to be educated for a better future'. Fraudulent or coerced consent, the promising, giving or receipt of unlawful payments or benefits to achieve consent of parents are means that are prohibited under international law, particularly the 1926 Slavery Convention which prohibits 'any or all of the powers attaching to the right of ownership' (article 2).

Many managers and agents work in total impunity, even though some are assisted by criminal networks operating in the countries in which they recruit. In April 2000, the Luxembourg police uncovered a criminal network operating between Portugal and Brazil that sold stolen passports. When the passport of Leonardo, a Brazilian aged 17 at the time, was investigated by Rotterdam's public prosecutor, it was found that he was working on a false Portuguese passport to evade immigration restrictions (International Organization for Migration 2001: 188).

FIFA does try to control and regulate the activity of football managers through its Players' Agents Regulations. Licences are only issued to managers who have passed a written examination and have either taken out a professional liability insurance or have deposited a guarantee of 100,000 Swiss francs (US$ 80,000) in a Swiss bank (articles 6 and 7). Licensed players' agents also commit themselves to respect the Code of Professional Conduct (article 8). Article 2 of the regulations state that 'Players and clubs are forbidden from using the services of a non-licensed players' agent', even though article 3 stipulates that an agent does not require a FIFA licence if 'the agent acting on behalf of the player or club is legally authorised to practise as a lawyer in compliance with the rules in force in his country of domicile' (FIFA 2002a). In practice hundreds of non-licensed managers are working all over the world and FIFA remains powerless. 'If non-licensed agents take part in transactions of players without causing any problems, our organisation does not get involved. We only intervene upon denunciation,' explained FIFA spokesperson Andreas Herren (Rodrik 1999: 13).

Only article 12.12 of the Players' Agents Regulations refers to minors: 'Minors may not sign a representation contract without the express permission of their legal guardian(s) in compliance with national law of the country in which the player is domiciled.' The provision is relatively weak as it does not define the age of 'minors', which can vary from one country to another, and refers only to national law for the 'express permission of their legal guardian(s)' which in some countries might lead to weak protection. In addition, the rules do not subject the manager or agent to any obligation with regard to the transaction process and the follow-up of any international transfer involving minors. Many countries have no specific domestic legislation adequately covering the rights and obligations of agents and, therefore, any reference in this field to national law remains theoretical and inadequate. The Code of Professional Conduct annexed to the Players' Agents Regulations is also weak, especially with regard to the respect of human rights which are not reflected in the document.

At present, there are 26 players' agents in Africa compared with more than 1,000 in Western Europe. African football officials often accuse FIFA of excluding them; professional liability insurance is expensive and the deposit required in the absence of insurance is excessively high by African standards. So, around the world, but especially in Africa and Latin America, hundreds of unofficial agents work in parallel with the official system. Some simply use the services of a lawyer to sign all official documents.

In this jungle, the rights of minors are not properly addressed and protected. Young players may end up living in complete illegality on the margins of Western society, with no risk to the agents. The agents themselves admit that not all of their ilk are trustworthy. Belgian agent Louis de Vries, who was accused in 1999 of trafficking young players from Africa but who claimed his innocence, admitted the existence of a serious problem: 'There is a genuine trade in human flesh going on, and everyone knows which agents are guilty' (Henley 1998).

The French governmental inquiry (1999a: 11) on the recruitment of young non-European players severely criticized football agents and considered that FIFA's safeguards 'appear to be relatively inefficient'. The report maintained that frequently 'clubs deal (directly or indirectly) with unlicensed FIFA "agents" … intermediaries build up a relationship with parents or legal guardians which is often occult and exorbitant (in this respect, the assimilation to slavery is not unjust)'.

In the Americas, the work of baseball agents also remains largely unregulated. Angel Vargas (2000: 25), president of the Venezuelan Baseball Players Association and general secretary of the Caribbean Baseball Players

Confederation, declared: 'The greatest legal concern about how Latino children are contacted is that actions of scouts, *buscones*, and agents are unregulated in the two biggest markets: Venezuela and the Dominican Republic.'

Financial agreements vary enormously and usually depend on the agent's approach and the status of the player. The more vulnerable a player is, the weaker his chances are of signing a fair deal. Some agents receive between 3 to 10 per cent of the transaction cost and may keep some rights over the player; others receive between 5 to 10 per cent of all gains made over a period of time. But when it comes to non-European players involved in illegal transfers, contracts often contain unjust clauses that have not been negotiated openly, such as the payment of 50 per cent of their earnings or the retrocession of all their rights to the agent for several years. Young African and Latin American players and their parents may be hardly involved at all in establishing contractual rights, except when it comes to signing on the dotted line (*Centre pour l'égalité des chances et la lutte contre le racisme* 1998: 48).

In January 2001, the Dutch Ministry of Justice launched an inquiry into the trafficking and sale of young football players from Africa and Latin America (*De Telegraaf* 2001). A few months earlier, 24 Brazilian football players, aged 17 and older, had been arrested in Aruba, a self-governing Dutch territory in the Caribbean, on their way to the Netherlands for trials with football clubs (Schoorl 2001).

The following month, the Dutch media revealed that young footballers were being recruited from centres for asylum seekers (Schoorl and Wagendorp 2001; Weidemann 2001). Club managers now regularly visit refugee centres to scout for new talent among young asylum seekers. Professional teams have recruited and contracted them, even though the Dutch authorities may not grant them asylum and may decide to send them back to their home countries at any moment. Asylum-seeking and refugee children are in a particularly precarious position and need to receive special protection. Article 22 of the Convention on the Rights of the Child states that:

> States Parties shall take appropriate measures to ensure that a child who is seeking refugee status ... whether unaccompanied or accompanied by his or her parents or by any other person, shall receive *appropriate protection and humanitarian assistance in the enjoyment of applicable rights* set forth in the present Convention and in other international human rights or humanitarian instruments to which the States are Parties. [emphasis added]

In the junior teams of Heerenveen, another top Dutch club which participated in the 2000–1 Champions League, 13 per cent of players in 2001 were asylum seekers (Weidemann 2001). Alain Kabiba Fundi Memba, a 14-year-old asylum seeker from the Democratic Republic of the Congo, is considered one of the club's most promising young players. Many other Dutch teams have also recruited asylum seekers: Feyenoord, Ajax Amsterdam, De Graafschap, Fortuna Sittard and PSV. Professor van Kalmthout, a Dutch criminal law specialist, declared: 'Whether you transport a Brazilian football player or a Chinese cook, it is the same. As if in sports it is not all about financial profit and the traffickers were not exploiting the young boys' (Schoorl 2001).

THE TRANSFER MARKET AND ITS IMPACT ON CHILDREN

Obviously, all transfers of athletes from one club to another do not result from an illegal human trade. However, they do concern very young athletes and may be based on abusive behaviour, such as excessive pressure to sign or false promises.

In theory, young athletes may wish to change clubs for a number of reasons. They may want to join friends in another club or play in a more competitive and better structured club, or their parents may relocate to another area. But since the 1970s, the transfer of young talented athletes has moved away from the individual to the club and the transfer system's rationale is no longer motivated by the best interests of the child, but is geared to the cut-throat competition that exists between clubs. The entry into the commercial world of sports takes place at an ever-younger age for gifted children. In no other official activity do children work professionally at such a young age.

Transfer for financial compensation – for either the club or the athlete – is limited in most Western European countries to athletes aged 14 to 16 or over, according to sport association rules. But since the 1980s, federations have found it more and more difficult to enforce these rules. Children as young as 12 have been involved in deals whereby clubs offer them contracts in which the rights on the player's first contract are reserved for the club; the athlete is then under the contractual obligation to sign a 'real' contract as soon as the minimum age required is reached.

In the United States, the MLB opened a scouting bureau in 1974 to assist professional teams to identify and contract young prospects. The bureau employs 34 full-time and 13 part-time scouts across the country to search for young talents. What is the advantage for teams to go through a centralized scouting agency? 'They're getting a lot more bang for the buck,' replied Frank Marcos, of the MLB scouting bureau (Major League Baseball 2001).

In major sports such as American football, basketball, football and ice hockey, the identification and pursuit of very young talented athletes in order to get them under contract became systematic in the early 1980s. Now, hundreds of adolescents sign contracts with amateur, semi-professional or professional teams in North America and Europe every year, sometimes at such an early age that they cannot assess and evaluate the significance of the proposed deal. Such deals can increase the pressure to succeed on children as it can be difficult to live with the idea that they are worth a lot of money to a lot of people. This situation does not exist on this scale in any other domain; only the entertainment and fashion industries come close, although fewer children are involved in these activities than in sports.

The big junior football tournaments are ideal occasions for recruiters to approach young players. Every year, the Montaigu (France) tournament for national youth (under 15 years) squads attracts hordes of agents and managers from all over Europe. Trainers need to keep their eyes open: 'I must watch out to ensure that agents do not approach the children,' said Luc Rabat, former French trainer (Glo 2001a: 96). Coaches often even modify the best players' names on the official programmes of these high-level competitions in order to protect the children by confusing scouts and agents. Despite everything, talented children are often harassed by managers and agents offering them contracts to sign. One French mother explained that clubs hoping to sign her 15-year-old son phoned her four times a day for several months (Glo 2001a: 97).

Increasingly, parents, football clubs and authorities, disturbed and angry about the brutal and aggressive techniques used by scouts or agents – who approach children wherever they can, with no respect for their right to privacy (see also Chapter 15) – have started to react. In April 2001, the Dutch football club, Ajax Amsterdam, requested that all agents and managers they work with should in future respect a code of behaviour. The club now forbids scouts and agents from entering the locker rooms and talking to young players (aged 14 to 16) in De Toekomst ('the future'), its sport complex.

Since the Bosman case (1995), clubs in countries such as Belgium, Denmark, France, Germany, the Netherlands, Sweden and Switzerland see their young football talents 'stolen' by wealthier teams from England, Italy and Spain who offer better-paid contracts. In 1999, Huub Stevens, coach of the German team Schalke 04, said, after a talented 16-year-old footballer had transferred to an English club for 300,000 euros a year, 'We do not wish to compete on these transfers, otherwise in the long term clubs will kill the market' (Wekking 1999: 29).

There are several hundred professional football teams in Europe and, today, all of them have signed up talented under-18s. Some young players already earn large salaries, and have generated income for their agents and clubs of origin. Disturbed by the large amounts of money some athletes can make at an early age, Louis van Gaal, a Dutch football trainer who was famous for his tough educational approach towards junior players, stated:

> It is ridiculous that young players already earn millions. In addition they are treated as heroes. It is bad for their mental development. It costs them a huge amount of energy to keep living in line with normal norms and values … I deliberately kept the salaries of young players within certain norms. I did not allow them to drive expensive sports cars. But at a certain point the market mechanisms were stronger: if you do not follow it you lose them. If you want to stay at the top, you have no choice but to give in. It is a dilemma: do you stick to principles, or do you give in and try to combat the symptom? I chose the latter, with pain in my heart.
>
> (Verbraak 2000: 22)

The French parliament adopted a new law in December 1999 which prohibits any third party (sports club, agent or manager, legal representative or private company) from making a profit on an agreement signed by an athlete under 18 years old with a sports club. This law – so far, the only one of its kind in the world – does not stop young athletes from signing a contract, but prohibits adults or groups from reaping financial benefits by exploiting the athlete's talent (Government of France 1999a: article 6). In Belgium, the appeal court of Liege considered in 2001 that the commission paid to managers each time a football player is transferred – whether a minor or an adult – is illegal under a 1995 law, which prohibits the renumeration of one person for the work of another (Vandenbergh 2001).

In the United States, competitive sport is usually organized through the education system, so the transfer business starts with athletes aged between 12 and 14, i.e., before they enter high school. According to *Sports Illustrated*, 'fishy transfers and illicit recruiting are nothing new to high school sports, but they are becoming alarmingly commonplace' (Wahl and Zimmerman 1998: 27).

Athletics associations exist in every American state precisely to protect very young athletes from being harassed by coaches to join a specific high school. The rules of these associations usually proscribe contact between members of the school's sports programme and athletes outside the school zone. But this has been criticized by some groups as being an infringement of the American constitution's first amendment, freedom of speech.

In 1997, a conflict arose between the Tennessee Secondary School Athletic Association (TSSAA) and a Tennessee high school, Brentwood Academy. The TSSAA accused the school of violating TSSAA recruiting rules by contacting a group of young students and informing them in detail about the school's sports programme. The TSSAA rule regulating the recruitment of student athletes prohibits the use of undue influence on students or their parents 'to secure or to retain a student for athletic purposes' (Dulabon 2000). Brentwood Academy sued the TSSAA, claiming that its recruiting rules were unconstitutional as, by prohibiting coaches and other officials from talking to young athletes, they violated the first amendment. A Tennessee court found for the academy, and the TSSAA appealed the decision. The appeals court, however, ruled that it could not address the issue, as in its view the TSSAA did not constitute a state actor for the purposes of constitutional law and that the association's actions could not be attributable to the state of Tennessee. In 2001, the US Supreme Court ruled 'that the association's [TSSAA] regulatory activity may and should be treated as State action' and reversed the judgement of the appeals court, therefore recognizing that the rules established to protect children from illicit recruitment could not violate the fundamental individual right to freedom of speech.

THE TRADE AND EXPLOITATION OF CHILD JOCKEYS

In September 1986, a very short article went almost unnoticed in *Dawn*, one of the main daily newspapers in Karachi, Pakistan. It was probably the first article reporting the trafficking, sale and exploitation of child jockeys. *Dawn* related that Pakistani officials had arrested six men accompanying seven children, aged between three and five, as they were about to fly to Dubai in the United Arab Emirates (UAE). The children's passports indicated that they were 'camel drivers' (David 1995: 87).

Trafficking and sale of child jockeys is unique in the context of competitive sports: the children are trafficked across international borders; separated from their parents and taken to a place they do not know and whose language they do not understand; forced to engage in a hazardous and dangerous activity; and are subject to abusive treatment, including crash diets and physical beatings. Engaging children as child camel jockeys contravenes several provisions of the Convention, to which all Gulf states are party, especially the rights not to be separated from their parents (article 9), to be free from all forms of violence (article 19), to education (article 28), to be protected from economic exploitation (article 32), and to be free from any form of trafficking and sale (article 35). It also violates several fundamental provisions of ILO Conventions, No. 29 on forced labour, No. 138 on minimum age for access to employment and No. 182 on the worst forms of child labour.

Camel races are an old Bedouin tradition, but since the oil boom of the 1970s the nature of these races has changed radically to a more business-oriented sport and, through gambling, camel owners can win US$ 100,000 in a single race. The best camels are worth over US$ 1 million (David 1992: 18). This has created a greater market for young camel jockeys.

Two qualities are essential for camel jockeys: they must be very light so that camels run faster, and have a shrill voice to scream at the animals and make them run quickly. Young children, aged between five and ten, are therefore ideal. But, to stay light, they are often underfed and forced to diet. 'I would get a few biscuits and a glass of milk for meals,' said a five-year-old Pakistani, after being released by the police of Dubai and sent back to his parents (Hussain 1999). The races are over ten kilometres long, exhausting and dangerous: at any moment, the jockey may get trapped underneath the camel, fall, be dragged along or trampled. Camels can run very fast – 45 kilometres an hour and even faster over short distances. There have been cases of children stamped to death by the animals. To avoid any scandal, camel owners usually offer financial compensation to the victim's parents (David 1995: 88). A Mauritanian child jockey who returned home after spending ten months in the UAE testified:

> They would take us and attach us with a cord to the camels' backs, then they would make them run down a little track covered in sand and boarded [sic] with large pointed iron posts and barbed wire. The camels had to run within this space, and the animals and children who fell were trampled by the [other] frightened animals. Those [child jockeys] who refused or who were scared were beaten and forced onto the camels … we were frightened of falling or dying.
> (Anti-Slavery International 1998)

The father of two child jockeys from Pakistan declared:

Imtiaz, 7 years old, was my youngest son. He was sent to Abu Dhabi for camel races through an agent, Sharif Sindhi, under the guardianship of his elder brother, Akram. During the race, Imtiaz fell from the back of the camel and received an injury to his head. He was operated on but did not survive. His brother Akram filed a petition for compensation in the court against the concerned Sheikh and we received 375,000 rupees [US\$ 6,000]. I was not fully aware of the danger involved in camel races. It is an inhuman game and should be stopped. We were a poor family, but now we have our own house and all the needs for business and livelihood.

(David 1993: 29)

Bangladesh, India, Pakistan and Sri Lanka have long been the traditional reservoir of child jockeys. Children are recruited through intermediaries who 'rent' or buy them; in the poorest and most vulnerable communities, they may even be abducted. Usually, child jockeys are also exploited as domestic servants, workers or as stable boys. Parents can earn US\$ 30 a month, sometimes more, by 'renting' their children, while each child sold secures up to US\$ 1,000 for the intermediary. Some NGOs believe that between 1,000 and 2,000 children a year are sold in this traffic. The Lawyers Committee for Human Rights and Legal Aid of Pakistan estimated that 19,000 boys, aged two to 11, from the region had been trafficked and exploited as child jockeys in the Middle East in the 1990s (Tumlin 2000: 5). During the 1990s, traffickers began seeking children from other very poor countries, including Eritrea, Mauritania and Sudan, where the practice of slavery is still very much alive.

Children may bring in money to their 'owners', but earn almost nothing themselves. Saddam Hussain, a Pakistani camel jockey who was smuggled into the UAE when he was five, declared: 'I won three races, for which my owner received a car, gold ornaments and a large amount of prize money, but I was just given a few dirhams [less than one dollar]' (Hussain 1999). In addition, during the off-season, the exploitation of these children often continued: they were forced to work, mainly in the stables.

Parents and children are lured into this traffic, hoping the child will become a star and bring home wealth, pride and hope. The reality is that they are thrust into a life of danger, misery and loneliness. Nevertheless, children sometimes rebel if they are arrested and returned to their villages, for they think they have lost the chance to become wealthy. This phenomenon has been described as the 'Dubai syndrome' (David 1995: 88).

Pressure on the Gulf states to stop using very young children in camel races started to increase during the early 1990s. Anti-Slavery International (ASI) and Defence for Children International (DCI), two international NGOS, led the campaign to raise public awareness and halt the practice. In 1993, the case of child jockeys was denounced for the first time before the UN Commission on Human Rights by Vitit Muntarbhorn, from Thailand, then Special Rapporteur on sale of children, child prostitution and child pornography (UN Commission on Human Rights 1993: 39–41). While the countries of origin of the trafficked and exploited children (mainly the Indian subcontinent) began to raise their voices against the practice, Saudi Arabia and the UAE replied to the Special Rapporteur's enquiries with letters of denial.

However, to counter international pressure, the UAE took measures in September 1993, requesting that the Emirates Camel Racing Federation review its rules. The Federation prohibited the employment of children in camel races (but did not specify an age limit), fixed the minimum weight of riders at 45 kilograms and obliged all jockeys to wear helmets. Seven years later, the UAE made the regulation law and banned racing for jockeys under 15 years of age. But according to NGOs, press reports and the ILO, hundreds of child jockeys are still smuggled to the Gulf states every year. In 1999, the Special Rapporteur on sale of children, child prostitution and child pornography, Orfelia Calcetas-Santos, denounced the practices and stated that she had found evidence that:

> clearly indicates that the rules are blatantly ignored. In February 1998, ten boys, generally from Pakistan and Bangladesh, were rescued while being smuggled to become camel jockeys. The boys had been lured away from their poor families with the promise of high-paying jobs.
>
> (UN Commission on Human Rights 1999: para. 79)

International pressure increased in 2001 after the UN and the ILO monitored respect for international norms and standards in the Gulf region. The ILO's Committee of Experts stated in June 2001 that:

> children of 5 or 6 years of age are taken to the United Arab Emirates to be used as jockeys in camel races. These children are often kidnapped, sold by their parents or taken under false pretences. They are thereby separated from their families and taken to a country where the people, culture and language are completely unknown to them. The boys are underfed and subjected to severe diets before races so they are as light as possible.

In the second half of 2001, the Committee on the Rights of the Child monitored the situation of child rights in Oman, Qatar and the UAE. It expressed serious concern that 'sometimes very young children are involved; are trafficked, particularly from Africa (i.e. Sudan) and South Asia; are denied education and healthcare; and that such involvement produces serious injuries, even fatalities' (UN Committee on the Rights of the Child 2001c: para. 57). When questioned about camel races, members of the delegation from Oman explained to the Committee that: 'Camel riding was considered a sport, not a job, and the participation of children in it was a source of pride for both children and their parents' (UN Committee on the Rights of the Child 2001d: para. 50), while the representatives from Qatar stated that 'addressing the sensitive issue of the involvement of children in camel racing was a priority for the Government' (UN Committee on the Rights of the Child 2001e: para. 40).

Part V
Empowering young athletes

14 Writing on the wall

The right to education

I cannot do anything other than gymnastics. Without it, what am I? I've become entirely dependent, bound hand and foot.

(Alexei Nemov, top gymnast during the 1990s, in Donzé 2000b: 21)

Education is one of the most fundamental rights for all human beings and is essential for the optimal development of children, whatever the culture and environment they live in. Almost all international human rights treaties include a reference to education. Article 26 of the 1948 Universal Declaration of Human Rights states:

Everyone has the right to education. Education shall be free, at least in the elementary and fundamental stages. Elementary education shall be compulsory. Technical and professional education shall be made generally available and higher education shall be equally accessible to all on the basis of merit.

The Convention on the Rights of the Child recognizes in article 28 the right to education and defines the aims of education in article 29. Education, as referred to in the Convention, is not limited to formal instruction delivered in schools, it covers all forms of social learning. The UN Committee on the Rights of the Child (2001: para. 2) noted:

Education in this context goes far beyond formal schooling to embrace the broad range of life experiences and learning processes which enable children, individually and collectively, to develop their personalities, talents, abilities and to live a full satisfying life within society.

Today's young athletes start intensive training at an early age and are confronted with the challenge of having to succeed at school and in sport. The risk, of course, is that the pressure becomes excessive and some children will fail at both, dropping out of school at an early age but unable to make a living through sport. The Committee on the Rights of the Child considers it essential that 'no child leaves school without being equipped to face the challenges he or she can expect to be confronted with in life' (UN Committee on the Rights of the Child 2001: para. 9).

Under the Convention, all states are obliged to 'make primary education compulsory and available free to all' (article 28), although no upper age limit marking the end of compulsory education has been fixed. In most developed countries, the legal limit is between 14 and 16 years old; in developing countries, it is lower, often around 12 years of age. If a child leaves school before ending his or her primary education, the state has failed to respect its legal obligations.

Young elite athletes devote most, if not all, of their time, energy and concentration to learning at school and training at sport. They often spend over 30 hours a week at school plus another 20 hours in training. At the end of their primary-school career, many athletes are faced with the crucial decision of whether to focus on sports exclusively and neglect their education or vice versa (Kidd 2003). Former Dutch football star and top coach, Johan Cruyff, warned, 'Today, football and sports in general destroy many adolescents. At 16, a footballer, a swimmer or a track and field athlete has to make a choice. For 90 per cent it will be sports, with the risk of failure' (Coadic 1998: 112).

French cyclist Richard Virenque dropped out of school at 16. When justifying the reasons that had led him to take heavy doses of illegal performance-enhancing drugs, he explained, 'With my level of education I had no choice: either I made a career in sports or I would have earned the minimum wage for the rest of my life' (Droussant 1998: 56).

Professional sport cultivates the illusion that in the short term it offers much more potential for a successful career and financial gain than schooling. While this might be true for a handful of child athletes, it is not so for the overwhelming majority. For one Serena Williams or Michael Owen, thousands of others will fail and may suffer for the rest of their lives from their lack of education. Some parents are influenced by the 'get-rich-quick' illusion and allow their children to invest all their energy and time in competitive sports, by neglecting their education or dropping out of school altogether.

The problem is not that sport stars, such as Martina Hingis and Tara Lipinski, left school at 13 and do not have university degrees, for they don't need a diploma to ensure a decent income so that they can live the rest of their life in dignity. But when these exceptions become role models and are perceived as the norm, it poses an enormous problem: the message that parents and other adults receive is that a talented child athlete can or even should drop out of school in order to succeed in their sporting career.

Andrea Jaeger was already a top tennis player in her teens in the early 1980s. She was only 13 when her father insisted she leave school to train full time. Over ten years later she explained: 'I think that we thought that if we put 150 per cent into tennis, we'd get it all back later on' (Deford 1995: 29). Her tennis career was successful, albeit very brief, and she left professional tennis at the age of only 21, totally burned out physically and psychologically.

Many studies have shown that, in a conducive environment and with sufficient time, young elite athletes can do very well at school (TOYA 1993b; Etnier *et al.* 1997). But, given that the demands of professional sport are so great today, the value of education is often overlooked by many coaches, officials and parents. French athlete Stéphane Diagana, world 400-metre hurdles champion in 1998, was able to combine both studies and sports at high level. Of today's young athletes, he has said:

> I see young athletes who have participated in the European Youth Championships and they say to me, 'I train eight times a week. But I'll have to give up my studies so that I can train 14 times a week' ... I tell them: 'Find a solution, carry on studying as well as training and protect your future'. But I don't think they listen to me.
>
> (*L'Equipe Magazine* 2001b: 31)

Athletes who have done well in sports and studies are rarely respected for their academic achievements. In 2001, Vince Carter, a top American basketball player, celebrated his graduation from university on the same day that his team played – and lost – a crucial game. The following day, a *New York Times* editorial noted:

> The fundamental hypocrisy of education and elite sport was on sanctimonious display yesterday. The National Basketball Association trots out a new literacy campaign, and Commissioner David Stern lectures that undergraduates should stay in school and get their degrees [before joining professional teams]. Then Carter goes to pick up his, only to hear his coach and teammates grumble ... In truth, amateur and professional leagues want their players pliant and obedient, not particularly well educated and free thinking ... We want our athletes smart and articulate, but unwilling to offer contentious opinion. Or to take independent actions, such as attending graduation the day of a big game.
>
> (Longman 2001)

The lure of financial gain and celebrity is more appealing than schoolbooks. Tom McMillen, a former National Basketball Association (NBA) player and US Congressman, claimed:

> The overall message being drilled into our kids is clear and dangerous ... Superstars sign five-year contracts for US$ 20 million. Teachers sign one-year contracts for US$ 20,000. In those circumstances, to whom will you listen, your teacher or your coach? Where will you spend your time, in the library or the gym?
>
> (Coakley 1998: 437)

Parents and coaches may become obsessed about their child's sporting career, encouraging them to train intensively to the detriment of their studies. In Geneva, Switzerland, a father was condemned in 2000 to pay a 300-euro fine for having systematically encouraged his 11-year-old son to practise ice hockey during school hours. Despite repeated warnings from the school authorities, the boy frequently missed lessons to train. The court imposed the fine because the father had clearly given priority to his son's sporting career over his legal obligation to ensure that the boy attended school (Mansour 2000).

Not all elite athletes drop out of school, although they often need the help of a tutor or a correspondence course to keep up. But many involved in intensive training are unable to finish secondary school simply because they do not have the time to study. The problem is that if they leave school at 14 or 15 to devote themselves to sport, there is no guarantee that they will succeed in a sporting career. Most trainers and coaches agree that it is very difficult to assess how a young athlete, even if very talented and dedicated, will evolve physically and mentally. This has occurred time and again. In 1994, for example, the best young English and Swiss footballers (under 15) played an international game at Wembley; today hardly any of them play professional football (Walters 1994: 19). Only a few of the players who were members of England's national school squad in 1986 or in 1996 went on to succeed in a professional career (Conn 2002).

A very few top athletes do leave sports to concentrate on their schooling. William Gates, a talented American basketball player, decided to focus on his studies, despite the pressure on him to become an NBA player. He explained:

> All my brothers had the dream of me making the pros. When they found out, they tried to talk me out of it ... I realized what mattered most was getting my degree. And I wasn't going to get it if I kept concentrating on the game ... [After leaving sports] was the best time of my life – I wouldn't change anything. I never had so much free time. It felt good to come home from class and not have to rush off to practice and get yelled at ... They [college officials] made basketball more of a business, more a job, than a sport to play.
>
> (Joravsky 1995: 271–96)

HARDLY ANY CHANCE OF SUCCESS

Few statistics are collected and analysed about the success rates of junior champions once they are old enough to compete with adults. But obviously, the chance of becoming a professional athlete for a young talent is minimal, even for the most gifted among them. And the older an athlete gets, the tougher it is to stay in the elite. The National Collegiate Athletic Association (NCAA) in the United States is one of the rare institutions that collects such data, mainly concerning high-school (aged 15–18 years) and college (17–20) students. The NCAA found, for example, that only 2.6 per cent of high-school basketballers become college players. Of that 2.6 per cent, only 1.9 per cent will join America's most prestigious professional league, the NBA. In American football, 6.6 per cent of high-school athletes become college athletes, and 3.3 per cent of college players make it to the professional leagues (NCAA 1997). In this respect, as in the arts, music and politics, sport is a pyramid where only a privileged few make it to the top.

Too often the best interests of the child are not taken into consideration when a decision has to be made as to whether a child opts for intensive sport training or continues studying. Adults – parents, coaches, sponsors – tend to impose their choice on the young athlete. At a conference on the exploitation of young Kenyan athletes, Paul Ereng, 800-metre champion at the 1988 Seoul Olympics, denounced the fact that some foreign sport agents were encouraging youngsters to drop out of school to run races for money (Associated Press 1999c). Chinese diver Fu Mingxia was Olympic champion at the age of 13 and again four years later. When she was 18, she explained that she 'really wanted to study' but she was told by her coach Xu Yiming that she could not retire so young and that '[t]he Sport Commission, her regional team and even her parents would not allow her to' (Issert 2000: 10). She did retire from sports for three years to take up her studies before competing again successfully in the 1999 World University Games.

In any case, no child should drop out of school before finishing compulsory, primary schooling which represents the absolute minimal education level and is a universal obligation under law. This minimum requirement is now, for example, included in the Age Eligibility Rule of the Women's Tennis Association (WTA) which came under pressure in the mid-1990s to stop adults from encouraging young players to leave school. The rule states that: 'Players are required to complete the minimum educational requirements of their country of residence' (WTA 2000). While the WTA's ruling implicitly recognizes that a problem does exist and provides clear guidance, it is still up to sports and public authorities to enforce legal provisions on compulsory schooling.

Several sport stars have proven that it is possible to reach the top without dropping out of school at a young age. Tennis players such as Lindsay Davenport and Arnaud Clément finished secondary school, while Serena and Venus Williams insisted on studying for as long as possible. Talking about her father, Venus Williams said: 'He also made me stay in school. You don't need to practise five hours a day to be a champion. I practised about two hours every afternoon' (Kleinhenz 2000: 23).

Most elite female figure skaters and gymnasts do not even have the option of remaining in school as these sports are best performed by athletes aged between 15 and 18 years, a key period that is usually dedicated to ending secondary schooling. 'I don't like that kids don't go to school … because there's so much more in life than skating,' said Nancy Kerrigan, silver medallist at the 1998 Nagano Winter Olympics. 'You break your ankle and it could be over' (Brennan 1999: 209).

FAILURE OF THE EDUCATION SYSTEM

In an ideal world, young athletes would have a sound environment in which to follow two parallel careers, schooling and sports. This objective justifies in theory the establishment of specialized centres or schools; even there, however, it is very difficult to reconcile both. A trainer at the French sports institute, INSEP, asserted:

> They [young athletes] live their life at a crazy pace, with too little time for recovery. A professional is given time to rest and relax between two games. This is not the case with professional apprentices: they have to live up to the expectations of their parents, trainers, schools ... and the competition is sometimes harsh.
>
> (Thomas 1998: 19)

In many countries, the academic standards in sports schools have often been questioned. Education is rarely a priority in these centres, rather just enough tuition is given to respect a minimum moral and legal obligation and to reassure parents (see also Chapter 12). Some sport schools, in France and the US for example, have been accused in the past of giving grades too generously to athletes (Byers and Hammer 1995: 297–320). Under a 2001 law decree, the state in France is responsible for ensuring a minimum standard of education in sport centres, which public authorities can close if they do not meet this standard (Government of France 2001c). That year, the authorities inquired into two professional football clubs, AJ Auxerre and RC Lens, which were suspected of neglecting their educational obligations towards their young players (Le Coeur and Potet 2001).

An American footballer with the Washington Redskins team, Dexter Manley, admitted to a US panel on illiteracy that despite spending four years at the Oklahoma State University, he had neither graduated nor learned to read. A senator commented, 'You did not fail, sir. The system failed you' (Byers and Hammer 1995: 298).

The theoretical advantage of the American system, where competitive sports are incorporated in regular schools, is that students involved in intensive training follow an educational curriculum. In reality, however, most student athletes are given neither the time nor the means to follow both paths (see also Chapter 12). In addition, the contrast between the quality of the sports programme and that of the educational curriculum is often shocking.

Many American college and university athletes receive a scholarship and most sign a contract to play for a specific institution. They are thus contracted to do their best to serve the sporting and financial interests of their college or university. But what are the educational institution's obligations towards the athlete? Surely, their mission must first and foremost be to educate students, not to ensure that they perform well in sports. Once again, the reality does not live up to the intentions, and sports are generally given precedence over education (Byers and Hammer 1995: 301; Shulman and Bowen 2001).

Some student athletes have taken their case to court blaming their school for educational malpractice, but in general courts have not responded favourably to these types of claims. However, in one case in 1992 (*Ross v. Creighton University*), the court held that, when universities make identifiable contractual promises to a student athlete, they may be in breach of contract if they do not make a 'good faith effort' to keep their promises (Hilborn 1995).

The fact that in the United States the main programme of many high schools, colleges and universities focuses on sports excellence rather than on other academic skills has been regularly criticized as disrupting the quality of education in the long run (Duderstadt 2000; Sperber 2000; Shulman and Bowen 2001). The increasing involvement of commercial interests in high-school and college sport is accelerating this trend. Some educational institutions have annual deals with commercial sponsors and television companies worth several million dollars. Schools are tempted to compensate the high costs of the education system with the lucrative income generated by the sport system, especially television rights.

In this intercollegiate sport system, many schools and universities build their educational reputation on their sport teams' results rather than on the quality of their educational programmes. According to many researchers, education has been lagging behind college sport since the latter began to attract huge live television audiences in the 1970s. In his provocative book, *Beer and Circus. How Big-Time College Sports is Crippling Undergraduate Education*, American author Murray Sperber claimed in 2000 that the 'success' of intercollegiate sports is mainly responsible for the decline of American education. Sociologist Jay Coakley noted (1998: 465) that:

> evidence supports the notion that when sport programmes become big business, financial concerns tend to take priority over educational concerns. When media rights to games are sold, the academic progress of the college players often becomes less important than television ratings and network profits. Corporate sponsors are not concerned with educational issues; their survival depends on profits. Educational concerns may not be given top priority when people having nothing to do with higher education are making many of the decisions affecting intercollegiate sports.

Walter Byers and Charles Hammer concluded in 1995 that college students are exploited by the educational system and the NCAA, its supporting federation, which benefit financially from their young athletes' skills without in turn respecting their rights: 'The most depressing aspect is the continuing disregard for the rights of individual interests of young athletes. Here, the NCAA colleges regularly endorsed generalized statements about "student-athlete welfare" but rejected proposals for student-athlete freedom' (Byers and Hammer 1995: 397).

Intercollegiate sport has generated a system in which coaches earn up to 25 times more than an average college professor. In 2001, it was estimated that 17 college coaches were earning at least US$ 1 million a year (the highest income was US$ 2.2 million), while the annual average salary of a professor is US$ 72,000

(Wieberg 2001: 1). The ever-increasing salaries of college coaches have recently provoked strong reactions from professors of large universities. A number have passed resolutions condemning the 'arms race' of spending for coaches' salaries and stadiums. James Earl, a professor of English at the University of Oregon who spearheaded the resolution, said: 'How higher education ever went into the same bed with the entertainment industry – that's a historical weirdness we have to try to undo. It's turned the campuses into sports franchises and it's changed the whole country's attitude toward education' (Wilgoren 2001: 10). 'We are a nation of competitors,' responded the university presidents (Wieberg 2001: 2).

John Gerdy, a college-sports reformer and former professional basketball player in the US, declared in his book, *Sports in high school* (2000), that, 'To continue to blindly invest significant resources in an activity [sports] that falls short of meeting its educational objectives is irresponsible.'

An increasing number of young players, especially in sports such as basketball and football, no longer follow this traditional American path – high school to university to (sometimes) professional club. They are now directly recruited by professional teams, some even before they reach their majority, which means that their educational needs are often completely overlooked. Once again, the interests of sport reign supreme. This trend, which already exists in Europe and Latin America, is taking hold in the United States, largely because, as the coach of the Washington DC United football team pointed out, 'When a player goes to college he can lose some very important years in his [sport] development' (Thomsen 2000). Washington DC United recruited 16-year-old Bobby Convey directly from high school in 2000. When questioned about this new trend, Todd Durbin, the vice-president of the Major League Soccer (MLS), the US professional football league, replied:

> College does a good job, but it doesn't develop players at the rate of our league. All research we've done shows that young players benefit from getting in a professional environment – not just the on-field stuff. A lot of it is off the field: the travel, living in hotels … plus they're surrounded by players whose pay-check depends on their ability to stay in the field. They're locked into that environment of competing and striving to succeed.
>
> (Thomsen 2000)

15 A power of good
Civil rights of young athletes

In the case of athletes, as with other low-power groups, both securing rights and assuring their enforcement is problematic. In the absence of both an ethic of care and legal statements and protection of athletes' rights, athletics as an institution, and athletes in particular, are left with a norm of expected inequity.

(Duquin 1984: 299)

Athletes do not have free speech or the right to a fair trial [within the context of athletic programmes]. If they challenge the athletic power structure, they will lose their scholarship and eligibility. Athletes who have a grievance are on their own. They have no union, no arbitration board, and rarely do they have representation on campus communities.

(Eitzen 1992: E3)

During the twentieth century, a culture of human rights developed to a certain extent in activities such as the arts and politics. This was not the case for sport, probably due to its nature, history and intrinsic characteristics. Competitive sport grew up around traditional values – such as paternalism, military organization, strict discipline, authoritarianism, hierarchy and masculinity – that are not necessarily compatible with international human rights standards.

Mary Duquin (1984: 295) qualified competitive sport as being 'supported by the ideology of a benevolent dictatorship', while Michael Burke (1999: 1) considered that: 'There is a long-standing tradition in sport that suggests that it is beneficial for the athlete to endure limitations of their freedom because it is conducive to good performance.'

Since the revival of sports during the second part of the nineteenth century, democratic values have but weakly permeated the dominant sporting culture. Many core human rights values, such as equality, non-discrimination, individual freedoms, accountability, transparency and scrutiny have not gained much ground. Athletes are generally not empowered individuals; they largely depend on actions and decisions taken by others, such as trainers, coaches, officials and agents. Ultimate power resides with the athletic establishment, not with athletes. According to sports sociologist Jay Coakley (1998: 519):

Athletes control their sport skills, but the formation of their public personas is largely under the control of others, including team publicity departments, people in the media, agents and corporate advertising who create and use athletes' images and personas to promote and sell products and to hype sport events.

Coaches are expected to control, athletes to be controlled. The latter 'are cemented in a pattern of dominance and subordination' (Duquin 1984: 301) and any attempt on their part to challenge authority or to claim rights and redress might directly threaten their career.

A general assumption in sports is that empowering athletes by recognizing their rights will weaken the authority and power of coaches and other sport officials. Rarely are rights of athletes perceived as an agent of positive development, change and achievement. Celia Brackenridge (2001: 13) has said:

> Since athletes are often treated as children, in terms of their restricted rights in sports, and talented children are often defined as adults, in terms of performance expectations in sport, it is no wonder that there is confusion about both moral and sexual boundaries in sport.

Trainers and coaches often become defensive if young athletes under their wing do speak out and claim some autonomy. Two months before the 2001 World Gymnastics Championships, Mariana Bitang, one of the Romanian coaches, complained about the new generation of gymnasts:

> Look, you can't tell a gymnast she's fat any more because she'll start to cry immediately. However the risk of getting injured is greater when they are overweight. It puts more strain on their backs. Thousands of girls have made these sacrifices up until now but they think they only have rights. Now they are billionaires and they have cars. It's not right. A lot of money is invested in them.
>
> (Prosport 2001)

Within their rigid sporting environment, athletes are tacitly requested to refrain from any political or social statements. The sport establishment perceives all forms of extra-sporting empowerment – especially political – as a threat to the entire system, and still forcefully promotes the illusion that it can function in total independence and is free from politics and social problems. Sports authorities, whether local or international, have failed time and again to respond properly when challenged by their own athletes.

Two American athletes, Tommy Smith and John Carlos, were both students and members of the Olympic Project for Human Rights when they competed for their country in the 1968 Mexico City Olympics. Both won medals and, on the podium, they held their arms high in the 'black power' salute. They were immediately excluded for life from the sport movement and marginalized by society. Their case is significant: individual athletes showed their allegiance to non-discrimination, a cause considered just by many, but were heavily sanctioned by the sports establishment who felt it had been radically challenged. In comparison, people in the United States didn't sanction in the same way singers or politicians who expressed the same political feelings. Dwight Hayes, a sports specialist, noted (1993: 16): 'Overall, athletes are loved by everybody until their consciousness is raised and they start to speak out on social issues.'

The sports system also comes down hard on athletes who wish to express their political opinions. One example is Australian athlete Cathy Freeman, who is of Aboriginal origin. Before the 2000 Sydney Olympics she suggested that, if she won, she might show the Aborigine rather than the Australian flag. The International Olympic Committee (IOC) immediately made it clear that she would be excluded and that her title or medal would be automatically withdrawn. Freeman went on to win the 400-metre race, and did her lap of honour with *both* Australian and Aborigine flags.

In 2000, French tennis player and 1998 Wimbledon finalist, Nathalie Tauziat, published a book, *Les dessous du tennis féminin* (The underworld of female tennis). In it, she openly criticized some policies and decisions of both the French Tennis Federation (FFT), which had turned Tauziat down when she was 13 years old, and the Women's Tennis Association (WTA), the international sporting authority for female tennis. A few months later, the FFT chose the four players to represent France at the Sydney Olympics, but failed to select Tauziat, even though she was at the time the number-one ranked French player (Mary Pierce was better ranked but not eligible to play in the Olympics). The FFT clearly sanctioned Tauziat for having criticized it. She unsuccessfully appealed the decision, first at the French National Olympic Committee and then at the Court of Arbitration for Sport (CAS) in Lausanne, Switzerland.

The concept of empowerment is marginal in the traditional sports environment. Canada is one of the very few countries where athletes advocate nationally for the respect of their rights. The Canadian Association of National Team Athletes (CAN) was established in 1992 and its mission 'is to work with others in leadership, advocacy and education to ensure a fair, responsive, and supportive sport system for Canadian high performance athletes' (CAN 1999). In 1994, CAN's steering committee for sport policy in Canada stated that the people responsible 'for leadership and decision-making in sport must include the athlete in both defining the needs and goals and in determining how to meet them; i.e. the athlete should be the active subject in, not the object of, sporting programmes'.

CAN has defined ten criteria that need to be applied to shape an 'athlete-centred sport': accountability; mutual respect; empowerment; equity and fairness; excellence; extended and mutual responsibility; health; informed participation; mutual support; and athletes' rights. These criteria, most of which are directly inspired by the human rights ideology, can also be used as benchmarks to assess the quality of the environment in which young athletes are competing.

In addition to aiming at improving the protection of all human beings under 18 years of age, one of the main objectives of the Convention on the Rights of the Child is to recognize them as full subjects of rights. Children are holders of fundamental human rights; in accordance with their evolving capacity and maturity they are recognized as having the capacity to exercise those rights (Lansdown 2000: 1). This innovative vision of the child is at the heart of the concept of the 'human rights of children', as defined in the Convention. It strongly implies that children have the right to be given visibility in society and participate actively in all decision-making processes (De Winter 1998; Hart 1998). If the protection of children has been a concern of society for a relatively long time, the status of children as active rights-holders has only been recognized through the Convention for the past ten years and is to some extent still in an experimental phase. This new dimension is considerable and directly challenges adults and society as a whole.

One of the most fundamental aims of human rights is to empower people so that they can protect themselves and ensure that they fully enjoy and exercise their rights as recognized under law. Human rights also offer a legal tool for redress and compensation in case of violation. But human rights can only be enjoyed by individuals when properly reflected in law and deeply anchored in the culture, political and societal traditions of the place they live in.

According to the Convention, all young people under the age of 18 should have the following civil rights and freedoms: to express their opinion freely (article 12); to freedom of expression (article 13); to freedom of thought, conscience and religion (article 14); to freedom of association (article 15); to privacy (article 16); and to access appropriate information (article 17). These civil rights were explicitly granted only to human beings *over* 18 before the entry into force of the Convention in 1990 (especially in the 1948 Universal Declaration of Human Rights and the 1966 International Covenant on Civil and Political Rights). Since 1990, every child has become a rights-holder in accordance with his or her evolving capacity, and no longer solely a passive recipient of adult protection and compassion (Van Bueren 1995: xix and 1).

It is important to note that the signification and implications of the civil rights of children have not yet been extensively researched and understood and they are still resisted by many parties (David 2002: 260–2). Most states recognize in their constitutions or laws the rights to freedom of expression, thought, conscience, religion and association and the right of protection of privacy to 'everyone', but very rarely explicitly to children. Consequently, judicial courts and administrative bodies need to interpret these provisions in a progressive manner to apply them to young people who do not yet have full legal capacity. Until now, only a handful of countries have specifically recognized these civil rights to children in their constitutions or laws, even though it is an obligation under the Convention and is systematically requested by the Committee on the Rights of the Child (UN Committee on the Rights of the Child 1996: para. 48).

All these participatory rights – especially children's right to express their opinion freely and to have their opinion given due weight in all matters affecting them – are strongly interrelated with all of the Convention's other provisions; they should be fully respected whenever another right is implemented. These civil rights are meant to allow children to become responsible adult citizens in a free and democratic society and to recognize their inherent dignity as a human being; they do not provide children with full autonomy, self-determination or the right to ride roughshod over the rights of their parents. 'Children's participation is not about giving them the *last* word, it is about giving them *a* word,' remarked UNICEF (2001a).

By recognizing civil rights and freedoms to children, the international community has not only given them a tool to increase their participation in society, it has also offered a new channel to improve the protection of children from all forms of abuse, neglect, violence and exploitation. Through participation, empowered children can challenge abuses and provide first-hand information that is crucial for their own protection. Children can also effectively participate in the design and implementation of child protection laws, regulations and policies, especially at community level.

RIGHT TO EXPRESS THEIR VIEWS FREELY

The Convention promotes the right to participation (Flekkoy and Kaufman 1997; Santos Pais 1997: 427), but the context of competitive sports does not necessarily provide a favourable environment for young athletes to exercise this right. The culture of participation, self-reliance, self-organization, individual involvement in decision-making and progressive autonomy are present in spontaneous sport and street games organized by children themselves, but this is not the case in sports organized by adults.

Article 12 of the Convention is undoubtedly a key provision and has been identified by the Committee on the Rights of the Child as one of the Convention's four general principles.[1] It has had a considerable impact on society in the last decade (Flekkoy and Kaufman 1997; Lansdown 2000: 1; Santos Pais 1996: 246). It affirms that:

> States Parties shall assure to the child who is capable of forming his or her views the right to express those views freely in *all matters* affecting the child, the views of the child being given due weight in accordance with the age and maturity of the child. [emphasis added]

Recognizing the right of the child to express its views on all matters is a sound way to ensure that their best interests are fully respected (as defined in article 3 of the Convention). As Van Bueren (1995: xxii) has pointed out:

> the central issue is not one of law, but of respect, and of recognition that children as human beings are entitled not only to care and protection, but also to participate in decisions involving their own destinies to a greater extent than is generally recognised.

Trainers, parents and managers of young athletes may have a tendency to over-shadow their children by pulling at all the strings and leaving little space for them to express their views and develop their own personality. Tennis player Mary Pierce, who was once one of the world's top players, explained that her father did not allow her to take decisions or to set her own objectives: 'It was my father who decided and spoke on my behalf. "We have to win," he repeated to me' (Sainte-Rose 2000: 82). South Korean Se Ri Pak, a top female golf player and winner of the US Open and Ladies' Professional Golf Association (LPGA) tour in 2000, explained that her father pushed her to become a champion during her childhood and that she didn't have any choice in the matter. She was often weary of her routine of playing and practising: 'Many, many times I cried ... because I just wanted my dad to give me more rest; he didn't do that' (O'Connor 1999: 1C).

Views of young athletes are rarely taken into account when decisions affecting their own life and career are taken. Marat Safin was the world's top tennis player in 2002, but a year later, aged 24, he struggled with a lack of motivation and mental burn-out. Referring to the fact that his mother, Rauza, sent him away from his home in Russia to live and train in Spain at the age of 13, he said: 'I learned everything in Spain, but I left home much too early. Nobody asked me my opinion, and who would have listened anyway?' (Despont 2004).

Some parents treat young athletes as if they owned them, leaving little space for self-reliance, development and fulfilment. The father of former French water-skiing child prodigy, Patrice Martin, tried (unsuccessfully) to stop him, then aged over 30, from getting married. Martin said: 'My father made me and always believed he owned me' (Terrani 2000b: 18). This perception of owning a child is in complete opposition to that of the child regarded as subject of rights and acquiring progressive autonomy as suggested by the Convention (Flekkoy 1992).

By nature, competitive sport is selective and young athletes are usually not involved in the selection process. 'Selection programmes have problems related to decision-making. Does the child have a voice in the selection process? Are parents involved?' asked Robert Malina, director of the Institute for the Study of Youth Sport (USA) in 1997. He went on to note:

> Accounts of electronic and print media often highlight parents who are seemingly more interested in their child's success than is the child. Are deci-sions made independently by coaches or other sport authorities? What kind of guidance is available for the child, or parents, when he or she is selected? What are the implications of being labelled 'talented' for individual and parental expectations?
>
> (Malina 1997)

Listening to young athletes and taking their views into account is a process that may prevent and protect them from harm, abuse or exploitation. 'The adult cre-ates an atmosphere and environment where the athlete feels that his/her bodily integrity, sexual self-determination and possibilities to move are safeguarded,' remarked the Finnish Sports Federation (2002: 9–10), adding 'The adult listens to the child or young person and takes his/her opinion seriously.' Children may have information that is crucial to their own protection, but if their environment is not one of trust and confidence, they will not be encouraged to share this information with adults.

Research overwhelmingly shows that vulnerable children are most at risk of abuse; those who are empowered being best placed to protect themselves (Lansdown 2000: 7). A British female survivor of sexual abuse in sport said:

> We should have been able to make decisions about when we could go no further … I mean you know within your own body, if you're so sick that you should not be training, you should be allowed to say 'I can't come today' … You should be able to have a day off every week, you should be able to make decisions about your own career in sport, and about what your level of involvement would be. You shouldn't have to accept the coach's view on everything, you should be able to make your own choice on what level of sport you want to be on.
>
> (Brackenridge 2001: 230)

To ensure adequate protection, adults must also be ready to listen to young athletes and act in their interests. Elodie Lussac, from France, was 15 years old and a world-class gymnast when she fell from the balance beam during the 1994 world championships and sustained back injuries that forced her to end her career. She had complained several times the day before about severe back pains resulting from another injury. But her coaches and medical staff did not take her comments seriously and pushed her to compete despite her pain. 'They told me that I had to compete,' she recalled bitterly (Hirzel 1996: 51).

In a highly structured and hierarchical activity such as competitive sport, young athletes are a low-power group and are not always given sufficient space to exercise their freedom of expression. In article 13, the Convention guarantees that:

> The child shall have the right to freedom of expression; this right shall include freedom to seek, receive and impart information and ideas of all kinds, regardless of frontiers, either orally, in writing or in print, in the form of art, or through any other media of the child's choice.

In collective sports especially, athletes have to be careful when talking to outsiders, in order to respect the interests of the team, group, association and even the country they represent. For example, during the 2000 Sydney Olympics, officials asked the American female football team not to discuss in public the issue of homosexuality and to refrain from making any revelations to the media (*Tribune de Genève* 2000: 37).

Traditionally, competitive sport has not given much value to open criticism and evaluation, which are often perceived as indicative of a losing or selfish attitude on the part of an athlete. Trainers and managers feel they need to speak on behalf of the athletes, especially those under 18 years of age, in order to protect them. While this feeling might be justified in some situations, it reflects a lack of confidence in the ability of the young and may lead to abuse. Young athletes might also be pressured by their environment to say what adults expect them to say rather than what they want to say.

Contrary to artists or politicians, athletes cannot criticize in public any form of authority and they are bound to respect a confidentiality clause almost as restrictive as those that civil servants sign up to, in which they agree to keep certain information confidential. While the limitation may seem excessive, most athletes accept this self-censorship to preserve their own interests. 'Players are paid to play, not to speak,' said Bobby Robson, Newcastle Football Club's manager in 2002 after one of his players spoke to journalists about a series of disappointing results (*L'Equipe* 2002: 11). In a great number of cases where athletes have spoken out within the legally acceptable framework of freedom of expression, their sport association or federation has sanctioned them.

FREEDOM OF ASSOCIATION

In the context of competitive sports, freedom of association for young athletes comes into question in three specific situations: if they want to take up responsibilities in their sports club (right to participate in governance) (Kidd 2003); if they want to change club or team; or if they wish to join labour unions. Article 15 of the Convention provides that 'States Parties recognize the right of the child to freedom of association and to freedom of peaceful assembly'.

In most countries, the decision-making bodies of sports clubs are in practice composed of adults (aged generally over 30). Although there is nothing to stop management bodies being open to adolescent athletes, whose participation should be encouraged, young people usually prefer to focus their time and energy on practising rather than managing. A Belgian study on swimmers concluded that, 'Young swimmers indicated that they know little with regard to management nor are they interested in policy. They expect members of the board to listen to youth members, to take into account youth members and to be kind' (De Martelaer *et al.* 1997: 3).

The age to be eligible to vote as members of sport clubs or associations should also in principle be set lower than 18, normally between 14 and 16 (Meier 1997: 269). The Convention implicitly encourages political participation (Franklin 1998) and it is significant to note that, since its entry into force, nine states have lowered the voting age at national level and, in some other countries, the debate about this issue has been intense.[2]

Young athletes should have the right – legally – to set up their own sports clubs. And in existing clubs or teams, they should be more systematically involved in the daily life and policy-making, so that their views and opinions are better integrated. They should, for example, have a say on the type of sponsors with whom their team signs a contract. This is rarely the case. In 1998, Krystle

Newquist, a 14-year-old American baseball player, refused to wear on her shirt an advertisement for a bar selling alcohol. Her team was not consulted about the sponsor; they proposed to play games with tape covering the publicity in question. Finally, the bar's owners decided to withdraw their sponsorship to avoid any conflict (Associated Press 1998c).

Snowboarding as a sport appeared in the early 1990s, and provides an interesting – and almost unique – example of a sport that tried to develop around its own athletes through self-management and individual empowerment, strongly based on the concepts of 'fun, freedom and friendship'. Athletes, many of them teenagers under 18 years old, organized their own competitions and successfully approached the media and sponsors to raise funds. The International Snowboard Federation (ISF) was created in 1991. Success was immediate: the competitions attracted much attention and athletes remained in control of their sport. But with the approach of the 1998 Nagano Olympics, the IOC decided to recognize the sport officially and include it in the winter Olympic programme. But the IOC refused to recognize the ISF, as the International Ski Federation (FIS) had, since 1994, been its official counterpart for all skiing sports, including snowboard. Snowboarders were informed that they could only qualify for the Olympics if they took part in competitions organized by the FIS. Swiss champion Ueli Kestenholz, who won a bronze medal at the Nagano Olympics, strongly disapproved of the IOC's policy:

> Contrary to the International Snowboard Federation, where snowboarders decide for themselves, with the International Ski Federation 'riders' are the hostages of bureaucrats. They lose their freedom. They are obliged to run for their national teams and they cannot choose their own trainers. They are put in a mould. Consequently, they lose the possibility to say whether their own sport is going in the right direction or not … The essence of snowboard is freedom; that does not prevent us from behaving like professionals.
>
> (Buss 2002)

In 2002, 11 years of self-determination came to an end when the ISF, short of funds, was forced to merge with the FIS. Gilles Jacquet, a Swiss athlete who was twice world champion, explained: 'Under the ISF we had some influence on the rules of the game; we were consulted before decisions were taken. This isn't the case any more' (Buss 2002a: 43).

FREEDOM OF MOVEMENT

Millions of children worldwide are members of an official sports club and involved in organized competitive sports. They generally pay a fee for their membership. If talented young athletes want to change clubs, their original club may request that a compensation fee be paid to recompense its work in developing the athletes' potential before it releases them. Sporting authorities have allowed and even legitimized these transfer practices, which are especially common in the

most popular sports. But they may severely infringe the right to freedom of association of young athletes by conditioning their freedom of movement with the
payment of a transfer sum. Young athletes can be transferred against their will if
their club wants to make profit through selling their players or they may be frustrated in their desire to change clubs if the transfer sum requested is considered
excessive by other clubs.

Such serious threats to the freedom of association of young athletes have been
denounced and brought to court in both Belgium and Luxembourg (Blanpain
1993) and parents of young athletes have established associations to protect their
children's rights, such as *Jeunesse-Football-Liberté* (Youth-Football-Freedom).
One case taken to court, that of Eddy Michel, a 15-year-old basketball player,
made jurisprudence. The young athlete wanted to leave his club, Ensival, for
Club Pepinster. But Ensival refused on the basis of existing basketball rules and
demanded an excessively high transfer fee. In September 1994, the civil court of
Verviers condemned Ensival and the Belgian Basketball Association, ordering
them to free the young player immediately and offer him a new licence to play.
The public prosecutor's office severely condemned the transfer rules and practices between sports clubs:

> ... considering that the new basketball rules show by themselves that ath-
> letes remain in their eyes negotiable 'commodities' ... considering that a
> sport rule – far from truly wanting to compensate the real costs of formation
> ... wishes to organize and market in a constraining manner something that is
> in reality an 'acquisition' ... of human beings as if they were crude com-
> modities, the objects of speculation, evidently forgets that slavery has been
> abolished for many centuries in our country and that human beings ... are
> always and in whatever circumstances, outside commerce ...
>
> (*Journal du Droit des Jeunes* 1994: 29)

In another Belgian case concerning a 15-year-old football player, the judge argued
that it was not up to a sports club to decide what the interests of a young player
were, but that parents must be believed when they claimed their son wanted to
join another club. Another judge considered that the dignity of a 16-year-old
footballer was threatened, especially in view of his young age, by being treated as
a simple commodity and therefore exposed to the law of supply and demand (De
Smet 1993: 14).

Freedom of association of young athletes should also provide a legal basis for
young professional athletes who wish to form or join labour unions. Article 15 of
the Convention on freedom of association does not explicitly recognize this right
to young people under 18, though it clearly does not exclude the possibility; but
the International Covenant on Civil and Political Rights does recognize this
right to 'everyone' in its article 22. In the light of article 3 (best interests), article
12 (right of children to have their opinions heard), article 32 (protection from
economic exploitation) and article 41 (highest attainable standard), it would
seem acceptable that the most mature young athletes working legally under

labour contracts, at least those over 15 years of age (the minimum employment age for industrialized countries set by ILO Convention No. 138), be given the possibility by law to form or join unions and bargain collectively. Nevertheless, it appears that no such cases exist anywhere in the world.

RIGHT TO PRIVACY

Almost all state constitutions protect the right of 'everyone' to privacy but, in most countries until recently, this right has not been taken seriously when applied to young people under 18 years old. The Convention's entry into force has given more weight to the child's right to be protected from 'arbitrary or unlawful interference with his or her privacy, family, home or correspondence, [or to] unlawful attacks on his or her honour and reputation' (article 16.1). Nevertheless, in practice this right is still weakly enforced and not systematically guaranteed to children by adults, judicial courts and public authorities, who still consider children as simple objects in the hands of adults.

Young athletes' right to privacy can be threatened mainly if they are suspected of doping or if they attract media attention. The Convention guarantees that any child has the right 'to be presumed innocent until proven guilty according to the law' (article 40.2.b.i). In reality, if athletes (of any age) are suspected of having used illegal products or other forms of doping, their identities are sometimes revealed 'in the interest of the public', even before scientific testing, judicial or other proceedings are complete.

Young athletes' right to privacy was a major issue of controversy in the United States in the early 1990s. The question arose as to whether state schools could impose on all student athletes random drug tests without violating their constitutional right to privacy, including that of not being subjected to unreasonable searches. Many young athletes in Vernonia (Oregon) were found to be using illicit products and the high schools' prevention measures had failed to decrease the trend. The schools decided, with the support of parents, to make students, chosen at random, undergo a urine analysis to test for traces of drugs. Students taking part in inter-school athletics and their parents had to sign a form agreeing these tests. Those who refused to sign, like 12-year-old football player James Acton, could not participate in the schools' teams. James's parents also refused to sign as they felt that such random testing in the absence of any evidence of drug use was a violation of his right to privacy. They took the case to court and it went to the United States' Supreme Court, which decided in 1995 that the Vernonia school district's drug testing policy did not violate students' federal and constitutional right to privacy (US Supreme Court 47J US 1995). Some groups and scholars strongly disagreed with the court's decision and believed that it was excessively influenced and biased by the government's 'war on drugs' policy at that time and argued that within school context, courts have consistently stated that students 'do not shed their constitutional rights ... at the school gate' (Shulter 1996; Ettman 1997).

ROLE AND OBLIGATIONS OF THE MEDIA

As a result of their success, some outstanding young athletes suddenly become public figures, which can easily lead to their right to privacy being threatened in view of the overwhelming interest that sports generate in most societies. While public figures should expect and accept some degree of intrusion by the media in their private life, children and adolescents are still vulnerable and should benefit from special protection.

In 1998, the International Federation of Journalists (IFJ) adopted guidelines and principles for reporting issues involving children in light of the Convention on the Rights of the Child, which recognize that 'children have an absolute right to privacy ... journalistic activity ... should always be carried out with appreciation of the vulnerable situation of children', and recommends that journalists and the media 'consider carefully the consequences of publication of any material concerning children and shall minimise harm to children; guard against visually or otherwise identifying children unless it is demonstrably in the public interest' (IFJ 1999; 2002). The Convention also encourages the media to protect the child 'from information and material injurious to his or her well-being' (article 17.e).

Athletes and their coaches and clubs (or federations) often need the media to get sufficient exposure to attract fans and financial support. But young athletes need some protection to ensure that excessive publicity does not hurt their development in the long term. When she was 12, figure skater Tara Lipinski's parents welcomed all requests for information and interviews from journalists to ensure their daughter's high visibility in the media: 'It's hard to say "no" to the media,' admitted her mother (Brennan 1999: 55).

In 1998, 17-year-old tennis player Martina Hingis attracted major media attention not for her sporting results but due to her 'first romance'. When French tennis player Amélie Mauresmo was 19, she reached the final of the 1999 Australian Open, and she also publicly announced her homosexuality. Thereafter, the media seemed only interested in her private life. 'After all I have done for tennis, the only thing they talk about is my private life,' she said (Agence France Presse 1999). Diego Maradona, the Argentinean football prodigy of the 1980s, remembered often feeling harassed and powerless with respect to the media when he was young. He explained:

> at the age of 15, everybody expected me to be able to face men with 40 years of experience in football and others who had spent 50 years in journalism ... nobody has ever understood that a kid of 15 feels lost and does not know how to protect himself.
>
> (*Voetbal International* 2000: 9)

The privacy and identity of young athletes who are victims of any form of abuse or exploitation should especially be respected, particularly in serious situations such as sexual abuse or trafficking and sale. By reporting with sensitivity on these issues, the media can play a positive role in protecting children; however, it can also aggravate dramatic situations by publishing unnecessary private details and sensationalist stories. In Canada (1996) and the Netherlands (1997), media strategies were developed to raise the awareness of the press prior to the publication of a report on sexual harassment and abuse at Olympic level in order to protect the right to privacy of the victims (Council of Europe 2000a: 10). Some sports federations have also adopted guidelines for athletes in their dealings with the media. This is the case of the Canadian Hockey Association (1997) which recognized that 'sport administrators can use media as a tool not only to communicate policy but to help keep the sport environment safe'. But it drew attention to:

> hidden dangers in providing too much information to the public ... when children under legal age are involved. Administrators should be careful about what information is available in event programmes, media guides or web pages. Parents need to be knowledgeable and sign a consent form before information is publicized about their minor child. For example, administrators might set up a web page which includes photos and home addresses for adolescent athletes that could very well help raise the profile of the sport and/or club or association. Unfortunately such information also is a gold mine for those with bad intent such as sexual predators.

The right to privacy of young athletes can also be threatened in other types of situations. Medical information and test results, for example, should remain in the private sphere but are too often revealed to the media without the athlete's consent (Orchard 2002; Kidd 2003).

Respect for privacy also includes the right of everyone to control their own image, including whether their image can be published or not. While this obviously does not apply to a photo published in relation to a sports competition, for example, young athletes have the right to protect the use of their image without their consent in events that are not public. In many countries, a child's parent or guardian can also oppose the publication of a photograph of a young athlete (André-Simonet 2000: 271–8).

NOTES

1 The Convention's three other general principles identified by the Committee on the Rights of the Child are non-discrimination (article 2); the principle of the best interests of the child (article 3); and the right to life, survival and development (article 6).
2 The nine states are Bosnia and Herzegovina, Brazil, Croatia, Cuba, Iran, Nicaragua, the Philippines, Serbia and Montenegro, and Slovenia (Lansdown 2000: 6). The debate on lowering the national-level voting age to under 18 was intense in countries such as Germany, Switzerland and the United Kingdom in 2003.

16 A fair field
Non-discrimination

You're black, you're a young male, all you're supposed to do is deal drugs and mug women. The only reason why you're here is because you can make their team win. If their teams win, these schools get a lot of money. This whole thing is revolving around money.

(Film-maker Spike Lee, in Joravsky 1995: 219)

Sports are a reflection of society and, as such, are not free from discrimination, despite the fact that the right to be protected from all forms of discrimination is one of the most fundamental human rights and is recognized as an essential principle by all major international human rights treaties. This right is deeply rooted in the belief that every individual is equal under the law and receives equal protection and access to services from the state without discrimination.

The only international human rights treaty to recognize explicitly the right not to be discriminated against in access to sports is the Convention on the Elimination of All Forms of Discrimination Against Women (1979), which states in its article 10 that:

> States Parties shall take all appropriate measures to eliminate discrimination against women in order to ensure to them equal rights with men in the field of education and in particular to ensure, on a basis of equality of men and women: ... (g) the same opportunities to participate actively in sports and physical education.

In addition, one international treaty specifically addresses the issue of non-discrimination and other forms of intolerance, such as segregation, in sports: the Convention against Apartheid in Sports which entered into force on 3 April 1988. It included a provision banning all competitions between sports clubs from South Africa and clubs from other countries. For the same reason, South Africa was at the time excluded from the International Olympic Committee (IOC) and all other international sporting federations. But this convention lost its *raison d'être* when the apartheid regime fell in South Africa in 1990.

Discrimination in the access to sport is a vast subject that has been extensively researched (Carroll and Hollinshead 1993; McGuire and Collins 1998; Rowe and Champion 2000) and deserves an entire book to itself. This book will limit itself to issues of discrimination that directly relate to children involved in intensive training and competition.

Young athletes can be affected by discrimination based on, for example, gender, racial or social class, among others. Juan Antonio Samaranch, IOC president from 1980 to 2001, stated:

> Our duty is to be at the service of the athletes, to place them on an equal footing, whatever the political or economic system to which they belong, to make them independent, foster their development and combat all forms of discrimination which could hinder their personal growth or integration into society.
>
> (IOC 2001: 6)

The Convention on the Rights of the Child offers a comprehensive non-discrimination provision which declares that children should not be discriminated against for 'race, colour, sex, language, religion, political or other opinion, national, ethnic or social origin, property, disability, birth or other status' (article 2.1). The Committee on the Rights of the Child identified this provision as one of the Convention's four overarching principles, to be applied when implementing any other right (see note 1, Chapter 15). States have a twofold obligation: not to discriminate in any way against children and not to allow others to discriminate against them. Under domestic law, public authorities should not only prevent and combat discrimination actively, but they should also take measures to rectify instances of discrimination.

But what about private associations or clubs? Do they have the right to impose discriminatory rules? Can they refuse access to individuals on the basis of their personal status? The question is an important one. International human rights law is still ambivalent about the effects of human rights treaties on private entities, as ultimately it is states that are accountable under legally binding treaties (Clapham 1995; Addo 1999). Nevertheless, courts and human rights experts and bodies increasingly recognize that private associations or clubs do have some responsibility, and states must take preventive measures to ensure that, within the private sphere, individuals' human rights are protected (UN Committee on Economic, Social and Cultural Rights 2000; UN Committee on the Rights of the Child 2002b).

Courts have usually tried to draw a fine line between the right to associate freely and the right to be free from non-discrimination. In sports, they generally consider that, as these private entities are open to the public, they should respect the non-discrimination principle (Frank 1994). In the United States, for example, girls could not become members of the Little League Baseball association – and therefore couldn't play official games – until 1974, when a New Jersey court declared their exclusion illegal. Discrimination still exists regarding access to private sport associations or clubs; in Western countries, some sports – such as golf, tennis and polo – were long reserved for privileged social classes and some of these sports' clubs still deny membership to minority groups.

Despite increased awareness and sensitization campaigns by public and sport authorities, racial discrimination is still very present in everyday sport (Rowe and Champion 2000; Carrington and McDonald 2001). Young athletes, due to their inherent vulnerability and lack of empowerment, are especially exposed to racism and xenophobia. Racist experiences are clearly a significant factor accounting for low sport participation among minority groups in many countries (Fleming 1993).

GENDER

For a long time, girls and women have been systematically discriminated against in competitive sports, experiencing: very poor access and even exclusion; insufficient political and financial support and encouragement; low salaries; little interest among (male) sport officials and others, including the media; and weak representation in coaching and decision-making bodies. Sports have traditionally been strongly male-oriented (from 1894 to 1981, for example, there were no women IOC members). It is only since the 1990s that competitive sport has grown closer to achieving gender equity.

For decades, women who wanted to take part in world championships or the Olympic Games were forced to undergo controversial gender verification tests. These tests were based on tacit sexism that implied that men would try to pass themselves off as a woman because the competition would be easier, whereas women could not pretend to be a man. A few male athletes were caught competing in women's events, but other means of verification could have been instituted. Although many national medical associations opposed the test, it was only banned in 1999 by the IOC, which reserved the right to carry out such tests if it considered them necessary.

A wide range of factors has fuelled the recent evolution that led to increasing female participation in competitive sports. First, since the 1970s, many sports federations and clubs have established girls' teams and opened up their structures to women. Second, since the late 1960s, the pressure exercised by the women's rights movement has obliged public authorities to take the non-discrimination principle more seriously and forced governments to provide equal access and treatment to girls within sports. Third, during the late 1970s and early 1980s, both women and men discovered the health benefits of sports. Finally, girls and women have been encouraged to join competitive sports for commercial reasons. During the 1980s, many multinational corporations realized that, by actively advocating for women's emancipation and their involvement in sports, they could potentially double the number of consumers. Increased media coverage of female sports followed in the wake of this new market. In 1996, for example, Nike aired the following advertisement:

If you let me play – I will like myself more, I will have more self-confidence, I will suffer less depression, I will be 60 percent less likely to get breast cancer, I will be more likely to leave a man who beats me, I will be less likely to get pregnant before I want to, I will learn what it means to be strong – if you let me play sports.

(Coakley 1998: 210)

But some experts warn that this evolution is still cosmetic. Brackenridge (2001: 10) observed:

Despite more than three decades of research into institutionalised sexism in sport, however, public awareness of sex discrimination has prompted only limited policy responses and brought about only limited improvements for women ... overall, the progress of the women's sport movement has been characterised by liberal accommodation rather than radical change.

Access to some sports was – and in some cases still is – restricted according to gender. Women and girls have only been permitted to run long-distance races (marathon, 5,000 and 10,000 metres) since the 1980s or to take part in pole-vaulting since the 1990s. And it was not until the late 1970s or early 1980s that pre-puberty girls were allowed to join junior boys' teams in sports such as basketball, volleyball, football or field hockey. A landmark court case in the United Kingdom in 1978 concluded that a schoolgirl (aged 11 at the time of the hearing) was discriminated against as she could not join a boys' football team (at that time, female football hardly existed and there were no junior girls' teams). The Football Association did not permit mixed teams in league competitions. The girl lost in first instance but won the appeal. In Canada, Justine Blainey, a 12-year-old ice-hockey player, challenged in 1986 the Ontario Hockey Association's decision to forbid her to play with a boys' team and the court found that the association had infringed the Ontario Human Rights Code provision on 'equal treatment with respect to services and facilities' (Clapham 1993: 169–71). Girls and women are still not allowed to compete either separately or together with boys and men in some sports such as baseball, American football, ski jumping and wrestling (though female wrestling has been admitted at the 2004 Olympic Games in Athens).

Discrimination also exists against boys and men in rhythmic gymnastics and synchronized swimming; sport federations do not let them compete in official competitions, although in some countries they are allowed to participate at local level. The French Gymnastics Federation refused to allow Gregory Petit (15), to take part in the 2000 National Rhythmic Gymnastics Championships, even though he was considered one of the best athletes in his category (*L'Equipe Magazine* 2000c: 42). The IOC refused to allow American Bill May, the world's best male synchronized swimmer, to participate in the 2000 Sydney Olympics. 'I don't believe that synchronized swimming is made for men. They do not have enough grace for it,' said Edith Boss, a member of the Swiss Swimming Federation (Donzé 2001).

In the United States, a court decided in October 2000 that Duke University had discriminated against a female student, Heather Sue Mercer, who was dismissed from an American football team because of her gender. Condemned to pay US$ 1 million in compensatory damages and US$ 2 million in punitive damages, the university appealed the decision in June 2001, but only contesting the amount of punitive damages awarded, not the verdict (Associated Press 2001a). During her first two years at Duke, Mercer was selected for the university's team and was officially licensed with the National Collegiate Athletic Association. Her trainer dropped her from the team for, he claimed, insufficient performances. Mercer maintained that she was dropped due to her gender and that other male players, though less talented, were kept on the team. The jurors ruled that sex was the motivating factor in the way she was treated and that university officials, informed of her complaints, had failed to act to protect her right not to be discriminated against.

The National Federation of State High School Associations (NFSH) estimates that every year almost 1,000 girls play American football in male teams at high-school level; nearly 1,200 girls wrestle with boys' teams; and over 1,300 girls play baseball in male squads (Bostian 2000). Needless to say, women and girls often face prejudice when playing with male teams. Kellee Sikes, a 24-year-old American ice-hockey player, explained that when she started playing, 'There were no other women … seven years ago; some of the guys wouldn't even get on the ice when I was playing' (Coakley 1998: 210). In 2003 one of the world's top ice-hockey players, Hayley Wickenheiser, a 24-year-old Canadian, was the first woman to sign a professional contract with a Finnish male professional team. The Finnish Ice Hockey Federation approved the deal, contrary to the Italian federation which refused to allow Wickenheiser to play with an Italian men's team.

ATHLETES WITH DISABILITIES

Though access to competitive sports for athletes with disabilities has improved enormously since the 1980s, they are sometimes denied the right to participate in ordinary events. The key issue is related to the definition given to 'disability' and its impact on excluding an athlete from regular sport programmes and competitions. Can young athletes be barred from joining a sport association or school (and possibly benefit from a scholarship) because they have serious learning disabilities, a light functional disorder or have only one kidney? Can they compete in regular events? These are difficult issues for which the best interests of the child, as recognized by article 3 of the Convention, need to be carefully considered, in light of the right to life and development (article 6), the right to participate (articles 12–17), the right to health (article 24) and the right to leisure activities (article 31). Article 23 of the Convention directly protects the rights of children with disabilities, recognizing their right to 'enjoy a full and decent life, in conditions which ensure *dignity*, *promote self-reliance* and facilitate the child's *active participation in the community* [and foresees the child's] fullest *social integration* and individual development' (emphases added).

Respecting the right of disabled child athletes therefore means that, as far as possible, they should be given a chance to participate in regular sport programmes and events with other children. The Committee on the Rights of the Child has systematically advocated such an inclusive approach (UN Committee on the Rights of the Child 1997: paras. 310–39). This principle of inclusion is also enshrined in the UN Standard Rules on Equalization of Opportunities for Persons with Disabilities, a non-binding set of international standards adopted by the UN General Assembly in 1993, which states specifically in relation to sports (Rule 11.3) that: 'Sports organisations should be encouraged to develop opportunities for participation by persons with disabilities in sports activities ... States should support the participation of persons with disabilities in national and international events.'

So far, the international community has not agreed to adopt a legally binding international treaty specifically aimed at promoting and protecting the rights of disabled people, although specific provisions on disability are included in most of the main international human rights treaties. In 2002 a UN working group mandated to draft an international treaty to promote and protect the rights of people with disabilities was established. A first international legally binding treaty might result from this process.

In the United States, where intense competition exists among athletes to obtain sport scholarships for schools and universities, some student athletes with disabilities have been denied access to financial support due to their special status and the health risks inherent in elite sports. Many of these cases ended in court. Generally, the judiciary held that it was up to the individual and not the school to decide whether the risk is acceptable or not. In one case, the court held a school board responsible for violating the US Rehabilitation Act (1973) when it refused to let a student, a minor who only had one kidney, wrestle. The school board based its decision on a fear of injury to the student's remaining kidney and its obligation to protect children from injury. The court disagreed, judging that the student had been discriminated against as the risk of injury was true for any member of the wrestling team (Milani 1998).

Even when health risks are not involved, disabled children have occasionally been banned from ordinary competitions. In Italy, for example, Mauro Muscas, who has Down's syndrome, was not allowed to take part in the 1999 national roller-skating championships even though he was a regional champion. The decision was based on a 1982 law prohibiting any disabled person from competing in sports events that are not specially designed and reserved for the disabled. His parents successfully challenged the decision before parliament and the Italian Olympic Committee (Camera dei Deputati 1999: 44–7). Muscas took part in the championships and won the gold medal in his category.

OTHER FORMS OF DISCRIMINATION

Some young athletes have claimed that they have been discriminated against on the basis of their age and were not given the opportunity to compete in the category they wanted to. For example, the parents of an American tennis player, Monique Viele, threatened to sue the Women's Tennis Association (WTA) as they felt that their daughter (14 at the time) was a victim of WTA's allegedly discriminatory age rules. The WTA forbids players under 15 years old to turn fully professional in order to protect them from any form of abuse or exploitation and encourage them to end compulsory education. Finally, Viele's parents did not file the complaint (Homsi 1999).

In 2002, the US National Basketball Association (NBA) commissioner, David Stern, proposed to set at 20 the minimum age to play in the NBA, as he considered that even the most talented teenagers should stay in college, rather than join the frenetic NBA world. His proposition generated outrage, and players, coaches and managers all rejected it. Some considered that the NBA had no legal basis to impose such an age restriction and that it was discriminatory. Mark Conrad, professor of sports law at Fordham University (USA), said that imposing a minimum age limit to young players 'wouldn't stand a chance in court' (Shook 2002). So far, no limit has been set.

Young HIV-positive athletes can be victims of discrimination both in and outside the sporting context. What happens when a child infected by HIV/AIDS wants to compete in a contact or non-contact sport? The response is a balance between the individual's right not to be discriminated against and the need to protect public health (Appenzeller 2000: 129–32). Risk of transmission during sporting activities is believed to be extremely low and so far only one unsubstantiated report described possible transmission during a collision between soccer players in Italy. The American Academy of Pediatrics (2000a) considers the risk so low that it recommends that 'athletes infected with HIV should be allowed to participate in all competitive sports'. Jurisprudence is still almost non-existent in this field; however, in view of the magnitude of the HIV/AIDS pandemic worldwide, cases of infected young athletes claiming the right to play and compete will increase rapidly. In one of the very rare cases to reach the judiciary, the US Court of Appeals rejected in 1999 the right of 12-year-old Michael Montalvo to participate in group karate classes, because the court considered he represented a threat to his peers as karate involves violent body contact, with a high risk of injuries and bleeding. He was, however, offered private courses. The court said that the decision 'did not violate Title III of the ADA [American Disability Act]' because 'Michael posed a significant risk to the health and safety of others that could not be eliminated by a reasonable modification' (US Fourth Circuit Court of Appeals 1999).

The UN Convention on the Rights of the Child protects children from being discriminated against due to their 'parents' or legal guardian's … political or other opinion' (article 2.1). Such discrimination is not rare. In December 2002, the Court of Arbitration for Sport (CAS) was seized for the first time ever with such a case. Three children from the same family had been formally excluded from their ice-hockey team in Geneva (Switzerland) due to disagreement between their parents and club officials, though the latter recognized that the three players had an excellent record in the club (Jan-Hess 2002: 55). The case was admissible under the jurisdiction of CAS as the sports club concerned had explicitly mentioned in its by-laws that any conflict would be referred to the CAS. In May 2003, the CAS adopted a judgement on the case, but decided that it should be kept confidential.

Part VI
Is it just a game?
Responsibilities of adults

17 Reaping the fruits

Responsibilities, rights and duties of the parents

When my daughter made the Olympic team, I told her, 'You didn't make the Olympic team, I did'.

(Carol Stack, mother of gymnast Chelle Stack, in Ryan 1995: 148)

What I'd tell other parents is it's not worth it. It's just a sport. Don't do it. Don't do it at all. Enjoy your children as they grow up. It was child abuse what we did, what coaches did ... The only thing I don't apologize for is wanting her to do as well as she could do. But how do you draw the line between encouraging and pushing? I certainly couldn't.

(Carol Jackson, father of gymnast Amy Jackson, in Ryan 1995: 168)

Contrary to popular belief, the rights and responsibilities of parents or other adults are not threatened by recognizing children's human rights. It comes as no surprise to find that those who are against the Convention are generally to be found among society's most conservative and radical political and religious groups, who consider that the concept of child rights erodes the traditional family setting (David 1995: 34–8). The Heritage Foundation (USA), an ultra-conservative think tank, claims:

Few Americans are aware that agencies of the United Nations system are involved in a campaign to undermine the foundations of society – the two-parent, married family, religions that espouse primary importance to marriage and traditional sexual morality, and the legal and social structures that protect these institutions.

(Fagan 2001)

The Convention on the Rights of the Child promotes consultation, progressive autonomy, empowerment and self-reliability of the child, but also fully recognizes the 'responsibilities, rights and duties of parents' (article 5) and their 'primary responsibility for the upbringing and development of the child' (article 18).

For any parent, raising their child – something that cannot be learned in advance – is one of the biggest challenges in their life. Parents obviously have a great influence on their children. In the case of most athletes, it was their parents who encouraged them to take up sports and join teams, sometimes at an early age (Woolger and Power 1993). In Belgium, a 1995 survey of athletes aged between nine and 12 revealed that 46 per cent were introduced to their sport club by their parents. The remainder were influenced by their peers, schoolteachers or coaches (University of Antwerp 1995: 25). A 1999 survey covering young people in England showed that 46 per cent of parents strongly encouraged them to take part in sport (Sport England 2001a: 172).

Article 18 of the Convention, which recognizes the primary responsibility of parents in the upbringing of their children, also clearly states that 'the best interests of the child will be their basic concerns'. This concept of 'best interest' is obviously crucial in the field of child rights, and is the principle most frequently evoked in situations of conflict of interest. But it is not always easy to define and can be misused, having been used on occasion to justify treatment of children that amounts to human rights violations, such as forced separation from the family, deprivation of liberty or corporal punishment. 'What is remarkable about this standard, however, is its persistence taken alongside its complete lack of definite, or seemingly necessary, content,' argues one expert (Wolfson 1992: 7).

Nevertheless, respecting the best interests of the child means that, in the implementation of one right, the Convention's rights as a whole should be respected. In the context of intensive training, parents do not always respect their child's right to express their views freely and to have them duly taken into account (article 12). Reports of children who are pressured into intensive training and almost threatened if they want to stop and leave competitive sports are increasing (see Chapter 8).

When parents fail to protect their child, public authorities have the obligation to do so, as foreseen in article 19 of the Convention. In the context of competitive sports, this responsibility to protect the child also binds 'any other person who has the care of the child' (article 19.1), such as coaches and officials, especially in situations where young athletes train intensively and spend more time with those involved in their sporting environment than with their biological parents. Most societies still resist to a certain extent the fact that the state can intervene in domestic affairs in order to protect children (Kelly and Mullender 2000); the sporting world shares the same sort of resistance in facing outside scrutiny and intervention.

An enormous number of parents all over the world get involved in the sports their children practise, though the reasons why they do so are not always well understood. Sport psychologist Shane Murphy (1999: 42) has identified a number of motivational factors: bonding with a child; providing a supervised structure for free time and excitement; supporting the child's physical development and health; teaching the child self-control; and developing talent and socialization.

Since the 1980s, many forms of child abuse have been identified in families and in society as a whole (Gelles and Cornell 1983). Some parents' behaviour can be considered abusive if they are excessively involved in their children's sporting careers. Some parents talk as if they are 'addicted' to their child's sporting activities. The mother of a figure skater explained that she:

> got hooked the first time I saw Tess [her daughter] on the medal stand ... I kept coming back for more. Winning an event was never enough ... After a while I stopped listening to Tess. I wanted her to win. For me, I think, I needed it ... Tess wanted out a long time before I realized that it had to be that way. She was angry with me for the last few years. I just hope I didn't waste her childhood.
>
> (Murphy 1999: 84)

EXCESSIVE IDENTIFICATION AND SELF-SATISFACTION

For many young athletes, sport and competition provide an environment in which they can progressively develop their autonomy and self-reliance, boost their self-esteem and become agents of their own development. They can also create a new social network, different from those at home and in school.

Raising children is neither an exact science nor an art. What may work for one child will not for another. Parents are constantly challenged: they need to be attentive to their children and show genuine interest in their activities while respecting their progressive development and autonomy. When young athletes take sport very seriously and train over two hours a day, it is normal that parents become closely involved. Transportation, relations with trainers, changes in meal times, financial implications, attending competitions: there are many reasons for parents to become absorbed in their child's sporting life.

Joan Ryan, author of the bestselling book, *Little girls in pretty boxes*, declared:

> almost every successful child athlete rides to the top on the shoulders of a parent undaunted by sacrifice and extremes – whether this means sending a child far away to train, mortgaging a home to foot the bills, taking a child out of school so he can train longer hours, abusing her physically or verbally for not performing, or even giving up custody. All skating and gymnastics parents worth their salt own four things: a car, an alarm clock, a checking account and a vision – sometimes their child's, often their own.
>
> (Ryan 1995: 146)

While it is true that few athletes became successful without the involvement of their parents, it is wrong to assume that athletes cannot succeed without their parents pushing them. The father of Michael Jordan, the world's most successful basketball player, always kept some distance during his son's early involvement in sports. He told the *Chicago Tribune* in 1990: 'I had no idea all this would happen and maybe that's better. If I had, I might've pushed him too hard.'

Competitive sports can threaten children by projecting them at a very early age into an adult world. Parents are responsible for protecting them (see Table 17.1) but without being overprotective. Jon Hellestedt considered that parents can be under-involved, moderately involved or over-involved in their child's competitive sports activities. However, his research indicated, as does that of other researchers, that children may be made more vulnerable to abuse if their parents fail to take an active interest in their sporting activity (Hellestedt 1987; Brackenridge 1997). Once again, the problem many parents face is how to protect without being overprotective.

Competition among parents is not a particularity of sports; it can occur in any field of activity of children, whether education, arts or music. But, caught up by their obsession for success, some parents can lose control and go too far. Ryan (1995: 147) explained that:

> no parent sets out to destroy a girl's life. Yet so many lose their way, seduced by the possibilities. Parents speak of being swept in a maelstrom of competitiveness and ambition so intense they often use the word 'insane' to describe their behaviour at the time.

Table 17.1 Convention on the Rights of the Child: key obligations for parents with regard to young athletes

Situation	Relevant provision(s) of the Convention
Never force children to participate in sport	Articles 2, 3, 6 and 12
Show proper attention and interest with regard to children's sporting activities and provide appropriate guidance. Be properly informed about the people caring for children during their sporting activities	Article 5
Always listen to children's opinions and take them duly into account in all matters. Discuss and respect their sport objectives	Article 12
Empower children progressively in order to provide them with tools for their own empowerment and protection	Articles 12 to 17
Respect children's privacy.	Article 16
Ensure that children are not forced to train excessively and that they are not pushed into illicit unhealthy behaviour (such as doping)	Articles 3, 6,19 and 24
Behave with fair play and respect towards others, such as opponents and sport officials	Articles 5 and 29
Ensure that children's right to education is not overshadowed by considerations concerning a sporting career	Articles 3 and 28
Encourage sound skill development.	Article 29
Protect children from any form of economic exploitation	Article 32

Parents do not always have the emotional distance, analytical capacity and sport culture to understand fully their children's athletic capabilities. In 1997, Robert Malina, former director of the Institute for the Study of Sports at Michigan State University (USA), noted:

> Parents of children labelled as talented may develop a false sense of potential for their child's success in sport either in the form of a college scholarship or a professional career ... Early identification of 'talent' is no guarantee of success in sport during childhood, let alone during adolescence and adulthood. There are simply too many intervening variables associated with normal growth, maturation and development, and the sport system itself.

Parents might also be tempted to live their own frustrated ambitions through their children's career and live the success of their children as their own. This behaviour has been identified by psychologists as 'achievement by proxy'. The mother of twin figure-skating champions said:

> The first competition one of my daughters won, we were hooked ... It's just an amazing feeling. It's like horse racing. That's your horse. That's your prized possession. That's your showpiece. And when they do well, it's easy for a parent's need for recognition, for filling unfulfilled dreams, to surface ... We all became junkies of our kids' success.
>
> (Ryan 1995: 151)

Many champions may have been forced into competitive sport in order to please their parents, but others benefited from their parents' advice and guidance. American Marion Jones, Olympic champion sprinter, explained that, in 1992 at the age of 16, she qualified for the US Olympic relay: 'I was really a kid ... I hesitated and discussed with my mother and we decided to withdraw from the selection. My body was not ready, nor was I mentally mature' (Inizan 2000a: 42).

Parents' ambitions may also be fuelled by motives such as money, social recognition, glory, prestige and self-esteem, with the best interests of the child left selfishly to one side. Some athletes were forced into competitive sport in order to please a parent. 'My dad forced me into it [boxing] when I was 11 but I didn't like it at all,' said English boxer Danny Williams. 'Since I was a little baby he just kept saying I was going to be a champion' (Reuters 1994). The parental duty to provide '*appropriate* direction and guidance in the exercise by the child of the rights recognized in the Convention' (article 5, emphasis added) can be drawn into a maelstrom of irresponsible acts.

Mike Agassi, the father of American tennis player Andre Agassi and a tennis teacher, had his son on the courts at the age of three. When asked by a French television journalist what would have happened if little Andre hadn't liked the sport, Mike Agassi, a former low-ranked boxer, replied: 'He had no choice. Kids want to do something so that their parents are happy and the more he would train the more I was happy.' According to Paul Banman, author of a biography on Andre Agassi, his older sister Rita had a real 'potential but her father was too hard on her'.

Competitive sport should not become the dream of parents and the nightmare of young athletes. It has to be an enjoyable pursuit for the child athlete, even when training and competing. But the line between encouraging children and applying excessive pressure is fine. Parents' high expectations can be an additional factor of stress for a child already under pressure from coaches, officials and the media to obtain good results. A study of 46 elite Olympic athletes showed that, while 95 per cent of them said their parents were their main source of encouragement in sports, a large percentage also stated that their parents were a source of stress to them. One Olympic athlete recalled:

> I didn't understand my dad's harsh attitudes. I just wanted to go out and have fun, basically, and of course my dad wanted me to go out there and kick ass and take names. That took all the fun out of it.
>
> (Murphy 1999: 93)

Disproportionate expectations may also trap child athletes and limit their ability to take independent decisions, such as leaving the sport when they feel they want to quit. 'It would break my dad's heart if I gave up. It means everything to him,' explained a British gymnast (TOYA 1992: 8). A Canadian skater noted that her mother 'freaked out' and did not speak to her for three weeks after she announced that she was quitting (Donnelly 1993: 102). American gymnast Amy Jackson felt overwhelmed by her father's ambitions:

> I was kind of worried that my father was so excited about it. I was scared, scared of learning new things, scared I wasn't going to be good enough, that I wouldn't be able to do anything to please him. I was already thinking of quitting. I always did what I was told. I was scared of what my dad would say if I said anything.
>
> (Ryan 1995: 163)

Sport associations and clubs increasingly offer support, information tools and training to parents about children's involvement in sports in order to prevent false expectations, inappropriate behaviour, personal conflicts and other harmful situations. In the United States, the Parents Association for Youth Sports (PAYS) adopted a code of ethics, which states, *inter alia*:

> I will encourage good sportsmanship by demonstrating positive support for all players, coaches, and officials at every game, practice or other youth sport event ... I will insist that my child plays in a healthy environment ... I will remember that the game is for youth – not adults.
>
> (National Alliance for Youth Sports 2000)

In amateur sports, clubs and associations rely heavily on parents' involvement as coaches. Even political authorities encourage them. British Sports Minister, Richard Caborn, suggested in September 2001 that parents become volunteer coaches for youth and the British government's special adviser on sport, Sue Campbell, said: 'Parents who become coaches are revered in Australia and the United States of America, and here they could play a very important role by helping to enthuse, motivate and teach potential stars of tomorrow' (Campbell 2001).

SPORTS AS A FAMILY FINANCIAL INVESTMENT

Since the 1980s, the sports entertainment business has enabled athletes in a number of sports to make a decent living from their sport. But involvement in intensive training programmes and competitive sports – travel, equipment, club fees, training camps and especially private coaches – can also constitute a considerable financial burden on family budgets.

In some sports, such as figure skating and gymnastics, a top child athlete might cost up to US$ 30,000 a season in coaching alone. With sports becoming constantly more sophisticated and organized, coaches are offered ever-higher salaries and are sometimes caught up in bidding wars between clubs. In figure skating or gymnastics, for example, it is not uncommon for the best American coaches to earn over US$ 100,000 for training children under 14 (Brennan 1999: 111). Less well-known coaches can earn up to US$ 60,000 in the US and the UK.

In many families around the world, parents invest every penny in their children's education, some even contracting lifelong debts. In a large majority of cases, the investment finally pays off when the student completes his or her studies and begins qualified work. With sport, the financial investment is far more risky; even if the child works as hard as possible, there is absolutely no guarantee of success and only a minority of child athletes will ultimately make a living from their sport. Tom Rusedski, the father of Greg, a top British-Canadian tennis player, admitted having spent all his money on his son, US$ 400,000 in four years, to support him in his early years. He mortgaged his house to cover these costs (Bouveret 1994: 2).

Investing a lot of money to offer children the best training environment increases the pressure on them to succeed and may lead to their parents becoming exploitative, rather than protective. What pleasure can young athletes have in their sport if they realize their parents are calculating whether or not they are 'cost-effective'? Carol Stack, the mother of Chelle, who was in the 1988 US Olympic gymnastics team, admitted that:

> The more money you put into it, the more you want to see. It gets to the point where it's real vicious ... you want your kid to be the best, and you're going to push, scream, yell and holler – 'Hey I paid for this'.
>
> (Ryan 1995: 152)

When her daughter told her she wanted to quit three months before the Olympic trials, Carol Stack replied: 'I put this much time and effort into this and, by God, if you think I'm going to let you quit now, you're crazy. If I have to beat you every day, you're going to do it' (Ryan 1995: 153).

The time, emotions and finances invested by their parents can put such pressure on some young athletes that they cannot cope with it. They may feel they are competing for adults rather than for themselves and feel guilty if they do not meet expectations or wish to quit. One top 15-year-old American figure skater said: 'It's no fun anymore. I hate practice sessions, I hate the competitions. But how can I tell my parents? They spent US$ 50,000 on me ... How can I let them down?' (Murphy 1999: 121). In Murphy's opinion, 'There have always been pushy parents. It's just much more common these days because those dollar signs are out there' (Kleinhenz 2000: 23).

In some countries, especially the United States, the most talented athletes may be eligible for an educational scholarship. In principle, the existence of scholarships offers a wonderful opportunity for young athletes from all social classes to continue with their education. In reality, the lure of a scholarship can oblige the young athlete to succeed in order to alleviate financial pressure on the parents. Again children might run into a conflict of interests with their elders: competitive sport goes beyond personal pleasure; it becomes a financial investment.

For some young athletes, having to obtain a scholarship can be an additional burden and generate high levels of stress. One father who pushed his 11-year-old daughter to train intensively in softball so that she could obtain a college scholarship stated: 'All I want is for Stephanie to be good enough to deserve a full ride to one of those schools she needs to go to.' But Stephanie saw it differently, her motivation did not go beyond pleasure, and she felt her father considered her an investment that must pay off (Murphy 1999: 54–5).

Competitive sport can fuel ambitions of parents living in poverty, and may in some cases be a lever to eliminate social barriers, in both industrialized and developing societies. A handful of talented basketball players will leave their American ghetto every year for privileged neighbourhoods; a few football players will escape the slums of Brazil or Nigeria to join the wealthy suburbs of Paris, London or Barcelona. But this is for the lucky few – it will not happen for most young athletes, despite the hopes and high expectations of their parents. When she sees parents bringing their five-year-old daughters to the gymnastics hall, Romanian trainer Elena Chankelia, European finalist during the 1960s, has said that she thinks, cynically, 'Maybe it's not glory that interests them, but rather the money their child might bring home. They believe that they are going to get wealthier thanks to their daughter' (Arte 2001).

PARENTAL VIOLENCE

For many parents, sport is a passion, generating such intensive emotions and feelings that they may lose all sense of perspective and self-control. Child abuse and violence is not unique to sports and occurs in families in all social classes, religions and cultures. But although it is recognized as a universal phenomenon (see Chapter 6), in most countries it is still taboo and underreported (Gelles and Cornell 1983), mainly due to the fact that children cannot get appropriate support easily and, even with such help, it is very difficult for them denounce their own parents. Although very little research has been undertaken, there have been cases of parental, especially paternal, violence towards child athletes.

In the absence of comprehensive studies, anecdotal evidence cannot give a reliable idea of the scope of the phenomenon, but it does indicate that the problem needs to be addressed. In tennis and gymnastics, for example, cases of fathers physically and mentally abusing their daughters have been regularly reported. The fathers of teenage tennis stars such as Andrea Jaeger, Andrea Temeswari, Mary Pierce and Mirjana Lucic have behaved violently towards their daughters, sometimes in front of millions of television viewers. Jim Pierce used to scream, 'Kill the bitch!' while his teenage daughter Mary was playing (Kleinhenz 2000: 23).

It is very difficult for victims of paternal violence to speak out, but Hungarian Andrea Temeswari explained: 'I don't see my father any more. He feels he's lost his golden daughter and that I betrayed him because I did not become the player he dreamed of,' even though, when she was only 15, Temeswari was one of the top ten women tennis players in the world (Inizan 1995: 52). But at 16 she started to rebel against his abuse and left competitive sports before she was 20. When American gymnast Dominique Monceanu took her parents to court for misuse of her personal earnings (see Chapter 11), she told the press: 'I am terrified by my father. I believe that all my father's actions are intended to result in physical harm, bodily injury or assault to me or my friends' (Associated Press 1998d). She also said: 'When I went to compete when I was young, I always was in fear because I would get yelled at by my father' (*Houston Chronicle* 1998: 1S). She admitted that he hit her 'a couple of times'.

Violent behaviour also occurs among adults in sports, mainly between athletes' fathers, or between fathers and sports officials, such as referees. It is not rare that parents use verbal aggression towards officials or the parents of members of the opponents' team if they are disappointed and frustrated by a negative result or disagree with a referee's decision. In the absence of comprehensive studies and official records of incidents (except to some extent in the United States), it is very difficult to assess whether, in absolute terms and as has been suggested, the cases of violence around the playing fields have increased since the early 1990s. However, while the number of reported cases would seem to concur with such a conclusion, it must be borne in mind that the number of games and competitions involving child athletes has exploded since the 1980s in most countries.

Fred Engh, the president of the National Alliance for Youth Sports, an organization that promotes fun and safety in sports in the United States and that counts 2,200 chapters around the country, considered that:

> from road rage to airplane rage to cell-phone rage, children in sport aren't immune to all of this. Now we have sideline rage. The parent of today is much different than the parent of five years ago. It used to be maybe 5 percent of the people stepped over the line. It's growing now to about 15 percent.
>
> (Dahlberg 2001: 1)

The US National Association of Sports Officials (NASO) said in 1998 that assaults on umpires were reported two to three times a week, and especially around fields or arenas where children play. Many of these incidents ended up in court. For example, in California in 2000, a father was sentenced to 45 days in jail for beating and berating a coach who had taken his 11-year-old son out of a baseball game. In Ohio, the girls' soccer league decided in 1999 to ban crowd noise during all of its games for a whole weekend as a result of constant verbal abuse by parents and coaches from the sidelines (Associated Press 1999a). The most extreme case of violence, which shocked the American public, was the killing of one father by another in a fight after their two 12-year-old sons had played an ice-hockey match (Nack and Munson 2000).

The problem of violence against sport officials became so frequent during the 1990s that, since 1998, NASO has insured all its members against assault and almost 20 American states have enacted laws specifically mandating penalties for people who assault sports officials. Some sports associations offer classes to raise parents' awareness about the objectives of sports and their responsibilities. PAYS, for example, estimates that these measures have reduced violence around sport fields. In recent years, over 15,000 parents have been 'trained' in El Paso, Texas, a city where violence around sport fields was frequent; a 1999 brawl at a youth sporting event involved 30 parents, 10 of whom were arrested (National Alliance for Youth Sports 2001).

In Canada, too, many cases of parents over-reacting have been reported in the past five years, especially in ice hockey, the national sport. 'I think parents' expectations are greater than they have ever been,' said Steve Larmer, a 40-year-old retired NHL player and now a volunteer coach for children aged seven and eight. 'They expect more not just from their kids, but from coaches and referees too' (Deacon *et al.* 2001). Sport authorities in many regions of Canada have taken preventive measures to combat parents' abusive behaviour. Since 1994, some Canadian ice-hockey associations oblige parents wanting to enrol their child to sign a pledge that they will behave themselves at games. If they refuse to sign, their child cannot join the team and play.

Violence around sports fields is not only a North American phenomenon, as incidents are regularly reported in Latin America and Western and Eastern Europe. In France, a wave of violence hit football fields near Paris in 1999 and serious assaults were reported. The regional football federations decided to stop all games for several weeks, including junior matches, and then took drastic measures such as appointing police officers to at-risk games (Potet 2000). A year later, the French Minister for Sports declared proudly that violent incidents had decreased by 43 per cent (Buffet 2000).

CHEATING

In their quest for victory, some parents may be tempted to cheat with illegal means so that their child might have a greater chance of winning. In South Korea, for example, parents, college managers, team officials and umpires were implicated in 1998 in a corruption scandal. Football officials were arrested on charges of illegal recruiting, having accepted money from over-ambitious parents who paid to ensure that their children enter college on an athletic basis or play in national junior teams (JoongAng 1998).

In many countries, parents have been caught breaking the rules by altering birth certificates and lying about the age of junior athletes (see also Chapter 5). In August 2001, cheating hit baseball's US Little League World Series, one of the world's most prestigious sport events for children, which attracts millions of television viewers. The parents of Danny Almonte from the Dominican Republic, one of the stars of the event, pretended he was 12 years old, but *Sports Illustrated* discovered that he was officially registered twice under different dates in the Dominican Republic and that, in reality, he was two years older. Eligibility for the Little League is set at 12 years maximum. Almonte's parents at first denied the facts but evidence later showed that they abused the trust of the Little League officials (Thomsen and Llosa 2001).

Another reported case of birth certificate alteration was revealed after a tragic accident during which a 11-year-old American football player lost his life in September 2001 after a fatal collision with two players. An inquiry by the 'Pee-Wee' league revealed that the young player's mother had altered his birth certificate by three months so her son could play in a division normally limited to children aged between 9 and 11 (National Alliance for Youth Sports 2001a).

The most extreme cheating behaviour in which some parents participate is doping. Cases of parents giving their own child illicit performance-enhancing products are reportedly on the increase (see also Chapter 10). Gilbert Duclos-Lassale, former French cyclist and twice winner of the Paris–Roubaix race, has seen this happen in junior teams:

> Once a father asked me: 'What do you think of this product?' It was a substance that we do not use even to race the Tour de France! I said to him: 'If you give this to your child, by the end of the year he won't be able to cycle any more.' At the end of that year I saw the boy again, he had stopped cycling. Today the kid has his own life, but he is destroyed for sports. His body is destroyed …'
>
> (*L'Equipe Magazine* 1992a)

18 Pass the baton

Accountability of coaches, officials and managers

I just want athletes who are ready to compete at a high level. You can no longer wait to develop athletes. If you're not coming in at a certain level, you're wasting a scholarship for two years.

(Harvey Glance, coach at the University of Alabama, USA, in *The NCAA News* 2001)

Mankind owes to the child the best it has to give.

(Declaration on the Rights of the Child 1959: preamble)

For an adult, to train or coach young people can be an extremely exciting and satisfying activity. The overwhelming majority of coaches, whether volunteer or professional, train children and adolescents in full respect of their human rights. The main challenge for every coach or official involved in youth sports is to reconcile the ultimate objective of competitive sports – winning – with the need to protect children from any form of abuse, violence or exploitation. Success must not come at the expense of a negative impact on the child athlete's dignity and integrity.

All over the world, competitive sport is based on the work of volunteers and most sport associations depend heavily upon parents and others to give some of their free time to train an amateur youth team. During the 1990s, the increase in sports leagues and categories in many countries was such that now it is difficult to find sufficient volunteers to sustain these sporting activities. The European Commission estimates that there are almost one million sport clubs and associations in its member states and that approximately 100,000 professional coaches and trainers work outside of the formal school system (European Commission 1999: 16 and 36). Because of this phenomenal demand, it is all too easy for some adults, whether poorly prepared or even ill-intentioned, to find an entry into a sports club. 'The relative social and legal freedom afforded to voluntary sport allows large numbers of young girls and boys to be entrusted to adults about whom parents know very little, other than their coaching qualifications,' noted Celia Brackenridge (2001: 71).

Youth sports may attract certain trainers precisely because it gives them the opportunity to approach children directly. Sport England, the governmental body for sports in England, stated that 'sports organisations are becoming increasingly aware that some individuals, who want to harm and abuse children, will use sport as a medium to gain access to them' (Sport England 2001: 3). However, the threat of abusive behaviour does not only enter sports from the outside, it exists within the world of competitive sport, in which certain behaviours, such as intensive training, high pressure and discipline, paternalism, abusive physical contacts, etc., have long been present and which, in excess, might turn into abuse.

Competitive sport is entirely adult-driven and young athletes rely on adults during training and competitions. Under international law, parents have 'the primary responsibility for the upbringing and development of the child' and 'the best interest of the child will be their basic concern', according to article 18.1 of the UN Convention on the Rights of the Child. Other adults who are regularly in contact with children and assume some level of care and responsibilities, including making decisions concerning careers in some cases, are also required, under article 19, to protect the child from all forms of violence, injury or abuse, neglect or negligent treatment, maltreatment or exploitation. According to many experts, family social systems and the sporting world are structured the same way; child athletes often regard the sport club as a 'surrogate family' with the coach or trainer functioning as a substitute parent (Bizzini and Piffaretti 1998: 51; Donnelly 1999). In this context, under existing state policies and legislation, sports clubs and associations have major responsibilities with regard to protecting the rights of young athletes, especially in ensuring that they receive good-quality, safe training and coaching (see Table 18.1).

UNQUALIFIED TRAINERS

Young athletes, when questioned, generally want their coaches to be qualified. A Belgian study showed that 87.5 per cent of athletes aged between nine and 12 years considered it 'very important' to have a qualified coach, while 10.8 per cent considered it 'important'. The same study also showed that 98 per cent of the children felt that having qualified trainers is the most important criterion for a good sports environment. Other aspects considered important included having friends (89 per cent) and having pleasure (87 per cent). The two criteria considered least important for a sound sporting environment were winning (48 per cent) and being exhausted (39 per cent) (University of Antwerp 1995). 'More than anything else, poorly qualified coaches limit young people's opportunities to derive the full benefits from sport participation. In fact such coaches can cause physical and psychological harm,' said Rainer Martens (2001: 48), a respected sport psychologist and founder of the American Sport Education College, whose maxim is 'Athletes first; winning second'.

Increasingly, local and national sport authorities offer training opportunities to volunteer and professional coaches. In the field of human rights, training is

Table 18.1 Convention on the Rights of the Child: key obligations for coaches, and volunteers and professionals in sports with regard to young athletes

Situation	Relevant provision(s) of the Convention
Ensure that the sport system, including programmes, rules and regulations are child-sensitive	Articles 3, 12 and 31.1
Discuss and respect the objectives of young athletes, even if, for them, fun is considered more important than winning. Seek their opinion in all decision-making processes, and take them duly into account	Articles 3, 12 and 13
Respect the physical, sexual and psychological integrity of the child	Article 19
Never discriminate against an athlete	Article 2
Respect the dignity of the child; do not abuse power	Articles 3 and 12
Create a healthy environment conducive to the holistic development of the child	Articles 3 and 6
Ensure that athletes receive sound and appropriate training, advice and guidance from competent individuals	Articles 5 and 42
Respect the child's right to participate in training programmes and competitions adapted to his or her capacities. Never force a child to train or compete	Articles 3, 6, 12 and 31.1
Always first consider the child and his or her human rights before looking at the champion	Article 3
Protect the right to health of athletes, including with regard to doping	Article 24
Respect the right of young athletes to education; encourage young athletes to gain positive educational achievements	Article 28
Respect the right to rest of the child	Article 31
Do not impose commercial commitments on young athletes, except when proven to be in their best interests	Articles 3 and 32
Ensure that sport is practised in a culture of understanding, peace, tolerance, equality of sexes, friendship and fair play among all people	Article 29
Accept that sport programmes are periodically and independently monitored and that athletes are given access to an appropriate complaint mechanism	Article 3, 4 and 25
Keep the concept of the child's holistic development as the core objective of any sporting activity, rather than valuing only victory	Articles 3, 6 and 12
Always provide athletes with access to adequate information, including with regard to their own health	Articles 17 and 24
Respect athletes' decisions regarding transfer between two sport associations	Articles 12 and 15
Respect the child's interests and activities other than sports	Article 12
Respect the right to privacy of young athletes	Article 16

recognized as an essential tool to improve respect for domestic and international standards. But such training can only bring sound results if it is part of a wider human rights movement that includes a fair system of justice, respect for the rule of law, political leadership favouring human rights, an efficient and independent redress mechanism, sound monitoring and institutional confidence. When reviewing the situation of child rights worldwide, the Committee on the Rights of the Child systematically recommends that public authorities provide or facilitate access to qualitative and periodic training – especially on children's human rights – to all those who work with or for children (Hodgkin and Newell 2002: 615–6). This recommendation relating to training is based on articles 4 and 42 of the Convention. Article 42 affirms: 'States Parties undertake to make the principles and provisions of the Convention widely known, by appropriate and active means, to adults and children alike.'

Although in many countries significant progress has been made since the early 1990s, millions of volunteer and professional coaches around the world are involved in competitive sports without ever having attended a basic training course or education programme. No country has legal requirements for individuals to attain certain minimum standards before they can coach young athletes. According to some experts, the lack of coherence in credential, certification, registration, licensing and screening systems in the profession is likely to lead to child abuse (De Knop *et al.* 1996: 311). A Belgian study revealed in 1998 that, of 1,147 gymnastics trainers, only 42.8 per cent had a certificate (Van Hoecke and De Knop 1998: 33).

In the United States, the Positive Coaching Alliance (PCA) has advocated since the late 1990s for a positive approach to sport coaching. The alliance (2002) declared:

> The youth sports experience provides opportunities for children to learn important lessons about determination, commitment, hard work, teamwork, and empathy while acquiring increased self-confidence and positive character traits. Unfortunately, these opportunities are all too often squandered for a variety of reasons, among them: a) youth coaches and parents blindly emulate the win-at-all-cost mentality that filters down from the professional sports entertainment business, b) youth coaches are untrained in and unfamiliar with principles of effective motivation and age-appropriate teaching strategies. Grassroots youth sports organizations are staffed by volunteers unprepared to lead a complex volunteer educational organization. The time is ripe for a systematic approach that deals with the causes and not just the symptoms of these problems.

The PCA (2002a) has proposed a strategy to transform coaches into what it calls a 'double-goal coach', for whom winning is important, but whose second, more important, goal is 'to help players develop positive character traits, so they can be successful in life'. The alliance offers training for coaches, parents and officials to a wide range of organizations.

Sport associations in many countries have adopted or developed policy statements, codes of conduct or ethical charters, to ensure that coaches and other officials are competent, irreproachable in their behaviour, respect ethical standards and accept the principle of sanctions should they breach them. In the 1990s, for example, The Football Association in England adopted an 11-point code of conduct for its coaches. The first principle states that 'coaches must respect the rights, dignity and worth of each and every person and treat each equally within the context of the sport' and 'coaches must not exert undue influence to obtain personal benefit or reward'. Coaches must also 'ensure that the activities they direct or advocate are appropriate for the age, maturity and experience and ability of players' (The Football Association 2001c). The Australian Sports Commission's anti-harassment policy (ASC and Active Australia 1998a: 9) recommended that all sport organizations declare that they are 'committed to providing a work and sport environment free from harassment and that harassment will not be tolerated; ... setting out what situations are covered by the policy; a statement that harassment is against the law'.

The advantages of such statements are at least fourfold (McNamee 1998). First, they clearly explain the sport activity's objectives and safeguards to all those involved. Second, they define a policy composed of standards and criteria that serve as a benchmark to guide practitioners and evaluate the quality of provision of services. Third, such a policy serves as a neutral framework for negotiating and resolving conflicts. Finally, it sets clear moral and ethical values that, in case of violation, may serve as a tool for sanction.

MORAL PANIC AND ACCOUNTABILITY OF SPORT ORGANIZATIONS

During the 1990s, a number of Western countries, mainly Australia, the United Kingdom and the United States, witnessed a phenomenon identified by some researchers as a 'moral panic'. According to Brackenridge (2001a: 7), this arose 'because of unjustified and sometimes hysterical fears about sexual abuse – and specifically paedophilia'. However, she noted that if child abuse statistics (in the UK) are considered, 'it is clear that sexual abuse is only one part of a much bigger picture'. In the United States, even the respected weekly, *Sports Illustrated*, succumbed to the paranoia, publishing a special, rather sensationalist report entitled 'Every parent's nightmare' (1999).

This 'moral panic' led to a number of constructive reactions in the sports community. After an initial phase of denial and self-protection, officials and trainers realized that many parents were no longer confident that they were leaving their children in safe hands and some organizations adopted or reviewed child protection policies. Remarkable progress has since been achieved, especially in the United Kingdom, but also in other countries, such as Australia, Canada, New Zealand and the United States (see Chapter 19). But the child protection measures set up in these countries focus heavily on sexual abuse and tend to neglect other important child protection issues that may occur in sports, such as children's involvment in intensive training.

As the respect, protection and fulfilment of human rights imply legal obligations, the question of accountability also needs to be addressed in the sporting context. As seen in Chapter 1, if the state is ultimately responsible for ensuring respect for children's rights in sports, sport organizations have an obligation to protect the rights of young athletes, especially when one of their employees acts unlawfully. They cannot escape their responsibilities by failing to prevent violations or refusing to act upon them. But in practice, due to the tradition of self-policing, paternalism, a fierce resistance to independent criticism and a refusal to accept that sport is not always 'pure' and free from society's problems, the principles of accountability and scrutiny are still inadequately respected by the sporting world, or at best looked upon with suspicion.

The state's responsibility is engaged when sport organizations are partly or fully funded by public authorities. In many Western European countries, sport associations depend – at least partly – on public funding. Public funding gives the state a legitimate lever to scrutinize the sports world, including to ensure that sport federations respect the rights of young athletes. In France, a decree adopted in September 2001 concerning sport funding by public authorities, specifies that all training centres have to provide children with a minimum level of schooling or vocational training and that sport organizations must undertake actions to prevent violence in sports. If these requirements are not met, sports clubs and centres can lose their subsidies, which can attain 2.8 million euros a year (Government of France 2001c). In 2001, the French ministries of sport and education investigated two professional football clubs, RC Lens and AJ Auxerre, for not conforming to the established educational minimum standards (Potet 2001). In the United Kingdom, gender equity became a criterion for subsidies and lottery awards during the 1990s (Brackenridge 2001: 168). In March 2001, Sport England decided that any sport association requesting public funding must have a child protection policy in place in order to be eligible (Brackenridge 2001: 194).

TENSION BETWEEN THE OBJECTIVES OF CHILDREN AND ADULTS

As has been shown in preceding chapters, young athletes may become instruments of the excessive ambition of adult coaches or officials. Only very rarely does the sporting world – where the power of adults is unchallenged – allow these young athletes to be seriously involved in discussions about their objectives. In its code of conduct, The Football Association clearly recognizes the need to discuss objectives and mutual expectations with young athletes, parents and coaches in order to avoid misunderstandings, tensions and disappointment: 'Coaches should, at the outset, clarify with the player (and, where appropriate, their parents) exactly what is expected of them and also what they are entitled to expect from their coach' (The Football Association 2001d).

Coaches and trainers should be able to take young athletes to their limit, but not push them over it. Their skills and expertise should be used for the benefit of children, and not only to obtain results. But some coaches push children too far to satisfy their own ambitions. A 12-year-old elite Romanian gymnast, who trained in the national centre in Onesti, admitted: 'It's true they [the trainers] are hard. But they are hard on us for our own interest, so that we can reach the highest level. That's what they want' (Arte 2001).

Coaches and sport managers also need to be made aware of children's developmental stages, which influence the way they perceive competition. A seven-year-old child cannot be trained in the same way as an adolescent ten years older. This might seem evident, but too often young athletes are trained with the same concepts and techniques as adults.

A sports club or association's survival is endangered by poor results – it risks losing credibility, visibility, membership, sponsorship and other indispensable support. 'We need good results, otherwise we lose financial support from the state and that would be catastrophic,' explained Sirje Lubi, secretary general of the Estonian Table Tennis Association (Council of Europe 2001). So, young athletes can rarely escape the imperative to win and reinforce the reputation of their club or federation. This is not necessarily wrong or bad, as long as serious safeguards are put in place to ensure that their rights are taken into consideration.

HOW ADULTS SHAPE COMPETITIVE SPORTS FOR CHILDREN

Research overwhelmingly shows that the major motivation factor for young children to get involved in sports is fun and socializing; winning is at best only part of a wider group of factors (Weiss 1993; TOYA 1995a; Rowe and Champion 2000: 170–1). A British study revealed that 'enjoyment' was the main value for young competitors (rated 4.22 on a scale of importance ranged between 1 and 5) and winning came in last with a rate of only 1.27 (English Sports Council 1998: 9). 'Having fun is the main reason for playing sports given by children aged 5 to 17,' declared American sport psychologist Shane Murphy (1999: 60). Despite this, adults frequently shape competitive sport around the concept of winning by duplicating adult sports models. Successful sports programmes manage to combine fun with competition.

Except in rare cases, the opinions of children are totally ignored when sport programmes and competitions are designed. In the past 20 years, sport's universal success has led to a progressive lowering of the age at which children can compete in national and international competitions (see also Chapter 5). A consequence of this is that, although they can still compete at local or regional events, some of them are selected to take part in national and international competitions at a very young age. Does an athlete aged seven or nine years really need to compete at these levels? Do sport officials know whether this corresponds to a real need among child athletes, or is it simply a selfish aspiration among adults? Or is the involvement of the youngest athletes in national and international events a natural result of growth of the sport movement, globalization and increased professionalism?

Since the 1980s, the importance that adults lend to competitive youth sports has increased – so much so that often young athletes are perceived as adults and required to perform and behave not only as grown-ups but as potential champions, rather than as the children they are. When American figure-skating star Michelle Kwan was only 13, her trainer Frank Caroll did not want judges to consider her 'only' as a junior, so he insisted that she cut her ponytail and start wearing make-up in order to appear more mature. One day during a competition, Kwan arrived for practice with her old ponytail and was told by Caroll: 'Never appear again at an important practice with a ponytail! You have to look the part. Your grooming shows that you care about this. You want to do everything to be the best!' (Brennan 1999: 82).

Before the 1980s, there were very few official competitions involving children under ten years old. Since then, however, children are encouraged to join sports as early as five years of age and they can usually participate immediately in official competitions, although at this age they cannot entirely understand the meaning, implications and strategies of the game. In Romania, young gymnasts are often identified, selected and recruited between the ages of three and four in day-care facilities. Has the lowest age limit been reached, or will even younger children one day be involved in the identification and selection processes of competitive sports? Will child athletes be identified on the basis of their genetic code (see Chapter 10)? Or will champions be encouraged to breed better athletes? 'The child born of this couple will for sure be a champion,' said Nick Bolitieri, the American tennis coach referring on French television in 2001 to the wedding between Andre Agassi and Steffi Graf. Children are increasingly required to function in sports systems shaped by adults, leaving little or no space for creative, spontaneous and unstructured play or fun – activities that are, for such young children, fully compatible with the objective of 'grooming' champion athletes.

The social and economic success and importance of competitive sports all over the world mean that the pressure of a highly publicized system is brought to bear on child athletes. Major youth competitions now attract a national – and sometimes international – television audience. In the United States, baseball's Little League World Series (for children under 12) has been televised since 1953 (live since 1960) and fills 42,000-seat stadiums. Since the 1990s, other junior competitions have followed this trend and are shown on national and international television. Junior (under-14s) gymnastics competitions sometimes receive important television coverage. In 2002, the Danone Nations Cup, a football world championship for players aged ten to 12 years, was held, sponsored by Danone, Nike, Playstation and Eurosport television with the support of the International Football Federation (FIFA). The final of the unofficial tennis world championship for 12- to 14-year-old players was shown live in February 2002 on Eurosport television. Does this really serve the best interests of the child or is it simply bringing more promotion and greater financial profit to sport organizations that are responding to commercial marketing needs?

If these events are viewed solely from the child's viewpoint, what is the added value of having live television coverage of junior events? Is the best interest of the child seriously taken into account when sport organizations contract media corporations? It comes as no surprise to learn that the Association of National Olympic Committees formally suggested a project for a Junior (under-18s) Olympic Games during their 2001 annual congress, to be organized by the International Olympic Committee (IOC) (Agence France Presse 2001d). A year later, the association adopted a resolution in favour of the organization of World Games for Youth (IOC 2002a: 32). Many youth 'Olympic' festivals already exist worldwide, but these are not owned and organized by the IOC and focus more on the importance of cultural exchange and socializing than on purely competitive aspects.

Part VII

Reversing trends

Human rights as a powerful tool

19 Forging a new future

Towards a child-centred sport system

> You cannot assume a coaching risk management programme has been effective if winning is the only measurement.
>
> (Belmonte 1997: 115)

> I know you won't believe me when I say this, but I wish kids, especially black kids, didn't dream so much about playing in the NBA.
>
> (Charles Barkley, 1992 Olympic basketball champion and former NBA star, in Joravsky 1995: 9)

Generally, sport and public authorities have given limited attention to respecting the rights of young athletes. There is still a very low level of awareness and understanding about the specific human rights issues generated by intensive training and competitive sports. Due to their vulnerability, children can be put at risk in any situation, whether in or outside their family environment, in sports or in other activities. But to ensure the rights of young athletes, safeguards must be put in place, and in this regard, society as a whole has too often been unsuccessful, mainly because it has failed to acknowledge that sport can carry serious and potentially harmful side effects. Historically, the clichés surrounding sport have been overwhelmingly flattering; today, however, evidence clearly shows that it is susceptible to many forms of abuse, exploitation and violence that are also common outside the sporting world. Additionally, due to its unique particularities, competitive sport generates specific situations, such as transfer conflicts, intensive training, doping and pressure to win, that may threaten children and that rarely occur at such a young age in any other context.

Modern sport was born more than 100 years ago, but it is only in the past 30 years or so that young athletes have been systematically involved in both mass and elite sport. To promote sports among young people, pre-existing models were used, but these were all based on adult views, needs and requirements. Only since the 1990s has the sporting world systematically integrated specific structural changes in order the better to address the developmental needs of young athletes.

Many people (especially sports officials and coaches) believe that competitive sport is not compatible with respecting young athletes' rights, which they see as an obstacle to moulding a champion. On the contrary, competitive sport can be an ideal vector to fulfil children's rights, as long as the necessary safeguards are in place. Already, most young athletes largely benefit from their positive experiences in competitive sport, even though the efforts taken by sport and public authorities to protect their rights have on the whole been insufficient. More than ten years have passed since the entry into force of the Convention on the Rights of the Child, and it is now urgent for authorities to take more systematic and in-depth measures for two main reasons:

- **Respect for the rule of law** The sporting world, like any other, is bound by human rights laws and policies and can no longer remain an entirely closed and hermetic system.
- **Elimination of harmful side effects** In order to ensure that competitive sport remains a largely positive experience for young people, its potentially harmful side effects must be addressed, so that the number of athletes whose holistic development is irreversibly affected is kept to a minimum.

As stated in Chapter 1, we might assume that today approximately 70 per cent of young athletes largely benefit from competitive sport, 20 per cent are at risk and 10 per cent have some of their rights violated. Although this estimate is certainly not a scientific one, it provides a rough idea of where sport stands in relation to the respect of human rights of young athletes. As very little work has been done so far in this field by sport and public authorities, the scope for progress is, logically, immense. But if nothing is done, the number of children benefiting from competitive sport could decrease, leaving room for more abuse and exploitation.

A TEN-POINT CHILD RIGHTS AGENDA

As seen earlier (Part V), competitive sport does not necessarily empower athletes nor does it offer them an environment conducive to the enjoyment of their individual rights. As one British athlete explained:

> sometimes the sport organisations [say] ... athletes don't want to be part of decision-making ... Well, 60 percent said they would be athlete representatives and so I think athletes really want to be able to talk about these kinds of things but we ... feel so vulnerable ... they're afraid that a person will be blacklisted ... afraid because it could affect them personally and jeopardise their position on the team, or maybe some people would agree to speak out but somebody would back down, and then where would it leave the ones who did speak out, they'd be penalised.
>
> (Brackenridge 2001: 231)

Athletes have established very few organizations to ensure that their views are adequately taken into account. One exception is the Canadian Association of

National Team Athletes (CAN), an advocacy group aiming to empower top athletes (see also Chapter 15). In 1994, CAN adopted an 'athlete-centred' policy statement to ensure an 'effective athlete leadership' (CAN 1999). It is not often that adult athletes argue for their own human rights, and it is even less often that they seriously support and empower young athletes.

In most instances, youth competitive sport developed during the 1970s along adult models, sometimes with basic, but largely insufficient and inappropriate, adaptation to the needs of young athletes. The most radical errors made during this period of rapid growth have since been corrected by the sporting community. For example, at that time children aged under eight or ten years were expected to play on a full-sized football field with goals that were so wide that it was almost impossible to defend them properly. The same applies to very young children playing basketball on adult-sized pitches. But young footballers still often play with adult-sized balls which increases their vulnerability to injuries, especially for goalkeepers. A 2001 study showed that young goalkeepers were four to five times more likely to incur injuries as a direct result of not playing with specific junior balls (Boyd *et al.* 2001). Today, in a number of sports such as basketball, football, rugby or field hockey, children play on an infrastructure and in an environment that is in accordance with their physical and psychological aptitudes. This requirement is guaranteed under article 31.1 of the Convention which affirms that 'States Parties recognize the right of the child to rest and leisure, to engage in play and recreational *activities appropriate to the age of the child ...*' (emphasis added).

While youth sport has to a great extent overcome these structural shortcomings, it has failed to impose a child-centred sport system which aims at both developing competitive talent among young athletes and fulfilling their human rights and dignity. Sports bodies that organize youth competitions often claim to follow this dual objective, but those that in reality propose an environment in which the rights of the athlete override the objective of developing a champion are very rare indeed. Enabling children to develop holistically through competitive sports would require a child-sensitive sport system, which endorses and respects the following ten fundamental principles (see Table 19.1):

Table 19.1 A child-centred sport system: ten fundamental principles

1	Equity, non-discrimination, fairness
2	Best interests of the child: children first
3	Evolving capacities of the child
4	Subject of rights; exercise of rights
5	Consultation, the child's opinion, informed participation
6	Appropriate direction and guidance
7	Mutual respect, support and responsibility
8	Highest attainable standard of health
9	Transparency, accountability, monitoring
10	Excellence

1 Equity, non-discrimination, fairness

Equity is a core value in human rights just as fair play is in the sport movement. Equity implies non-discriminative and equal treatment of all athletes. Competition can only be justified when driven by principles of equity, non-discrimination and fairness.

2 Best interests of the child: children first

The principle of the best interests of the child is strongly anchored in the Convention (article 3) and is recognized as an overarching provision that should always be applied when any child rights are considered. The Convention states that: 'In all actions concerning children … the best interests of the child *shall be a primary consideration*' (article 3.1, emphasis added). The principle implies that, if there is conflict of interest, children should be given proper visibility, power and status in the decision-making processes. Some groups, especially UNICEF, use the slogan, 'Children first', to emphasize that, as a priority, all decisions in society need to focus on their potential impact on children.

3 Evolving capacities of the child

The fact that between birth and the age of 18, human beings are developing all the time is largely unchallenged. When considering the human rights of children, due consideration needs to be given to their evolving capacities and their age, maturity and capacity for discernment. The concept of evolving capacities is crucial in the process of empowering young people and in creating an environment in which they can become actors of their own development.

Recognizing children's evolving capacities also implies that each child has his or her own developmental rhythms and needs. All young athletes, even of the same age, cannot train and compete at the same levels; they have the right to participate at a level commensurate with their capacities. Young athletes have the right not to be a champion.

4 Subject of rights; exercise of rights

Since the entry into force of the Convention, children need to be considered as fully fledged subjects of rights, entitled to be treated with dignity, and not simply as passive recipients of services and protection measures. The Convention's entire philosophy and legal implications are to recognize that children should be gradually empowered to maximize the quality of their development and to prepare them to live their adult lives in dignity, responsibility, freedom, justice and peace. In addition, children who are able to exercise their rights in accordance with their evolving capacity are less vulnerable to abuse and exploitation.

5 Consultation, the child's opinion, informed participation

In all situations, children need to be treated as partners in decision-making processes and it is up to adults to find creative ways of involving them. This principle is framed in article 12 which affirms that: 'States Parties shall assure to the child who is capable of forming his or her own views the right to express those views *freely in all matters affecting the child, the views of the child being given due weight* in accordance with the age and maturity of the child' (emphasis added). Consulting children so as to integrate their opinion in any decision that affects them is not an option, it is an obligation. When designing and implementing child protection policies and programmes, it is essential to consult children and take their opinions into account.

To be meaningfully empowered and involved in decision-making processes, children need to be systematically given the opportunity to access appropriate information, as foreseen in article 17, which affirms that states 'shall ensure that the child has access to information and material from a diversity of national and international sources, *especially those aimed at the promotion of his or her social, spiritual and moral well-being and physical and mental health*' (emphasis added).

6 Appropriate direction and guidance

Young athletes have the right to expect appropriate guidance and direction from adults involved in competitive sports, including parents, coaches and officials (article 5). Children deserve 'competent supervision', as referred to in article 3.3.

7 Mutual respect, support and responsibility

By promoting empowerment and the principle of equality, the Convention implies the concept of mutual respect between children, their peers and adults. It also implies that empowered children are able to enjoy their rights and to understand and respect their responsibilities within their social setting.

8 Highest attainable standard of health

From a human rights perspective, competitive sport can only be justified and legitimized if it respects the highest attainable standard of health for all athletes. In this context, health must be understood as widely as possible, covering physical, psychological, spiritual, social and cultural grounds. Young athletes have the right to rest, and adults, sports organizations and public authorities have the obligation to respect this right.

9 Transparency, accountability, monitoring

Transparency and accountability are two fundamental principles applied in human rights. In the context of competitive youth sport, adults, sport organizations and public authorities assume essential legal obligations in order to protect the rights of young athletes and are therefore held accountable under existing sport rules and regulations, as well as civil and penal law. Transparency needs to be guaranteed by all parties in order to respect all human rights and is a prerequisite for any system to function democratically. The sport system must accept independent monitoring, an indispensable safeguard of the application of rights and to evaluate the quality of sport services offered.

10 Excellence

The Convention advocates for the 'development of the child's personality, talents and mental and physical abilities to their *fullest potential*' (article 29.1.a, emphasis added). This means that excellence should be promoted in all domains, as long as all the rights and safeguards recognized in the Convention are respected. In this context, excellence does not refer exclusively to winning; more importantly, it is a process that aims at challenging and surpassing one's own limits, targeting perfection, respecting opponents, promoting a culture of sportsmanship, mastering physical and mental self-control, and accepting the negative aspects of sports, especially defeat. The 'winning at any cost' mentality is the opposite of excellence.

TAKING STOCK OF POSITIVE DEVELOPMENTS

During the 1970s, Western countries witnessed the first significant development of mass sport programmes for children, some 10 or 20 years after those developed in the Communist bloc. At that time, young people's involvement in competitive sports was overwhelmingly considered positive, as sport was perceived as an instrument of public health and social cohesion. Little attention was paid to possible side effects. During this initial period, many sport structures and rules were not adapted to children's developmental needs, and a body of critical analysis started to grow, mainly in academic and health fields, rather than in the world of sport. In 1976, the American Alliance for Health, Physical Education and Recreation adopted a visionary tool: the 'Bill of Rights for Young Athletes'. This ten-point charter covered issues such as 'the right to participate at a level commensurate with each child's developmental level; the right to have a qualified adult leadership; the right to participate in safe and healthy environments; the right to play as a child and not as an adult; the right to proper preparation ... to equal opportunity ... to be treated with dignity ... to have fun in sports' (Martens 1978: 360). Significantly, the bill of rights also referred to 'the right of children to share in the leadership and decision-making of their sport participation' almost 15 years before this innovative principle was given force of law by the Convention on the Rights of the Child. While its impact is hard to assess scientifically, it was certainly the first tool for positive change in both mass and elite youth sport.

The bill of rights inspired others. In Switzerland, for example, two leading sport doctors and a psychologist adopted a charter of child rights in sport in 1988; the charter was updated 12 years later. It reaffirmed the same rights as the bill but added the right to practise sport in an environment free of doping and the right to rest. It strongly influenced Geneva's sports policies by helping to shape the (at that time) newly established state schools for elite athletes. These schools do not focus on producing champions, but on helping potential champions to enjoy a sound and holistic human development (see Chapter 12). The charter was also endorsed by Geneva's public authorities and widely disseminated to the region's sport clubs in order to raise awareness and to stimulate debate. Nevertheless, Geneva did not link compliance with the charter to public funding, although much amateur sport is partly funded by the canton.

Geneva's charter of child rights in sport in turn inspired Panathlon International, which was founded in 1951 and is active around the world, but mainly in Europe and Latin America. It adopted the charter in the early 1990s to promote its objectives, which are to further the positive values of sports, such as fair play, non-discrimination, non-violence and inter-cultural exchanges, through awareness-raising, research and services supporting access to sports for vulnerable groups (the disabled, drug addicts, etc.). Despite its international scope, the work of Panathlon's clubs has had a limited impact on the sports movement and the federations in charge of it.

During the 1980s, the sporting world still systematically denied the need for child protection within sport, even though problems such as doping, excessive intensive training, sexual abuse and trafficking of young football players had started to emerge, mainly in sporadic press reports. External criticism, even in its most constructive, non-militant and scientific forms, did not succeed in penetrating the sporting movement. Sport did not escape the rhetoric of the cold war: Western criticism concerning competitive sports targeted the 'enemy', the Soviet Union and its satellite states (and vice versa). Communist countries were accused of not respecting young athletes' human rights, at a time when the West was ignoring the same issues at home.

The 1990s saw for the first time some sports organizations acknowledge the existence of serious child-related problems, despite the continued resistance of other sporting bodies. The systematic involvement of very young players in intensive training schemes meant that some sports federations suddenly realized that their best players were under-aged. If the International Tennis Federation rapidly and energetically addressed the issue (see Chapter 5), the International Federation of Gymnastics was unable to find the ways or the political consensus to solve the problem.

Abuses – whether financial and political corruption, doping or other forms of cheating – were also revealed more systematically during the 1990s. Sports organizations, even the prestigious International Olympic Committee, were forced to open themselves up, to some extent at least, to scrutiny, transparency and demands for accountability. At the same time, the first serious media accounts of abusive practices against children in sport (sexual and physical abuse, doping, trafficking, contractual rights, etc.) appeared in many Western countries.

The first serious, institutional responses at national level to child rights issues emerged during the second half of the 1990s. In almost all cases these responses came as a *reaction* – rather than as a preventive process – to widely publicized cases of sexual abuse of teenagers. For example, the cases of Graham James (an ice-hockey coach convicted of sexual abuse, Canada), Paul Hickson (a swimming coach convicted of rape and sentenced to 17 years in prison, United Kingdom), Derry O'Rourke (a swimming coach, sentenced to 12 years in prison for sexually abusing 19 teenage girls from 1976 to 1992, Ireland) and Peter Ooms (a judo coach, convicted of sexual abuse and suspended for three years by the Dutch judo federation) clearly increased institutional response. Such responses to child protection needs, however, were almost always a reaction to sexual abuse scandals and not to other types of child rights violations, such as doping or excessive intensive training. Sexual abuse easily attracts media attention and often shocks the general public. These responses to sexual violence and harassment did not necessarily target children only, but also women, and were often initiated by women's rights groups, such as the Canadian Association for the Advancement of Women in Sport.

The most sustained and significant institutional reactions to child protection issues in sports took place in some English-speaking countries, mainly Australia (Australian Sports Commission, 1998), Canada (Canadian Red Cross, 1997; Canadian Hockey Association, 1997), New Zealand (Hillary Commission for Sport Fitness and Leisure, late 1990s), the United Kingdom (National Coaching Foundation, 1993; National Society for the Prevention of Cruelty to Children and Sport England, 2000) and the United States (American Sport Education Program, 1981; National Alliance for Youth Sports, 1990s; Positive Coaching Alliance, 1990s – see Chapter 18). With the exception of the US, institutional responses in these countries were openly backed, and in some cases led, by political support for public authorities. In these countries, child protection measures have mainly focused on:

- adoption of child protection policies and ethical charters;
- criminal record checks (of trainers or coaches);
- awareness-raising and training of athletes, parents, coaches and other officials;
- appointment of child protection officers in sports clubs and federations;
- establishment of telephone helplines;
- establishment of conflict resolution and litigation mechanisms;
- quality control management and labelling; and
- research on child protection in sport issues.

An interesting initiative was the decision of the Irish Sports Council and the Sports Council for Northern Ireland in 2001 to unite and adopt a 'Code of Ethics and Good Practice for Children's Sport in Ireland' (2001: 4), which affirms that:

As citizens, adults have a responsibility to protect children from harm and to abide by government guidelines in responding to and reporting child protection concerns. This responsibility exists wherever such concerns might arise, whether inside or outside sport. Guidelines contained in the Code of Ethics and Good Practice for Children's Sport in Ireland *took account of the UN Convention on the Rights of the Child* and are in accordance with government guidelines ... [emphasis added]

The Code further considers that 'a child centred approach to children's sport will return many benefits in terms of the health and well being of our future adult population' (Irish Sports Council and the Sports Council for Northern Ireland 2001: 9).

Other countries also took action. In France, with its centralized 'top-down' form of government, the government directly took the lead to protect children involved in sports. Under Marie-Georges Buffet, Minister of Sports from 1997 to 2002, the French authorities were mainly active in protecting child athletes from economic exploitation (including trafficking of players and illegal transfers), precocious involvement in intensive training, doping and sexual abuse. Some positive actions, though not always sufficiently sustained and developed, also took place in the Nordic countries, Belgium, the Netherlands and some regions of Germany.

Many grass-roots initiatives also developed during the 1990s, especially in the United States. They all focused on certain aspects of the youth sport environment, including sport parenting (Center for Sports Parenting, Nurturing Parenting.com), coaching education (American Sport Education Program, National Institute for Child Centred Coaching), safety issues (National Youth Sport Safety Foundation), spectator behaviour from a mother's perspective (UnitedHockeyMoms), moral educational values (Charactercounts, GoodSport), women's rights (Women Sports Foundation) and nutrition (Sports, Cardiovascular and Wellness Nutritionists, Australian Institute of Sport). These groups function mainly as support groups for parents, educators, coaches, officials, etc., and offer specialized information, training and expert advice through their websites.

However, it was probably in the United Kingdom that the most advanced initiative in relation to the protection of young athletes took place at the end of the 1990s. After the 'moral panic' that shook sports in England (see Chapter 18), the government established a National Child Protection in Sport Task Force in 1999, following a seminar organized the same year by the National Society for the Prevention of Cruelty to Children (NSPCC), the UK's largest welfare organization. In its plan of action, the task force requested as a priority the establishment of a Child Protection in Sport Unit (CPSU), which was opened in 2001, the first of its kind in the world (Sport England and NSPCC 2000). The unit is a focal point and establishes systems for dealing with allegations of abuse, develops standards, provides education and training, minimizes the chance of having inappropriate individuals enter the sports world, and provides expert advice on child protection issues and policies. The UK's largest and most powerful sport federations, such as The Football Association, have committed their support to the CPSU. In 2002, in order to understand the situation in its own sport, The Football Association commissioned a five-year research project, which will be the biggest in-depth, broad-based study on child protection in British sports, and established an Ethics Strategy Group to investigate wider issues.

QUALITY CONTROL MANAGEMENT AND LABELLING

In the United Kingdom, after the widely publicized scandal of British Olympic swimming coach Paul Hickson sexually abusing athletes, the Amateur Swimming Association (ASA) took several measures, including the establishment of 'Aquamark', a quality control label. Quality control has been a management tool in the private sector for several decades and is increasingly used by the public sector. In sports it has only just begun to emerge as a possible response to the failure of sport organizations to provide high-quality, safe services. Some sport federations have started 'risk management' programmes, such as the Australian Office of Sport and Recreation (1999) and the Belgian (Flemish) gymnastics federation (Van Hoecke and De Knop 1998). A few European football and ice-hockey teams have recently acquired ISO (International Organization for Standardization) labelling to guarantee quality management. The World Anti-Doping Agency (WADA) and ISO also collaborate in combating doping in sports (ISO 2001).

The Aquamark scheme comprises three main elements: 20 programme criteria (including child protection); self assessment; and assessment carried out by industry experts who are trained as assessors. This quality-control scheme is designed for local authorities, private leisure contractors, swimming clubs, private swimming schools and local education authorities (ASA 1999). The main challenge of such a 'labelling' policy is to monitor independently and periodically the application and respect of established criteria and take meaningful measures when these are no longer guaranteed. This independent monitoring and assessment is critical to maintain a quality-control system, but it is a very costly, politically sensitive and demanding requirement. Bestowing awards is another approach to encourage sport service quality. In the UK, Sportsmark and Sportsmark Gold provide 'a mark of special distinction for schools whose sport policies exceeded the basic criteria across a number of important requirements' (Government of the United Kingdom 1999b: para. 9.65.14).

Quality-control management is still in its early days in sports, but it shows a great potential for growth. In 2002, the Belgian Football Association became one of the first major national sport federations to agree to have an outside group of researchers (from the Free University of Brussels) evaluate the quality of the youth programmes of its 36 main professional football teams. 'The aim is not to criticize and undermine the youth programmes in these clubs; our objective is to

provide all these clubs with an instrument to improve the quality of their training programmes for young players,' said Professor Paul de Knop, head of the
research team, who thought that only 15 per cent of the clubs would meet the
criteria. Four main criteria were evaluated: social qualities (health and ethics,
integration of the views of the young athlete, etc.); qualities for the user (pleasure, level of pressure, access to information, etc.); qualities of the product
(variety of the training schemes, etc.) and qualities of the process (effective and
efficient organization). Only clubs attaining 70 per cent of requirements were
given a label of quality (Mercy 2001: 11).

The institutional developments referred to above are very important, but they
are few and far between and represent only the initial phase of a much wider and
complex movement to achieve the protection of child rights in competitive
sports. The most delicate phase of these projects is the one of implementation.
Celia Brackenridge (2001: 203), a British expert, noted:

> The proliferation of anti-harassment and child protection policy statements
> over recent years in British sport organisations is an indication of growing
> commitment to the issue. But looked at more critically, this development
> has been neither efficient nor creative. Many of the agencies that support
> sport, for example, through state funding, sponsorship or voluntary contribu-
> tions, have failed to attend to implementation issues or to the monitoring
> and evaluation processes by which accountability can be assured. Policy
> without implementation is like a car with no engine; it may look good but
> it's going nowhere.

Obviously, child protection measures should not become just an alibi to reassure
parents, please donors, serve politics and deal with internal and external pressures. Child protection policies and programmes need to be monitored and
evaluated periodically and independently in order to understand their real
impact on reducing the number of victims and improving the quality of experience of all children.

INTERNATIONAL (IN)ACTION

Thus far, the two major actors in the field, the International Olympic
Committee (IOC) and the United Nations (UN), have not yet adequately
addressed the promotion and protection of child rights in competitive sports.
The general objectives of both institutions include the promotion and protection
of every individual's human rights, but no serious consideration has been given to
the issue. In February 2001, former Swiss president, Adolf Ogi, was named
Special Adviser to the UN Secretary-General on Sport for Development and
Peace, but he has yet to include the protection of children's rights in competitive
sports, or human rights in general, in his work.

The UN Commission for Human Rights and the UN Committee on the Rights of the Child have paid very little attention to child rights issues in sports: they have dealt sporadically with the question of camel jockeys and, on one occasion, the trafficking of football players. Nor have UNICEF or the Office of the UN High Commissioner for Human Rights (the guardian of human rights treaties) ever looked closely at the phenomenon. FIFA has established programmes, with the support of the International Labour Organization (ILO) and UNICEF, to combat the use of child labour in the manufacturing of footballs, especially in Pakistan. FIFA and UNICEF also declared that they would 'dedicate the 2002 World Cup to children'. 'I am very much looking forward to this cooperation with UNICEF,' declared FIFA's president, Joseph Blatter, six months before the 2002 football World Cup. 'It is FIFA's obligation as a global organization to help children all over the world, because football offers fun and hope based on tolerance, respect and fair play' (UNICEF 2001). During the African Football Cup of Nations in Mali (2002), the ILO also launched a campaign against child labour, called 'Red card to child labour', in partnership with the African Football Federation (ILO 2002a). In other situations, the ILO has remained silent on athletes' labour rights. Only the World Health Organization (WHO) has undertaken since the early 1990s systematic and sustained work on the specific issue of doping of athletes, though with no specific focus on young athletes.

Whilst it had never before addressed the rights of young athletes, the UN Educational, Scientific and Cultural Organization (UNESCO) organized in early 2003 a round table of ministers and senior officials responsible for physical education and sport from 103 states. Remarkably, the meeting adopted the most sophisticated UN statement ever:

> The protection of young athletes should be understood in the perspective of the principles stated in the UN Convention on the Rights of the Child. That is why protection should not be understood solely in terms of health as well as physical and psychological integrity. It also involves quality education that facilitates long-term personal and professional development. To this end, flexible modalities of educational provisions should be provided which meet the educational needs of young athletes. Protection also includes safeguarding against such dangers such as child labour, violence, doping, early specialization, over-training, and exploitative forms of commercialization as well as less visible threats and deprivations, such as the premature severance of family bonds and the loss of sporting, social and cultural ties.
>
> (UNESCO 2003:2)

A year later (2004), the UNESCO statement was discussed at the UN General Assembly. The Assembly adopted resolution 58/5, 'Sport as a means to promote education, health, development and peace', in which the General Assembly recognized for the first time that sports could lead to the abuse and exploitation of young

athletes. The resolution, which gives the United Nations the potential to pay serious attention and take measures to protect young athletes in the future, states:

> Taking note of the communiqué issued by the round table of ministers
> responsible for sports and physical education, held in Paris on 9 and 10
> January 2003 ... Recalling the Convention on the Rights of the Child ...
> Acknowledging with concern the dangers faced by sportsmen and sports-
> women, in particular young athletes, including, inter alia, child labour,
> violence, doping, early specialization, over-training and exploitative forms
> of commercialization, as well as less visible threats and deprivations, such as
> the premature severance of family bonds and the loss of sporting, social and
> cultural ties ...
>
> (United Nations 2004)

So far, the most active intergovernmental institution for the protection of the
human rights of athletes is undoubtedly the Council of Europe. Since the early
1990s, the Council has established norms and standards, and encouraged member states to adopt laws, policies and programmes, especially in the fields of
doping, violence, sportsmanship, and abuse and exploitation of athletes.

The Council has adopted three important international instruments relating
to sports, one of which is legally binding, the 1989 Convention against Doping
(see Chapter 10), and two non-binding, the European Sport Charter (1992) and
the Code of Sport Ethics (1992). The European Sport Charter aims, *inter alia*:

> to protect and develop the moral and ethical bases of sport and the *human*
> *dignity* and safety of those involved in sport, by safeguarding sport, sportsmen
> and women from *exploitation for political, commercial and financial gain and*
> *from practices that are abusive,* or debasing including the abuse of drugs and
> the sexual harassment and abuse, particularly of children, young people and
> women.
>
> (Council of Europe 2001c; article 1.ii., emphases added)

The Code of Sport Ethics intends to address the downsides of modern competitive sports as it aims to provide 'a sound ethical framework to combat the
pressures in modern day society which appear to be undermining the traditional
foundations of sport – foundations built on fair play and sportsmanship, and on
the voluntary movement' (Council of Europe 2001b). The Code's scope covers
many fields related to child rights as it claims that fair play 'incorporates issues
concerned with the elimination of cheating, gamesmanship, doping, violence
(both physical and verbal), the sexual harassment and abuse of children, young
people and women, exploitation, unequal opportunities, excessive commercialisation and corruption'. It is almost impossible to assess the concrete impact of
these instruments among Council members, but it is safe to say that they have
prompted some level of political debate and at best influenced policy- and law-
makers in a number of countries.

Since 1992, the Council of Europe's Committee for the Development of Sport (CDDS) has worked both at democratizing and promoting the practice of sport and at protecting and reinforcing the core ethical values of sport. At the end of the 1990s, the CDDS focused attention on gender equality and protecting athletes, especially women and children, from sexual harassment and abuse. In 2000, the Council adopted a comprehensive resolution on the prevention of sexual harassment in sport, which prompted much debate among member states as it was the first time the Council had promoted to such an extent a human rights issue in sports (Council of Europe 2000b).

The relative political success of the CDDS's initiative encouraged the Council of Europe to engage in the broader issue of child protection in sport. In September 2001, it organized its first regional workshop on child protection in sport and asked the author and two other specialists to provide guidance on the issue. The recommendations adopted by representatives of member states and of sport organizations focused on the following main areas (Council of Europe 2001a):

- ensure compatibility of all sporting rules and regulations with child protection laws particularly the Convention on the Rights of the Child;
- encourage all sport authorities, federations, associations, etc., to adopt a child rights and protection policy (which could be linked to funding);
- ensure that child protection policies which already exist are enforced in sport;
- ensure proper investigation of all violence to and abuse of the rights of the child and if appropriate the prosecution of the perpetrators;
- ensure and monitor the complaints mechanism itself;
- stimulate independent comprehensive research on child rights issues in both competitive and recreational sport;
- foresee independent monitoring of sports centres and institutions especially those of a residential nature and those in which intensive, long-term training takes place;
- ensure that all sports centres have appropriate mechanisms for young athletes to file individual complaints, and guarantee that such complaints are properly investigated;
- foresee the provision of support systems and follow-up to those reporting abuse;
- ask the CDDS to explore the possibility of drafting a specific European convention on the protection of children and young people in sport;
- teach parents and trainers to recognize the signs that denote that a child may be suffering any kind of abuse: in the same way that parents might detect abuse in a child from a sports trainer, so too are sports trainers often in a position to note that a child may be suffering abuse or neglect from within the home and family;
- circulate information through networking; for example, attention must be drawn to the ways in which coaches or trainers, with a record of sexual

harassment and abuse, have been known to move freely to another country and continue training young athletes; and

- develop codes of practice for trainers and child protection policies, etc., at the pan-European level in all countries, to act as either a counterweight or a prevention tool in the areas of child protection and sexual harassment and abuse in children, young people and women in sport.

At the non-governmental level, little, if any, attention has been given internationally to the issue of child rights in competitive sports. The Swiss section of Defence for Children International, a child rights NGO, published a booklet on the protection of children's rights in high-level competitive sport (David 1993), which was used – mainly in Switzerland – by sport organizations to raise awareness or train their members. Other child rights or human rights organizations, including the largest ones such as Amnesty International, Human Rights Watch and Save the Children, have never shown any interest in giving the topic an international profile.

Another international initiative that broke some ground was the organization in 1998 of the first international conference on child rights and sports by the International Institute for the Rights of the Child in Sion, Switzerland (Zermatten 1999). A multi-disciplinary working group, set up as a result of the conference, examined whether an international mechanism to deal with the promotion and protection of child rights in sports was necessary. In 2001, the working group recommended that an international centre for the promotion and protection of child rights in sports be established.

In future initiatives, child protection in sport should only remain part of a broader picture, the human rights of children. The latter does not just consist and relate to *protection* but importantly also includes *freedoms, participation* and *empowerment*. Most people understand and accept the idea of protecting children, but their participation in affairs that concern them and their empowerment is still by and large resisted, misunderstood and undermined.

20 Olympic values and the rights of the child

I don't understand. Why should anyone be playing against anyone else?
(Dalai Lama, watching a ball game, in Dellatre 1978: 40)

The debate about the moral values of sport is not new, but rather an ancient and persistent one that goes back to Aristotle's philosophical treatises, if not before. People associated with the world of competitive sport generally confer very positive moral values on sport, which they feel justifies the activity itself. Most critics of this view are outsiders who rarely belong to the sporting community. Those 'in the middle' consider that sport is an accurate reflection of both the good and the bad aspects of society as a whole. The Olympic motto, *Citius, altius, fortius* (Faster, higher, stronger), can therefore be interpreted in various ways according to one's standpoint: as an almost metaphysical search for purity and excellence; as an ideology of power, destruction and domination; or as a reflection of a combination of positive and harmful forces in society. The essential value of these interpretations is to suggest that only by constantly challenging our interpretations can knowledge of the moral values in competitive sports be improved.

Moral values are an essential element of any educational process. The Convention on the Rights of the Child recognizes that 'the education of the child shall be directed to: ... his or her own cultural identity, language and values, for the national values of the country in which the child is living, the country from which he or she may originate, and for civilizations different from his or her own' (article 29.1.c). Therefore the question arises whether competitive sport represents for children a valuable educational tool or not. While a majority of those involved in sport would without hesitation agree with the affirmation, some specialists in education believe that:

> it would not seem that physical activities are in any way indispensable for the practice of moral education, so that a person might lack moral qualities by virtue of never having experienced physical education; indeed, I am inclined to the plausible enough view that other school subjects such as literature and history are probably far better vehicles of moral education than, say, games or metalwork.

(Carr 1998: 130)

The established moral values of the global sport community are embodied in the Olympic charter of the International Olympic Committee (IOC). The charter combines a set of philosophical and moral guiding principles with a set of practical structural and institutional rules organizing the Olympic movement. The Olympic charter's 'fundamental principles' establish an ambitious framework for the sporting community:

> Olympism is a philosophy of life, exalting and combining in a balanced whole the qualities of body, will and mind. Blending sport with culture and education, Olympism seeks to create a way of life based on the joy found in effort, the educational value of good example and respect for universal fundamental ethical principles. The goal of Olympism is to place everywhere sport at the service of the harmonious development of man, with a view to encouraging the establishment of a peaceful society concerned with the preservation of human dignity.
>
> (IOC 2002: fundamental principles, articles 2 and 3)

When discussing child rights and competitive sports, it is important to recognize that the Olympic charter is articulated around fundamental human rights principles that mutually reinforce those enshrined in the Convention on the Rights of the Child. On the basis of these commonalities, the charter could lend impetus to the promotion and protection of child rights; similarly, the Convention has the potential to reinforce Olympic values. As the implementation of the Convention on the Rights of the Child is, in all countries except Somalia and the United States, now a *universal legal obligation*, sport could help to make children and adults more responsive to a human rights culture. The highest sport authorities – the IOC and international sport federations – rarely refer to nor use as a yardstick the Olympic charter's values or fundamental principles. Does this mean that the sporting movement does not focus sufficiently on promoting and protecting its values? Has it attempted to reduce tensions between its values and the political and commercial nature of its work? Does the IOC frame its action in or outside the philosophical principles of its charter?

Human rights are ethical values that have been given force of law in order to protect individuals from any form of state abuse. But human rights laws are only meaningful when certain criteria are respected: citizens have to be adequately informed about their rights; they need easy access to an independent judiciary; and they have to trust their political and judicial systems. If citizens' rights are crushed by public or private entities and if the justice system and the state administration are corrupt, then human rights provisions are meaningless. The same applies to the Olympic charter's fundamental principles: they can only shape the sporting spirit of young athletes if they are constantly respected and promoted by those who govern sport.

Once again, it can be argued that the Olympic movement has not yet succeeded in giving young people strong moral leadership. Despite the Olympic Games' commercial success, the IOC has so far struggled to create an environment of trust and credibility conducive to promoting the values embodied in its charter. During the twentieth century, the IOC was plagued by corruption scandals and, despite its humanistic ideology, it has not always succeeded in decreasing the gap between its official speech and concrete acts. In his last year as IOC president, Juan Antonio Samaranch said:

> Sport is a school of justice, democracy and human rights. The first rules that we learn are those linked to the Games and to sports. Moreover, sport, a universal language, creates, in all circumstances, national unity, political consensus, solidarity and mutual understanding.
>
> (IOC 2001: 7)

To ensure that it could not be manipulated and corrupted by political and economic powers, the IOC should have – but as yet has not – systematically promoted and integrated in its work fundamental human rights principles such as transparency, accountability, equality, empowerment, independent monitoring and scrutiny, non-impunity, independence, due process and redress. Failure to do so led to a public scandal in 1999 when one senior member of the IOC and its Executive Board, Marc Hodler from Switzerland, openly denounced the deep-rooted ill-functioning of the institution, including the widespread corruption. This was the first time ever that the IOC was criticized from inside. An extraordinary session of the IOC was organized and its members publicly reacted by expelling ten members for their unethical behaviour. In March 1999, the IOC established an ethics commission to prevent and combat corruption, which would be:

> responsible for ensuring that the ethical principles, with which IOC members must comply, are clear, correctly applied and enforced. The mission of the Ethics Commission is to provide advice and guidance on how the IOC operates in accordance with the best practices of international business and government.
>
> (IOC 2002b)

The IOC affirms that: 'The Ethics Commission will use the Olympic charter as a reference to ensure that the fundamental principles of the Olympic Movement are respected. It is their aim to promote ethics and ensure clarity and accountability' (IOC 2002a). So far, the work of the Commission to promote Olympic values and ensure compliance within its own constituency has been extremely discreet; it has rarely taken a significant public stand on ethical conflicts in sports. But it adopted both a code of ethics in 2000 and, despite strong internal resistance, new conflict-of-interest rules for Olympic parties in 2002.

IOC president since 2001, Jacques Rogge from Belgium, openly acknowledged the crisis in sports values and believes that the Olympic movement needs to promote more vigorously its moral values:

I love to paraphrase the Olympic motto 'Faster, higher and stronger' by applying it to the current context of sport: 'More pure, more solidarity and more humane' ... I have seen athletes with appalling injuries caused by intensive training. I have also observed that some athletes find it difficult to enter the professional world once their career is over. The world of sports has a moral responsibility in these situations ... When ... I denounce racism and doping, when I affirm that we cannot give in to the pressure of sponsors who want to change the rules of the games in their own interest, I am referring to the Olympic values. I would like to promote this sense of humanism among all members of the Olympic movement, athletes, coaches, etc.

(Donzé 2001: 19)

BRINGING BACK HUMAN RIGHTS TO THE OLYMPIC MOVEMENT

The IOC affirms that:

According to the Olympic Charter, established by Pierre de Coubertin, the goal of the Olympic Movement is to contribute to building a peaceful and better world by educating youth through sport practised without discrimination of any kind and in the Olympic spirit, which requires mutual understanding with a spirit of friendship, solidarity and fair play.

(IOC 2002)

The Olympic fundamental principles have several aims: they guide the IOC in its decision-making processes and policy development and implementation; they protect athletes against all forms of abuse of power; they guarantee fair and equal treatment of all athletes, coaches, sport officials, etc.; and they enable the promotion of a universal system of values for sport.

From a child rights perspective, the Olympic charter clearly proclaims values that are relevant to young athletes. When the charter states that the 'goal of Olympism is to place everywhere sport at the service of the harmonious development of man, with a view to encouraging the establishment of a peaceful society concerned with the preservation of human dignity' (fundamental principle no. 3), it shares the ultimate objective of the Convention on the Rights of the Child which aims at ensuring the 'full and harmonious development' (Preamble) of the child and its 'inherent dignity' (article 37). Olympism further seeks to 'promote peace' (principle no. 3), just as the Convention commits states to 'the preparation of the child for responsible life in a free society, in the spirit of understanding, peace, tolerance, equality of sexes, and friendship among all peoples, ethnic, national and religious groups and persons of indigenous origin' (article 29.1.d). The Olympic charter also declares that: 'The practice of sport is a human right' (principle no. 8) that should be 'practised without discrimination of any kind and in the Olympic spirit, which requires mutual understanding with a spirit of friendship, solidarity and fair play' (principle no. 6). Non-discrimination, which is a cornerstone of the human rights system and an overarching general principle of the Convention (article 2), is also a key value of Olympism. In this regard, it 'strongly encourages, by appropriate means, the promotion of women in sport in all levels and all structures' (Role of the IOC, article 5).

Whilst these fundamental principles are key to the sports movement, the Olympic charter embodies five other values which are fundamental to the promotion and protection of young athletes' human rights: prohibition of violence (Role of the IOC, article 7), the fight against doping (article 8), not to endanger the health of athletes (article 9), oppose any political or commercial abuse of sport and athletes (article 10), and provide for the social and professional future of athletes (article 11). These IOC objectives are clearly reinforced by human rights provisions enshrined in the Convention: right to protection from all forms of violence (article 19); right to the highest standard of health (article 24); right to be free from all forms of political and commercial exploitation (articles 32 and 36); and right to education and social reintegration (articles 28, 29 and 39). This convergence of interests between the Olympic values and child rights provisions, and the latter's legally binding nature, seem to be a unique asset to enforce child rights in sport. It is a paradox that the Olympic movement has as yet given so little voice and teeth to its own human rights values, despite the fact that they are recognized in the domestic legislation of a majority of countries around the world.

In addition to its charter, the Olympic movement, after the revelation of the internal scandals in 1999, adopted a Code of Ethics in order to reinforce the Olympic ideal. The code reinforces the charter in its objective to protect athletes and prohibit corruption among all individuals involved in the Olympic movement.

In order to promote and protect human rights in sports, the IOC need only turn to existing international and domestic human rights law. The Convention on the Rights of the Child could be a powerful tool in the IOC's negotiations with private and public entities. In any policy or decision that affects children, whether minimum ages for participating in the Olympic Games (see Chapter 5) or transfer regulations (see Chapter 13), the IOC should be guided by the Convention's provisions and principles.

The scope of the work of the IOC's Commission for Culture and Olympic Education and its Olympic Academy remains of relatively low impact. If the IOC were to use the Convention as a reference tool to protect the rights of young athletes, it would also help to promote the Convention among a larger audience of young and adult athletes, coaches, supporters, sport officials, etc., thus taking an active part in the universal effort to promote and protect children's rights. Such an action would undoubtedly increase the IOC's credibility with regard to its action for children and adolescents.

REBIRTH OF SPORTSMANSHIP?

'Fair play' and 'sportsmanship' have been extolled as the predominant foundations of modern sport since its 'rebirth' over a century ago. Their real
signification, however, has not been seriously addressed within the sporting community. The concepts of fair play and sportsmanship are associated with positive
values and are perceived by most people as an absolute objective, in the same
way as peace is perceived as a goal for society at large. Both concepts remain
strongly linked to the sporting movement and, to some extent, owned by it. But
this quasi-ownership does not provide any clear definition of the meaning and
scope of either concept. The Olympic charter refers to fair play, but doesn't
define it. Yet what the concept means can vary enormously according to age,
moral values, culture, socio-economic and religious backgrounds and type of
sport. For example, a study which examined the behaviour of 15- to 18-year-old
footballers in England, Finland and Sweden showed major differences in their
interpretation of fair play (Loland 1998: 79–80).

Knowledge and research about ethical values and attitudes among young
sports competitors is still limited, although growing slowly. Such knowledge is
indispensable in order to understand what motivates young athletes and to
design appropriate youth sport programmes and policies. A British survey of
young people and sport showed that 89 per cent of athletes said they did not like
playing with people who cheat or break the rules, while 72 per cent 'mind[ed] a
lot'. The same study concluded that a third of young people said they didn't mind
losing (32 per cent), while 9 per cent 'mind[ed] a lot'. Two-thirds regard fair play
as an important part of sport (Rowe and Champion 2000: 170–1). Another study
revealed that coaches, teachers and friends have the strongest influences on children's sporting values, parental influence remaining marginal (English Sports
Council 1998: 9). In this study, young athletes place 'sportsmanship' as the third
most important value in sport, just after 'enjoyment' and 'personal achievement',
while winning is ranked the least important value. Fair play usually suggests
behaviour respecting the written rules of the game, but in many cases it goes
beyond this, relying on less definable criteria, such as the *spirit of the game*.

The provision of human rights education is an obligation for states that are
party to at least one of the seven main international human rights treaties, and
the Convention foresees that human rights education should be part of the
school curriculum (article 29.1.b). The Committee on the Rights of the Child
considers this a core requirement to establish a sound human rights system. The
contents of human rights education should strive for '[t]he preparation of the
child for a *responsible* life in a free society, in the *spirit of understanding, peace, tolerance, equality of sexes, and friendship among all peoples, ethnic, national and
religious groups and persons of indigenous origin*' (article 29.1.d, emphases added).
This provision could, to some extent, serve as a starting guideline for defining fair
play among young athletes in addition to the existing written rules of the game,
thereby illustrating the complementarity between human rights education and
Olympic education.

21 The human rights approach
An added value for the competitive sport system

> The International Law on the Rights of the Child is based on the premise that international law is a valuable tool for those seeking to improve the daily lives of children.
>
> (Van Bueren 1995: xix)

> Sport is a school of justice, democracy and human rights.
> (Juan Antonio Samaranch, IOC President 1980–2001, in IOC 2001: 7)

Respecting human rights is not an *option* for sport authorities, it is an *obligation* that derives from the responsibilities of states under the rule of law. For decades, the sporting world has been largely autonomous and self-regulating, but that era is coming to an end. Sport also remains one of the rare domains – if not the only one – that has been impermeable to the legal obligations to promote and protect child rights. The Convention on the Rights of the Child could help to reduce the number of young athletes at risk of human rights violations, even though, as yet, the use of the human rights approach to guarantee the rights of all athletes and achieve justice in the sporting world has been the object of very little research.

The Convention is not simply *another tool* to protect children during their sporting activity. Since the 1970s, several declarations and charters, policy statements, resolutions and recommendations have been adopted by a wealth of sport and non-sport organizations; but none is based on a legally binding framework. Implementing child rights in the sports context is a process based on law enforcement, as enshrined in the Convention. Even in countries where sports are in the hands of non-state actors, respect for the rights of children remains a legal obligation. However, human rights and competitive sports are not incompatible. It is possible to form champions and at the same time fully respect their rights. Competitive sport as an educative and socio-economic process must be subject to the legal, moral and ethical imperatives expressed in international human rights law.

Since the 1970s, sports have rapidly developed worldwide into a successful professional enterprise in which several million young athletes are involved every day. This success has also, almost inevitably, generated conflicts at very different levels – human, socio-economic, legal, political. Human rights tools have rarely been used to resolve these disputes, even though they could easily guide the design of sound policy decisions, inspire administrative and court decisions and be a suitable reference for the sustainable development of competitive sport.

In any field, the added value of human rights is at least threefold as it provides a legal, analytical and procedural framework:

- **Legal framework** Human rights are recognized under law and are therefore not optional. Not only should laws be scrupulously observed, but all sport rules, by-laws and regulations must respect human rights standards and principles. All human rights rely on fundamental precepts, such as empowerment, participation, transparency, accountability, equality and non-discrimination, independent monitoring and scrutiny, non-impunity, independence and due process, redress and remedy, rehabilitation and reintegration, and compensation.
- **Analytical framework** Fundamental human rights are defined in international human rights treaties. These minimum international norms and standards provide a key reference frame for any analytical work. All promotion, policy-making, normative, assessment and monitoring work should be undertaken against these benchmarks.
- **Procedural framework** Human rights strongly imply a clear and comprehensive procedural framework, especially for victims of human rights violations seeking judicial or other type of redress. It also generally includes international public scrutiny, through the monitoring work of independent UN expert treaty bodies, and mechanisms for submitting individual complaints.

Traditionally, human rights obligations imply that the state and its agents are under the obligation to prevent and refrain from performing specific acts, such as torture, in order to protect the rights of individuals. Over the past two decades, this traditional thinking of human rights has been seriously weakened by the evolution of society – including globalization – in which the economic and political powers of private entities have challenged the monopoly of public authorities. Initially, no legal human rights obligations were recognized regarding private entities, but today human rights thinking is more nuanced, evolving towards a more balanced share of responsibilities. Public authorities are still perceived as carrying ultimate obligations, but private entities can no longer deny some level of responsibility. Nevertheless, the definition and implications of legal obligations for private entities still remain a controversial and open debate (Clapham 1995; Addo 1999).

In the specific field of children's rights, the pyramidical approach of human rights between public and private entities is of a slightly different nature, as the child is not considered to be legally autonomous by the state. Therefore a third party (usually, but not necessarily, the parents) has the primary responsibility for the upbringing and development of the child, including guaranteeing his or her human rights (article 18.1 of the Convention). As discussed throughout this book, in this legal context, private parties in charge of the care of children, such as sport authorities, have clear human rights obligations under the Convention. Nonetheless, at this very early stage of the process of integrating a human rights perspective into youth competitive sports, the initial challenge is simply the *recognition* by both public and private entities of these obligations towards young athletes.

HUMAN RIGHTS AT ALL COSTS

If the sports system is to become human rights sensitive, it must integrate the fundamental principles recognized in international human rights law. With regard to respect for child rights, public and private authorities are obliged to ensure that the following measures are taken.

Normative review and law enforcement (article 4 of the Convention)

From local to international level, public and private authorities need to ensure full *compatibility* of all bodies of relevant legislation, sporting rules, regulations and by-laws with the provisions and principles of the Convention on the Rights of the Child. For example, the International Football Federation (FIFA) revised its transfer rules in 2001, and attempted to address the issue of sale and trafficking of young football players in order to protect them from such violations. And court decisions in the 1990s forced the Belgian Football Federation and the Belgian Basketball Federation to review their transfer rules in order to make them compatible with the right to freedom of association of young players, as recognized in the Convention.

Public authorities need to be serious and vigilant about the *law enforcement* of existing child rights legislation *within* the sports sphere and to use the same principles and criteria as those generally applied elsewhere to protect children's rights, whether the children live with their families or in social welfare institutions. When incidents occur, public authorities need to ensure proper *investigation* of child rights violations and, when appropriate, *prosecution* of abusers in the sporting context (physical and sexual abuse or trafficking and sale, for example). Respect for the private sphere cannot be a justification for non-intervention when credible elements of suspicion exist about instances of abuse or violence against children. If there is any conflict of interest with adults, it is essential that the principle of the best interests of the child (article 3 of the Convention) guide any decision regarding potential intervention. Further, when cases of abuse are investigated and addressed through judicial or non-judicial means, the *rights of victims*, especially in light of the vulnerability of children, need to be carefully taken into consideration during the entire process.

Allocation of budgetary resources (article 4)

Under the Convention, public authorities commit themselves to take measures to implement children's rights 'to the *maximum extent* of their available resources' (article 4, emphasis added). In order to fulfil their obligations towards children, these provisions must be distinct from budgetary allocations for adults in general.

Monitoring and individual complaint mechanisms (articles 4, 12 and 25)

Monitoring is a natural component of human rights as it is the main tool used to collect factual information independently and analyse a given situation. Therefore public and private authorities involved in sports need to ensure *periodic and independent monitoring* of all sport programmes, centres and institutions, especially those where intensive training takes place. More generally the behaviour of coaches, parents, officials and all others involved in training programmes and games should be supervised on a regular basis by sport teams, clubs and associations.

International scrutiny is essential in any monitoring system, not only to serve as a supra-national watchdog but also to provide neutral and expert analysis and advice. The Committee on the Rights of the Child should pay more attention to sport-related issues and problems in order to provide expert recommendations to states parties to the Convention and private sport institutions.

Both public and private authorities also need to ensure that all sports teams and centres have established an appropriate *mechanism* for young athletes to access and file *individual complaints* easily; and guarantee that these complaints are properly addressed. In order to avoid duplication, these mechanisms can link with existing ones outside the sports world, such as telephone helplines, social and legal services, child rights 'shops' (multi-disciplinary advice and assistance centres established mainly in Belgium, Israel and the Netherlands), ombudspersons or commissioners for children, or independent national human rights institutions.

In view of the blatant absence of data and research, public and private authorities need to stimulate and provide access to financial and other resources in order to boost independent comprehensive *scientific research* on child rights issues in competitive sports. The current absence of such data and research puts very serious limitations on any kind of awareness-raising measures, policy-making and, ultimately, sound reform of the sporting system.

Awareness-raising and training (articles 4, 29 and 42)

Change processes often start with *awareness-raising and training* measures. All adults involved in youth competitive sports, especially trainers, coaches, medical and para-medical staff, officials, managers, etc., need to become aware of and trained in children's human rights. Children themselves need to be properly informed about their own rights. Under the Convention (article 29.1.b), states are obliged to ensure that all young people, including athletes, are given *human rights education* in and/or outside school.

The International Olympic Committee should upgrade its education programmes to *promote Olympic values* and its officials should promote more vigorously the values established by the Olympic charter and establish links with the rights of young athletes.

Empowerment (articles 12-17)

All parties working for and with children need to ensure that *the right of children to express their views freely in all matters affecting them* is enforced. They must also take all measures to guarantee that intensive training and competitive sports take place in an *environment of trust* so that young athletes feel confident enough to discuss their problems. Information regarding the effects of doping, or about child abuse, or the right to freedom of association in the context of transfer between two teams, are examples of situations for which access to information can be crucial for sound decision-making.

Redress and remedy (article 4, and article 2.3 of the International Covenant on Civil and Political Rights)

The *access to redress* mechanism is a basic human rights principle. Every human being should have the right to redress and remedy under law.[1] Child victims of conflicts of interests, abuse, neglect, violence or exploitation during their sporting activity should always be given appropriate access to redress and remedy. Legal and other advice and assistance are crucial in this regard, as the child might need support to protect his or her own rights.

Judicial redress should only be sought when appropriate and as a last resort. Often remedy can be attained through non-judicial and less traumatic means for the young victim, such as *conflict resolution*, *mediation*, *arbitration* or other procedures outside of the court system. Non-judicial approaches often offer child-sensitive procedures; nevertheless, they need to respect human rights norms and principles, especially due and fair process. In Canada, the Centre for Sport and Law has a programme specifically designed for the sport community: the alternative dispute resolution programme for amateur sport (ADR).

Compensation and rehabilitation (article 39, article 14 of the Convention against Torture and articles 9.5 and 10.3, International Covenant on Civil and Political Rights)

The principle that child victims receive support for physical and psychological recovery and social reintegration is recognized under the Convention. In many countries, however, this right is very often denied to victims who are left to their own devices after having suffered serious physical injury or psychological trauma or another type of human rights violation. The right to compensation is not recognized explicitly by the Convention, though appropriate provisions recognized under other main international human rights treaties apply to children. Here too, the principle of compensation of victims is still weakly recognized and enforced in most states; though with regard to violations of the rights of adult athletes jurisprudence is slowly building in North America and Western Europe.

The power of rights

Many states and private entities refrain from using human rights as a governance tool because they fear its alleged political sensitivity. Many sport authorities are in a similar position, almost totally ignoring the concept of rights as they dread any kind of backlash in the form of political or legal claims. In fact these potential claims could be effectively *reduced* through mainstreaming the concept of human rights, if the latter were perceived as a prevention and promotional tool for the sports system, rather than the opposite.

Systematic promotion and respect of human rights by public and sports authorities could reinforce the *positive* values repeatedly put forward by the sports community and help it to enhance its own traditional arguments, such as:

- **Sport combats discrimination** by facilitating the *integration of groups suffering from discrimination*, such as children belonging to minority or marginalized groups, children living in poverty, children with disabilities, girls, etc. (article 2).
- **Sport provides easy and equal access to sports to all groups of children in need of special protection**, including children with disabilities, children living in social and other institutions, children living in detention centres, child refugees, children in rehabilitative care, working children, etc. (articles 20, 22, 23 and 31).
- **Sport empowers youth,** allowing them to experience *progressive participation and autonomy, self-reliance and empowerment* with due regard to the maturity and evolving capacity of the child, and respecting the rights and responsibilities of adults. In addition, sports can boost self-confidence (articles 5, and 12 to 17).
- **Sport promotes non-violence** and, by developing self-control and positive use of physical and mental strength, it encourages fair play and channels potential violence (articles 19 and 29).
- **Sport is healthy** and, by promoting and ensuring *healthy and safe sporting conditions*, it enhances public health (article 24).
- **Sport talent needs to be supported,** and measures can be taken to ensure that all gifted youngsters are given the opportunity *to develop to their fullest potential* (article 29.1.a).
- **Sport promotes peace, tolerance and friendship** by promoting the *ethical values of sport*, namely peace, tolerance, understanding, equality and friendship.

- **Sport is a positive recreational activity**: the practice of sport keeps children and adolescents *away from deviant behaviours* (article 31).
- **Sport is a rehabilitation and reintegration tool** and child victims can use sport to support their physical or psychological *rehabilitation*; the same applies for social *reintegration* (article 39).

In making use of the human rights concept, public and private authorities dealing with sports could gain credibility and efficiency in promoting their activity and preventing all forms of abuse, violence and exploitation.

DOING THE RIGHT THING – RIGHT NOW

On 13 September 1930, Pierre de Coubertin presented at the University of Geneva (Switzerland) his 'Charter of Sports Reform'. The charter was adopted by the IOC, 'but its articles demand too great a sacrifice and self-denial from those concerned for them to be willing to put the provisions into practice right away. This can only be done slowly, step by step' (de Coubertin 1997: 234).

De Courbertin's charter for the reform of sports stated:

> The criticisms made against sport can be reduced to three types of complaints: *Excessive physical strain*; *Contribution to intellectual decline*; *Growth of the commercial spirit and love of gain*.
>
> It is impossible to deny the existence of these dangers, but it is not athletes who are responsible. Those to blame are: the parents, teachers, public authorities and, to a lesser extent, the heads of federations and members of the press.
>
> The necessary remedies are as follows:
>
> ... prohibition of spectators at all competitions for juniors under 16 years of age; creation of school sports associations under whose colours alone schoolchildren will be allowed to take part in competitions; postponement of the age of enrolment of boy scouts; ... encouragement given by all means for the practice of sport by individual adults as opposed to adolescents among whom, on the contrary, an attempt should be made to slow it down a little ...
>
> (de Coubertin 1997: 234–5)

Over 70 years later, de Coubertin's charter still seems valid. Over-training and excessive commercialization of the sports system are frequently identified as two of the main threats to the integrity of athletes. The overarching question posed in this book is: can the integration of human rights in the sport system improve its quality and the status of athletes, including the youngest ones? As yet, there is no straightforward answer, because – as Chapter 3 shows – human rights norms and standards have just scratched the surface of the sports world, and it is an obligation of public authorities to ensure respect for the rule of law in all sectors of society.

For historical and political reasons, the sports movement and the human rights community have kept each other at arm's length and the challenge will be to lessen the rift between them, as potential mistrust and misunderstandings subsist. The Convention's main value is its utility as a universal yardstick at local and national levels for policy-setting, law-making, programme design and judicial or other types of redress. Its minimum norms and standards are only meaningful if they are translated into the reality of every child's daily life.

Looking back on the 1990s, there is room for quiet optimism: even though the sports community remains on the whole insensitive to child rights, the decade did see some members begin to acknowledge that young athletes have specific requirements and to initiate measures to prevent them becoming victims of human rights violations. Many serious obstacles – political, behavioural, societal and financial – still need to be lifted by sport and public authorities to guarantee child rights in competitive sports. First, they will have to acknowledge that human rights is a useful tool rather than perceiving it as an intrusive threat to their autonomy and authority. Second, those involved in competitive sports will need to recognize and respect children as human beings not only in their entitlement to care and protection, but also as full subjects of rights capable of progressively participating in decision-making and, if necessary, using appropriate procedures to obtain redress. Finally, sport and public authorities will have to be willing to spend the amounts necessary to establish preventive mechanisms.

One problem facing many people working in the field of human rights is that they may focus too much on rights' violations and risk losing sight of the global picture. As seen in Chapter 2, it is often difficult to analyse scientifically the levels of respect for human rights. When I started to study young athletes' human rights in the early 1990s, I often felt very isolated: knowledge of the subject was extremely limited and debate non-existent. The sports community often judged my work excessive or controversial, while the human rights community considered the rights of athletes as a minor, or even artificial, problem that, compared to 'serious' human rights violations, deserved little attention. Therefore, as it covers a new area of research, this book needed to be articulated, whenever possible, around scientific evidence as well as the accounts of victims, perpetrators and other adults involved in competitive sport.

Anyone engaging in a new field of research will find the road paved with long periods of doubt. I sometimes asked myself whether it was really necessary to bother about the human rights of young athletes. Was the sports community right in ignoring them? An easy response came back in no time: 'It is simply unacceptable that children who voluntarily engage in a sporting activity run the risk of being given illegal drugs or being physically ill-treated, sexually abused or trafficked.' But this response, although perfectly justified, does not fully satisfy me. It is too superficial an answer, a violation-based response. And the human rights of children in sports are far more than that: they are a life process.

A story that often comes back to me is one of a girl whom I shall call Maarit. She was a 14-year-old top gymnast from Finland. One day, she came home and told her mother: 'Mum, today is the happiest day of my life!' Her mother looked at her, astonished: 'Did you qualify for the Olympics?' she asked. Maarit smiled and replied: 'No, Mum, I've decided to quit gymnastics!' Her mother was in a state of shock for a week before she was able to accept her daughter's decision. Behind this story is a young adolescent who had lost all pleasure in her sport, mainly due to what she saw as too much time spent training excessively hard, extreme pressure for results from her trainers and parents, and the difficulties she encountered in trying to keep up at school and have a normal social life. Talking about these problems did not lead to any change for Maarit; she felt she had only one way out: leave her sport before she became bitter and jeopardized her childhood, education and social life. Maarit tried to discuss her problems to solve them, but when that didn't work she felt confident enough to decide for herself. Today Maarit still lives in peace with her decision, and looks back with pride and satisfaction at her excellent sporting career. She recognizes that competitive sport was not all negative and that she learned lessons that have been useful for her personal development and fulfilment; she is thankful to her environment for – eventually – having accepted her decision.

Like any other human activity, competitive sport carries its rights and wrongs. Human rights aim at limiting, and even eliminating, the wrongs. For most children, competitive sport remains an excellent channel for human development and a rare source of joy. A human rights approach must build on this reality to ensure the dignity and integrity of all young athletes. Indeed, the sports system can help spread this universal message. Most important of all, young athletes deserve to have their rights respected through a child-sensitive sport system.

NOTES

1 Article 3 of the ICCPR states: 'Each State Party to the present Covenant undertakes: (a) To ensure that any person whose rights or freedoms as herein recognized are violated shall have an effective remedy, notwithstanding that the violation has been committed by persons acting in an official capacity; (b) To ensure that any person claiming such a remedy shall have his right thereto determined by competent judicial, administrative or legislative authorities, or by any other competent authority provided for by the legal system of the State, and to develop the possibilities of judicial remedy; (c) To ensure that the competent authorities shall enforce such remedies when granted.'

Appendix
UN Convention on the Rights of the Child

Adopted and opened for signature, ratification and accession by United Nation's General Assembly resolution 44/25 of 20 November 1989.

Entry into force 2 September 1990, in accordance with article 49.

PREAMBLE

The States Parties to the present Convention,

Considering that, in accordance with the principles proclaimed in the Charter of the United Nations, recognition of the inherent dignity and of the equal and inalienable rights of all members of the human family is the foundation of freedom, justice and peace in the world,

Bearing in mind that the peoples of the United Nations have, in the Charter, reaffirmed their faith in fundamental human rights and in the dignity and worth of the human person, and have determined to promote social progress and better standards of life in larger freedom,

Recognizing that the United Nations has, in the Universal Declaration of Human Rights and in the International Covenants on Human Rights, proclaimed and agreed that everyone is entitled to all the rights and freedoms set forth therein, without distinction of any kind, such as race, colour, sex, language, religion, political or other opinion, national or social origin, property, birth or other status,

Recalling that, in the Universal Declaration of Human Rights, the United Nations has proclaimed that childhood is entitled to special care and assistance,

Convinced that the family, as the fundamental group of society and the natural environment for the growth and well-being of all its members and particularly children, should be afforded the necessary protection and assistance so that it can fully assume its responsibilities within the community,

Recognizing that the child, for the full and harmonious development of his or her personality, should grow up in a family environment, in an atmosphere of happiness, love and understanding,

Considering that the child should be fully prepared to live an individual life in society, and brought up in the spirit of the ideals proclaimed in the Charter of the United Nations, and in particular in the spirit of peace, dignity, tolerance, freedom, equality and solidarity,

Bearing in mind that the need to extend particular care to the child has been stated in the Geneva Declaration of the Rights of the Child of 1924 and in the Declaration of the Rights of the Child adopted by the General Assembly on 20 November 1959 and recognized in the Universal Declaration of Human Rights, in the International Covenant on Civil and Political Rights (in particular in articles 23 and 24), in the International Covenant on Economic, Social and Cultural Rights (in particular in article 10) and in the statutes and relevant instruments of specialized agencies and international organizations concerned with the welfare of children,

Bearing in mind that, as indicated in the Declaration of the Rights of the Child, "the child, by reason of his physical and mental immaturity, needs special safeguards and care, including appropriate legal protection, before as well as after birth",

Recalling the provisions of the Declaration on Social and Legal Principles relating to the Protection and Welfare of Children, with Special Reference to Foster Placement and Adoption Nationally and Internationally; the United Nations Standard Minimum Rules for the Administration of Juvenile Justice (The Beijing Rules); and the Declaration on the Protection of Women and Children in Emergency and Armed Conflict,

Recognizing that, in all countries in the world, there are children living in exceptionally difficult conditions, and that such children need special consideration,

Taking due account of the importance of the traditions and cultural values of each people for the protection and harmonious development of the child,

Recognizing the importance of international co-operation for improving the living conditions of children in every country, in particular in the developing countries,

Have agreed as follows:

PART 1

Article 1

For the purposes of the present Convention, a child means every human being below the age of eighteen years unless under the law applicable to the child, majority is attained earlier.

Article 2

1   States Parties shall respect and ensure the rights set forth in the present Convention to each child within their jurisdiction without discrimination of any kind, irrespective of the child's or his or her parent's or legal guardian's race, colour, sex, language, religion, political or other opinion, national, ethnic or social origin, property, disability, birth or other status.

2   States Parties shall take all appropriate measures to ensure that the child is protected against all forms of discrimination or punishment on the basis of the status, activities, expressed opinions, or beliefs of the child's parents, legal guardians, or family members.

Article 3

1   In all actions concerning children, whether undertaken by public or private social welfare institutions, courts of law, administrative authorities or legislative bodies, the best interests of the child shall be a primary consideration.

2   States Parties undertake to ensure the child such protection and care as is necessary for his or her well-being, taking into account the rights and duties of his or her parents, legal guardians, or other individuals legally responsible for him or her, and, to this end, shall take all appropriate legislative and administrative measures.

3   States Parties shall ensure that the institutions, services and facilities responsible for the care or protection of children shall conform with the standards established by competent authorities, particularly in the areas of safety, health, in the number and suitability of their staff, as well as competent supervision.

Article 4

States Parties shall undertake all appropriate legislative, administrative, and other measures for the implementation of the rights recognized in the present Convention. With regard to economic, social and cultural rights, States Parties shall undertake such measures to the maximum extent of their available resources and, where needed, within the framework of international co-operation.

Article 5

States Parties shall respect the responsibilities, rights and duties of parents or, where applicable, the members of the extended family or community as provided for by local custom, legal guardians or other persons legally responsible for the child, to provide, in a manner consistent with the evolving capacities of the child, appropriate direction and guidance in the exercise by the child of the rights recognized in the present Convention.

Article 6

1   States Parties recognize that every child has the inherent right to life.
2   States Parties shall ensure to the maximum extent possible the survival and development of the child.

Article 7

1   The child shall be registered immediately after birth and shall have the right from birth to a name, the right to acquire a nationality and, as far as possible, the right to know and be cared for by his or her parents.
2   States Parties shall ensure the implementation of these rights in accordance with their national law and their obligations under the relevant international instruments in this field, in particular where the child would otherwise be stateless.

Article 8

1   States Parties undertake to respect the right of the child to preserve his or her identity, including nationality, name and family relations as recognized by law without unlawful interference.
2   Where a child is illegally deprived of some or all of the elements of his or her identity, States Parties shall provide appropriate assistance and protection, with a view to re-establishing speedily his or her identity.

Article 9

1   States Parties shall ensure that a child shall not be separated from his or her parents against their will, except when competent authorities subject to judicial review determine, in accordance with applicable law and proce-dures, that such separation is necessary for the best interests of the child. Such determination may be necessary in a particular case such as one involving abuse or neglect of the child by the parents, or one where the par-ents are living separately and a decision must be made as to the child's place of residence.
2   In any proceedings pursuant to paragraph 1 of the present article, all inter-ested parties shall be given an opportunity to participate in the proceedings and make their views known.
3   States Parties shall respect the right of the child who is separated from one or both parents to maintain personal relations and direct contact with both parents on a regular basis, except if it is contrary to the child's best interests.
4   Where such separation results from any action initiated by a State Party, such as the detention, imprisonment, exile, deportation or death (including death arising from any cause while the person is in the custody of the State) of one or both parents or of the child, that State Party shall, upon request,

provide the parents, the child or, if appropriate, another member of the family with the essential information concerning the whereabouts of the absent member(s) of the family unless the provision of the information would be detrimental to the well-being of the child. States Parties shall further ensure that the submission of such a request shall of itself entail no adverse consequences for the person(s) concerned.

Article 10

1   In accordance with the obligation of States Parties under article 9, paragraph 1, applications by a child or his or her parents to enter or leave a State Party for the purpose of family reunification shall be dealt with by States Parties in a positive, humane and expeditious manner. States Parties shall further ensure that the submission of such a request shall entail no adverse consequences for the applicants and for the members of their family.

2   A child whose parents reside in different States shall have the right to maintain on a regular basis, save in exceptional circumstances personal relations and direct contacts with both parents. Towards that end and in accordance with the obligation of States Parties under article 9, paragraph 1, States Parties shall respect the right of the child and his or her parents to leave any country, including their own, and to enter their own country. The right to leave any country shall be subject only to such restrictions as are prescribed by law and which are necessary to protect the national security, public order (ordre public), public health or morals or the rights and freedoms of others and are consistent with the other rights recognized in the present Convention.

Article 11

1   States Parties shall take measures to combat the illicit transfer and non-return of children abroad.

2   To this end, States Parties shall promote the conclusion of bilateral or multilateral agreements or accession to existing agreements.

Article 12

1   States Parties shall assure to the child who is capable of forming his or her own views the right to express those views freely in all matters affecting the child, the views of the child being given due weight in accordance with the age and maturity of the child.

2   For this purpose, the child shall in particular be provided the opportunity to be heard in any judicial and administrative proceedings affecting the child, either directly, or through a representative or an appropriate body, in a manner consistent with the procedural rules of national law.

Article 13

1 The child shall have the right to freedom of expression; this right shall include freedom to seek, receive and impart information and ideas of all kinds, regardless of frontiers, either orally, in writing or in print, in the form of art, or through any other media of the child's choice.
2 The exercise of this right may be subject to certain restrictions, but these shall only be such as are provided by law and are necessary:

   (a) For respect of the rights or reputations of others; or
   (b) For the protection of national security or of public order (ordre public), or of public health or morals.

Article 14

1 States Parties shall respect the right of the child to freedom of thought, conscience and religion.
2 States Parties shall respect the rights and duties of the parents and, when applicable, legal guardians, to provide direction to the child in the exercise of his or her right in a manner consistent with the evolving capacities of the child.
3 Freedom to manifest one's religion or beliefs may be subject only to such limitations as are prescribed by law and are necessary to protect public safety, order, health or morals, or the fundamental rights and freedoms of others.

Article 15

1 States Parties recognize the rights of the child to freedom of association and to freedom of peaceful assembly.
2 No restrictions may be placed on the exercise of these rights other than those imposed in conformity with the law and which are necessary in a democratic society in the interests of national security or public safety, public order (ordre public), the protection of public health or morals or the protection of the rights and freedoms of others.

Article 16

1 No child shall be subjected to arbitrary or unlawful interference with his or her privacy, family, home or correspondence, nor to unlawful attacks on his or her honour and reputation.
2 The child has the right to the protection of the law against such interference or attacks.

Article 17

States Parties recognize the important function performed by the mass media and shall ensure that the child has access to information and material from a diversity of national and international sources, especially those aimed at the promotion of his or her social, spiritual and moral well-being and physical and mental health. To this end, States Parties shall:

(a) Encourage the mass media to disseminate information and material of social and cultural benefit to the child and in accordance with the spirit of article 29;
(b) Encourage international co-operation in the production, exchange and dissemination of such information and material from a diversity of cultural, national and international sources;
(c) Encourage the production and dissemination of children's books;
(d) Encourage the mass media to have particular regard to the linguistic needs of the child who belongs to a minority group or who is indigenous;
(e) Encourage the development of appropriate guidelines for the protection of the child from information and material injurious to his or her well-being, bearing in mind the provisions of articles 13 and 18.

Article 18

1   States Parties shall use their best efforts to ensure recognition of the principle that both parents have common responsibilities for the upbringing and development of the child. Parents or, as the case may be, legal guardians, have the primary responsibility for the upbringing and development of the child. The best interests of the child will be their basic concern.
2   For the purpose of guaranteeing and promoting the rights set forth in the present Convention, States Parties shall render appropriate assistance to parents and legal guardians in the performance of their child-rearing responsibilities and shall ensure the development of institutions, facilities and services for the care of children.
3   States Parties shall take all appropriate measures to ensure that children of working parents have the right to benefit from child-care services and facilities for which they are eligible.

Article 19

1   States Parties shall take all appropriate legislative, administrative, social and educational measures to protect the child from all forms of physical or mental violence, injury or abuse, neglect or negligent treatment, maltreatment or exploitation, including sexual abuse, while in the care of parent(s), legal guardian(s) or any other person who has the care of the child.
2   Such protective measures should, as appropriate, include effective procedures for the establishment of social programmes to provide necessary support for the child and for those who have the care of the child, as well as for other forms of prevention and for identification, reporting, referral, investigation, treatment and follow-up of instances of child maltreatment described heretofore, and, as appropriate, for judicial involvement.

Article 20

1   A child temporarily or permanently deprived of his or her family environment, or in whose own best interests cannot be allowed to remain in that environment, shall be entitled to special protection and assistance provided by the State.
2   States Parties shall in accordance with their national laws ensure alternative care for such a child.
3   Such care could include, inter alia, foster placement, kafalah of Islamic law, adoption or if necessary placement in suitable institutions for the care of children. When considering solutions, due regard shall be paid to the desirability of continuity in a child's upbringing and to the child's ethnic, religious, cultural and linguistic background.

Article 21

States Parties that recognize and/or permit the system of adoption shall ensure that the best interests of the child shall be the paramount consideration and they shall:

(a) Ensure that the adoption of a child is authorized only by competent authorities who determine, in accordance with applicable law and procedures and on the basis of all pertinent and reliable information, that the adoption is permissible in view of the child's status concerning parents, relatives and legal guardians and that, if required, the persons concerned have given their informed consent to the adoption on the basis of such counselling as may be necessary;
(b) Recognize that inter-country adoption may be considered as an alternative means of child's care, if the child cannot be placed in a foster or an adoptive family or cannot in any suitable manner be cared for in the child's country of origin;
(c) Ensure that the child concerned by inter-country adoption enjoys safeguards and standards equivalent to those existing in the case of national adoption;
(d) Take all appropriate measures to ensure that, in inter-country adoption, the placement does not result in improper financial gain for those involved in it;
(e) Promote, where appropriate, the objectives of the present article by concluding bilateral or multilateral arrangements or agreements, and endeavour, within this framework, to ensure that the placement of the child in another country is carried out by competent authorities or organs.

Article 22

1   States Parties shall take appropriate measures to ensure that a child who is seeking refugee status or who is considered a refugee in accordance with applicable international or domestic law and procedures shall, whether

unaccompanied or accompanied by his or her parents or by any other person, receive appropriate protection and humanitarian assistance in the enjoyment of applicable rights set forth in the present Convention and in other international human rights or humanitarian instruments to which the said States are Parties.

2   For this purpose, States Parties shall provide, as they consider appropriate, co-operation in any efforts by the United Nations and other competent intergovernmental organizations or non-governmental organizations co-operating with the United Nations to protect and assist such a child and to trace the parents or other members of the family of any refugee child in order to obtain information necessary for reunification with his or her family. In cases where no parents or other members of the family can be found, the child shall be accorded the same protection as any other child permanently or temporarily deprived of his or her family environment for any reason , as set forth in the present Convention.

Article 23

1   States Parties recognize that a mentally or physically disabled child should enjoy a full and decent life, in conditions which ensure dignity, promote self-reliance and facilitate the child's active participation in the community.

2   States Parties recognize the right of the disabled child to special care and shall encourage and ensure the extension, subject to available resources, to the eligible child and those responsible for his or her care, of assistance for which application is made and which is appropriate to the child's condition and to the circumstances of the parents or others caring for the child.

3   Recognizing the special needs of a disabled child, assistance extended in accordance with paragraph 2 of the present article shall be provided free of charge, whenever possible, taking into account the financial resources of the parents or others caring for the child, and shall be designed to ensure that the disabled child has effective access to and receives education, training, health care services, rehabilitation services, preparation for employment and recreation opportunities in a manner conducive to the child's achieving the fullest possible social integration and individual development, including his or her cultural and spiritual development.

4   States Parties shall promote, in the spirit of international cooperation, the exchange of appropriate information in the field of preventive health care and of medical, psychological and functional treatment of disabled children, including dissemination of and access to information concerning methods of rehabilitation, education and vocational services, with the aim of enabling States Parties to improve their capabilities and skills and to widen their experience in these areas. In this regard, particular account shall be taken of the needs of developing countries.

Article 24

1   States Parties recognize the right of the child to the enjoyment of the highest attainable standard of health and to facilities for the treatment of illness and rehabilitation of health. States Parties shall strive to ensure that no child is deprived of his or her right of access to such health care services.

2   States Parties shall pursue full implementation of this right and, in particular, shall take appropriate measures:

(a) To diminish infant and child mortality;

(b) To ensure the provision of necessary medical assistance and health care to all children with emphasis on the development of primary health care;

(c) To combat disease and malnutrition, including within the framework of primary health care, through, inter alia, the application of readily available technology and through the provision of adequate nutritious foods and clean drinking-water, taking into consideration the dangers and risks of environmental pollution;

(d) To ensure appropriate pre-natal and post-natal health care for mothers;

(e) To ensure that all segments of society, in particular parents and children, are informed, have access to education and are supported in the use of basic knowledge of child health and nutrition, the advantages of breastfeeding, hygiene and environmental sanitation and the prevention of accidents;

(f) To develop preventive health care, guidance for parents and family planning education and services.

3   States Parties shall take all effective and appropriate measures with a view to abolishing traditional practices prejudicial to the health of children.

4   States Parties undertake to promote and encourage international co-operation with a view to achieving progressively the full realization of the right recognized in the present article. In this regard, particular account shall be taken of the needs of developing countries.

Article 25

States Parties recognize the right of a child who has been placed by the competent authorities for the purposes of care, protection or treatment of his or her physical or mental health, to a periodic review of the treatment provided to the child and all other circumstances relevant to his or her placement.

Article 26

1   States Parties shall recognize for every child the right to benefit from social security, including social insurance, and shall take the necessary measures to achieve the full realization of this right in accordance with their national law.

2   The benefits should, where appropriate, be granted, taking into account the resources and the circumstances of the child and persons having responsibility for the maintenance of the child, as well as any other consideration relevant to an application for benefits made by or on behalf of the child.

Article 27

1   States Parties recognize the right of every child to a standard of living adequate for the child's physical, mental, spiritual, moral and social development.
2   The parent(s) or others responsible for the child have the primary responsibility to secure, within their abilities and financial capacities, the conditions of living necessary for the child's development.
3   States Parties, in accordance with national conditions and within their means, shall take appropriate measures to assist parents and others responsible for the child to implement this right and shall in case of need provide material assistance and support programmes, particularly with regard to nutrition, clothing and housing.
4   States Parties shall take all appropriate measures to secure the recovery of maintenance for the child from the parents or other persons having financial responsibility for the child, both within the State Party and from abroad. In particular, where the person having financial responsibility for the child lives in a State different from that of the child, States Parties shall promote the accession to international agreements or the conclusion of such agreements, as well as the making of other appropriate arrangements.

Article 28

1   States Parties recognize the right of the child to education, and with a view to achieving this right progressively and on the basis of equal opportunity, they shall, in particular:

(a) Make primary education compulsory and available free to all;
(b) Encourage the development of different forms of secondary education, including general and vocational education, make them available and accessible to every child, and take appropriate measures such as the introduction of free education and offering financial assistance in case of need;
(c) Make higher education accessible to all on the basis of capacity by every appropriate means;
(d) Make educational and vocational information and guidance available and accessible to all children;
(e) Take measures to encourage regular attendance at schools and the reduction of drop-out rates.

2   States Parties shall take all appropriate measures to ensure that school discipline is administered in a manner consistent with the child's human dignity and in conformity with the present Convention.

3   States Parties shall promote and encourage international cooperation in matters relating to education, in particular with a view to contributing to the elimination of ignorance and illiteracy throughout the world and facilitating access to scientific and technical knowledge and modern teaching methods. In this regard, particular account shall be taken of the needs of developing countries.

Article 29

1   States Parties agree that the education of the child shall be directed to:

(a) The development of the child's personality, talents and mental and physical abilities to their fullest potential;

(b) The development of respect for human rights and fundamental freedoms, and for the principles enshrined in the Charter of the United Nations;

(c) The development of respect for the child's parents, his or her own cultural identity, language and values, for the national values of the country in which the child is living, the country from which he or she may originate, and for civilizations different from his or her own;

(d) The preparation of the child for responsible life in a free society, in the spirit of understanding, peace, tolerance, equality of sexes, and friendship among all peoples, ethnic, national and religious groups and persons of indigenous origin;

(e) The development of respect for the natural environment.

2   No part of the present article or article 28 shall be construed so as to interfere with the liberty of individuals and bodies to establish and direct educational institutions, subject always to the observance of the principle set forth in paragraph 1 of the present article and to the requirements that the education given in such institutions shall conform to such minimum standards as may be laid down by the State.

Article 30

In those States in which ethnic, religious or linguistic minorities or persons of indigenous origin exist, a child belonging to such a minority or who is indigenous shall not be denied the right, in community with other members of his or her group, to enjoy his or her own culture, to profess and practise his or her own religion, or to use his or her own language.

Article 31

1 States Parties recognize the right of the child to rest and leisure, to engage in play and recreational activities appropriate to the age of the child and to participate freely in cultural life and the arts.
2 States Parties shall respect and promote the right of the child to participate fully in cultural and artistic life and shall encourage the provision of appropriate and equal opportunities for cultural, artistic, recreational and leisure activity.

Article 32

1 States Parties recognize the right of the child to be protected from economic exploitation and from performing any work that is likely to be hazardous or to interfere with the child's education, or to be harmful to the child's health or physical, mental, spiritual, moral or social development.
2 States Parties shall take legislative, administrative, social and educational measures to ensure the implementation of the present article. To this end, and having regard to the relevant provisions of other international instruments, States Parties shall in particular:

 (a) Provide for a minimum age or minimum ages for admission to employment;
 (b) Provide for appropriate regulation of the hours and conditions of employment;
 (c) Provide for appropriate penalties or other sanctions to ensure the effective enforcement of the present article.

Article 33

States Parties shall take all appropriate measures, including legislative, administrative, social and educational measures, to protect children from the illicit use of narcotic drugs and psychotropic substances as defined in the relevant international treaties, and to prevent the use of children in the illicit production and trafficking of such substances.

Article 34

States Parties undertake to protect the child from all forms of sexual exploitation and sexual abuse. For these purposes, States Parties shall in particular take all appropriate national, bilateral and multilateral measures to prevent:

(a) The inducement or coercion of a child to engage in any unlawful sexual activity;

(b) The exploitative use of children in prostitution or other unlawful sexual practices;

(c) The exploitative use of children in pornographic performances and materials.

Article 35

States Parties shall take all appropriate national, bilateral and multilateral measures to prevent the abduction of, the sale of or traffic in children for any purpose or in any form.

Article 36

States Parties shall protect the child against all other forms of exploitation prejudicial to any aspects of the child's welfare.

Article 37

States Parties shall ensure that:

(a) No child shall be subjected to torture or other cruel, inhuman or degrading treatment or punishment. Neither capital punishment nor life imprisonment without possibility of release shall be imposed for offences committed by persons below eighteen years of age;

(b) No child shall be deprived of his or her liberty unlawfully or arbitrarily. The arrest, detention or imprisonment of a child shall be in conformity with the law and shall be used only as a measure of last resort and for the shortest appropriate period of time;

(c) Every child deprived of liberty shall be treated with humanity and respect for the inherent dignity of the human person, and in a manner which takes into account the needs of persons of his or her age. In particular, every child deprived of liberty shall be separated from adults unless it is considered in the child's best interest not to do so and shall have the right to maintain contact with his or her family through correspondence and visits, save in exceptional circumstances;

(d) Every child deprived of his or her liberty shall have the right to prompt access to legal and other appropriate assistance, as well as the right to challenge the legality of the deprivation of his or her liberty before a court or other competent, independent and impartial authority, and to a prompt decision on any such action.

Article 38

1   States Parties undertake to respect and to ensure respect for rules of international humanitarian law applicable to them in armed conflicts which are relevant to the child.
2   States Parties shall take all feasible measures to ensure that persons who have not attained the age of fifteen years do not take a direct part in hostilities.
3   States Parties shall refrain from recruiting any person who has not attained the age of fifteen years into their armed forces. In recruiting among those persons who have attained the age of fifteen years but who have not attained the age of eighteen years, States Parties shall endeavour to give priority to those who are oldest.
4   In accordance with their obligations under international humanitarian law to protect the civilian population in armed conflicts, States Parties shall take all feasible measures to ensure protection and care of children who are affected by an armed conflict.

Article 39

States Parties shall take all appropriate measures to promote physical and psychological recovery and social reintegration of a child victim of: any form of neglect, exploitation, or abuse; torture or any other form of cruel, inhuman or degrading treatment or punishment; or armed conflicts. Such recovery and reintegration shall take place in an environment which fosters the health, self-respect and dignity of the child.

Article 40

1   States Parties recognize the right of every child alleged as, accused of, or recognized as having infringed the penal law to be treated in a manner consistent with the promotion of the child's sense of dignity and worth, which reinforces the child's respect for the human rights and fundamental freedoms of others and which takes into account the child's age and the desirability of promoting the child's reintegration and the child's assuming a constructive role in society.
2   To this end, and having regard to the relevant provisions of international instruments, States Parties shall, in particular, ensure that:

   (a) No child shall be alleged as, be accused of, or recognized as having infringed the penal law by reason of acts or omissions that were not prohibited by national or international law at the time they were committed;
   (b) Every child alleged as or accused of having infringed the penal law has at least the following guarantees:

(i)   To be presumed innocent until proven guilty according to law;

(ii)   To be informed promptly and directly of the charges against him or her, and, if appropriate, through his or her parents or legal guardians, and to have legal or other appropriate assistance in the preparation and presentation of his or her defence;

(iii) To have the matter determined without delay by a competent, independent and impartial authority or judicial body in a fair hearing according to law, in the presence of legal or other appropriate assistance and, unless it is considered not to be in the best interest of the child, in particular, taking into account his or her age or situation, his or her parents or legal guardians;

(iv)   Not to be compelled to give testimony or to confess guilt; to examine or have examined adverse witnesses and to obtain the participation and examination of witnesses on his or her behalf under conditions of equality;

(v)   If considered to have infringed the penal law, to have this decision and any measures imposed in consequence thereof reviewed by a higher competent, independent and impartial authority or judicial body according to law;

(vi)   To have the free assistance of an interpreter if the child cannot understand or speak the language used;

(vii) To have his or her privacy fully respected at all stages of the proceedings.

3   States Parties shall seek to promote the establishment of laws, procedures, authorities and institutions specifically applicable to children alleged as, accused of, or recognized as having infringed the penal law and in particular:

(a)   The establishment of a minimum age below which children shall be presumed not to have the capacity to infringe the penal law;

(b)   Whenever appropriate and desirable, measures for dealing with such children without resorting to judicial proceedings, providing that human rights and legal safeguards are fully respected.

4   A variety of dispositions, such as care, guidance and supervision orders; counselling; probation; foster care; education and vocational training programmes and other alternatives to institutional care shall be available to ensure that children are dealt with in a manner appropriate to their well-being and proportionate both to their circumstances and the offence.

Article 41

Nothing in the present Convention shall affect any provisions which are more conducive to the realization of the rights of the child and which may be contained in:

(a) The law of a State party; or

(b) International law in force for that State.

PART II

Article 42

States Parties undertake to make the principles and provisions of the Convention widely known, by appropriate and active means, to adults and children alike.

Article 43

1   For the purpose of examining the progress made by States Parties in achieving the realization of the obligations undertaken in the present Convention, there shall be established a Committee on the Rights of the Child, which shall carry out the functions hereinafter provided.

2   The Committee shall consist of ten experts of high moral standing and recognized competence in the field covered by this Convention. The members of the Committee shall be elected by States Parties from among their nationals and shall serve in their personal capacity, consideration being given to equitable geographical distribution, as well as to the principal legal systems.

3   The members of the Committee shall be elected by secret ballot from a list of persons nominated by States Parties. Each State Party may nominate one person from among its own nationals.

4   The initial election to the Committee shall be held no later than six months after the date of the entry into force of the present Convention and thereafter every second year. At least four months before the date of each election, the Secretary-General of the United Nations shall address a letter to States Parties inviting them to submit their nominations within two months. The Secretary-General shall subsequently prepare a list in alphabetical order of all persons thus nominated, indicating States Parties which have nominated them, and shall submit it to the States Parties to the present Convention.

5   The elections shall be held at meetings of States Parties convened by the Secretary-General at United Nations Headquarters. At those meetings, for which two thirds of States Parties shall constitute a quorum, the persons elected to the Committee shall be those who obtain the largest number of votes and an absolute majority of the votes of the representatives of States Parties present and voting.

6   The members of the Committee shall be elected for a term of four years. They shall be eligible for re-election if renominated. The term of five of the members elected at the first election shall expire at the end of two years;

immediately after the first election, the names of these five members shall be chosen by lot by the Chairman of the meeting.

7   If a member of the Committee dies or resigns or declares that for any other cause he or she can no longer perform the duties of the Committee, the State Party which nominated the member shall appoint another expert from among its nationals to serve for the remainder of the term, subject to the approval of the Committee.

8   The Committee shall establish its own rules of procedure.

9   The Committee shall elect its officers for a period of two years.

10   The meetings of the Committee shall normally be held at United Nations Headquarters or at any other convenient place as determined by the Committee. The Committee shall normally meet annually. The duration of the meetings of the Committee shall be determined, and reviewed, if necessary, by a meeting of the States Parties to the present Convention, subject to the approval of the General Assembly.

11   The Secretary-General of the United Nations shall provide the necessary staff and facilities for the effective performance of the functions of the Committee under the present Convention.

12   With the approval of the General Assembly, the members of the Committee established under the present Convention shall receive emoluments from United Nations resources on such terms and conditions as the Assembly may decide.

Article 44

1   States Parties undertake to submit to the Committee, through the Secretary-General of the United Nations, reports on the measures they have adopted which give effect to the rights recognized herein and on the progress made on the enjoyment of those rights:

(a) Within two years of the entry into force of the Convention for the State Party concerned;

(b) Thereafter every five years.

2   Reports made under the present article shall indicate factors and difficulties, if any, affecting the degree of fulfilment of the obligations under the present Convention. Reports shall also contain sufficient information to provide the Committee with a comprehensive understanding of the implementation of the Convention in the country concerned.

3   A State Party which has submitted a comprehensive initial report to the Committee need not, in its subsequent reports submitted in accordance with paragraph 1 (b) of the present article, repeat basic information previously provided.

4   The Committee may request from States Parties further information relevant to the implementation of the Convention.

5 The Committee shall submit to the General Assembly, through the Economic and Social Council, every two years, reports on its activities.

6 States Parties shall make their reports widely available to the public in their own countries.

Article 45

In order to foster the effective implementation of the Convention and to encourage international co-operation in the field covered by the Convention:

(a) The specialized agencies, the United Nations Children's Fund, and other United Nations organs shall be entitled to be represented at the consideration of the implementation of such provisions of the present Convention as fall within the scope of their mandate. The Committee may invite the specialized agencies, the United Nations Children's Fund and other competent bodies as it may consider appropriate to provide expert advice on the implementation of the Convention in areas falling within the scope of their respective mandates. The Committee may invite the specialized agencies, the United Nations Children's Fund, and other United Nations organs to submit reports on the implementation of the Convention in areas falling within the scope of their activities;

(b) The Committee shall transmit, as it may consider appropriate, to the specialized agencies, the United Nations Children's Fund and other competent bodies, any reports from States Parties that contain a request, or indicate a need, for technical advice or assistance, along with the Committee's observations and suggestions, if any, on these requests or indications;

(c) The Committee may recommend to the General Assembly to request the Secretary-General to undertake on its behalf studies on specific issues relating to the rights of the child;

(d) The Committee may make suggestions and general recommendations based on information received pursuant to articles 44 and 45 of the present Convention. Such suggestions and general recommendations shall be transmitted to any State Party concerned and reported to the General Assembly, together with comments, if any, from States Parties.

PART III

Article 46

The present Convention shall be open for signature by all States.

Article 47

The present Convention is subject to ratification. Instruments of ratification shall be deposited with the Secretary-General of the United Nations.

Article 48

The present Convention shall remain open for accession by any State. The instruments of accession shall be deposited with the Secretary-General of the United Nations.

Article 49

1   The present Convention shall enter into force on the thirtieth day following the date of deposit with the Secretary-General of the United Nations of the twentieth instrument of ratification or accession.
2   For each State ratifying or acceding to the Convention after the deposit of the twentieth instrument of ratification or accession, the Convention shall enter into force on the thirtieth day after the deposit by such State of its instrument of ratification or accession.

Article 50

1   Any State Party may propose an amendment and file it with the Secretary-General of the United Nations. The Secretary-General shall thereupon communicate the proposed amendment to States Parties, with a request that they indicate whether they favour a conference of States Parties for the purpose of considering and voting upon the proposals. In the event that, within four months from the date of such communication, at least one third of the States Parties favour such a conference, the Secretary-General shall convene the conference under the auspices of the United Nations. Any amendment adopted by a majority of States Parties present and voting at the conference shall be submitted to the General Assembly for approval.
2   An amendment adopted in accordance with paragraph 1 of the present article shall enter into force when it has been approved by the General Assembly of the United Nations and accepted by a two-thirds majority of States Parties.

3 When an amendment enters into force, it shall be binding on those States Parties which have accepted it, other States Parties still being bound by the provisions of the present Convention and any earlier amendments which they have accepted.

Article 51

1 The Secretary-General of the United Nations shall receive and circulate to all States the text of reservations made by States at the time of ratification or accession.
2 A reservation incompatible with the object and purpose of the present Convention shall not be permitted.
3 Reservations may be withdrawn at any time by notification to that effect addressed to the Secretary-General of the United Nations, who shall then inform all States. Such notification shall take effect on the date on which it is received by the Secretary-General.

Article 52

A State Party may denounce the present Convention by written notification to the Secretary-General of the United Nations. Denunciation becomes effective one year after the date of receipt of the notification by the Secretary-General.

Article 53

The Secretary-General of the United Nations is designated as the depositary of the present Convention.

Article 54

The original of the present Convention, of which the Arabic, Chinese, English, French, Russian and Spanish texts are equally authentic, shall be deposited with the Secretary-General of the United Nations.

IN WITNESS THEREOF the undersigned plenipotentiaries, being duly authorized thereto by their respective governments, have signed the present Convention.

Bibliography

ABC News (1999) *5PM News Journal*, New York, 23 December.

Academy for Eating Disorders (2002) *Information on eating disorders*. Online. Available HTTP: <http:// www.aedweb.org> (accessed 14 April 2002).

Addo, M.K. (ed.) (1999) *Human rights standards and the responsibility of transnational corporations*, The Hague: Kluwer Law International.

African Football Management (2001) *AFM Homepage*. Online. Available HTTP: <http://www.geocities.com/africanfootman/presentazione> (accessed 21 April 2001).

Agence France Presse (2001) *Sport: Indonesian boxer dies after match*, 29 October.

Agence France Presse (2001a) *Karol Hingis, père meurti* (Karol Hingis, wounded father), 6 January.

Agence France Presse (2001b) *L'habit ne fait pas le moine* ... (Clothing is not all ...), 18 October.

Agence France Presse (2001c) *La ligue polonaise veut faire jouer ses basketteuses en slip* ... (The Polish league wants its players to compete in their briefs ...), 19 October.

Agence France Presse (2001d) *Projet de Jeux Olympiques pour les juniors* (Junior Olympic Games project), 29 September.

Agence France Presse (1999) *Mauresmo déçue par Martina* (Mauresmo disappointed by Martina), 30 January.

Agence Télégraphique Suisse (2001) *Football: plus de 700 footballeurs brésiliens expatriés en 2001* (Football: over 700 Brazilian football players sent abroad in 2001), 26 December.

Ajax Amsterdam (2001) *Jan Pruijn: Manager of the International Training Programme*. Online. Available HTTP: <http://www.ajax.nl/international> (accessed 10 March 2001).

Ajax Amsterdam (2000) *Tower topic: youth development*. Online. Available HTTP: <http://www.ajax.nl/international> (accessed 2 February 2000).

Albuy, G. (1993) 'Un entretien avec Juan Antonio Samaranch' (A conversation with Juan Antonio Samaranch), *Le Monde*, 21 September.

Alpert, B.S. and Wilmore, J.H. (1994) 'Physical activity and blood pressure in adolescents', *Paediatric Exercise Science*, 6: 381–405.

Alston, P. (1996) 'Establishing accountability: some current challenges in relation to human rights monitoring', in Verhellen, E. (ed.) *Monitoring children's rights*, The Hague: Martinus Nijhoff.

Amateur Swimming Association (1999) *Have your swimming programme quality assured*. Online. Available HTTP: <http://www.britishswimming.org> (accessed 20 April 2000).

American Academy of Pediatrics (2000) 'Intensive training and sports specialization in young athletes', *Pediatrics* 106, 1: 154–7.

American Academy of Pediatrics (2000a) 'Human Immunodeficiency Virus and other related blood-borne viral pathogens in the athletic setting', *Pediatrics* 104, 6: 1400–3.

American Academy of Pediatrics (1997) 'Adolescent and anabolic steroids: a subject review, Policy statement', *Pediatrics* 99, 6.

American College of Sports Medicine (2000) 'The physiological and health effects of oral creatine supplementation', *Medicine and Science in Sports and Exercise* 32, 706–17.

American College of Sports Medicine (1996) 'Weight-loss in wrestlers', *Medicine and Science in Sports and Exercise* 28, ix–xii.

Andersen, A.E. (1999) 'Gender-related aspects of eating disorders: a guide to practice', *The Journal of Gender-Specific Medicine*, vol. 2, 1: 47–54.

Andersen, R.E., Bartlett, S.G., Morgan, N.D. and Brownell, K.D. (1995) 'Weight loss, psychological and nutritional patterns in competitive male body builders', *International Journal of Eating Disorders*, 18: 49–57.

Anderson, S. and Cavanagh, J. (1996) *The top 200*, Washington: Institute for Policy Studies.

Anderson, W.F. (1992) 'Uses and abuses of human gene transfer', *Human Gene Therapy* 3, 1: 1–2.

André-Simonet, M. (2000) *Le droit du sport et les jeunes* (Sports law and the youth), Paris: Editions Jeunesse et Droit.

Anti-Slavery International (1998) *Child camel jockeys in the Gulf States*, London: ASI.

Appenzeller, T. (2000) *Youth sport and the law. A guide to legal issues*, Durham, NC: Carolina Academic Press.

Aristotle (1995) *Politics*, Oxford World's Classics, Oxford: Oxford University Press.

Arlott, J. (1975) *The Oxford companion to sports and games*, Oxford: Oxford University Press.

Arte (2001) *Roumanie, la gymnastique de la rigueur* (Romania: gymnastics of rigour), Equipe TV and PDJ Productions, Strasbourg: Arte.

Assavanonda, A. and Susanpoolthong, S. (1999) 'Child exploitation, Boxers attack block on under-age bouts. Parliament protest to gain the right to fight', *Bangkok Post*, 28 May.

Associated Press (2004) *Former East German athletes compensated for doping damage*, 2 February.

Associated Press (2002) *L'âge des gymnastes roumaines falsifié* (The age of Romanian gymnasts falsified), 2 May.

Associated Press (2001) *Senate finds exploitation of Brazilian, African youngsters in European soccer*, 19 March.

Associated Press (2001a) *Duke files appeal in case against female kicker*, 4 June.

Associated Press (2000) *Text of court decision on Raducan*, 28 September.

Associated Press (2000a) *Raducan's appeal rejected*, 12 December.

Associated Press (1999) *Women's tennis increasingly turning toward glamour*, 27 March.

Associated Press (1999a) *Youth soccer league bans crowd noise*, 30 September.

Associated Press (1999b) *EU probes FIFA rules on player agents*, 21 October.

Associated Press (1999c) *The heart of the matter. Conference addressed welfare of young Kenyan athletes*, 25 October.

Associated Press (1999d) *Illegal trade? Agent says Dodgers were scouting Cubans*, 19 November.

Associated Press (1999e) *Dodgers fined for signing young Beltre*, 21 December.

Associated Press (1999f) *President offers athletes rewards*, 25 December.

Associated Press (1998) *North Korean women underage?*, 9 December.

Associated Press (1998a) *"I need to compete" Defying doctors to compete in national championships*, 19 August.

Associated Press (1998b) *Monceanu gets her freedom*, 27 October.

Associated Press (1998c) *Beer strikes out. Bar drops Little League sponsorship over uniform furore*, 20 August.

Associated Press (1998d) *Gymnast accuses dad of stalking her*, 1 December.

Australian Institute of Sport (2001) *Acts on online: gymnastics*. Online. Available HTTP: <http://www.ausport.gov.au/aisgym.html> (accessed 19 March 2001).

Australian Institute of Sport (2001a) *AIS sports nutrition, a winning diet*. Online. Available HTTP: <http://www.ausport.gov.au/nutrition/WinDiet.html> (accessed 19 March 2001).

Australian Sports Commission (2000) *Harassment-free Sport. Protecting children from abuse*, Canberra.

Australian Sports Commission (1995) *Don't stand for sexual harassment, Aussie sport action*, *A publication of the Australian Sports Commission*, V6(4), Canberra.

Australian Sports Commission and Active Australia (1998) *Harassment-free sport: Guidelines for athletes*, Canberra.

Australian Sports Commission and Active Australia (1998a) *Harassment-free sport: Guidelines for sport administrators*, Canberra.

Australian Sports Commission, Confederation of Australian Sport, School Sport Australia, Standing Committee on Sport and Recreation, Committee of Education Systems Chief Executive Officers (1999) *National Junior Sport Policy (1994) a review: Final report*, National Junior Sport Policy Working Group.

Ballester, P. (2001) 'Le TAS frappe ferme' (The CAS hits hard), *L'Equipe*, 13 January.

Baumann, E. (1976) *Le grand livre des Jeux Olympiques: Montréal 1976* (The big book of the Olympic Games: Montreal 1976), Künzelzau, Germany: Sigloch.

Baupère, M. (2001) 'Jenny, fille de fer' (Jenny, iron girl), *L'Equipe*, 28 January.

Baxter-Jones, A.D.G. and Maffuli, N. (2002) 'Intensive training in elite young female athletes', *British Journal of Sports Medicine*, 36: 13–15.

Béguin, J.-M. (2000) 'A l'école de la rage de vaincre' (The raring-to-win school), *Le Temps*, 2 May.

Belgium, Government of (2001) *Proposition visant à instituer une commission d'enquête parlementaire chargée d'enquêter sur les causes et les mécanismes de la traite des êtres humains dans certains secteurs* (Proposal to establish a parliamantary commission of inquiry to investigate the causes and mechanisms of the sale of human beings in specific sectors) 2–694/1, 19 March.

Belgium, Government of (2000) *Deelneming aan wielerwedstrijden en proeven* (Participation in cycling competitions), Flemish parliament, Decree proposal, advice by the Commissioner for Children, Document 102, No. 2.

Belgium, Government of (1995) *Loi du 15 Décembre 1980 sur l'accès au territoire, le séjour, l'établissement et l'éloignement des étrangers, amendement No1142/4 du 30 mars 1995* (Law of 15 December 1980 on access to the territory, the stay, establishment and removal of foreigners, amendment No. 1142/4 of 30 March 1995).

Belmonte, V. (1997) *Hurting Athletes II: Prevention, care and response*, USA Hockey, United States Olympic Congress, 4 November, Orlando, Florida.

Ben-Ismaïl, K. (2000) 'L'empire du judo' (Judo's empire), *L'Equipe Magazine*, no. 957, 2 September.

Bernard, J.-P. (1999) 'Erwann Menthéour: Celui qui a le meilleur médecin finit par triompher' (Erwann Menthéour: The one with the best doctor always wins), *Le Temps*, 12 February.

Bernès, F. (2002) 'Dans les pas de Ravva' (Following Ravva's steps), *L'Equipe*, 11 May.

Bianchi, F. and Curro, E. (1999) 'Tratta di baby-calciatori: stop sotto I sedici anni' (Trade of baby-footballers: stop until 16 years old), *La Repubblica*, 10 November.

Bichon, F. (1995) 'Un jeune athlète américain sur quatre serait prêt à se doper' (One young American athlete in four prepared to use drugs), *Le Nouveau Quotidien*, 21 September.

Bielderman, E. (2000) 'Transferts: la partie d'échecs' (Transfers: a game of chess), *L'Equipe Magazine*, no. 964, 21 October.

Bigelow, B., Moroney, T. and Hall, L. (2001) *How to stop other adults from ruining your child's fun and success in youth sports*, Deerfield Beach, FL, Health Communications.

Bitensky, S.H. (1998) 'Spare the rod, embrace our humanity: towards a new legal regime prohibiting corporal punishment of children', *Journal of Law Reform*, University of Michigan, vol. 31, 2: 353–474.

Bizzini, L. (1993) 'Avant-Propos' (Foreword) in David, P. *La protection des droits de l'enfant dans le sport de haute compétition* (The protection of children's rights in high-level competitive sports), Geneva: Defence of Children International.

Bizzini, L. (1989) *Le sport, la compétition et l'enfant. Approche psychologique et psychopédagogique* (Sport, competition and the child. Psychological and psychopedagogical approaches), Départment de l'instruction publique du canton de Genève.

Bizzini, L. and Piffaretti, M. (1998) 'Evolution psychologique et stress psychique chez le footballeur adolescent: notes addressées aux entraineurs' (Psychological evolution and psychic stress in young adolescent footballers: notes for trainers), in Bizzini, L., Haubert, C.-A. and Piffaretti, M. (eds) *Etudes et recherches du GISS: 6*, Editions Médecine & Hygiène.

Blanpain, R. (1993) *Les gladiateurs du sport, la mafia du sport* (Sport gladiators, the sport mafia), Brussels: La Charte.

Bochud, F. (2000) 'La détermination de l'âge des requérants d'asile minuers non-accompagnés et ses conséquencs juridiques' (Age determination of unaccompanied asylum seekers and its legal consequences), *Bulletin Suisse des Droits de l'Enfant*, vol. 6, 2: 12–14.

Bonamy, E. (1999) 'On ne se soigne plus, on ne guérit plus' (You no longer cure, you no longer recover), *L'Equipe*, 30 January.

Bostian, T. (2000) *Making the cut*. Online. Available HTTP: <http://www.sportsjones.com/sj/107.shtml> (accessed 15 April 2000).

Boston Globe (1995) 16 July.

Bouchard, C., Shepard, R.J. and Stephens, T. (eds) (1994) *Physical activity, fitness and health*, Champaign, IL: Human Kinetics Publishers.

Bouveret, N. (1994) 'Les revers de la famille Rusedski' (The difficulties of the Rusedski family), *L'Equipe*, 25 August.

Boyd, K.T., Brownson, P. and Hunter, J.B. (2001) 'Distal radial fractures in young goal-keepers: a case for an appropriately sized soccer ball', *British Journal of Sports Medicine*, 35: 409–11.

Brackenridge, C.H. (2001) *Spoilsports, understanding and preventing sexual exploitation in sports*, Ethics and Sports series, London: Routledge.

Brackenridge, C.H. (2001a) *Developments in child protection policy and practice: experiences of the United Kingdom*, SPRINT seminar on the protection of children, young people and women in sport: how to guarantee human dignity and equal rights for these groups, Committee for the Development of Sport (CDDS), Council of Europe, Helsinki, 14–16 September 2001.

Brackenridge, C.H. (2000) 'Harassment, sexual abuse, and safety of the female athlete', *Clinics in Sports Medicine* 19, 2: 187–98.

Brackenridge, C.H. (1997) '"He owned me basically": women's experience of sexual abuse in sport', *International Review for the Sociology of Sports* 32, 2: 115–30.

Brackenridge, C.H. and Kirby, S. (1997) 'Playing safe? Assessing the risk of sexual abuse to elite child athletes', *International Review of the Sociology of Sports*, 32, 4: 407–18.

Brecht, Bertolt (1928) 'Die Krisis des Sportes' (The crises of sports), in Meisl, W. (ed.), *Der Sport am Scheidewege* (Sport at the crossroads), Heidelberg: Iris Verlag.

Brennan, C. (1993) 'An exercise in self-control', *Washington Post*, 25 December (D1–D5).

Brennan, C. (1999) *Edge of glory, the inside story of the quest for figure skating's Olympic gold medals*, New York: Penguin Books.

Breton, M. (1997) 'Lost in New York: Baseball's Latin Ghetto', *APF Reporter*, vol. 8, no. 2.

Breton, M. and Villegas, J.-L. (1999) *Away games: the life and times of a Latin ball*, Albuquerque: University of New Mexico Press.

British Broadcasting Corporation (2000) *Minister rejects boxing ban*. Online. Available HTTP: <http://www.bbc.co.uk> (accessed 18 December 2000).

British Broadcasting Corporation (2000a) *Gold winner fails drug test*. Online. Available HTTP: <http://www.bbc.co.uk> (accessed 18 December 2000).

British Broadcasting Corporation (2000b) *Tour riders test positive*. Online. Available HTTP: <http://www.bbc.co.uk> (accessed 18 December 2000).

British Broadcasting Corporation (1999) *Special report feature: Belgium's football slave trade*. Online. Available HTTP: <http://www.bbc.co.uk> (accessed 20 April 1999).

British Broadcasting Corporation (1999a) *Boxing: the health risks*. Online. Available HTTP: <http://www.bbc.co.uk> (accessed 18 December 2000).

British Broadcasting Corporation (1998) *Boxing's deadly toll*. Online. Available HTTP: <http://www.bbc.co.uk> (accessed 18 December 2000).

British Journal of Sports Medicine (2001) 'No pain, no gain. The dilemma of a team physician', 35: 141–2.

British Law Commission (1994) *Consent and offences against the person*, Law Commission Consultation Paper No. 134, London.

British Medical Association (1996) *Sport and medicine: policy and provision*, Board of Science and Education, London: British Medical Association.

Brohm, J.-M. (1981) *Le mythe olympique* (The Olympic myth), Paris: Christian Bourgeois.

Browne, K. *et al.* (2002) *Child abuse and neglect in Romanian families: a national prevalence study 2000*, Copenhagen: WHO Regional Office for Europe.

Brunel, P., Coltier, A. and Ladouce, A. (1998) 'La dérive n'épargne aucun continent' (No continent is free of doping) *L'Equipe Magazine*, no. 856, 19 September.

Buffet, M.-G. (2000) *Le discours de la Ministre* (Statement by the Minister), Paris: Ministère de la Jeunesse et des Sports.

Buisman, A., De Knop, P. and Theeboorn, M. (1998) 'Kwaliteit van jeugdsport: naar en pedagodisch kader' (Quality of youth sport: towards a paedagogical framework), in De Knop, P. and Buisman, A. *Quality of youth sport*, Brussels: VUB Press.

Burke, M. (1999) *Coach–athlete relationship and sexual abuse: radical feminist interventions*, Melbourne: Victoria University.

Burley, J. (ed.) (1999) *The genetic revolution and human rights*, Oxford: Oxford University Press.

Buss, P.-E. (2002) 'Ueli Kestenho`lz, un champion pressé d'en finir avec les Jeux Olympiques de Salt Lake City' (Ueli Kestenholz, a champion in a hurry to finish with the Salt Lake City Olympics), *Le Temps*, 5 February.

Buss, P.-E. (2002a) 'Gilles Jacquet : c'est une page qui se tourne' (Gilles Jacquet. A page is turning), *Le Temps*, 20 December.

Buss, P.-E. (2001) 'Icône sportive et publicitaire, Martina Hingis est omniprésente en marge de Roland-Garros' (Sport and publicity icon, Martina Hingis is omnipresent around Roland-Garros), *Le Temps*, 6 June.

Byers, W. and Hammer, C. (1995) *Unsportsmanlike conduct. Exploiting college athletes*, Ann Arbor: The University of Michigan Press.

Cahill, B.R. and Pearl, A.J. (eds), *Intensive participation in children's sports*, American Orthopedic Society for Sports Medicine, Champaign, IL: Human Kinetics Publishers.

Camera dei Deputati (1999) *XIII Legislatura, discussioni, seduta del 28 Aprile 1999–N. 527* (13th Legislature, discussions, decision of 28 April 1999–N527), Rome.

Campbell D. (2001) 'Sport Minister urges parents to lead coaching revolution', *The Observer*, 23 September.

Campbell D. (2000) 'What the future holds', *The Guardian*, 23 May.

Canadian Association of National Team Athletes (CAN) (1999) *Effective athlete leadership*, Ontario: CAN.

Canadian Hockey Association (1999) *Policy against harassment and abuse*.

Canadian Hockey Association (1997) *Harassment in sport handbook: dealing with the media*.

Cantwell, N. (1998) 'The history, content and impact of the Convention on the Rights of the Child', in Verhellen, E. (ed.) *Understanding children's rights*, Ghent: University of Ghent.

Carr, D. (1998) 'What moral significance has physical education', in MacNamee, M. and Parry, S.J. (eds), *Ethics and sports*, London: Routledge.

Carrington, B. and McDonald, I. (eds) (2001) *Race, sport and British society*, London: Routledge.

Carroll, B. and Hollinshead, G. (1993) 'Ethnicity and conflict in physical education', *British Educational Research Journal* 19, 1: 59–76.

CASA (National Commission on Sports and Substance Abuse) (2000) *Winning at any cost: doping in Olympic sport*, New York: Columbia University.

Casas, F. (1996) 'Monitoring children's rights and monitoring childhood: different tasks?', in Verhellen, E. (ed.) *Monitoring children's rights*, The Hague: Martinus Nijhoff.

Centre pour l'égalité des chances et la lutte contre le racisme (1998) *Rapport annuel d'é-valuation sur l'évolution et les résultats de la lutte contre la traite des êtres humains* (Annual evaluation report on the evolution and the results of the fight against trafficking in human beings), Brussels.

Champel, E. (2000) 'Chemins d'exil' (Roads of exile), *L'Equipe Magazine*, no. 970, 2 December.

Chandra, P.S., Shah, J., Shenoy, U., Kumar, U., Verghese, M., Bhatti, R.S. and Channabasavanna, S.M. (1995) 'Family pathology and anorexia in the Indian context', *International Journal of Social Psychiatry*, 41: 292–8.

Citroen, N. (2001) *Interview with Andrea Raducan*. Online. Available HTTP: <http://members.tripodnet.nl/AndreaRaducan/quotes.html> (accessed 19 September 2001).

Clapham, A. (1995) 'The Privatisation of Human Rights', *European Human Rights Law Review*, Launch issue: 20–32.

Clapham, A. (1993) *Human rights in the private sphere*, Oxford: Clarendon.

Clarke, J. (2000) 'Anabolic steroids – a growing problem', *Network Northwest*, no. 10, Liverpool: Healthwise Liverpool.

Cleveland Plain Dealer (1995), 19 May.

CNN/SI.com (2001) Online. Available HTTP: <http://www.si.com> (accessed 13 December 2001).

Coadic, L. (1998) 'Le sportif est une victime' ('The sportsman is a victim'), *L'Equipe Magazine*, no. 858, 19 September.

Coadic, L. (1998a) 'Entraîneur et médecin, le tandem ambigu' (Coach and doctor, the ambiguous couple), *L'Equipe Magazine*, no. 866, 14 November.

Coadic, L. (1998b) 'Sport et médecins, le grand malaise' (Sport and doctors: big misunderstandings), *L'Equipe Magazine*, no. 874, 23 January.

Coakley, J. (1998) *Sport in society, issues and controversies*, Boston: WCB McGraw-Hill.

Coakley, J. (1993) 'Social dimension of intensive training and participation in youth sports', in Cahill, B.R. and Pearl, A.J. (eds), *Intensive participation in children's sports*, American Orthopedic Society for Sports Medicine, Champaign, IL: Human Kinetics Publishers.

Columbus Dispatch (1994) 'The gymnastics obsession', 15 August.

Conn, D. (2002) 'Whatever happened to the likely lads?', *The Observer*, 4 August.

Costa, G. (2000) 'Lausanne reste en lice pour acceuillir le siège permanent de l'Agence mondiale antidopage' (Lausanne remains in the running to obtain the World Agency Against Doping), *Le Temps*, 19 September 2000.

Council of Europe (2001) *SPRINT seminar on the protection of children, young people and women in sport: how to guarantee human dignity and equal rights for these groups*, oral statement, Committee for the Development of Sport (CDDS), Helsinki, 14–16 September.

Council of Europe (2001a) *The protection of children, young people and women in sport: how to guarantee human dignity and equal rights for these groups*, final statement, Document CDDS (2001) 60, Committee for the Development of Sport (CDDS), Finnish Sports Federation, the Finnish Ministry of Education, Hanasaari, Helsinki, 14–16 September.

Council of Europe (2001b) *Preamble of the Recommendation No. R(92)14 Rev of the Committee of Ministers to Member States on the Revised Code of Sport Ethics, adopted by the Committee of Ministers on 24 September 1992 at the 480th meeting of the Ministers' Deputies and revised at their 752nd meeting on 16 May 2001*, Strasbourg: Council of Europe.

Council of Europe (2001c) *Preamble of the Recommendation No. R(92)13 Rev of the Committee of Ministers to Member States on the Revised Code of Sport Ethics, adopted by the Committee of Ministers on 24 September 1992 at the 480th meeting of the Ministers' Deputies and revised at their 752nd meeting on 16 May 2001*, Strasbourg: Council of Europe.

Council of Europe (2000) *Report on the Commission report to the European Council with a view to safeguarding current sport structures and maintaining the social function of sport within the Community framework, The Helsinki report on sport*, (COM(1999)644-C5-0088/2000 – 2000/2055(COS)), Committee on culture, youth, education, the media and sport, Final A5-0208/2000, Strasbourg: Council of Europe.

Council of Europe (2000a) *Background studies on the problem of sexual harassment in sport, especially with regard to women and children*, Brackenbridge, C. and Fasting, K., 9th Council of Europe Conference of Ministers responsible for sport – 'A clean and healthy sport for the 3rd millennium', Bratislava, Slovakia, 30–31 May.

Council of Europe (2000b) *Resolution No3/2000 on the sexual harassment and abuse of women, young people and children in sport*, 9th Council of Europe Conference of Ministers responsible for sport – 'A clean and healthy sport for the 3rd millennium', Bratislava, Slovakia, 30–31 May.

Council of Europe (1999) 'Sports in Europe', *Eur-op news*, 2/99.

Council of Europe (1999a) *Sports information bulletin*, Sport for all clearing house, CDDS, No. 51–2, Strasbourg: Council of Europe.

Council of Europe (1996) *Recommendation 1292 on young people in high-level sport*, Parliamentary Assembly, Report of the Committee on Culture and Education, Document 7459, Strasbourg: Council of Europe.

Council of Europe (1989) *Anti-Doping Convention*, ETS No. 135.

Council of Europe (1979) *Recommendation 874 on a European Charter on the Rights of the Child*, Parliamentary Assembly, Report of the Committee on Social and Health Questions, Document 4376, Strasbourg: Council of Europe.

Cumming, P. (2001) *The use of creatine supplements in youth sports*, Institute for the Study of Youth Sports, Michigan State University and Todd Bartee Department of Kinesiology and Health.

Cyrulnik, B. (2002) *Un merveilleux malheur* (A marvellous misfortune), Paris: Odile Jacob.

Dabscheck, B. (2000) 'Sport, human rights and industrial relations', *How you play the game, the contribution of sport to the protection of human rights*, The first international conference on sports and human rights, conference proceedings, Sydney: University of Technology.

Dahlberg, T. (2001) 'On U.S. playing fields, parents escalate the violence', *International Herald Tribune*, 4 June.

Dalton, S.E. (1992) 'Overuse injuries in adolescent athletes', *Sports Medicine*, 13: 58–70.

Daly, R.L., Bass, S.L. and Finch, C.F. (2001) 'Balancing the risk of injury to gymnasts: how effective are the counter measures?', *British Journal of Sports Medicine*, vol. 35.

Damato, M. (1999) 'Le Brésil dans la tourmente' (Brazilian football in a turmoil), *L'Equipe*, 20 December.

Daniels, J. (2001) *Dominican Diamonds. In the Dominican Republic, baseball isn't just a pastime – it's an obsession*. Online. Available HTTP: <http://www.cigaraficionado.com> (accessed 26 March 2001).

Davet, G. (2002) 'Zinédine Zidane veut vivre le sommet de sa carrière à Madrid' (Zinédine Zidane wants to reach his peak in Madrid), *Le Monde*, 21 January.

David, P. (2002) 'Implementing the rights of the child: six reasons why the human rights of children remain a constant challenge', *International Review of Education* 48, 3–4: 259–63.

David, P. (1999) 'Children's rights and sports. Young athletes and competitive sports: exploit and exploitation', *International Journal of Children's Rights*, 7: 53–81.

David, P. (1999a) *Preventing and combating all forms of physical punishment, achievements and challenges of the Committee on the Rights of the Child*, Seville: Save the Children-Spain.

David, P. (1995) *Enfants sans Enfance* (Children without childhood), Collection Pluriel Inédit, Paris: Hachette.

David, P. (1993) *La protection des droits de l'enfant dans le sport de haute compétition* (The protection of children's rights in high-level competitive sports), Geneva: Defence for Children International.

David, P. (1993a) *Le rôle des organisations non-gouvernementales (ONG) dans le projet d'élaboration et la mise en œuvre de la Convention des Nations Unies relative aux droits de l'enfant* (The role of non-governmental organizations (NGOs) in the drafting and implementation of the United Nations Convention on the Rights of the Child), unpublished.

David, P. (1992) 'The exploitation of child-jockeys', *International Children's Rights Monitor* 9, 3–4: 16–18, Geneva: Defence for Children International.

Davie, R. (1996) 'Partnerships with children: the advancing trend', in Davie, R., Upton, G. and Varma, V. (eds), *The voice of the child: a handbook for professionals*, London: The Falmer Press.

Davies, T. (1994) 'Intercollegiate athletics: competing models and conflicting realities', *Rutgers Law Journal*, 269.

Davin, A. (1999) 'What is a child?', in Fletcher, A. and Hussey, S. (eds) *Childhood in question. Children, parents and the State*, Manchester: Manchester University Press.

Dawson, R.T. (2001) 'Hormones in sport. Drugs in sport – the role of the physician', *Journal of Endocrinology*, 170: 55–61.

Dayton Daily News (1997) 7 July.

Deacon, J., Branswell, B., McClelland, M. and Smart, D. (2001) 'Rink rage. Screaming, shouting, hitting – abusive parents spoiling their kids' sports', *Maclean's*, 26 March.

Deak, D. (1999) 'Out of bounds: how sexual abuse of athletes at the hands of their coaches is costing the world of sports millions', *Secton Hall Journal of Sport Law* 9, 1: 171–95.

Debonnaire, Y. (2000) 'Le temps … de prendre son temps' (Time … to take time), *Le Temps*, 10 June.

de Coubertin, P. (1997) *Olympic Memoirs*, Lausanne: IOC.

Defence for Children International (1993) Child-jockeys: devastating testimony, *International Children's Rights Monitor* 10, 3: 28–9, Geneva: DCI.

Deford, F. (1995) 'Trouble on the court', *Vanity Fair*, August.

De Knop, P. (1998) 'The best interest of the child in sport and the current situation in Flanders', in Zermatten, J. (ed.) *Un champion à tout prix? Les droits de l'enfant et le sport* (A champion at all costs? Child rights and sport) Sion, Switzerland: International Children's Rights Institute and Kurt Bösch Academic Institute.

De Knop, P. and De Martelaer, K. (2001) 'Quantitative and qualitative evaluation of youth sport in Flanders and the Netherlands: a case study', *Sport, Education and Society*, 6 (1): 35–51.

De Knop, P., Engström, L.-M., Skirstad, B. and Weiss, M.R. (1996) *Worldwide trends in youth sports*, Champaign, IL: Human Kinetics Publishers.

Dellatre, P. (1978) *Tales of a Dalai Lama, Celestial Sports*, Berkeley, CA: Creative Arts Books.

De Martelaer, K., De Knop, P., Theeboom, M. and Harthoorn, S. (1997) *Youth-centered simming: a matter of policy and pedagogy*, Brussels: Free University.

De Martelaer, K., De Knop, P., Theeboom, M. and Van Heddegem, L. (2000) 'The UN Convention as a basis for elaborating rights of children in sport', *Journal of Leisurability*, vol. 27, 2: 3–10.

De Mause, L. (1974) 'The evolution of childhood', in De Mause, L. (ed.) *The history of childhood*, Northvale, NJ: Jason Aronson.

DePalma, M.T., Koszewski, M., Case, J.G., Barile, R.J., De Palma, B.F. and Oliaro, S.M. (1993) 'Weight control practices of lightweight football players,' *Medicine and Research in Sports and Exercise*, 25: 694–701.

DePalma, M.T., Koszewski, M., Case, J.G., Romani, W., Zuiderhof, N.J. and McCoy, P. (2002) 'Identifying college athletes at risk for pathogenic eating', *British Journal of Sports Medicine*, 36: 45–50.

De Smet, L. (1993) 'In Belgian sport, more and more cases go to court', *International Children's Rights Monitor*, 10: 4.

Despont, C. (2004) 'Marat Safin, chef-d'oeuvre en péril' (Marat Safin, a jewel in danger), *Le Temps*, 22 January.

De Telegraaf (2002) 'IOC op kruispunt' (IOC at the crossroads), 5 February.

De Telegraaf (2001) 'Onderzoek justitie naar mensenhandel voetballers' (Ministry of Justice inquires about football slavery), 12 January.

De Telegraaf (2001a) 'Van de Leur verrast zichzelf' (Van de Leur surprises herself), 28 March.

De Telegraaf (1999) 'Illegale opleiding in betaald voetbal' (Illegal players in professional football), 16 November.

Detrick, S. (1999) *A Commentary on the United Nations Convention on the Rights of the Child*, The Hague: Martinus Nijhoff.

Detrick, S. (1992) *The United Nations Convention on the Rights of the Child, a Guide to the 'Travaux préparatoires'*, The Hague: Martinus Nijhoff.

De Winter, M. (1998) 'Social participation of children and young people as a fundamental element of children's rights', in Verhellen, E. (ed.) *Understanding children's rights*, Ghent: University of Ghent.

Dhaliwal, G.K., Gauzas, L., Anotonowicz, D.H. and Ross, R.R. (1996) 'Adult male survivors of childhood sexual abuse: prevalence, sexual abuse characteristics and long term effects', *Clinical Psychological Review*, vol. 16, 6: 19–39.

DiFiori, J.P. (1999) 'Overuse injuries in children and adolescents', *The Physician and Sports Medicine*, vol. 27: 1.

Dixon, M. and Fricker, P. (1990) 'Injuries to elite gymnasts over 10 years', *Medical Science Sports Exercise*, 2: 209–29.

Doherty, E.M. (1999) 'Winning isn't everything … it's the only thing: a critique of teenaged girls participation in sports', *Marquette Sports Law Journal* 10, 1: 127–60.

Dominican Republic, Government of (1985) *Presidential Regulation 3450 of 1985* (translated into English in *International Sports Law and Business*, no. 2, 1997, p. 889).

Donnelly, P. (1999) 'Who's fair game? Sport, sexual harassment and abuse', in White, P. and Young, K. (eds) *Sport and Gender in Canada*, Toronto: Oxford University Press.

Donnelly, P. (1997) 'Child labour, sport labour. Applying child labour laws to sport', *International Review for Sociology of Sport* 32, 4: 389–406.

Donnelly, P. (1993) 'Problems associated with young involvement in high-performance sport', in Cahill, B.R. and Pearl, A.J. (eds) *Intensive participation in children's sports*, American Orthopedic Society for Sports Medicine, Champaign, IL: Human Kinetics Publishers.

Donzé, F. (2001) 'J'imagine un sport plus pur, plus human' (I imagine a purer sport, more human), *Le Temps*, 21 July.

Donzé, F. (2000) 'En effeuillant les volleyeuse' (Stripping volleyball players), *Le Temps*, 5 January 2000.

Donzé, F. (2000a) 'Alex Popov: Je ne suis pas une machine' (Alex Popov: I am not a machine), *Le Temps*, 28 March.

Donzé, F. (2000b) 'Alexei Nemov, parcours d'une star mondiale de la gym qui a sacrifié sa vie à la compétition' (Alexei Nemov, the path of a world gymnastics star who sacrificed his life to competiton), *Le Temps*, 17 March.

Drape, J. (1997) 'Federation looks to parents, refuses to let sport be blamed', *Atlanta Journal and Constitution*, 5 September.

Driessen, V. (2001) 'Ajax ziet bestuursleden "satellietclub" GBA vertrekken' (Board members of Ajax's 'satellite' club leave), *De Telegraaf*, 13 February.

Droussant, C. (1998) 'Docteur Richard et ... mystère Virenque' (Dr. Richard and ... Mr. Virenque), *L'Equipe Magazine*, no. 863, 24 October.

Duda, J.L. and Gano-Overway, L. (1996) 'Anxiety in elite youth gymnastics, Part 1: definitions of stress and relaxation', *Technique*, vol. 16, no. 3, USA Gymnastics.

Duda, J.L. and Gano-Overway, L. (1996a) 'Anxiety in elite young gymnasts Part II: sources of stress', *Technique*, vol. 16, no. 6, USA Gymnastics.

Duderstadt, J.J. (2000) *Intercollegiate athletics and the American university. A university president perspective*, University of Michigan Press.

Dulabon, D.W. (2000) 'First Amendment and goal: high-school recruiting and the State actor theory', *Vanderbilt Journal of Entertainment Law and Practice*, 2.

Dupuis, P.-A. (2001) 'Reebok plonge dans le décolleté de Venus Williams pour gagner le match des marques' (Reebok dives into Venus Williams low-cut dress in order to win the brand game), *Le Temps*, 24 January.

Duquin, M.E. (1984) 'Power and authority: moral consensus and conformity in sport', *International Review for the Sociology of Sport* 19, 3–4: 295–303.

Durant, R.H., Escobedo, L.G. and Heath, G.W. (1995) 'Anabolic steroid use, strength training, and multiple drug use among adolescent in the United States', *Pediatrics*, 96: 1.

Durant, R.H., Rickert, V.I., Ashworth, C.S., Newman, C. and Slavens, G. (1993) 'Use of multiple drugs among adolescents who use anabolic steroids', *New England Journal of Medicine*, 328: 922–6.

Eagles, J.M., Johnston, M.I. and Hunter, D. (1995) 'Increasing incidence of anorexia nervosa in the female population of Northeast Scotland', *American Journal of Psychiatry*, 152: 1266–71.

Eitzen, S. (1992) 'Treatment of athletes is the problem with college sports', *The Coloradoan*, 29 November.

Elian, J. (1994) 'Mary Pierce joue le meilleur tennis' (Mary Pierce plays the best tennis), *L'Equipe*, 2 June.

Elliott, M., Browne, K. and Kilcoyne, J. (1995) 'Child sexual abuse prevention: what sex offenders tell us', *Child abuse and neglect* 19, 5: 579–94.

Emmerson, T. and Wehrfritz, G. (1996) 'China dives in', *Newsweek*, 24 June.

Engelhardt, G.N. (1995) 'Fighting behavior and winning National Hockey League games: a paradox, *Perceptual and motor skills*, 80: 416–18.

English Sports Council (1998) *Young people, sport and ethics. An examination of values and attitudes to fair play among youth sport competitors*, London: English Sports Council.

Ennew, J. and Miljeteig, P. (1996) 'Indicators for children's rights: progress report on a project', *International Journal of Children's Rights* 4: 213–37.

EPOCH Worldwide and Save the Children-Sweden (1999) *Hitting people is wrong – and children are people too.*

Ethiopia, Government of (1999) *Second periodic report on the implementation of the Convention on the Rights of the Child: Ethiopia*, CRC/C/70/Add.70, Geneva: United Nations.

Etnier, J.L., Salazar, W., Landers, D.M., Petruzello, S.J., Han, M. and Nowell, P. (1997) 'The influence of physical fitness and exercise upon cognitive functioning: a meta-analysis', *Journal of Sport and Exercise Psychology* 19, 3: 249–77.

Ettman, J.M. (1997) 'Veronia case comment: high school students lose their rights when they don their uniforms', *New York Law School Journal of Human Rights*, no. 13.

European Commission (2001) *Outcome of discussions between the Commission and FIFA/UEFA on FIFA Regulations on international football transfers*, 5 March.

European Commission (2000) *Commission investigation into FIFA's transfer rules*, statement to the European Parliament by Viviane Reding, Commissioner for Sports, Culture and Education, 7 September.

European Commission (2000a) *The Community vision of sports*, statement by Viviane Reding, Commissioner for Sports, Culture and Education and Member of the European Commission, meeting of the European Commission and Sports Federations, 17 April.

European Commission (2000b) *Protection of young sportsmen and doping problems: a European answer is required*, statement by Viviane Reding, Member of the European Commission responsible for education and culture, opening ceremony of the ninth European Sports Forum, 26 October.

European Commission (1999) *The Helsinki report on sport*, Communication from the European Commission (COM (1999) 644 and/2), Brussels: European Commission.

European Commission (1999a) *The European model of sport*, consultation document of DG X, Brussels: European Commission.

European Commission (1999b) *Doping in sports, sports economics and statistics*, Secretariat-General, Directorate C, Secretariat of the European Group on Ethics in Science and New Technologies, Brussels: European Commission.

European Court of Human Rights (1998) *A. v. The United Kingdom*, 100/1997/884/1096, Strasbourg.

European Court of Human Rights (1997) *Aydin v. Turkey*, 57/1996/676/866, Strasbourg.

European Court of Human Rights (1982) *Campbell and Cosans* v. *The United Kingdom*, Strasbourg.

European Court of Human Rights (1980) *Republic of Ireland* v. *United Kingdom*, 2 European Human Rights Reports 25, 1979–1980, Strasbourg.

European Non-Governmental Sports Organisation (1998) *Guidelines for children and youth sport*, ENGSO.

European Union (1994) *Council Directive 94/33/EC of 22 June 1994 on the protection of young people at work*, Brussels: European Union.

Fagan, P. (2001) 'How UN Conventions on women's and children's rights undermine family, religion and sovereignty', *Heritage Foundation*. Online. Available HTTP: <http://www.heritage.org/library/backgrounder/bg1407.html> (accessed 21 September 2001).

Fairburn, C.G. and Beglin, S.J. (1990) 'Studies of the epidemiology of bulimia nervosa', *American Journal of Psychiatry*, 147: 401–8.

Farrey, T. (2001) *Athletes abusing athletes*, ESPN.com, 14 April.

Fasting, K., Brackenridge, C.H. and Sundgot-Borgen, J. (1998) *Sexual harassment in and outside sport*, unpublished data.

Fédération des Médecins Suisses (2001) 'Médicine du sport et déontologie. Text pour consultation' (Sport medicine and deontology. Text for consultation), *Bulletin des médecins suisses*, 31: 1655–8.

Feiner, S. (1997) 'The personal liability of sports officials: don't take the game into your own hands, take them to court!' *Sports Lawyers Journal* 4, 1: 213–15.

Fergusson, D.M. and Mullen, P.E. (1999) 'Childhood sexual abuse: an evidence based perspective', *Developmental Clinical Psychology and Psychiatry*, vol. 40, London: Sage.

FIFA (Fédération Internationale de Football Association/International Football Federation) (2002) 'Luciano Siqueira de Oliveira (AC Chievo Verona) provisionally suspended from all official or friendly international matches', *Media Information*, Zurich: FIFA.

FIFA (2002a) *FIFA licensed players' agents and annex.*

FIFA (2002b) *FIFA licensed players' agents by country.*

FIFA (2001) *Principles for the amendment of FIFA rules regarding international transfers.*

FIFA (2001a) *FIFA regulations for the status and transfer of players.*

FIFA (1995) 'FIFA Disciplinary Committee decision of 4 December 1995', *FIFA Newsletter*, December 1995.

FINA (Fédération Internationale de Natation/International Swimming Federation) (2001) *FINA Diving Rules, 2000–2001*, Lausanne: FINA.

Finkelhor, D. (1989) 'The international epidemiology of child sexual abuse', *Child Abuse and Neglect*, 13: 89–100.

Finn, R. (1992) 'The molding of a tennis prodigy', *New York Times*, 23 April.

Finnish Sports Federation (2002) *Allowed to care – allowed to intervene. Sexual harassment in sports. A guidebook for adults*, Slu: Finnish Sports Federation.

First International Conference on Concussion in Sport (2002), summary and agreement statement, *British Journal of Sports Medicine*, 36: 6–10.

FIVB (International Volleyball Federation) (1998) *FIVB rules changes*. Online. Available HTTP: <http://www.volleyball.org/rules/98fivb> (accessed 9 July 1999).

Flamand, J.-B. (1994) 'Jeunes et déjà au dope niveau' (Young and already doped), *L'Equipe*, 30 November.

Flekkoy, M.G. (1992) 'Attitudes to children – their consequences for work for children', in Freeman, M. and Veerman, P. (eds) *The ideologies of children's rights*, The Hague: Martinus Nijhoff.

Flekkoy, M.G. and Kaufman, N.H. (1997) *The participation rights of the child: rights and responsibilities in family and society*, London: Jessica Kingsley.

Fleming, J. (1993) *Equality, education and physical education*, London: Falmer Press.

Fletcher, A. and Hussey, S. (eds) (1999) *Childhood in question. Children, parents and the State*, Manchester: Manchester University Press.

Forbes.com (2000) *Forbes celebrity 1000*. Online. Available HTTP: <http://www.forbes.com> (accessed 9 July 2000).

Fournier, J.-F. (2001) 'La Suisse doit faire son examen de conscience' (Switzerland needs to re-examine its conscience), *Le Matin*, 26 August.

France 2 Television (2000) 'Le trafic des enfants footballeurs' (Trafficking of child football players), *Envoyé Spécial*, Paris, 19 October.

France 3 Television (1998) 'Dopage, la mort aux trousses' (Doping: on death row), *La Marche du Siècle*, Paris, 18 November.

France Football (1992) 'Luigi onze ans et déjà star' (Luigi, 11 years old and already a star), 24 June.

France, Government of (2001) 'Loi No. 86-610 du 16 juillet 1984 modifiée relative à l'organisation et à la promotion des activités physiques et sportives' (Law No. 86-610 of 16 July 1984 amended, on the organization and promotion of physical activities and sports), *Journal Officiel*, 6 June, unofficial translation.

France, Government of (2001a) 'Article 4 de l'Arrêté du 15 mai 2001 fixant les modalités de la délivrance et du retrait d'agrément des centres de formation en application de l'article 15-4 de la loi no 86-610 du 16 juillet 1984 modifiée relative à l'organisation et à la promotion des activités physiques et sportives' (Article 4 of the Decree of 15 May 2001 for the implementation of article 15-4 of Law no. 86-610 of 16 July 1984 amended, on the organization and promotion of physical activities and sports), *Journal Officiel*, 6 June, unofficial translation.

France, Government of (2001b) 'Article 5 du Décret du 6 septembre 2001 pris pour l'application de l'article 15-4 de la loi no. 86-610 du 16 juillet 1984 modifiée relative à l'organisation et à la promotion des activités physiques et sportives' (Article 5 of the Decree of 6 September 2001 for the implementation of article 15-4 of Law no. 86-610 of 16 July 1984 amended, on the organization and promotion of physical activities and sports), *Journal Officiel*, 13 September, unofficial translation.

France, Government of (2001c) 'Décret no. 2001 du 4 septembre 2001 pris pour l'application de l'article 19-3 de la loi no. 86-610 du 16 juillet 1984 modifiée relative à l'organisation et à la promotion des activités physiques et sportives' (Decree no. 2001 of 4 September 2001 for the implementation of article 19-3 of Law no. 86-610 of 16 July 1984 amended, on the organization and promotion of physical activities and sports), *Journal Officiel*, 12 September 2001, unofficial translation.

France, Government of (1999) 'Loi No. 99-223 du 23 mars 1999 relative à la protection de la santé des sportifs et à la lutte contre le dopage' (Law No. 99-223 of 23 March 1999 on the protection of athletes' health against doping), *Journal Officiel*, no. 70, 24 March, unofficial translation.

France, Government of (1999a) *Le recruitement, l'accueil et le suivi des jeunes étrangers (hors Union Européenne) dans les centres de formation des clubs de football professionnels en France* (The recruitment, reception and follow-up of young foreigners (ex-European Union) in the training centres run by professional football clubs in France), Paris: Ministère de la Jeunesse et des Sports, unofficial translation.

France, Government of (1999b) 'Loi No. 99–1124 du 28 décembre 1999 1990 portant diverses mesures relatives à l'organisation d'activités physique et sportives' (Law No. 99–1124 of 28 December 1999 covering measures for the organization of physical and sporting activities), *Journal Officiel*, 29 December, unofficial translation.

France, Government of (1998) 'Loi No. 98-468 du 17 juin 1998' (Law No. 98-468 of 17 June 1998), *Journal Officiel*, no. 139, 18 June, unofficial translation.

Frank, S. (1994) 'The key to unlocking the clubhouse door: the application of anti-discrimination laws to quasi-private clubs', *Michigan Journal of Gender and Law*, 27: 41.

Franke, W.W. and Berendonk, B. (1997) 'Hormonal doping and androgenization of athletes: a secret program of the German Democratic Republic Government', *Clinical Chemistry*, 43: 1262–79.

Franklin, B. (1998) 'Children's political rights', in Verhellen, E. (ed.) *Understanding children's rights*, Ghent: University of Ghent.

Freeman, M. (1992) 'Introduction: rights, ideology and children', in Freeman, M. and Veerman, P. (eds) *The ideologies of children's rights*, The Hague: Martinus Nijhoff.

Freeman, M. (1992a) 'The limits of children's rights', in Freeman, M. and Veerman, P. (eds) *The ideologies of children's rights*, The Hague: Martinus Nijhoff.

Fritscher, F. (2000) 'Enquête ministérielle sur les centres de formation de l'OGC Nice et de l'AS Cannes' (Ministerial inquiry on the training centres of the OGC Nice and AS Cannes), *Le Monde*, 15 February.

Frost, J., Wortham, S. and Reifel, S. (2001) *Play and child development*, New Jersey: Merrill/Prentice-Hall.

Furedi, F. (2000) 'The conceptualisation of risk in Anglo-Saxon countries', in *Youth sporting practices and risk behaviours*, seminar proceedings, Interministerial mission to combat drugs and drug addiction, 5–6 December, Paris: Ministry for Youth and Sports.

Gardaz, S. (2001) 'La jurisprudence' (Jurisprudence), *Le Temps*, 20 January.

Gardiner, S. (2000) 'Tackling from behind: interventions on the playing field', in Greenfield, S. and Osborn, G. (eds) *Law and sport in contemporary society*, London: Frank Cass.

Gardner, R. (1989) 'On performance-enhancing substances and the unfair advantage argument', *Journal of the Philosophy of Sport*, 16: 59–73.

Gatellier, J.-L. (2001) '"De mon plein gré", ou les confessions d'un as du vélo qui s'est retrouvé "junkie"' ('My own free will', confessions of a cycling star who ended up a 'junkie'), *Le Temps*, 21 February.

Gatellier, J.-L. (2000) 'Des coureurs dopés à leur insu? Ca n'existe pas, ce ne sont pas des gamins' (Cyclists drugged against their will? This does not exist; they are not kids), *Le Temps*, 22 December.

Gaudiano, N. (2001) '14 girls kicked off hockey team for hazing', *The Record*, New Jersey News, 6 September.

Gelles, R.J. and Cornell, P.C. (1983) 'International perspective on child abuse', *Child Abuse and Neglect*, vol. 7, 4: 375–86.

Gerbis, M. and Dunn, N. (2004) 'The emotional abuse of elite child athletes by their coaches', *Child Abuse Review*, 3:215–233.

Gerdy, J.R. (2000) *Sports in school, the future of an institution*, New York: Columbia University Teachers College Press.

Gerrard, D.F., Waller, A.E. and Bird, Y.N. (1994) 'The New Zealand rugby injury and performance project. II. Previous injury experience of a rugby-playing cohort', *British Journal of Sports Medicine*, 28: 229–33.

Glo, P. (2001) 'Carlos Kameni. Lion en cage' (Carlos Kameni. A lion in a cage), *L'Equipe Magazine*, no. 987, 7 April.

Glo, P. (2001a) 'Le Mondial du môme' (Kids World Cup), *L'Equipe Magazine*, no. 989, 21 April.

Glo, P. (2000) 'Comment Monaco ramène ses filets' (How Monaco fills its fishing nets), *L'Equipe Magazine*, no. 927, 5 February.

Glo, P. (2000a) 'Un peu de Brésil dans nos clubs' (A little bit of Brazil in our clubs), *L'Equipe Magazine*, no. 928, 12 February.

Goldberg, L., Elliot, D.L., Moe, E.L., MacKinnon, D.P., Clarke, G. and Cheong, J. (2000) 'The adolescents training and learning to avoid steroids program, preventing drug use and promoting health behaviours', *Archives of Pediatric and Adolescent Medicine*, 154: 332–8.

Goldberg, L., Elliot, D.L., Moe, E.L., MacKinnon, D.P., Clarke, N., Zaref, L., Green, C. and Wolf, S.L. (1996) 'The adolescents training and learning to avoid steroids (ATLAS) prevention program, background and results of a model intervention', *Archives of Pediatric and Adolescent Medicine*, 150: 713–21.

Gould, D. (1993) 'Intensive sport participation and the prepubescent athlete: competitive stress and burnout', in Cahill, B.R. and Pearl, A.J. (eds) *Intensive participation in children's sports*, American Orthopedic Society for Sports Medicine, Champaign, IL: Human Kinetics Publishers.

Grayson, E. (2000) 'The historical development of sport and law', in Greenfield, S. and Osborn, G., *Law and sport in contemporary society*, London: Frank Cass.

Green, T. (1996) *The dark side of the game, my life in the NFL*, New York: Warner Books.

Grondin, S. and Musch, J. (2000) *Unequal competition as an impediment to personal development, A review of the relative age effect in sport*, Universities of Bonn and Laval.

Grossekathöfer, M. and Pfeil, G. (2003) 'Skispringen: "Permanenter Terror"' (Ski jumping: permanent terror), *Der Spiegel, no. 51*, 15 December.

Guzman, E. (1998) 'Danger is among routines of gymnastics', *New York Times*, 23 July.

Haas-Wiss, U. and Holla, M. (2003) *Staatliche Rechtsgrundlagen. Das Dopingopferhilfsgesetz* (Domestic legal provisions. The law on assistance to victims of doping), Nationale Antidoping Agentur (National Anti-Doping Agency). Online. Available HTTP: <http://www.nada-bonn.de/deutsch/d_info/r_grund/staat_r/staat_r.htm> (accessed 20 January 2004).

Hack, D. (2004) 'Judge orders NFL to permit young athletes to enter draft', *New York Times*, 6 February.

Hainly, D.F. (1983) 'Drug and sex testing, regulations for international competition', *Clinical Sports Medicine*, 2: 13–17.

Halm, H. and Guterman, N. (2001) 'The emerging problem of physical child abuse in South Korea', *Child Maltreatment*, 6: 169–79.

Halperin, D.S., Bouvier, P. and Jaffe, P.D. (1996) 'Prevalence of child sexual abuse among adolescents in Geneva: results of a cross-sectional survey', *British Medical Journal*, 312: 1326–9.

Hammarberg, T. and Newell, P. (2000) 'The right not to be hit', *Children's rights, turning principles into practice*, Stockholm: Save the Children-Sweden, UNICEF.

Harris, D.J. (1991) *Cases and materials on international law*, London: Sweet and Maxwell.

Hart, J. (2000) 'L. Hamilton, premier des tous prochains' (L. Hamilton, first to come), *L'Equipe Magazine*, no. 938, 22 April.

Hart, R. (1998) 'Children's right to participate: some tools to stimulate discussion on the issue of different cultures', in Verhellen, E. (ed.) *Understanding children's rights*, Ghent: University of Ghent.

Hart, R. and Petren, A. (2000) 'The right to play', *Children's rights, turning principles into practice*, Stockholm: Save the Children-Sweden, UNICEF.

Hayes, D.W. (1993) 'Sport images and realities', *Black issues in higher education*, 10:15–19.

Heller, S.J. (1999) 'Legislative updates: the price of celebrity; when a child star-studded career amounts to nothing', *Journal of Arts and Entertainment Law*, 10: 161–75.

Hellestedt, J.C. (1987) 'The coach/parent/athlete relationship', *The Sport Psychologist*, 151–60.

Henley, J. (1998) 'Scandal of Belgium's football slave trade', *Daily Mail & Guardian*, 4 December. Online. Available HTTP: <http://www.mg.co.za/mg/news/98dec1/4dec-football.html> (accessed 27 April 2001).

Henry J. Kaiser Family Foundation (2000) 1999 unpublished data, in CASA (National Commission on Sports and Substance Abuse), *Winning at any cost: doping in Olympic sports*, New York: Columbia University.

Hermann, M. (1998) 'Steroids, a vague threat', *Newsday*, 30 October.

Heyns, C. and Viljoen, F. (2002) *The Impact of the United Nations Human Rights Treaties on the Domestic Level*, The Hague: Kluwer.

Hilborn, H.B. (1995) 'Student-athletes and judicial inconsistency: establishing a duty to educate as a means of fostering meaningful reform of intercollegiate athletics', *Northwestern University Law Review*, 89.

Hirzel, F. (1996) 'Elodie Lussac, le rêve brisé' (Elodie Lussac: broken dreams), *Le Matin*, 10 March.

Hoberman, J. (1992) *Mortal engines: the science of performance and the dehumanisation of sport*, New York: The Free Press.

Hodgkin, R. and Newell, P. (2002) *Implementation handbook for the Convention on the Rights of the Child*, 2nd edition, New York: UNICEF.

Hodgkin, R. and Holmberg, B. (2000) 'The evolving capacities of the child', *Children's rights, turning principles into practice*, Stockholm: Save the Children-Sweden, UNICEF.

Holander, D.B., Meyers, M.C. and LeUnes, A. (1995) 'Psychological factors associated with overtraining: implications for youth sport coaches', *Journal of Sport Behavior*, vol. 18, 1: 3–20.

Homsi, G. (1999) 'Monique Viele, l'ado des courts a les dents longues' (Monique Viele, tennis's ambitious adolescent), *L'Equipe Magazine*, no. 884, 3 April.

Hoover, N.C. (1999) *National Survey: initiation rites and athletic for NCCA sports teams*, New York: Alfred University.

Hoover, N.C. and Pollard, N. (2000) *Initiation Rites in American High Schools: A National Survey*, New York: Alfred University.

Houlihan, B. (1999) *Dying to win, doping in sport and the development of anti-doping policy*, Strasbourg: Council of Europe.

Houston Chronicle (1998) 'Gymnast, 17, sues to become a legal adult', 1 December.

Howard, J. and Munson, L. (1998) 'Betrayal of Trust', in Littlefield, B. (ed.) *The Best American Sports Writing 1998*. Boston: Houghton Mifflin Co.

Huertas, F. (2001) 'La filière sud-américaine : l'Amsud en a pour tous les goûts (The Latin American network: South America has something for everyone), *L'Equipe*, 20 December.

Hughes, F. (1999) *Children, play and development*, 3rd edition, Boston: Allyn & Bacon.

Huizinga, J. (1950) *Homo Ludens: a study of the play element in culture*, Boston: Beacon Press.

Hunt, V. (2000) 'Are high-school athletes caught up in creatine?', *National Athletic Trainers Association* (NATA).

Hussain, Z. (1999) 'Pakistan: a five-year-old sold as camel jockey', *Reuters*, 6 July.

IFOP Opinion Poll (1999) 'Le sport? Une grande partie de plaisir' (Sport? Play for fun), *L'Equipe Magazine*, no. 906, 4 September.

Imhof, M. (1999) 'La pédophilie dans le sport est enfin mise à l'enquête' (Finally an inquiry into paedophilia in sports) *Tribune de Genève*, 3 September.

Inizan, F. (2001) 'Kwan: rien ne la glace' (Kwan: nothing freezes her), *L'Equipe Magazine*, no. 984, 17 March.

Inizan, F. (2000) 'Usine à gymnastes' (Gymnasts' factory), *L'Equipe Magazine*, No. 954, 12 August.

Inizan, F. (2000a) 'Marion Jones: Sydney, je ne pense qu'à ça' (Marion Jones: I only think of Sydney), *L'Equipe Magazine*, no. 950, 15 July.

Inizan, F. (1999) 'Ce qu'il reste du sport de l'ex-RDA' (What's left of sports in the former GDR), *L'Equipe Magazine*, no. 915, 6 November.

Inizan, F. (1995) 'Délivrez-les du père!' (Deliver them from the father!), *L'Equipe Magazine*, no. 711, 28 October 1995.

International Council on Human Rights Policy (2002) *Beyond voluntarism. Human rights and the developing international legal obligations of companies*, Versoix, Switzerland: International Council on Human Rights Policy.

International Federation of Journalists (1999) *International Federation of Journalists' Guidelines and Principles for reporting on issues involving children* (revised 2002), Brussels: IFJ.

International Labour Organization (2002) *90th session of the Conference (2002)*, Governing Body, Geneva: ILO.

International Labour Organization (2002a) *Red card to child labour*, ILO, AFF and Organizing Committee of the African Cup of Nations.

International Labour Organization (1992) *World Labour Report 1992*, ILO: Geneva.

International Olympic Committee (IOC) (2002) *Olympic Charter*, Lausanne: IOC.

International Olympic Committee (2002a) *IOC Code of Ethics*, Lausanne: IOC.

International Olympic Committee (2002b) The Ethics Commission. Online. Available HTTP: <http://www.olympic.org> (accessed 22 August 2002).

International Olympic Committee (2001) 'Quotations by Juan Antonio Samaranch', *Olympic Review*, XXVII-39, June–July 2001, Lausanne: IOC.

International Organization for Migration (2001) *Trafficking in unaccompanied minors for sexual exploitation in the European Union*, Geneva: IOM.

International Organization for Standardization (2001) *ISO standard to help fight drug abuse*, press release, 3 December, Geneva: ISO.

Irish Sports Council and the Sports Council for Northern Ireland (2001) *Code of Ethics and Good Practice for Children's Sport in Ireland.*

Issert, P. (2000) 'Fu Mingxia, plongeons en or et années de plomb' (Fu Mingxia, golden diver and dark times), *L'Equipe Magazine*, no. 928, 12 February.

James, M. and Ziemer, T. (2000) 'Bad sports. With cues from adults, are kid athletes getting more aggressive?', *ABC News*, 8 August.

Jan-Hess, I. (2002) 'Leurs trois enfants sont exclus du club de hockey sur glace' (Their children are excluded from ice-hockey club), *Tribune de Genève*, 18 December.

Janofsky, M. (2000) 'USOC suppressed doping results, lawsuit charges', *New York Times*, 18 July.

JoongAng (1998) *Scout corruption in soccer*, 16 November. Online. Available HTTP: <http://english.joongang.co.kr> (accessed 20 November 1998).

Joravsky, B. (1995) *Hoop dreams, a true story of hardship and triumph*, New York: Harper Perennial.

Jordan, B., Ravdin, L. and Relkin, N. (1997), 'Apolopoprotein E epsilon 4 associated with traumatic brain injury in boxing', *Journal of the American Medical Association*, no. 278: 136–40.

Jouhaud, F. (1998) 'L'ex-Yougoslavie s'exporte bien' (Former Yugoslavs export well), *L'Equipe*, 19 December.

Journal du Droit des Jeunes (1994) 'Civ. Verviers (4e ch.)', no. 138, Liège, 4 January.

Kelly, L. and Mullender, A. (2000) 'Complexities and contradictions: living with domestic violence and the UN Convention on the Rights of the Child', *International Journal of Children's Rights*, 8: 229–41.

Kempe, C.H., Silverman, F.N., Steele, B.F., Drögemuller, W. and Silver, H.K. (1962) 'The battered child syndrome', *Journal of the American Medical Association*, 181: 17–24.

Kennedy, M.C. (1992) 'Anabolic steroid use and toxicology', *Australian and New Zealand Journal of Medicine*, 22.

Kentucky Gazette (1997) 17 June.

Kenya, Government of (2001) *Initial report on the implementation of the Convention on the Rights of the Child: Kenya*, CRC/C/3/Add.62, Geneva: United Nations.

Kerr, A. (1999) *Protecting disabled children and adults in sport and recreation: the guide*, Leeds, U.K.: National Coaching Foundation.

Kerrane, K. (1989) *Dollar sign on the muscle: the world of baseball scouting*, Tyler, Texas: Fireside Books.

Khan, K.M., Liu-Ambrose, T., Saran, M., Ashe, M.C., Donaldson, M.G. and Wark, J.D. (2002) 'New criteria for female triad syndrome?', *British Journal of Sports Medicine*, 36: 10–13.

Kidd, B. (2003) *Athletes' human rights*, University lectures on the Olympics, Barcelona: International Chair on Olympism.

Kidd, B. (1988) 'Philosophy of sport and physical activity: issues and concepts', in Glasso, P.J. (ed.) *The philosophy of excellence: Olympic performances, class power and the*

Canadian state, Toronto: Canadian Scholars' Press.

Kidd, B. and Donnelly, P. (2000) 'Human rights in sports', *International Review for the Sociology of Sports*, 35(2): 131–48.

Kindlundh, A., Isacso, D., Berglund, L. and Nyberg, F. (1998) 'Adolescent and use of doping agents: anabolic-androgenic steroids', *Scandinavian Journal of Social Medicine* 26, 1: 71–4.

Kirby, S.L. and Greaves, L. (1996) *Foul play: sexual abuse and harassment in sport*, Paper presented to the Pre-Olympic Scientific Congress, Dallas, 11–14 July.

Kirby, S.L. and Wintrup, G. (2002) 'Running the gauntlet: an examination of initiation/hazing and sexual abuse in sport', in Brackenridge, C. and Fasting, K. (eds) *Sexual harassment and abuse in sport. International research and policy perspectives*, London: Whiting & Birch.

Kirke, G. (1997) *Players first*, Canadian Hockey League.

Klein, A.M. (1991) *Sugarball: the American game, the Dominican dream*, New Haven: Yale University Press.

Klein, M. and Palzkill, B. (1998) *Gewalt gegen Mädchen und Frauen im sport* (Violence against girls and women in sport), Studie, Dokumente und Berichte 46 (Studies, Documents and Reports 46), Dusseldorf: Ministry for Women, Young People and Family, Nordrhein-Westfalen.

Klein, N. (2000) *No logo*, London: Flamingo.

Kleinhenz, L. (2000) 'My Dad's cool, but my Mom's a psycho', *The Independent on Sunday*, 25 June.

Kohler, I (2000) *Quand on fait du sport, les contacts physiques sont courants …* (When you practise sports, physical contact is frequent …), Berne: Association suisse pour la protection de l'enfant.

Kolt, G.S. and Kirby, R.J. (1995) 'Epidemiology of injury in Australian female gymnastics', *Sports Medicine and Training Rehabilitation*, 6: 223–31.

Koshland Jr., D. (1999) 'Ethics and safety', in Stock, G. and Campbell, J. (eds) *Engineering the human germline, An exploration of the science and ethics of altering the genes we pass to our children*, Oxford: Oxford University Press.

Kujala, M.O., Taimela, S., Antti-Piika, I., Orava, S., Tuominen, R. and Myllynen, P. (1995) 'Acute injuries in soccer, ice-hockey, volleyball, basketball, judo, and karate: analysis of national registry', *British Medical Journal*, 311: 1465–8.

Lansam, C., Fu, F.H., Robins, P.D. and Evans, C.H. (1997) 'Gene therapy in sports medicine', *Sports Medicine*, 25: 73–7.

Lansdown, G. (2000) 'The reporting process under the Convention on the rights of the child', in Alston, P. and Crawford, J. (eds) *The future of human rights treaty monitoring*, Cambridge: Cambridge University Press.

La Lettre du Sport (1999) 'Affaire Lussac: condamnation de la FFG', 21 July. Online. Available HTTP: <http://www.sport.fr/gym/576-21-799> (accessed 9 November 2001).

La Presse (1993) 'Nos adolescents rafolent des stéroïdes' (Our youngsters love steroids), 2 June.

Leahy, T., Pretty, G. and Tenebaum, G. (2002) 'Prevalence of sexual abuse in organised competitive sport in Australia', in Brackenridge, C. and Fasting, K. (eds) *Sexual harassment and abuse in sport. International research and policy perspectives*, London: Whiting & Birch.

Leaman, O. (1988) 'Cheating and fair-play in sport', in Morgan, W.J. and Meier, K.V. (eds) *Philosophic inquiry in sport*, Champaign, IL: Human Kinetics Publishers.

Leclerc, C. and Herrera, C.D. (1999) 'Sport medicine and the ethics of boxing', *British Journal of Sports Medicine*, 33: 426–9.

Le Coeur, P. (2001) 'Des sportifs français vont tester des systèmes hypoxiques' (French athletes will test hypoxic systems), *Le Monde*, 27 November.

Le Coeur, P. and Potet, F. (2001) 'Les centres de formation de Lens et d'Auxerre inquiètent le Ministère de la Jeunesse' (Auxerre's and Lens' training centres worry the Youth Ministry), *Le Monde*, 29 October.

Le Courrier (2001) 'Une campagne d'affichage tendancieuse' (A tendentious poster campaign), 9 March.

— (2001a) 'Un Américain de 16 ans contrôlé positif' (A 16-year-old American tests positive), 1 May.

— (1999) 'Une "académie" formera les Michael Owen du XXIe siècle' (An 'academy' will form 21st century Michael Owens), 28 January.

Leglise, M. (1997) *The protection of young people involved in high-level sport, Limits on young gymnastics' involvement in high level sport*, Strasbourg: Committee for the Development of Sports, Council of Europe.

L'Equipe (2002) 'Robson avertit Robert' (Robson warns Robert), 28 September.

L'Equipe (2001) 17 March.

L'Equipe (2001a) 23 March.

L'Equipe (2001b) 2 June.

L'Equipe (2000) 27 April.

L'Equipe (1999) 26 June.

L'Equipe (1985) 23 January.

L'Equipe Magazine (2001) no. 975, 13 January.

L'Equipe Magazine (2001a) no. 984, 17 March.

L'Equipe Magazine (2001b) no. 1004, 4 August.

L'Equipe Magazine (2000) no. 935, 1 April.

L'Equipe Magazine (2000a) no. 960, 23 September.

L'Equipe Magazine (2000b) no. 958, 9 September.

L'Equipe Magazine (2000c) no. 960, 23 September.

L'Equipe Magazine (1999) no. 892, 29 May.

L'Equipe Magazine (1996) no. 750, 3 August.

L'Equipe Magazine (1994) no. 624, 5 February.

L'Equipe Magazine (1993) no. 582, 23 April.

L'Equipe Magazine (1993a) no. 601, 7 August.

L'Equipe Magazine (1993b) no. 610, 2 October.

L'Equipe Magazine (1992) no. 551, 1 August.

L'Equipe Magazine (1992a) no. 547, 4 July.

Leroux, P. (1999) 'Michel Platini: Je ne connais pas la nostalgie' (Michel Platini: I'm not nostalgic), *L'Equipe Magazine*, no. 872, 9 January.

Le Soir (2000) 'L'Europe manque de législation uniforme en matière d'exploitation des jeunes joueurs non européens mais cela pourrait changer' (Europe lacks uniform legislation for young players, but this could change), 14 December.

Le Temps (2002) 'Justice sportive. Première vaudoise' (Justice and sport: a first in Vaud), 25 September.

L'Hermitte, S. (2000) 'Au fin fond du fond' (Deep inside long-distance running), *L'Equipe Magazine*, no. 956, 26 August.

Limber, S.P. and Melton, G.B. (1992) 'What children's rights mean to children: children's own views', in Freeman, M. and Veerman, P. (eds) *The ideologies of children's rights*, The Hague: Martinus Nijhoff.

Lindholt, L. and Sano, H.O. (2000) *Human rights indicators, a methodological and technical outline*, Copenhagen: Danish Centre for Human Rights.

Lions, B. (2001) 'Saviola, "El Pibe" du Barça' (Saviola, 'El Pibe' of Barcelona), *L'Equipe*, 8 December.

Litsky, F. (1999) 'At age 23, Capriati continues comeback', *New York Times*, 18 July.

Litsky, F. (1998) 'She's only 16, but Sorgi is a rising young talent in the diving world', *New York Times*, 26 July.

Liverpool FC (2000) *Liverpool FC has Europe's biggest soccer academy*. Online. Available HTTP: <http://www.liverpool.fc.net/general/club_details/academy> (accessed 1 May 2000).

Loe, S. (1998) 'Legal and epidemiological aspects of child maltreatment', *Journal of Legal Medicine*, no. 471.

Loesel, F. and Bliessener, T. (1990) 'Resilience in adolescence: a study on the generalizability of protective factors', in Hurrelamann, K. and Loesel, F. (eds) *Health hazards in adolescence*, New York: Walter de Gruyter.

Loland, S. (1998) 'Fair-play: historical anachronism or topical idea', in MacNamee, M. and Parry, S.J. (eds) *Ethics and sports*, London: Routledge.

Longman, J. (2001) 'Pro Leagues' ratings drop; nobody is quite sure why', *New York Times*, 29 July.

Longman, J. (2001a) 'Despite his critics, Carter was correct', *New York Times*, 21 May.

Longman, J. (1998) 'Widening drug use compromises faith in sport', *New York Times*, 26 December.

Loomis, J. (2001) 'The merging law of referee malpractice', *Seton Hall Journal of Sport Law* 11, 1: 73–102.

Los Angeles Times (1995), 19 October.

Losson, C. (1994) 'L'élève terrible de l'école russe' (The terrible apprentice of the Russian school), *Libération*, 8 October.

Lueschen, G. (1993) 'Doping in sport: the social structure of a deviant subculture', *Sport Science Review* 2, 1: 92–106.

Lurie J. (1998) 'Child protection and children's rights: impact on the Norwegian Child Protection Act of 1992', in Jaffé, P.D. (ed.) *Challenging mentalities, implementing the UN Convention on the Rights of the Child*, Ghent: University of Ghent.

MacGregor, M. (1998) 'Harassment and abuse in sport and recreation', *Cahperd Newsletter*, vol. 64, 2: 4–13, Canadian Association for Health, Physical Education, Recreation and Dance.

Mack, D.B. (1995) 'Reynolds v. International Amateur Athletic Federation: the need for an independent tribunal in international athletic disputes', *Connecticut Journal of International Law*.

MacMillan, H., Fleming. J, Trocme, N., Boyle, M., Wrong, M., Racine, Y., Beardslee, W. and Offord, D. (1997) 'Prevalence of child physical and sexual abuse in the community: results from the Ontario Health supplement', *Journal of the American Medical Association*, 278(2), 131–5.

Maffuli, N. (1998) 'At what age should a child begin regular continuous exercise at moderate or high intensity?' *British Journal of Sports Medicine*, 32: 298.

Major League Baseball (2001) *Major League Baseball Scouting Bureau Questions and Answers*. Online. Available HTTP: <http://www.mlb.com> (accessed 5 April 2001).

Malby, S. (2002) 'Human dignity and human reproductive cloning', *Health and Human Rights*, 6, 1: 3–35.

Malina, R.M. (1997) *Talent identification and selection in sport, Spotlight on youth sport*, International Institute for the Study of Sport newsletter, Spring 1997, University of Michigan.

Malina, R.M. (1994) 'Physical growth and biological maturation of young athletes', *Exercise Sport Science Review*, 22: 389–434.

Mandelbaum, B.R. (1993) 'Intensive training in the young athlete: pathoanatomic change', in Cahill, B.R. and Pearl, A.J. (eds) *Intensive participation in children's sports*, American Orthopedic Society for Sports Medicine, Champaign, IL: Human Kinetics Publishers.

Mangan, J.A. (2000) 'Series editor foreword', in Greenfield, S. and Osborn, G. (eds) *Law and sport in contemporary society*, London: Frank Cass.

Mansour, F. (2000) 'Un tribunal genevois rappelle que l'école passe avant le sport' (A Genevan court repeats that school comes before sports), *Le Temps*, 22 January.

Marcano, A.J.G. and Fidler, D.P. (2003) *Stealing lives*, Bloomington: Indiana University Press.

Marcano, A.J.G. and Fidler, D.P. (1999) 'The globalization of baseball: Major League Baseball and the mistreatment of Latin American baseball talent', *Indiana Journal of Global Legal Studies*, 6: 511–57.

Marchand, T. (2000) 'Dugarry, les raisons du coeur' (Dugarry, heart talks), *L'Equipe*, 15 January.

Martens, R. (2001) *Directing youth sports programs*, American Sport Education Program, Champaign, IL: Human Kinetics Publishers.

Martens, R. (ed.) (1978) *Joy and sadness in children's sports*, Champaign, IL: Human Kinetics Publishers.

Martinek, V., Fu, F.H. and Huard, J. (2000) 'Gene therapy and tissue engineering in sports medicine', *The physician and sports medicine*, 28: 2.

Maryland School of Public Affairs (1999) *One pill makes you smarter: an ethical appraisal of the rise of Ritalin*. Online. Available HTTP: <http://www.puaf.umd.edu/ippp> (accessed 8 March 2000).

McCrory, P. (2001) 'No pain, no gain. The dilemma of a team physician', *British Journal of Sports Medicine*, 35: 141–2.

McGuire, B. and Collins, D. (1998) 'Sport, ethnicity and racism: the experience of Asian heritage boys', *Sport, Education and Society* 3, 1: 79–88.

McNamee, M. (1998) 'Celebrating trust: virtues and rules in the ethical conduct of sport coaches,' in MacNamee, M. and Parry, S.J. (eds) *Ethics and sports*, London: Routledge.

McPherson, B.D. and Brown, B. (1988) 'The structure, processes, and consequences of sport for children', in Ash, M.J., Magill R.A., Smoll, F.L. (eds) *Children in sport*, Champaign, IL: Human Kinetics Publishers.

Meier, P. (1997) 'Minorité civile et activités sportives' (Minority and sporting activities), *Droit et Sport*, Bern: Stämpfli.

Meldrum, R. and Feinberg, J.R. (2002) 'Drug use by college athletes: is random testing an effective deterrent?', *The Sport Journal* 5, 1: 1–5.

Mercier, P. and Miquel, P. (2001) 'Trois questions à ... Frank Shorter' (Three questions to Frank Shorter), *Le Monde*, 25 April.

Mercy, M. (2001) 'Kwaliteitsmeting is geen inquisitie' (Measuring quality is not an inquisition), *De Standaard*, 9 December.

Messner, M. (1992) *Power at play: sports and the problem of masculinity*, Boston: Beacon Press.

Metzl, J.D. (2002) *The Young Athlete*, Boston: Little Brown.

Miah, A. (2004) *Genetically modified athletes: The ethical implications of genetic technologies in sport*, London: Routledge.

Miah, A. (2001) 'Genetic technologies and sport: the new ethical issue', *Journal of the Philosophy of Sport*, 28: 32–52.

Miah, A. (2000) 'The engineered athlete: human rights in the genetic revolution', *Culture. Sport. Society* 3, 3: 25–40.

Micheli, L.J., Glassman, R. and Klein, M. (2000) 'The prevention of sport injuries in children', *Pediatric and Adolescent Sports Injuries*, 19: 4.

Milani, A. (1998) *Can I play? The dilemma of the disabled athlete in interscholastic sports*, Alabama Law Review, no. 49: 817–60.

Milling, H.B. (1998) 'På graensen meelen beroring og befamling' (The limit between sexual touching and molesting), *Idraetsliv*, Copenhagen.

Minnesota Amateur Sport Commission (1993), *What is child maltreatment in youth sports?* Blaine, MN.

Monnard, B. (1992) 'Les bébés champions sont-ils des petits monstres?' (Are baby champions monsters?), *L'Hebdo*, no. 32, 6 August.

Monnat, A. (2001) 'La médecine du sport dans le code déontologique de la FMH, procédure de consultation' (Sport medicine in the FMH's code of deontology, consultative process), *Bulletin des médecins suisses*, 31: 1651–4.

Montaingnac, R. (1993) 'Gymnastique: l'inacceptable' (Gymnastics: the inacceptable), *L'Equipe*, 13 July 1993.

Morss, J.R. (1996) *Growing critical*, London: Routledge.

Munthe, C. (2000) 'Selected champions: making winners in the age of genetic technology', in Tännsjö, T. and Tamburrini, C. (eds) *Values in sport*, London: Routledge.

Murphy, S. (1999) *The cheers and the tears, a healthy alternative to the dark side of youth sports today*, San Francisco: Jossey-Bass.

Nack, W. and Munson, L. (2000) 'Out of control', *Sports Illustrated*, 20 July.

Nait-Challal, M. and Glo, P. (1999) 'Centres de formation: espoirs et dangers' (Training centres: hopes and dangers), *L'Equipe Magazine*, no. 878, 20 February.

National Alliance for Youth Sports (2001) *Mandatory PAYS programmes helping curb parental youth sports violence nationwide*. Online. Available HTTP: <http://www.nays.org> (accessed 25 October 2001).

National Alliance for Youth Sports (2001a) *Boy in fatal football play was over age*. Online. Available HTTP: <http://www.nays.org> (accessed 25 October 2001).

National Alliance for Youth Sports (2000) *Code of ethics, Parents Association for Youth Sports*. Online. Available HTTP: <http://www.nays.org> (accessed 3 February 2001).

National Athletic Trainers Association Research and Education Foundation (1998), press statement, 28 July, Dallas.

National Collegiate Athletic Association (NCAA) *NCAA Constitution*. Online Available HTTP <http://www.ncaa.org/library/membership/division_i_manual/2001-02/A02.pdf> (accessed 12 December 2002).

National Collegiate Athletic Association (NCAA) (2001) *The NCAA News*, 21 May.

National Collegiate Athletic Association (NCAA) (1997) *A career in professional athletics: a guide for making the transition*, NCAA Professional Sports Liaison Committee.

National Research Council and Institute of Medicine (2000) *Sleep needs, patterns, and difficulties of adolescents*, Summary of a workshop, Board on Children, Youth and Families, Washington DC: National Academy Press.

National Youth Sport Safety Foundation (NYSSF) (2001) *Fact sheet: emotional injuries*, Boston: NYSSF.

Nativ, A., Agostini, R. and Drinkwater, A.R.B. (1997) 'The female athlete triad. The inter-relatedness of disordered eating, amenorrhoea, and osteoporosis', *Clinical Sports Medicine and Exercise*, 29: 1–4.

Nestel, D. (1994) 'Batter up! Are youth baseball leagues overlooking the safety of their players?', *Seton Journal of Sport Law*.

Newell, P. (1998) 'Children's active participation as a role of government, in Verhellen, E. (ed.) *Monitoring children's rights*, The Hague: Martinus Nijhoff.

Nielsen, B. (1989) 'Controlling sport violence: too late for carrots – bring on the big stick', *Iowa Law Review*.

Nobes, G. and Smith, M. (1997) 'Physical punishment of children in two-parent families', *Clinical Child Psychology and Psychiatry*, Sage, vol. 2, 2: 271–81.

Nobes, G., Smith, M., Bee, P. and Heveren, A. (1999) 'Physical punishment by mothers and fathers in British homes', *Journal of Interpersonal Violence*, vol. 14, 8: 887–902.

Norway, Government of (1998) *Second periodic reports on the implementation of the Convention on the Rights of the Child: Norway*, CRC/C/70/Add.2, Geneva: United Nations.

Oberli, P. (2000) 'Le sport de haut niveau est nocif' (High-level sport is harmful), *Le Temps*, 4 May.

O'Connor, I. (2001) 'The bigger the NFL gets, the more dangerous it becomes', *The Journal News*, 2 August.

O'Connor, I. (1999) 'Price of success can be high when a parent is calling all the shots', *The Journal News*, 17 July.

Office of Sport and Recreation (1999) *A sporting chance. A risk management framework for the sport and recreation industry*, Tasmania, Australia.

Oliver, B. (2000) '"Slaves" on a fortune', *The Observer*, 13 February.

Oneill, D.B. and Micheli, L.J. (1988) 'Overuse injuries in the young athlete', *Clinical Sport Medicine*, 7: 591–610.

On the record for children (2002) 'UN General Assembly Special Session on Children: Text could waken references to refugees and avoid criminalizing the sale of children', vol. 3, no. 9, 2 May.

Orchard, J. (2002) 'Medical records: who owns the records?', *British Journal of Sports Medicine*, 36: 16–18.

Osava, M. (2001) 'Brazil: alarm sounds on trafficking soccer player to EU', *IPS*, 23 February.

Owen, D. (2001) *The chosen one. Tiger Woods and the dilemma of greatness*, New York: Simon and Schuster.

Papp, G. and Pristoka, A.G. (1995) 'Sportsmanship as an ethical value', *International Review for the Sociology of Sport*, 30:3/4: 375–90.

Payot, C. (2002), 'Stephan Eberharter entre dans la légende du ski alpin sur la pointe des spatules' (Stephan Eberharter enters the ski legend on the tips of his skis), *Le Temps*, 11 March.

Peake, A. (1989) 'Under-reporting: the sexual abuse of boys', in Christopherson, J., Furniss, T., O'Mahoney, B., Peake, A., Armstrong, H. and Hollows, A., *Working with sexually abused boys: an introduction for practitioners*, London: National Children's Bureau.

Pearn, J. (1998) 'Boxing, youth and children', *Journal of Paediatric Child Health*, 34: 311–13.

Pellegrini, A.D. and Smith, P.K. (1998) 'Physical activity play: the nature and function of a neglected aspect of play', *Child Development*, 69, 3: 577–98.

Pénouel, S. (1999) 'Vincenzo X, dix ans, future star du calcio?' (Vincenzo X, 10 years old, Italian football's future star?), *Le Matin*, 30 Janaury.

Piaget, J. (2001) *The psychology of intelligence*, London: Routledge (new edition).

Piccard, L. (1995) *Introduction to the ILO Convention 138 concerning the minimum age for admission to employment*, Geneva: Defence for Children International.

Positive Coaching Alliance (PCA) (2002) *Vision statement*. Online. Available HTTP: <http://www.positivecoach.org/index> (accessed 8 January 2002).

Positive Coaching Alliance (PCA) (2002a) *The positive coach mental model*. Online. Available HTTP: <http://www.positivecoach.org/index> (accessed 8 January 2002).

Potet, F. (2001) 'Les centres de formation de Lens et Auxerre inquiètent le Ministère de la jeunesse' (Training centres in Lens and Auxerre are cause of concern for the Minister for Youth), *Le Monde*, 29 October.

Potet, F. (2000) 'La violence serait en baisse sur les terrains de football de la Seine-Saint-Denis' (Violence believed to decrease on football fields in Seine-Saint-Denis), *Le Monde*, 4 April.

Potet, F. (2000a) 'Viviane Reding réclame l'intervention des Etats pour les transferts dans le football' (Viviane Reding calls for States' interventions in football tranfers), *Le Monde*, 1 December.

Pound, R.W. (2002) *Sport – Where talent and genetic manipulation collide*, keynote address at the workshop on 'Genetic enhancement of athletic performance', Banbury, USA, 18–20 March.

Prébois, G. (2001) 'Si la Fédération française le veut, nous lui fournirons les dossiers du dopage au Giro' (If French Federation wants, we'll give them the Giro doping files), *Le Temps*, 22 June.

Price, S.L. (2001) 'Vamp counsellors. Young players are pushed to show more than their A game', *Sports Illustrated*, 4 September.

Propson, R. (1995) 'A call for statutory regulation of elite child athletes', *The Wayne Law Review*, 41: 1773.

Prosport (2001) 3 September. Online. Available HTTP: <http://members.tripodnet.nl/ AndreaRaducan/September.html> (accessed 19 September 2001).

Puffen, J. (1986) 'The use of drugs in swimming', *Clinical Sports Medicine*, 5: 77.

Putman, H. (1999) 'Cloning people', in Burley, J. (ed.) *The genetic revolution and human rights*, Oxford: Oxford University Press.

Qasem, F.S., Mustapha, A.A., Kazem, N.A. and Shah, N.M. (1998), 'Attitudes of Kuwaiti parents toward physical punishment of children', *Child Abuse and Neglect*, vol. 22, 12: 1189–1202.

Quiner, K. (1997) *Dominique Monceanu, a gymnastic sensation*, New Jersey: The Bradford Book Company.

Raducan, Andrea (interview with) (2001). Online. Available HTTP: <http://members. tripodnet.nl/AndreaRaducan/quotes.html> (accessed 19 September 2001).

Ralbovsky, M. (1974) *Lords of the locker room. The American way of coaching and its effect on youth*, New York: Peter H. Wyden Publisher.

Randall, R.W., Gray, M. and Rodrigo, J.A. (2002) 'Anabolic steroids and pre-adolescent athletes: prevalence, knowledge and attitudes', *The Sport Journal*, 5, 3: 1–10.

Reebok (2003). Online. Available HTTP: <http://markwalker.reebok.com> (accessed 3 November 2003).

Regalado, S.O. (2000) 'Latin players on the cheap: Professional baseball recruitment in Latin America and the neo-colonialist tradition', *Indiana Journal of Global Legal Studies* 8, 9: 9–20.

Research Centre for Injury Studies (1999), *Injury issues monitor*, University of Adelaide, no. 16.

Reuters (2001) *Blatter says FIFA made a mistake over transfer row*, 21 January.

Reuters (2001a) *Soccer-Asia bans 16 over-age players for two years*, 10 May.

Reuters (2000) *'Slave ownership'. Pelé attacks transfers of young players*, 4 November.

Reuters (2000a) *Slavery is widespread, reports international crime conference*, 28 November.

Reuters (1999) *Arsenal signs 15-year-old*, 8 January.

Reuters (1995) 'Ma confesses – somewhat', *International Herald Tribune*, 23 May.

Reuters (1994) *English heavyweight chases ultimate crown*, 17 August.

Riordan, J. (1980) *Soviet sport*, Oxford: Basil Blackwell.

Roberts, G. (1980) 'Children in competition: a theoretical perspective and recommendations', *Motor skills: theory and practice*, 4: 37–50.

Roberts, J.V. and Stalans, L.J. (2000) *Public opinion, crime, and criminal justice*, Boulder, CO: Westview Press.

Roberts, T.J. and Hemphill, D.A. (1988) *Banning drugs in sport: ethical inconsistencies*, submission to the Senate Standing Committee on Environment, Recreation and the Arts, Australia.

Roberts, W.O. (1999) 'Hitting in amateur ice hockey: not worth the risk', *The Physician and Sportsmedicine*, vol. 27, no. 12.

Roberts, W.O., Brust, J.D. and Leonard, B. (1999) 'Youth ice hockey tournament injuries: rates and patterns to season play', *Medicine and Science in Sports and Exercise*, vol. 31, 1: 46–51.

Robinson, L. (1998) *Crossing the line: sexual harassment and abuse in Canada's national sport*, Toronto: McClelland and Stewart.

Rodeaud, M.-A. (2000) 'Dopage: malaise à l'italienne' (Doping: Italian-style unease), *L'Equipe Magazine*, 28 October.

Rodeaud, M.-A. (1999) 'L'Italie attend encore sa loi anti-dopage' (Italy is still waiting for its anti-doping legislation), *L'Equipe Magazine*, no. 918, 27 November.

Roderick, M., Waddington, I. and Parker, G. (2000) 'Playing hurt: managing injuries in English professional football', *International Review for the Sociology of Sport*, vol. 35, 2: 165–80.

Rodriguez, J. (2001) 'Meet Anna of the US', *Miami Herald*, 22 March.

Rodrik, P. (1999) 'Agent de joueur: un metier que la FIFA contrôle peu' (Players' agent: a job over which FIFA has little control), *Tribune de Genève*, 16 February.

Roger, G. (2000) 'Virenque: 'Si j'avais su … ?' (Virenque: If only I had known …), *L'Equipe*, 28 October.

Rongé, J. L. (2002) 'Les mineurs non-accompagnés en Europe' (Unaccompanied minors in Europe), *Bulletin Suisse des Droits de l'Enfant*, vol. 8, 3: 11–15.

Rosenberg, D. (1995) 'The concept of cheating in sport', *International Journal of Physical Education* 32, 2: 4–14.

Rowe, N. and Champion, R. (2000) *Sports participation and ethnicity in England. National Survey 1999/2000*, London: Sport England.

Rowland, T.W. (1993) 'The physiological impact of intensive training on the prepubertal athlete', in Cahill, B.R. and Pearl, A.J. (eds) *Intensive participation in children's sports*, American Orthopedic Society for Sports Medicine, Champaign, IL: Human Kinetics Publishers.

Rutter, M. (1992) 'Psychological resilience and protective mechanisms', in Rolf, J. and Masten, A.S. (eds) *Risk and protective factors in the development of psychopathology*, Cambridge University Press.

Ryan, J. (1995) *Little girls in pretty boxes, The making and breaking of elite gymnasts and figure skaters*, New York: Doubleday.

Sae-Lim, S. (1999) 'Is boxing bad for children?', *The Nation*, 4 April.

Sainte-Rose, V. (2000) 'Je n'ai jamais été aussi calme' (I have never been so calm), *L'Equipe Magazine*, no. 930, 26 February.

Sainte-Rose, V. (2000a) 'Mais à quoi jouent-elles?' (What game are they playing?), *L'Equipe Magazine*, no. 956, 28 August.

Salah-el-din-Attia, M., Youssef, R.M. and Kamel, I. (1998) 'Children experiencing violence I: parental use of corporal punishment', *Child Abuse and Neglect*, vol. 22, 10: 959–85.

Sandomir, R. (2000) 'Having style pays off for Venus Williams', *New York Times*, 23 December.

Sanex WTA Pro Shop (2001) Online. Available HTTP <http://www.wtatour.com> (accessed 25 January 2001).

Santos Pais, M. (1997) 'The Convention on the Rights of the Child', in *Office of the UN High Comissioner for Human Rights, Manual on human rights reporting*, Geneva: United Nations.

Santos Pais, M. (1996) 'Monitoring children's rights: a view from within', in Verhellen, E. (ed.) *Monitoring children's rights*, The Hague: Martinus Nijhoff.

Sapsomboon, S.R. (1999) 'Pro-Thai boxing lobby want age limit revised', *The Nation*, 28 May.

Scanlan, T.K., Stein, G.L. and Ravizza, K. (1991) 'An in-depth study of form elite figure skaters: III. Sources of stress', *Journal of Sport and Exercise Psychology*, pp. 208–26.

Schmid, H. (1999) *Sport, psychisches Befinden und Drogenkonsum bei Jugendlichen* (Sport, psychological attitude and drug consumption among young people), Lausanne: Schweizerische Fachstelle für Alkohol und andere Drogenprobleme (SFA).

Schoorl, J. (2001) 'Tweede Kamer wil einde aan handle in jonge voetballers' (High Chamber wants to end trafficking of young footballers), *de Volkskrant*, 11 January.

Schoorl, J. and Wagendorp, B. (2001) 'Hier loopt de hele wereld' (Here, the entire world is running around), *de Volkskrant*, 13 February.

Seymour, A. (1998) 'Aetiology of the sexual abuse of children: an extended feminist perspective', *Women's Studies International Forum*, vol. 21, 4: 415–27.

Sherif, C.W. (1976) 'The social context of competition', in Landers, D. (ed.) *Social problems in athletics*, Chicago: University of Illinois Press.

Shook, D. (2002) 'Seasoning basketball's young hopefuls', *Business Week*, 11 June.

Shulman, J.L. and Bowen, W.G. (2001) *College sports and educational values: the game of life*, Princeton: Princeton University Press.

Shulter, S.E. (1996) 'Supreme Court review: random, suspicionless drug testing of high school athletes, Samantha Elizabeth', *Journal of Criminal Law and Criminology*, no. 8.

Shupe, A. and Stacy, W. (1983) *The family secret*, Boston: Beacon Press.

Siegel, E. (2000) 'When parental interference goes too far: the need for adequate protection of child entertainers and athletes', *Cardozo Arts & Entertainment Law Journal*, 18: 427–67.

Silent Edge (1999) *Parents' survey results*. Online. Available HTTP: <http://www.silent-edge.org/parents/parentsresults.html> (accessed 3 August 2000).

Silent Edge (1999a) *Sexual harassment survey*. Online. Available HTTP: <http://www.silent-edge.org/sesurvey> (accessed 3 August 2000).

Skolnick, A.A. (1993) 'Female athlete triad: risk for women', *Journal of the American Medical Association*, vol. 2, 270: 921–3.

Smith, A. (1996) 'The female athlete triad: causes, diagnosis and treatment', *The Physician and Sportsmedicine*, 24: 7.

Sobsey, D. (1991) 'Patterns of sexual abuse and assault', *Sexuality and Disability*, 9, 3: 243–59.

Soccer Brazil (2001) *Project Soccer Brazil*. Online. Available HTTP: <http://www.soccerbrazil.com/project.html> (accessed 20 February 2001).

Solberg, E.E., Ingjer, F., Holen, A., Sundgot-Borgen, J., Nilsson, S. and Holme, I. (2000) 'Stress reactivity to and recovery from a standardised exercise bout: a study of 31 runners practising relaxation techniques', *British Journal of Sports Medicine*, 34: 268–72.

Solerti, G. (2000), 'Sport and doping, study and pilot project conducted in the Venice area', *Youth sporting practices and risk behaviours*, seminar proceedings, Interministerial mission to combat drugs and drug addiction, 5–6 December, Paris: Ministry for Youth and Sports.

Sopel, J. (2000) 'Africa's football "slave trade"', BBC, 14 February.

Sperber, M. (2000) *Beer and circus. How big-time college sports is crippling undergraduate education*, New York: Murray Sperber, Henry Holt and Company.

Sport England (2001) *Safeguarding the welfare of children in sport, towards a standard for sport in England*, London.

Sport England (2001a) *Young people and sport in England 1999. A survey of young people and PE teachers*, London.

Sport England and National Society for the Prevention of Cruelty to Children (NSPCC) (2000) *Child Protection in Sport Task Force, action plan*, London.

Sports Illustrated (1999) 'Every parent's nightmare' no. 35, 13 September.

Sports Industries Federation (2001) *The European sports good market*, London.

Sports Industries Federation (2001a) *The economic importance of sports in the UK*, Sports Data Online. Online. Available HTTP: <http://www.sportsdata.co.uk> (accessed 7 September 2001).

Sports Industries Federation (2001b) *Japan report 2000*, Sports Data Online. Online. Available HTTP: <http://www.sportsdata.co.uk> (accessed 7 September 2001).

Steen, S.N. (1998) *Nutrition for young athletes*, Eureka, CA: Nutrition Dimensions.

Steiner, H. J. and Alston, P. (1996) *International human rights in context. Law, politics and morals. Text and materials*, Oxford: Clarendon Press.

Stilger, V.G. and Yesalis, C.E. (1999) 'Anabolic-androgenic steroid use among high school football players', *Journal of Community Health* 24, 2: 131–45.

Stocks, C. (2000) 'Africa's worrying soccer exodus', BBC, 14 January.

Suisse, N., Fournier, G. and Hayoz, C. (1990) *A la recherche d'un deuxième souffle – La transition de carrière des sportifs et des artistes* (In search of a second wind – Changing careers among athletes and artists), Lausanne.

Sundgot-Borgen, J. (1999) 'Eating disorders among male and female athletes', *British Journal of Sports Medicine*, vol. 33, 4: 434.

Sundgot-Borgen, J., Klunglan, J. and Tortsveit, M. (1999) 'Prevalence of eating disorders in female elite athletes', *Medicine and Science in Sport and Exercise*, vol. 31.

SUVA (2001) *Mieux qu'une assurance, le goût du risque se paye* (More than an adventure, you pay for the risk), press release Schweizerische Unfallversicherungsanstalt.

Swift, E.M. (1999) 'Paralysing hit. A blind-side check put a teen's future on ice', *Sports Illustrated*, no. 24, 20 December.

Swift, E.M. and Yager, D. (2001) 'Man or mouse', *The Observer*, 2 September.

Swiss Olympic Association (2002) *Guide en cas d'abus sexuels survenant dans le cadre du sport* (Guidelines on sexual abuse in sports), Berne.

Switzerland, Government of (2002) 'Evolution du nombre de prescription de Ritalin dans le Canton de Neuchâtel entre 1996 et 2000' (Evolution of the number of prescriptions of Ritalin in the Canton of Neuchâtel between 1996 and 2000), *Bulletin* 15/02: 284–9, Office fédéral de la santé publique.

Switzerland, Government of (2001) 'Répercussions économiques du rapport entre santé et activité physique: premières estimations en Suisse' (Economic repercussions of the relationship between physical activity and health: first estimations in Switzerland), *Bulletin OFSPO*, 33: 604–7, Office fédéral du sport.

Switzerland, Government of (2000) 'Loi fédérale encourageant la gymnastique et le sport' (Federal legislation to encourage gymnastics and sport), *Feuille fédérale*, 28 December.

Switzerland, Government of (1992) *Enfance maltraitée en Suisse* (Ill-treatment of children in Switzerland), Groupe de travail 'Enfance maltraitée' (ed.), Rapport final présenté au Chef du Département fédéral de l'intérieur, Berne (Final report presented to the Head of the Federal Department of the Interior, Bern).

Symposium on talent detection in sport (1997) *Medische aspecten van talent ontdekking en ontwikkeling in sport* (Sports medical aspects of talent detection and development in sports), Ghent, 11 October 1997.

Tamburrini, C. (2000) 'What's wrong with doping, Claudio', in Tännsjö, T. and Tamburrini, C. (eds) *Values in sport*, London: Routledge.

Tanner, S.M., Miller, C.A. and Alongi, C. (1995) 'Anabolic steroid use by adolescents: prevalence, motives and knowledge or risks', *Clinical Journal of Sport*, 5: 108–15.

Tauziat, N. (2000) *Les dessous du tennis féminin* (The underworld of female tennis), Paris: Plon.

Télévision Suisse Romande (2000) 'Jeunes et Jeux Olympiques, pas de dopage, pas de JO?' (Youth and the Olympic Games: no doping, no Olympics?), *Droit de Cité*, 17 September.

Terrani, Y. (2001) 'La gymnastique rythmique a mis fin à la période des poupées anorexiques' (Rhythmic gymnastics has ended the era of anorexic dolls), *Le Temps*, 18 June. (Information confirmed to the author by the International Federation of Gymnastics on 20 June 2001).

Terrani, Y. (2000) 'Zinédine Zidane, une star qui cultive son jardin secret' (Zinédine Zidane, a star cultivating his secret garden), *Le Temps*, 2 March.

Terrani, Y. (2000a) 'Un spécialise du dopage estime que "l'accident" de Ronaldo est une sanction, pas une fatalité' (A doping specialist considers Ronaldo's 'accident' is a sanction, not a fatality'), *Le Temps*, 19 April.

Terrani, Y. (2000b) 'Patrice Martin, l'inusable carrière d'un champion qui rêve de gloire olympique en ski nautique' (Patrice Martin, the never-ending career of a champion dreaming of Olympic glory in water skiing), *Le Temps*, 2 August.

Terrani, Y. (1999) 'Un réservoir permanent de 2000 champions potentiels' (A permanent reservoir of 2,000 potential champions), *Le Temps*, 9 February.

The Economist (2000) 'Just not cricket in the Caribbean', 26 August.

The Economist (2000a) 'Youth, Inc.', 23 December.

The Football Association (2001) *Shooting for the stars*. Online. Available HTTP: <http://www.the-fa.org> (accessed 7 June 2001).

The Football Association (2001a) *Centres for excellence*. Online. Available HTTP: <http://www.the-fa.org> (accessed 21 October 2001).

The Football Association (2001b) *This is the Football Association*. Online. Available HTTP: <http://www.the-fa.org> (accessed 21 October 2001).

The Football Association (2001c) *Code of Conduct*. Online. Available HTTP: <http://www.the-fa.org> (accessed 2 December 2001).

The Lancet (1988) 'Sports medicine – is there lack of control?', 2: 612.

Thiel, A. (1993) 'Subclinical eating disorders in male athletes', *Acta Psychiatrica Scandinavica*, 88: 259–65.

Thomas, C. (1998) 'L'INSEP, le quotidien du haut niveau' (INSEP, daily life at the top level), *L'Equipe Magazine*, No. 863, 24 October.

Thomas, S. (1999) 'Thoughts on the ethics of germline engineering', in Stock, G. and Campbell, J. (eds) *Engineering the human germline, An exploration of the science and ethics of altering the genes we pass to our children*, Oxford: Oxford University Press.

Thomsen, I. (2000) *Sports Illustrated*, 16 March.

Thomsen, I. and Llosa, L.-F. (2001) 'One for the ages', *Sports Illustrated*, 27 August.

TMO/Sportlab poll on doping (2001) published in *Dimanche.ch*, 24 June.

Tofler, I.R., Stryer, B.K., Micheli, L.J. and Herman, L.R., (1996) 'Physical and emotional problems of elite gymnasts', *New England Journal of Medicine*, vol. 335, no. 4.

TOYA (1995) *Training of young athletes study (TOYA), TOYA and health*, London: The Sports Council.

TOYA (1995a) *Training of young athletes study (TOYA), TOYA and retirement*, London: The Sports Council.

TOYA (1993) *Training of young athletes study (TOYA), TOYA and intensive training*, London: The Sports Council.

TOYA (1993a) *Training of young athletes study (TOYA), TOYA and fair-play*, London: The Sports Council.

TOYA (1993b) *Training of young athletes study (TOYA), TOYA and education*, London: The Sports Council.

TOYA (1992) *Training of young athletes study (TOYA), TOYA and lifestyle*, London: The Sports Council.

TOYA (1992a) *Training of young athletes study (TOYA), Identification of talent*, London: The Sports Council.

Tribune de Genève (2000) 'Homosexualité, un sujet tabou' (Homosexuality, a taboo issue), 30 September.

Tshimanga Bakadiababu, E. (2001) *Le commerce et la traite des footballeurs africains et sud-américains en Europe* (Sale and trafficking of African and Latin American footballers to Europe), Paris: L'Harmattan.

Tschopp, M., Biedert, R.M., Hasler, H. and Marti, B. (2001) 'Orthopädische Probleme bei jugendichlen Spitzfussballern. Erste Ergebnisse einer 4-Jahres-Prospektivstudie' (Orthopaedic problems in young elite footballers. First results of a four-year initial study), *Sportorthopädie – Sporttraumatologie*, 17: 67–73

Tschoumy, R. (2004) 'Footballeuses ou mannequins?' (Football players or models?), *Le Matin*, 25 January.

Tumlin, K.C. (2000) *Trafficking in children and women: a regional overview*, Institute of Asian Studies, Chulalongkorn University, paper presented at the Asian Regional High-Level Meeting on Child Labour, Jakarta, 8–10 March.

Ungerleider, S. (2001) *Faust's gold. Inside the East German doping machine*, New York: St Martin Press.

United Kingdom, Government of (2000) *Children involved in prostitution*, Circular No. 20/2000, London: Home Office.

United Kingdom, Government of (1999) *Caring for young people and the vulnerable? Guidance for preventing abuse of trust*, London: Home Office.

United Kingdom, Government of (1999a) *Memorandum submitted by the Department for Education and Employment*, House of Commons – Culture, Media and Sports, Appendix 23.

United Kingdom, Government of (1999b) *Second periodic reports on the implementation of the Convention on the Rights of the Child: United Kingdom of Great Britain and Northern Ireland*, CRC/C/83/Add.3, Geneva: UN.

United Nations (UN) (2004) *Sport as a means to promote education, health, development and peace*, resolution 58/5 adopted by the General Assembly on 3 November 2004, New York: UN.

United Nations (UN) (1993) *Standard Rules for the Equalization of Opportunities for Persons with Disabilities*, Resolution adopted by the General Assembly on 20 December 1993, Report of the Third Committee, A/48/267, New York: UN.

United Nations (1989) *Convention on the Rights of the Child*, UN General Assembly resolution 44/25 on 20 November 1989, New York: UN. (Full text available online at http://www.unhchr.ch/html/menu2/6/crc/treaties/crc.htm)

United Nations (1959) *Declaration on the Rights of the Child*, Resolution 1386 (xiv) adopted by the General Assembly on 20 November 1959.

United Nations (1948) *Universal Declaration of Human Rights*, UN General Assembly resolution 217 A (III), New York: UN. (Full text available online at http://www.unhchr.ch/udhr/index.htm).

UN Commission on Human Rights (2000) *Report of the Special Rapporteur on the sale of children, child prostitution and child pornography*, 56th session, E/CN.4/2000/73, Geneva: UN.

UN Commission on Human Rights (2000a) *Contemporary forms of slavery, updated review of the implementation of and follow-up to the conventions on slavery, forms of slavery*, E/CN.4/Sub.2/2000/3/Add.1, 56th session, Geneva: UN.

UN Commission on Human Rights(2000b) *Report on the mission of the Special Rapporteur to Belgium and the Netherlands on the issue of commercial sexual exploitation of children*, E/CN.4/2000/73/Add.1, 56th session, Geneva: UN.

UN Commission on Human Rights (1999) *Report of the Special Rapporteur on the sale of children, child prostitution and child pornography*, E/CN.4/1999/71, 55th session, Geneva: UN.

UN Commission on Human Rights (1996) *Further promotion and encouragement of human rights and fundamental freedoms, including the question of the programme and methods of work of the Commission, The Olympic Ideal*, E/CN.4/1996/L.49, 52nd session, Geneva: UN.

UN Commission on Human Rights (1993) *Report of the Special Rapporteur on sale of children, child prostitution and child pornography*, E/CN.4/1993/67, 49th session, Geneva: UN.

UN Committee on Economic, Social and Cultural Rights (2000) *The right to the highest attainable standard of health, article 12 of the International Covenant on Economic, Social and Cultural Rights*, General Comment No. 14, E/C.12/2000/4, Geneva: UN.

UN Committee on the Rights of the Child (2002) *Report of the Committee on the Rights of the Child to the General Assembly*, A/57/41, New York: UN.

UN Committee on the Rights of the Child (2002a) *Concluding observations of the Committee on the Rights of the Child: Poland*, 31st session, CRC/C/15/Add.194, Geneva: UN.

UN Committee on the Rights of the Child (2002b) *Report of the 31st session*, CRC/C/121, Geneva: UN.

UN Committee on the Rights of the Child (2001) *General Comment No. 1 (2001), Article 29(1): the aims of education*, CRC/C/GC/2001/1, Geneva: UN.

UN Committee on the Rights of the Child (2001a) *Concluding observations of the Committee on the Rights of the Child: Saudi Arabia*, 24th session, CRC/C/15/Add.148, Geneva: UN.

UN Committee on the Rights of the Child (2001b) *Recommendations of the Discussion on 'Violence against Children, within the Family and in Schools'*, 28 September 2001, 28th session, CRC/C/111, Geneva: UN.

UN Committee on the Rights of the Child (2001c) *Concluding observations of the Committee on the Rights of the Child: Qatar*, 28th session, CRC/C/15/Add.163, Geneva: UN.

UN Committee on the Rights of the Child (2001d) *Summary Records of the 728th meeting of the Committee on the Rights of the Child*, 28th session, CRC/C/SR.728, Geneva: UN.

UN Committee on the Rights of the Child (2001e) *Summary Records of the 734th meeting of the Committee on the Rights of the Child*, 28th session, CRC/C/SR.734, Geneva: UN.

UN Committee on the Rights of the Child (2001f) *Summary Records of the 701st meeting of the Committee on the Rights of the Child*, 27th session, CRC/C/SR.701, Geneva: UN.

UN Committee on the Rights of the Child (2000) *Concluding observations of the Committee on the Rights of the Child: Iran*, 24th session, CRC/C/15/Add.123, Geneva: UN.

UN Committee on the Rights of the Child (1998) *Concluding observations of the Committee on the Rights of the Child: Japan*, 18th session, CRC/C/15/Add.90, Geneva: UN.

UN Committee on the Rights of the Child (1997) *The rights of the child with disabilities*, General discussion day of the Committee on the Rights of the Child, 6 October 1997, CRC/C/64, Geneva: UN.

UN Committee on the Rights of the Child (1996) *General guidelines regarding the form and content of periodic reports submitted by States Parties under article 44, paragraph 1 (B), of the Convention*, CRC/C/58, Geneva: UN.

UN Committee on the Rights of the Child (1994) *Summary Records*, CRC/C/SR.176, Geneva: UN.

UN Committee on the Rights of the Child (1994a) *Report of the sixth session*, CRC/C/29, Geneva: UN.

UN Committee on the Rights of the Child (1992) *Report of the second session*, CRC/C/10, Geneva: UN.

UN Development Programme (2002) *Human Development Report 2002, Deepening democracy in a fragmented world*, Oxford: Oxford University Press.

UN Development Programme (2000) *Human Development Report 2000, Human rights and human development*, Oxford: Oxford University Press.

UN Educational, Social and Cultural Organization (UNESCO) (2003) *Final Communiqué of the Round Table of Ministers and Senior Officials Responsible for Physical Education and Sport*, 10 January, Paris: UNESCO.

UN High Commissioner for Human Rights, Office of the (2004) *What is a rights-based approach to development?* Online. Available HTTP: <http://www.unhchr.ch/development/approaches-04.html> (accessed on 12 January 2004).

UN High Commissioner for Human Rights, Office of the (1997) *Manual on Human Rights Reporting*, Geneva: UN.

UNICEF (UN Children's Fund) (2002) *Birth registration, right from start*, Innocenti Digest no. 9, Florence: UNICEF Innocenti Research Centre.

UNICEF (UN Children's Fund) (2001) *Football and UNICEF unite to 'say yes for children'*, press release.

UNICEF (UN Children's Fund) (2001a) *Young voices, main findings, Opinion survey of children and young people in Europe and Central Asia*, Geneva: UNICEF.

UNICEF (UN Children's Fund) (2000) *Domestic violence against women and girls*, Innocenti Digest, no. 6, Florence: UNICEF Innocenti Research Centre.

UNICEF (UN Children's Fund) (1998) *The progress of nations*, New York: UNICEF.

UNICEF (UN Children's Fund) (1997) *The state of the world's children 1997*, New York: Oxford University Press.

UN International Narcotic Control Board (2001) *INCB Annual Report*, E/INCB/2000/1, Vienna: UN.

UN International Narcotic Control Board (2000) *INCB Annual Report*, E/INCB/1999/1, Vienna: UN.

UN International Narcotic Control Board (1995) *INCB Annual Report*, E/INCB/1994/1, Vienna: UN.

University of Antwerp (1995) *Sportbeleving bij kinderen* (Sport experiences of children), Antwerp.

USA Today (2000) 6 November.

USA Today (1998) 29 May.

USA Today (1996) 20 September.

US Fourth Circuit Court of Appeals (1999) *Montalvo v. Radcliffe*.

US News and World Report (1992) 1 June.

US Open (2001) *Transcribed interview of Ashley Harkleroad after her game against A. Tu (lost 6-4, 2-6, 6-0)*, 28 August. Online. Available HTTP: <http://www.usopen.org> (accessed 10 October 2001).

Valenti-Hein, D. and Schwartz, L. (1995) *The sexual abuse interview for those with developmental disabilities*, Santa Barbara: James Stanfeld.

Van Bueren, G. (1995) *The international law on the rights of the child*, The Hague: Martinus Nijhoff.

Vandenbergh, P. (2001) 'Les agents transfèrent illégalement' (Agents transfer illegally), *La Libre Belgique*, 2 July.

Van den Heuvel, J. (2000) 'Sportscholen verkopen massaal dope en drugs' (Sports schools sell massive amounts of doping and drugs), *De Telegraaf*, 5 April.

Van der Meyden, H. (2000) 'Martina Hingis: 'ik wil niet dood voor mijn dertigste' (Martina Hingis: I don't want to die by 30), *De Telegraaf*, 28 August 2000.

Vandeweghe, H. (2000), 'Te véél goud kan niet' (Too much gold is impossible), *Sport International*, October 2000.

Van Hoecke, J. and De Knop, P. (1998) 'A model for evaluating Flemish gymnastics clubs', *European Journal of Sport Management*, 5: 2.

Vanoyeke, V. (1992) *La naissance des Jeux Olympiques et le sport dans l'Antiquité* (The birth of the Olympic Games and sport during Antiquity), Paris: Les Belles Lettres.

Van Wijnen, J.F. (2000) 'Als Ajax niet wint, zakt de verkoop van shirties in' (When Ajax doesn't win, the sale of shirts collapses), *Vrij Nederland*, 22–24 October.

Vargas, A. (2000) 'The globalization of baseball: a Latin American perspective', *Indiana Journal of Global Legal Studies* 8, 9: 21–36.

Vargas N.A., Lopez, D., Perez, P., Zuniga, P., Toro, G. and Ciocca, P. (1995) 'Parental attitude and practice regarding physical punishment of school children in Santagio de Chile', *Child Abuse and Neglect*, vol. 19, 9; 1077–82.

Verbraak, C. (2000) 'De wetten binnen and buiten de poort' (The law inside and off the field), *Vrij Nederland*, 23 December.

Verhellen, E. (1992) 'Changes in the image of the child', in Freeman, M. and Veerman, P. (eds) *The ideologies of children's rights*, The Hague: Martinus Nijhoff.

Voetbal International (2000) 24 June.

Voy, R. (1991) *Drugs, sports and politics, the inside story about drug use in sport and its political cover-up*, Champaign, IL: Leisure Press.

Waddington, I. (2001) 'Doping in sport: a medical sociological perspective', *Proceedings from the workshop 'Research on doping in sport'*, Oslo: The Research Council of Norway.

Waddington, I. (2000) *Sport, health and drugs*, London: E & FN Spon.

Waddington, I. (1996) 'The development of sports medicine', *Sociology of Sport Journal*, 13: 176–96.

Wahl, G. and Zimmerman, P. (1998) 'Travelling violations', *Sports Illustrated*, 21 September.

Waller, E., Daniels, J.L., Weaver, N.L. and Robinson, P. (2000) 'Jockeys' injuries in the United States', *Journal of the American Medical Association* 283, 10: 1326–8.

Walters, R. (1994) 'Skilful schoolboys keep the stream of England junior talent flowing', *The Observer*, 13 March.

Weidemann, S. (2001) 'In Holland steigt Zahl junger Asylbewerber' (Number of young asylum seekers rises in Holland), *Süddeutsche Zeitung*, 16 February.

Weinberg, R.S. and Comar, W. (1994) 'The effectiveness of psychological interventions in competitive sports', *Sports Medicine*, 18: 406–18.

Weinberg, R.S. and Gould, D. (1995) *Foundations of sport and exercise psychology*, Champaign, IL: Human Kinetics Publishers.

Weiss, M.R. (1993) 'Psychological effects on intensive sport participation on children and youth: self-esteem and motivation', in Cahill, B.R. and Pearl, A.J. (eds) *Intensive participation in children's sports*, American Orthopedic Society for Sports Medicine, Champaign, IL: Human Kinetics Publishers.

Weissbrodt, D. (1988) 'Human rights: an historical perspective', in Davies, P. (ed.) *Human rights*, London: Routledge.

Wekking, P. (1999) 'Huub Stevens vercht tegen giftige pijlen' (Huub Stevens fights poisoned attacks) *Voetbal International*, 31 March.

Wenn, B. (1989) *Violence in sport*, Canberra: Australian Institute of Criminology.

Wen, P. (2001) 'Letting it go their heads', *The Boston Globe*, 24 January.

Wertheim, J. (2001) *Venus envy: a sensational season inside the women's tennis tour*, New York: Harper Collins.

Wetzel, D. and Yaleger, D. (2000) *Sole influence. Basketball, corporate greed, and the corruption of America's youth*, New York: Warner Books.

Wieberg, S. (2001) 'Top dollar, top coaches', *USA Today*, 3 August.

Wilgoren, J. (2001) 'Spiralling sports budgets draw fire from faculties', *New York Times*, 29 July.

Wilkinson, I. (2001) 'Spain sets up school for bullfighters', *Daily Telegraph*, 25 September.

Williamson, D.J. (1993) 'Anabolic steroid use among students at a British college of technology', *British Journal of Sports Medicine*, 27, 3: 200–1.

Willsher, K. (1995) 'The little girl who died for gold', *The Mail on Sunday*, 19 February.

Wolfson, S.A. (1992) 'Children's rights: the theoretical underpinning of the "best interests of the child"', in Freeman, M. and Veerman, P. (eds) *The ideologies of children's rights*, The Hague: Martinus Nijhoff.

Woll, L. (2000a) *The Convention on the Rights of the Child impact study*, Stockholm: Save the Children-Sweden.

Woll, L. (2000b) 'Reporting to the UN Committee on the Rights of the Child: a catalyst for domestic debate and policy change?', *International Journal for Children's Rights*, 8: 71–81.

Woolger, C. and Power, T.G. (1993) 'Parent and sport socialisation: views from the achievement literature', *Journal of Sport Behaviour* 16, 3: 171–87.

World Anti-Doping Agency (2002) *WADA Conference sheds light on the potential of gene doping*, press release, 20 March, Montreal: WADA.

World Conference on Human Rights (1993) *Vienna d§§eclaration and programme of action*, A/CONF/.157/23, Vienna: UN.

World Health Organization (2002) *World report on violence and health*, Krug, E.G., Dahlberg, L.L., Mercy, J.A., Zwi, A. and Lozano, R. (eds), Geneva: WHO.

World Health Organization (2001) *Prevention of child abuse and neglect. Making the links between human rights and public health*, submission from WHO to the Committee on the Rights of the Child for its Day of General Discussion, 28 September, Geneva: WHO.

World Health Organization (2001a) *Health and health behaviours among young people. Health behaviour in school-aged children: a WHO cross-national study (HBSC)*, *international report*, Currie, C., Hurrelmann, K., Setterbodulte, W., Smith, R. and Todd, J. (eds) Copenhagen: WHO.

World Health Organization (1999) *Report of the consultation on child abuse prevention*, 29–31 March 1999, WHO/HSC/PVI/99.1, Geneva: WHO.

World Health Organization (1998) 'Sports and children: consensus statement on organized sports for children', FIMS/WHO ad hoc Committee on Sports and Children, in *Bulletin of the World Health Organization*, no. 76(5), Geneva: WHO.

World Health Organization (1993) *Drug use and sport, current issues and implications for public health*, Hush, J., Geneva: WHO.

World Medical Association (1999) *Declaration on Principles of Health Care for Sports Medicine*, third revision adopted at the 51st General Assembly in Tel Aviv, Israel.

Writing Group for the PEPI Trial (1995) 'Effects of estrogen or estrogen/progestin regimens on heart disease risk factors in postmenopausal women: the postmenopausal estrogen/progestin interventions (PEPI) trial', *Journal of the American Medical Association*, vol. 273, 3: 199–208.

Yeager, K.K., Agostini, R. and Nattiv, A. (1993) 'The female athlete triad: disordered eating, amenorrhea, osteoporosis', *Medicine and Science in Sports and Exercise*, vol. 25, 7: 775–7.

Yesalis, C.E., Vicary, J.R. and Buckley, W.E. (1993) 'History of anabolic steroid use in sport and exercise', in Yesalis, C.E. (ed.) *Anabolic steroid in sport and exercise*, Champaign, Illinois: Human Kinetics, pp. 35–47.

Yonnet, P. (1998) *Systèmes de sports* (Sport systems), Paris: Gallimard.

Young, K. (1991) 'Violence in the workplace of professional sports', *International Review for the Sociology of Sports* 26, (1): 3–14.

Zermatten, J. (ed.) (1999) *Un champion à tout prix? Les droits de l'enfant et le sport* (A champion at any cost? Child rights and sport), Sion, Switzerland: International Children's Rights Institute and Kurt Bösch Academic Institute.

Index